A CONFIRMATION
OF
THE BOOK OF BOOKS

Once considered merely illustrative tales, the stories of the *Bible* now emerge as fascinating fact:

"As far as the famous manna is concerned, we have reliable information from the botanist . . .

"Experts from the Hebrew University at Jerusalem set out for the Sinai peninsula to clear up the disputed question of the existence of manna once and for all . . .

"Their report caused a sensation. They not only brought back the first photographs of manna . . . but also established the factual truth of the Biblical description of the desert migration of the people of Israel."

After thousands of years, the events, the people and places of the Book of Books take on a thrilling new reality documented by science.

THE BIBLE AS HISTORY

The Bible as History

A CONFIRMATION OF THE BOOK OF BOOKS

Werner Keller

translated by William Neil

*This low-priced Bantam Book
has been completely reset in a type face
designed for easy reading, and was printed
from new plates. It contains the complete
text of the original hard-cover edition.*
NOT ONE WORD HAS BEEN OMITTED.

RL 9, IL 9-up

THE BIBLE AS HISTORY
*A Bantam Book / published by arrangement with
William Morrow & Co., Inc.*

PRINTING HISTORY
*Originating publisher
Econ Verlag
Düsseldorf, Germany*

*William Morrow edition published October 1956
12 printings to May 1963
Revised William Morrow edition published October 1964*

2nd printing .. September 1965	*4th printing .... July 1971*
3rd printing .. September 1967	*5th printing .... December 1973*

A Book-Of-The-Month selection from 1956 to 1973

Bantam edition / June 1974

2nd printing .. September 1974	*4th printing .. September 1976*
3rd printing .... March 1975	*5th printing .... March 1978*
	6th printing .... June 1979

ISBN 0-553-12483-8

Published simultaneously in the United States and Canada

*Bantam Books are published by Bantam Books, Inc. Its trade-
mark, consisting of the words "Bantam Books" and the portrayal of a bantam, is Registered in U.S. Patent and Trademark
Office and in other countries. Marca Registrada. Bantam
Books, Inc., 666 Fifth Avenue, New York, New York 10019.*

PRINTED IN THE UNITED STATES OF AMERICA

To My Parents
and
My Friend Th. Ruth

Contents

DIGGING UP THE NEW TESTAMENT

I. Jesus of Nazareth

III. Let There Be Light!

Appendix

Illustrations

Drawings

Maps and Diagrams

Introduction

THE GREATEST HAPPINESS OF THE THINKING MAN
IS TO HAVE FATHOMED WHAT CAN BE FATHOMED,
AND QUIETLY TO REVERENCE WHAT IS UNFATHOM-
ABLE (Goethe).

When a nontheologian writes a book about the Bible, it
is a rare enough occurrence to entitle the reader to
ask for some explanation of how the writer managed to
make himself master of his subject.

As a journalist I have been for many years exclusively concerned with the results of modern science
and research. In 1950, in the course of my routine
work, I came across the reports of the French archaeologists Professors André Parrot and C. F. A. Schaeffer
on their excavations at Mari and Ugarit. Cuneiform
tablets discovered at Mari on the Euphrates were found
to contain Biblical names. As a result, narratives of
the patriarchs that had been for a long time regarded
as merely pious tales were unexpectedly transferred
into the realm of history. At Ugarit on the Mediterranean, evidence of the Canaanite worship of Baal
had for the first time come to light. By a coincidence,
a scroll of Isaiah discovered in a cave by the Dead
Sea was in the same year dated as pre-Christian. These
sensational reports—and, indeed, in view of the significance of these finds it is not too much to use the
word "sensational"—awakened in me the desire to
come to closer grips with Biblical archaeology, the
most recent and, generally speaking, least known province in the field of investigation into the ancient
world. I therefore ransacked German and foreign
literature for a comprehensive and intelligible sum-
mary of the results of previous research. I found none
for there was none to find. So I went to the sources
myself in the libraries of many lands—aided in this
bit of real detective work by my wife's enthusiasm—
and collected all the hitherto scientifically established
results of investigations which were to be found in

the learned works of Biblical archaeologists. The deeper I went into the matter the more exciting it became.

The door into the historical world of the Old Testament had already been thrown open by a Frenchman, Paul-Émile Botta, in 1843. In the course of excavations at Khorsabad in Mesopotamia he suddenly found himself confronted by reliefs of King Sargon II of Assyria, who ravaged Israel and led its people off into captivity. Accounts of this conqueror's campaigns deal with the conquest of Samaria, which is also described in the Bible.

For a century now, American, English, French, and German scholars have been digging in the Middle East, in Mesopotamia, Palestine, and Egypt. All the great nations have founded institutes and schools specifically for this type of research. The Palestine Exploration Fund began in 1869, the German Palestine Association in 1877, the Dominican École Biblique de St. Étienne in 1892. The German Oriental Society followed in 1898; then in 1900 the American Schools of Oriental Research and in 1901 the German Protestant Institute of Archaeology.

In Palestine, places and towns that are frequently mentioned in the Bible are being brought back once more into the light of day. They look exactly as the Bible describes them and lie exactly where the Bible locates them. On ancient inscriptions and monuments scholars encounter more and more characters from Old and New Testaments. Contemporary reliefs depict people whom we have hitherto known only by name. Their features, their clothes, their armor take shape before our eyes. Colossal figures and sculptures show us the Hittites with their big noses; the slim, tall Philistines; the elegant Canaanite chiefs with their "chariots of iron," which struck terror into the hearts of the Israelites; the kings of Mari, contemporary with Abraham, with their gentle smiles. During the thousands of years that divide us from them, the Assyrian Kings have lost nothing of their fierce and forbidding appearance: Tiglath Pileser III, well known as the Old Testament Pul; Sennacherib, who destroyed

Lachish and laid siege to Jerusalem; Esarhaddon, who put King Manesseh in chains; and Ashurbanipal, the "great and noble Asnapper" of the book of Ezra.

As they have done to Nineveh and Nimrod—old-time Calah—or to Ashur and Thebes, which the prophets called No-Amon, the scholars have also awakened from its ancient slumber the notorious Babel of Biblical story with its legendary tower. In the Nile Delta archaeologists have found the cities of Pithom and Raamses, where the resentful Hebrews toiled as slaves. They have laid bare strata that tell of the flames and destruction that accompanied the children of Israel on their conquering march into Canaan. In Gibeah they found Saul's mountain stronghold, the walls of which once echoed to the strains of David's harp. At Megiddo they came upon the vast stables of King Solomon, who had "12,000 horsemen."

From the world of the New Testament reappeared the palatial edifices of King Herod. In the heart of Old Jerusalem the Pavement was discovered where Jesus stood before Pilate, as is mentioned in St. John's gospel. Assyriologists deciphered on the astronomical tables of the Babylonians the exact dates on which the Star of Bethlehem was observed.

These breathtaking discoveries, whose significance it is impossible to grasp all at once, make it necessary for us to revise our views about the Bible. Many events that previously passed for pious tales must now be judged to be historical. Often the results of investigation correspond in detail with the Biblical narratives. They not only confirm but also illumine the historical situations out of which the Old Testament and the gospels grew. At the same time the changing fortunes of the ancient people of Israel are woven into a lively, colorful tapestry of daily life in the age in which they lived. They were also caught up in the political, cultural, and economic disputes of the nations and empires that struggled for power in Mesopotamia and on the Nile, from which the inhabitants of the tiny buffer state of Palestine were never able completely to detach themselves for over two thousand years.

The opinion has been, and still is, widely held that

the Bible is nothing but the story of man's salvation. a guarantee of the validity of their faith for Christians everywhere. At the same time it is a book about things that actually happened. Admittedly in this sense it has limitations, in that the Jewish people wrote their history in the light of their relationship to Yahweh, which meant writing it from the point of view of their own guilt and expiation. Nevertheless, the events themselves are historical facts and have been recorded with an accuracy that is nothing less than startling.

Thanks to the findings of the archaeologists, many of the Biblical narratives can be understood better now than ever before. There are, of course, theological insights which can only be dealt with in terms of the Word of God. But as Professor André Parrot, the world-famous French archaeologist, has said: "How can we understand the Word, unless we see it in its proper chronological, historical and geographical setting?"

Until now, knowledge of these extraordinary discoveries was confined to a small circle of experts. Only fifty years ago Professor Friedrich Delitzsch of Berlin was asking. "Why all this effort in these distant barren and dangerous lands? Why all this costly rummaging among the rubble of past ages when we know there is neither gold nor silver to be found there? Why this mad competition among different countries to get control of these dreary-looking mounds for the sole purpose of digging them up?" The German scholar Gustav Dalman gave him the right answer from Jerusalem itself when he expressed the hope that one day all that the archaeologists had "experienced and seen in their scientific labors would be turned to good account and would help to solve the practical problems of school and church." This latter hope has so far, however, remained unfulfilled.

No book in the whole history of mankind has had such a revolutionary influence, has so decisively affected the development of the western world, or had such a world-wide effect as the "Book of Books," the Bible. Today, after two thousand years, it has been translated into 1120 languages and dialects and gives no sign of having exhausted its triumphal progress.

In gathering together and working over the material for this book, which I in no way claim to be complete, it seemed to me that the time had come to share with those who read their Bibles and those who do not, with churchmen and agnostics alike, the exciting discoveries which have resulted from a careful examination of the combined results of scientific investigation along many different lines. In view of the overwhelming mass of authentic and well-attested evidence now available, as I thought of the skeptical criticism which from the eighteenth century onward would fain have demolished the Bible altogether, there kept hammering in my brain this one sentence: "The Bible is right after all!"

Werner Keller

Hamburg, September 1955

DIGGING UP
THE OLD TESTAMENT

I / The Coming of the Patriarchs: From Abraham to Jacob

CHAPTER 1 / In the Fertile Crescent

Four thousand years ago—Continents asleep—The great cradle of our civilization—Culture in the Ancient East—Arab tribes attack from the desert

If we draw a line from Egypt through the Mediterranean lands of Palestine and Syria, then, following the Tigris and Euphrates, through Mesopotamia to the Persian Gulf, the result is an unmistakable crescent.

Four thousand years ago this mighty semicircle around the Arabian Desert, which is called the "Fertile Crescent," embraced a multiplicity of civilizations lying side by side like a lustrous string of pearls. Rays of light streamed out from them into the surrounding darkness of mankind. Here lay the center of civilization from the Stone Age right up to the golden age of Greco-Roman culture.

About 2000 B.C., the farther we look beyond the Fertile Crescent, the deeper grows the darkness, and signs of civilization and culture decrease. But over the eastern Mediterranean, already a light is shining. It is the heyday of the Minoan kings of Crete, founders of the first sea power known to history. For a thousand years the fortress of Mycenae had protected its citizens, and a second Troy had long been standing upon the ruins of the first. In the nearby Balkans, however, the early Bronze Age had just begun. In Sardinia and western France the dead were being buried in vast stone tombs. These megalithic graves are the last great manifestation of the Stone Age.

In Britain they were building the most famous sanctuary of the megalithic age, the Temple of the Sun at Stonehenge, that giant circle of stones near Salisbury which is still one of the sights of England and about which many tales are told. In Germany they were tilling the soil with wooden plows.

At the foot of the Himalayas the flickering lamp of an isolated outpost of civilization in the Indus Valley was fast going out. Over China, over the vast steppes of Russia, over Africa, darkness reigned supreme. And beyond the waters of the Atlantic lay the Americas in predawn gloom.

In the Fertile Crescent and in Egypt, on the other hand, cultured and highly developed civilizations jostled each other in colorful and bewildering array. For a thousand years the Pharaohs had sat upon the throne. About 2000 B.C. it was occupied by the founder of the XIIth Dynasty, Amenemhet I. His sphere of influence ranged from Nubia, south of the second cataract of the Nile, beyond the Sinai peninsula to Canaan and Syria, a stretch of territory as large as Norway. Along the Mediterranean coast lay the wealthy seaports of the Phoenicians. In Asia Minor, in the heart of present-day Turkey, the powerful kingdom of the ancient Hittites stood on the threshold of its history. In Mesopotamia, between the Tigris and Euphrates, reigned the kings of Sumer and Akkad, who held in tribute all the smaller kingdoms from the Persian Gulf to the headwaters of the Euphrates.

Egypt's mighty pyramids and Mesopotamia's massive temples had for centuries watched the busy life around them. For two thousand years farms and plantations that were as large as any modern enterprise had been exporting corn, vegetables, and choice fruits from the artificially irrigated valleys of the Nile, the Euphrates, and the Tigris. Everywhere throughout the Fertile Crescent and in the empire of the Pharaohs the art of cuneiform and hieroglyphic writing was commonly known. Poets, court officials, and civil servants practiced it. For commerce it had long been a necessity.

The endless traffic in commodities of all sorts that the great import and export firms of Mesopotamia and Egypt dispatched by caravan routes or by sea from the Persian Gulf to Syria and Asia Minor, from the Nile to Cyprus and Crete and as far as the Black Sea, is reported in the business correspondence which was recorded on clay tablets or papyrus. Out of all the rich variety of costly wares the most keenly sought after were copper from the Egyptian mines in the mountains of Sinai, silver from the Taurus mines in

Asia Minor, gold and ivory from Somaliland in East Africa and from Nubia on the Nile, purple dyes from the Phoenician cities on the coast of Canaan, incense and rare spices from south Arabia, the magnificent linens that came from the Egyptian looms, and the wonderful vases from the island of Crete.

Literature and learning were flourishing. In Egypt the first novels and secular poetry were making their appearance. Mesopotamia was experiencing a renaissance. Philologists in Akkad, the great kingdom on the lower Euphrates, were compiling the first grammar and the first bilingual dictionary. The story of Gilgamesh and the old Sumerian legends of creation and flood were being woven into epics of dramatic power in the Akkadian tongue which was the language of the world. Egyptian doctors were producing their medicines in accordance with textbook methods from herbal compounds that had proved their worth. Their surgeons were no strangers to anatomical science. By

Fig. 1. The Fertile Crescent and Egypt—the great centers of civilization about 2000 B.C.

empirical means the mathematicians of the Nile reached the conclusion about the sides of a right-angled triangle which fifteen hundred years later Pythagoras in Greece embodied in the theorem which bears his name. Mesopotamian engineers were solving the problem of square measurement by trial and error. Astronomers, admittedly with an eye solely on astrological prediction, were making their calculations based on accurate observations of the course of the planets.

Peace and prosperity must have reigned in this world of Nile, Euphrates, and Tigris, for we have never yet discovered an inscription dating from this period that records any large-scale warlike activities.

Then suddenly from the heart of this great Fertile Crescent, from the sandy sterile wastes of the Arabian desert whose shores are lashed by the waters of the Indian Ocean, there burst in violent assaults on the north, on the northwest, on Mesopotamia, Syria, and Palestine a horde of nomadic tribes of Semitic stock. In endless waves these Amorites, "Westerners" as their name implies, surged against the kingdoms of the Fertile Crescent.

The empire of the kings of Sumer and Akkad collapsed in 1960 B.C. under their irresistible attack. The Amorites founded a number of states and dynasties. One of them was eventually to become supreme: the first dynasty of Babylon, which was the great center of power from 1830 to 1530 B.C. Its sixth king was the famous Hammurabi.

Meanwhile one of these tribes of Semitic nomads was destined to be of fateful significance for millions upon millions throughout the world up to the present day. It was a little group, perhaps only a family, as unknown and unimportant as a tiny grain of sand in a desert storm: the family of Abraham, forefather of the patriarchs.

*A station on the Baghdad railway—A staged tower of
bricks—Ruins with Biblical names—Archaeologists in
search of scriptural sites—A consul with a pick—The
archaeologist on the throne of Babylon—Expedition to Tell
al Muqayyar—History books from rubble—Tax receipts
on clay—Was Abraham a city dweller?*

AND TERAH TOOK ABRAM HIS SON, AND LOT THE SON
OF HARAN, HIS SON'S SON, AND SARAI, HIS DAUGH-
TER-IN-LAW, HIS SON ABRAM'S WIFE; AND THEY WENT
FORTH WITH THEM FROM UR OF THE CHALDEES. . . .
(Gen. 11:31)

*. . . and they went forth with them from Ur of the
Chaldees.* . . . Christians have been hearing these
words for almost two thousand years. Ur, a name as
mysterious and legendary as the bewildering variety
of names of kings and conquerors, powerful empires,
temples, and golden palaces with which the Bible re-
gales us. Nobody knew where Ur lay. Chaldea certainly pointed to Mesopotamia. Thirty years ago no
one could have guessed that the quest for the Ur mentioned in the Bible would lead to the discovery of
a civilization that would take us further into the twilight of prehistoric times than even the oldest traces
of man that had been found in Egypt.

Today Ur is a railway station about 120 miles north
of Basra, near the Persian Gulf, and one of the many
stops on the famous Baghdad railway. Punctually the
train makes a halt there in the gray light of early
morning. When the noise of the wheels on their northward journey has died away, the traveler who has
alighted here is surrounded by the silence of the desert.

His glance roams over the monotonous yellowish
brown of the endless stretch of sand. He seems to be
standing in the middle of an enormous flat dish intersected only by the railway line. Only at one point
is the shimmering expanse of desolation broken. As

9

the rays of the rising sun grow stronger, they pick out a massive dull red stump. It looks as though some Titan had hewn great notches in it.

To the Bedouins this solitary mound is an old friend. High up in its crevices the owls make their nests. From time immemorial the Arabs have known it and have given it the name Tell al Muqayyar—"mound of pitch." Their forefathers pitched their tents at its base. Still, as from time immemorial, it offers welcome protection from the danger of sand storms. Still, today, they feed their flocks at its base when the rains suddenly charm blades of grass out of the ground.

Once upon a time—four thousand years ago—broad fields of corn and barley swayed here. Market gardens, groves of date palms and fig trees stretched as far as the eye could see. These spacious estates could cheerfully bear comparison with Canadian wheat farms or the market gardens and fruit farms of California. The lush green fields and beds were interlaced by a system of dead-straight canals and ditches, a masterpiece of irrigation. Far back in the Stone Age experts among the natives had utilized the water of the great rivers; skillfully and methodically they diverted the precious moisture at the river banks and thereby converted desert wastes into rich and fruitful farmland.

Almost hidden by forests of shady palms the Euphrates in those days flowed past this spot. This great life-giving river carried a heavy traffic between Ur and the sea. At that time the Persian Gulf cut much deeper into the estuary of the Euphrates and the Tigris. Even before the first pyramid was built on the Nile, Tell al Muqayyar was towering into the blue skies. Four mighty cubes, built one upon the other in diminishing size, rose up into a 75-foot tower of gaily colored brick. Above the black of the square foundation block, its sides 120 feet long, shone the red and blue of the upper stages, each studded with trees. The uppermost stage provided a small plateau on which was enthroned a Holy Place shaded by a golden roof.

Silence reigned over this sanctuary, in which priests performed their office at the shrine of Nannar, the moon-god. The stir and noise of wealthy metropolitan

Ur, one of the oldest cities of the world, scarcely penetrated into it.

In the year 1854 a caravan of camels and donkeys laden with an unusual cargo of spades, picks, and surveyors' instruments approached the lonely red mound under the leadership of the British consul in Basra. J. E. Taylor was inspired neither by a lust for adventure nor, indeed, by any motive of his own. He had undertaken the journey at the instigation of the Foreign Office, which in its turn was complying with a request from the British Museum that a search should be made for ancient monuments in southern Mesopotamia, where the Euphrates and the Tigris came closest together just before entering the Persian Gulf. Taylor had often heard in Basra about the strange great heap of stones that his expedition was now approaching. It seemed to him a suitable site to investigate.

Fig. 2. The great staged tower at Ur (Reconstruction).

About the middle of the nineteenth century, all over Egypt, Mesopotamia, and Palestine investigations and excavations had started in response to a suddenly awakened desire to get a scientifically reliable picture of man's history in this part of the world. The goal of a long succession of expeditions was the Middle East.

Until then the Bible had been the only historical source for our knowledge of that part of Asia before about 550 B.C. Only the Bible had anything to say about a period of history that stretched back into the dim twilight of the past. In the Bible peoples and names cropped up about which even the Greeks and the Romans no longer knew anything.

Scholars swarmed impetuously into these lands of the ancient East. What these men with infinite pains extracted from the desert sand by the great rivers of Mesopotamia and Egypt deserved indeed the attention of mankind. Here, for the first time, science had forced open the door into the mysterious world of the Bible.

The French vice-consul in Mosul, Paul-Émile Botta, was an enthusiastic archaeologist. In 1843 he began to dig at Khorsabad on the Tigris and from the ruins of a four-thousand-year-old capital proudly brought to light the first witness to the Bible: Sargon, the fabulous ruler of Assyria. "In the year that Tartan came unto Ashdod, when Sargon the king of Assyria sent him," says Isaiah 20:1.

Two years later a young English diplomat and ex-cavator, A. H. Layard, uncovered Nimrud (Kalchu), the city which the Bible calls Calah (Gen. 10:11) and which now bears the name of the Nimrod of the Bible: "a mighty hunter before the Lord. And the beginning of his kingdom was Babel and Erech, and Akkad and Calneh in the land of Shinar. Out of that land he went forth into Assyria and builded Nineveh and Rehoboth-Ir and Calah. . . ." (Gen. 10:10-11)

Shortly after that, excavations under the direction of an English major, Henry Creswicke Rawlinson, one of the foremost Assyriologists, unearthed Nineveh, the Assyrian capital with the famous library of King Ashurbanipal. This is the Nineveh whose wickedness the Biblical prophets constantly denounced. (Jonah 1:2) In Palestine the American scholar Edward Robinson devoted himself in 1838 and 1852 to the reconstruction of the topography of the ancient world. From Germany, Richard Lepsius, later director of the Egyptian Museum in Berlin, recorded the monuments of the Nile area during an expedition which lasted from 1842 to 1846. Just as the Frenchman Champollion had the good fortune to decipher Egyptian hieroglyphics, so Rawlinson, the discoverer of Nineveh, was, among others, successful in solving the riddle of cuneiform writing. The ancient documents were beginning to speak.

Let us return to the caravan that is approaching Tell al Muqayyar.

Taylor pitched his tents at the foot of the red mound. He had neither scientific ambitions nor previous knowledge. Where was he to begin? Where was the best spot to deploy his native diggers? The great brick mound, architectural masterpiece of a shadowy past though it might be, conveyed nothing to him. Perhaps in the heart of it lay something which might eventually be exhibited in the museum and might interest the London experts. He thought vaguely of old statues, armor, ornaments, or even perhaps buried treasure. He took a closer look at the curious mound. Step by step he tapped its surface. No indication of a hollow cavity within; the great edifice appeared to be completely solid. Thirty feet above him the wall of the lowest block rose straight and sheer out of the sand. Two broad stone ramps led to the next and smaller stage above; then above them rose the third and fourth stages.

Taylor clambered up and down, crawled along the ledges on hands and knees in the broiling sun, finding only broken tiles. One day, bathed in sweat he reached the topmost platform, and a few owls flew startled from the dilapidated walls. Nothing more. However, he was not discouraged. In his efforts to get to the heart of the secrets of the mound he made a decision that today we can only deeply regret. He took his labor gangs away from the base of the mound and set them to work at the top.

What had survived for centuries, what had withstood sand storm and blazing sun alike, became now the victim of tireless pickaxes. Taylor gave orders to pull down the top story. The work of destruction began at the four corners simultaneously. Day after day masses of bricks crashed dully down the sides to the ground. After many weeks the chattering voices on the top of the mound were suddenly hushed, the clanging and banging of the pickaxes stopped abruptly. Falling over each other in their haste, a few men rushed down the side of the mound and up to Taylor's tent. In their hands they held little bars—cylinders—made of baked clay. Taylor was disappointed; he had expected more. As he carefully cleaned his finds, he recognized that the clay rolls were covered over and over with inscriptions. Cuneiform writing! He understood none of it, but he was highly delighted. The cylinders, carefully packed, were dispatched to London. The scholars on the Thames were not impressed —and small wonder. Those were the years during which the experts were looking to north Mesopotamia, where, under their fascinated gaze, the emergence from the hills of Nineveh and Khorsabad on the upper Tigris, of the palaces and colossal reliefs of the Assyrians, as well as thousands of clay tables and statues, was enough to put everything else in the shade. Compared with them, what significance had the little clay cylinders from Tell al Muqayyar? For two years more Taylor hopefully continued his search. But there were no further results from Tell al Muqayyar, and the expedition was abandoned.

It was seventy-five years later that the world learned what priceless treasures were still lying under that ancient mound.

As far as the experts were concerned Tell al Muqayyar was once more forgotten. But it was by no means neglected. No sooner had Taylor left than hordes of other visitors arrived. The broken walls and, above all, the top tier of the mound, which Taylor's laborers had shattered, provided a welcome and inexhaustible supply of inexpensive building material for the Arabs who over the years came from far and near and departed with as many bricks as their pack mules could carry. These bricks, fashioned by men's hands thousands of years before, still bore plainly the names of Ur-Nannu, the first great builder, and of Nabonidus, the Babylonian conqueror who restored the staged tower that they called the ziggurat. Sand storms, rain, wind, and the heat of the sun had all contributed to the process of destruction.

During the First World War, when British troops on the march to Baghdad in 1915 camped near this ancient structure, they found that its former appearance had been completely altered. It had become so flat owing to dilapidation and theft in the intervening years since 1854 that one of the soldiers was able to indulge in a piece of daredevilry. The step formation of the tower, which had previously been clearly marked, had disappeared so completely that he was able to ride his mule right to the summit of the mound.

By a lucky chance there was an expert among the officers of the party, R. Campbell Thompson, of the Intelligence Staff of the army in Mesopotamia. In peacetime he had been an assistant in the British Museum. Thompson rummaged with an expert eye through the huge heap of bricks and was shocked at the deterioration of the material. Examination of the terrain led him to suppose that there were additional areas worth investigating in the neighborhood of the Tell, ruins of settlements that lay buried under the sand. Thompson recorded all this with great care and sent an urgent message to London. His message prompted the Museum people to blow the dust off the insignificant-looking little clay cylinders, which had been almost forgotten, and to look at them again with greater attention. The inscriptions on them were then found to contain some extremely important information as well as a curious story.

Almost twenty-five hundred years before Taylor someone else had been searching and rummaging on the same spot and with the same concern—Nabonidus, king of Babylon in the sixth century B.C., venerator of the past, man of renown, ruler of a mighty kingdom, and archaeologist rolled into one. In his day he established that "the ziggurat was now old." But his tactics were different from Taylor's. "I restored this Ziggurat to its former state with mortar and baked bricks." When the weakened structure of the staged tower had been restored, he had caused the name of the first builder, which he had discovered, to be cut out on that little clay cylinder. His name, as the Babylonian had been able to decipher from a damaged in-

scription, had been King Ur-Nammu. Ur-Nammu?
Was the builder of the great staged tower the king of
the Ur that the Bible mentions? Was he the ruler of Ur
of the Chaldees?

It seemed highly probable. The same Biblical name
had cropped up several times since then. Ancient records recovered from other sites in Mesopotamia had
also mentioned Ur. It appeared from these cuneiform
writings that it was the capital city of the great
Sumerian people. At once the battered remnants of
Tell al Muqayyar aroused eager interest. Scholars from
the University of Pennsylvania Museum joined the
archaeologists from the British Museum in fresh investigations. The staged tower on the lower Euphrates
might hold the secret of this unknown Sumerian people—and of the Ur of the Bible. But it was not until
1923 that a joint American and British team of archaeologists could set out. They were spared the tiresome
journey on the backs of swaying camels. They went
by the Baghdad railway. Their equipment likewise
went by train: trucks, rails, picks, spades, baskets.

The archaeologists had enough funds at their disposal to turn up the whole countryside. They began
their carefully planned excavation on a large scale.
Since considerable finds might be expected, they reckoned on taking several years. In charge of the expedition was Sir Charles Leonard Woolley. The forty-
three-year-old Englishman had already won his spurs
on expeditions and digs in Egypt, Nubia, and
Carchemish on the upper Euphrates. Now this talented
and successful man made Tell al Muqayyar his life
work. Unlike the zealous but unsuspecting Taylor several decades before, his chief aim was not directed to
the staged tower at all. He was possessed with a desire
above all to investigate those flat mounds that rose all
round him out of the vast sandy plain.

Woolley's trained eye had not failed to note their
striking configuration. They looked like little table
mountains. Flat on top, they sloped downward in an
almost uniform pattern. Similar mounds exist in great
numbers, large and small, in the Middle East, on the
banks of the great rivers, in the midst of fertile plains,

by the waywide on the routes followed by caravans from time immemorial. No one has yet been able to count them. We find them from the delta of the Euphrates and Tigris on the Persian Gulf to the highlands of Asia Minor where the river Halys tumbles into the Black Sea, on the eastern shores of the Mediterranean, in the valleys of the Lebanon, on the Orontes in Syria, and in Palestine by the Jordan.

These little eminences are great quarries for archaeological finds, eagerly sought and often inexhaustible. They are not formed by the hand of Nature but are artificially created, piled high with the legacy of countless generations that came before; vast masses of rubble and rubbish from a bygone age that have accumulated from the remains of huts and houses, town walls, temples, and palaces. Each one of these hills took shape gradually in the same way through centuries or even millennia. At some point, after men had first settled there, the place was destroyed by war or was burned down or was deserted by its inhabitants. Then came the conquerors or the new settlers who built upon the selfsame spot. Generation after generation built their settlements and cities, one on top of the other, on the identical site. In the course of time the ruins and rubble of countless dwellings grew, layer by layer, foot by foot, into a sizable hill. The Arabs of today call such an artificial mound a tell. The same word was used even in ancient Babylon. Tell means "mound." We come across the word in the Bible in Joshua 11:13. During the conquest of Canaan, in which cities "that stood on their mounds" are spoken of, it is these Tulul, which is the plural of tell, that are meant. The Arabs make a clear distinction between a tell and a natural eminence, which they call a "jebel."

Every tell is at the same time a silent history book. Its strata are for the archaeologist as the leaves of a calendar. Page by page he can make the past come to life again. Every layer, if we read it correctly, tells of its own time, its life and customs, the craftsmanship and manners of its people. The skill of excavators in deciphering the message of the strata has reached astonishing heights of achievement.

Stones, hewn or rough, bricks, or traces of clay betray the nature of the buildings. Even decayed and
weathered stones or the remains of brick dust can indicate exactly the ground plan of a building. Dark shadows show where once a fireplace radiated its warming
glow.

Broken pottery, armor, household utensils, and
tools, which are to be found everywhere among the
ruins, afford further help in this detective work on the
past. How grateful are the scholars of today that the
ancient world knew nothing of municipal sanitation!
Anything that had become unusable or superfluous
was simply thrown out and left to the mercies of time
and the weather.

Today the different shapes, colors, and patterns of
pots and vases can be so clearly distinguished that
pottery has become archaeology's first and most reliable measurement of time. Single potsherds, sometimes merely fragments, make it possible to give a
precise dating. As far back as the second millennium
B.C. the greatest margin of error in establishing a date
in this way is, at the outside, about fifty years.

Priceless information was lost in the course of the
first great excavations of the last century because no
one paid attention to these apparently worthless bits
of broken pottery. They were thrown aside. The only
important things seemed to be great monuments, reliefs, statues, and jewels. Much that was of value was
thus lost forever. The activities of Heinrich Schliemann, the antiquary, are an example. Fired with am-
bition, he had only one end in view: to find Homer's
Troy. He set his gangs of laborers onto digging
straight down. Strata that might have been of great value in establishing dates were thrown aside as useless
rubbish. At length Schliemann unearthed a valuable
treasure amid general acclamation. But it was not, as
he thought, the treasure of Priam. His find belonged
to a period several centuries earlier. Schliemann had
missed the reward of his labors, which would have
meant so much to him, by digging past it and going far
too deep. Being a businessman, Schliemann was an
amateur, a layman. But the professionals were to begin

no better. Only in the last few decades have the archaeologists been working in accordance with approved methods. Beginning at the top and working down through the tell, they have examined every square inch of the ground. Every tiny object, every piece of pottery has been scrutinized. First they would dig a trench deep into a mound. The different colored strata would lie open, like a cut cake, and the trained eye of the expert could at a glance place in their historical perspective whatever ancient human habitations lay embedded there. In accordance with this tried method the Anglo-American expedition started work at Tell al Muqayyar in 1923.

In early December there arose a cloud of dust over the rubble heap that lay east of the ziggurat and only a few steps from the broad ramp up which ancient priests in solemn procession had approached the shrine of Nannar the moon-god. Fanned by a light wind, the dust spread across the site until the whole area around the old staged tower seemed shrouded in fine mist. Powdery sand whirling up from hundreds of spades indicated that the great dig had started.

From the moment that the first spade struck the ground, an atmosphere of excitement hovered over every shovelful. Each spadeful was like a journey into an unknown land where no one could foretell what surprises lay ahead. Excitement gripped even Woolley and his companions. Would some important find richly reward them for their toil and sweat upon the hill? Would Ur give up its secrets to them? None of these men could guess that for six long winters, until the spring of 1929, they would be kept in suspense. This large-scale excavation deep in southern Mesopotamia was to reveal bit by bit those far-off days when a new land arose out of the delta of the two great rivers and the first human settlers made their home there. Out of the painstaking research of these men, which carried them back to a time 7000 years earlier, events and names recorded in the Bible were more than once to take solid shape.

The first thing they brought to light was a sacred precinct with the remains of five temples, which had once surrounded King Ur-Nammu's ziggurat in a semi-circle. They were like fortresses, so thick were their walls. The largest one, which was 100 yards by 60 yards, was dedicated to the moon-god. Another temple honored Nin-Gal, goddess of the moon and wife of Nannar. Every temple had an inner court surrounded by a series of rooms. The old fountains were still standing, with long water troughs coated with bitumen. Deep grooves made with knives on the great brick tables showed where the sacrificial animals had been dissected. They were cooked as a common sacrificial meal on the hearths of the temple kitchens. Even the ovens for baking bread were there. "After 3800 years," noted Woolley in his diary, "we were able to light the fire again and put into commission once more the oldest kitchen in the world."

Nowadays, churches, law courts, tax offices, and factories are quite separate establishments. It was otherwise in Ur. The sacred area, the temple precinct, was not reserved exclusively for the worship of the gods. The priests had many other things to do besides their holy office. In addition to receiving the sacrifices, they collected the tithes and the taxes. These transactions did not take place, however, without written confirmation. Every payment was noted on a little clay tablet—probably the first tax receipts ever issued. The amounts received were entered by scribes in weekly, monthly, and yearly totals.

Since minted currency was not yet known, taxes were paid in kind: every inhabitant of Ur paid in his own coin. Oil, cereals, fruit, wool, and cattle made their way into vast warehouses; perishable articles went to the temple shops. Many goods were manufactured in factories owned by the temple, for example, the spinning mills which the priests managed. One workshop produced twelve different kinds of fashionable clothing. Tablets found in this place gave the names of the mill girls and their quota of rations. Even the weight of the wool given to each worker and the number of garments made from it were meticulously recorded. In one of the legal buildings they found copies of the sentences carefully stacked exactly as they are in the administrative offices of modern law courts.

For three winters the Anglo-American expedition worked on at the site of ancient Ur, and still this extraordinary museum of man's early history had not yielded up all its secrets. Outside the temple area the excavators had a further surprise.

South of the staged tower, as they were clearing away a series of mounds, there suddenly emerged from the rubble solid structures: row upon row of walls and façades one after the other. As the sand was cleared away, it revealed a complete checkerboard of dwellings, the ruins of which were still ten feet high in places. Between them ran little alleyways. Here and there open squares broke the line of the streets.

After several weeks of hard work and the removal of endless loads of rubble, the diggers were faced with an unforgettable sight.

Under the red slopes of Tell al Muqayyar lay a whole city, bathed in the bright sunshine, awakened from its long sleep after many thousand years by the patient burrowing of the archaeologists. Woolley and his companions were beside themselves with joy. For before them lay Ur, the "Ur of the Chaldees" to which the Bible refers.

And how well its citizens lived and in what spacious homes! No other Mesopotamian city has revealed such handsome and comfortable houses.

Compared with them the dwellings that have been preserved in Babylon are modest; in fact, miserable. Professor Koldewey, during German excavations there at the beginning of the twentieth century, found nothing but simple mud-brick buildings, one story high with three or four rooms surrounding an open courtyard. That was how people lived about 600 B.C. in the much admired and extolled metropolis of Nebuchadnezzar the Great of Babylon. But 1500 years before that the citizens of Ur were living in large two-story villas with thirteen or fourteen rooms. The lower flat was solidly built of burned brick; the upper flat, of mud brick. The walls were neatly covered with plaster and whitewashed.

A visitor would pass through the door into a small entrance hall where there was a basin to wash the dust off hands and feet. He then continued into the inner court, which was attractively paved. Round it were grouped the reception room, the kitchen, living rooms, and private rooms, and the domestic chapel. Up a stone staircase, which concealed a lavatory, the visitor would reach a gallery from which branched off the rooms belonging to members of the family and the guest rooms.

From beneath the debris of brick and plaster there emerged into the light of day all the things that these patrician houses had contained in the way of domestic appliances for ordinary use. Countless shards of pots, jugs, vases, and small clay tablets covered with writing combined to form a mosaic from which piece by piece a picture of everyday life in Ur could be reconstructed. Ur of the Chaldees was a powerful, prosperous, colorful, and busy capital city at the beginning of the second millennium B.C.

One idea was very much in Woolley's mind: Abraham is said to have come from Ur of the Chaldees. He must therefore have been born in one of these two-story patrician houses and must have grown up there. Woolley wandered through the alleyways, past the walls of the great temple, and as he looked up he glimpsed the huge staged tower with its black, red, and blue blocks and its fringe of trees. "We must radically alter," he wrote enthusiastically, "our view of the Hebrew patriarch when we see that his earlier years were passed in such sophisticated surroundings. He was the citizen of a great city and inherited the traditions of an old and highly organized civilisation. The houses themselves reveal comfort and even luxury. We found copies of the hymns which were used in the services of the temples and toegther with them mathematical tables. On these tables were anything ranging from plain addition sums to formulae for the extraction of square and cube roots. In other texts the writers had copied out the old building inscriptions to be found in the city and had compiled in this way a short history of the temples."

Abraham—no simple nomad, this Abraham, but a son of a great city of the second millennium B.C.

That was a sensational discovery and one difficult to grasp. Newspapers and magazines carried photographs of the crumbling old staged tower and the ruins of the metropolis. They caused a tremendous sensation. People looked with astonishment at a drawing that bore the title "A house of the time of Abraham," which Woolley had had done by an artist. It was a genuine reconstruction in accordance with the finds. It showed the inner court of a villa type of house, in which two tall jars stood on a tiled pavement and a wooden balustrade ran round the upper story shutting off the rooms from the courtyard. Was the old familiar picture of the patriarch Abraham, as it had been held for generations, which saw him surrounded by his family and his cattle, suddenly to be called in question?

Woolley's idea did not remain unchallenged. Very soon theologians and even archaeologists registered their dissent.

In favor of Woolley's idea were the words of Gen. 11:31: "And Terah took Abram his son and Lot . . . and they went forth . . . from Ur of the Chaldees." But there are other references in the Bible that point to some other place. When Abraham sent his old servant from Canaan to the city of Nahor, to fetch a wife for his son Isaac, he calls this place Nahor his "country" (Gen. 24:4), his "father's house," and "the land of my kindred" (Gen. 24:7). Nahor lay in the north of Mesopotamia. After the conquest of the Promised Land, Joshua addressed the people in these words: "Your fathers dwelt on the other side of the flood in old time, even Terah the father of Abraham and the father of Abraham and the father of Nahor" (Josh. 24:2). In this case the "flood" means, as in other places in the Bible, the Euphrates. The city of Ur was excavated on the right bank of the Euphrates: viewed from Canaan it lay on this side, not on the other side, of the "flood." Had Woolley been too hasty in his conclusions? What reliable evidence had the expedition produced that Terah and his son Abraham lived actually in the city of Ur?

"The earlier journey from Ur of the Chaldees to Haran has, apart from the discovery of the city itself, no archaeological foundation," declares Professor W. F. Albright, of Johns Hopkins University. This scholar, who has himself conducted successful excavations and is the foremost authority on the archaeology of Palestine and the Middle East, goes further. "The remarkable fact that the Greek translations (of the Bible) nowhere mention Ur but read instead the more natural 'Land (of the Chaldees)' might mean that the removal of Abraham's native place to Ur is possibly secondary and was not generally known in the third century B.C."

Ur emerged from the shadowy past as the capital city of the Sumerians, one of the oldest civilizations in Mesopotamia. As we know, the Sumerians were not Semites like the Hebrews. When the great invasion of Semitic nomads streamed out of the Arabian desert about 2000 B.C., its first encounter in the south was with the extensive plantations of Ur, its houses and its canals. It is possible that some recollection of that great journey through the lands of the Fertile Crescent, in which Ur was involved, has resulted in its being mentioned in the Bible. Painstaking research, particularly excavations in the last two decades make it almost certain that Abraham cannot ever have been a citizen of the Sumerian metropolis. It would conflict with all the descriptions that the Old Testament gives of the kind of life lived by the patriarch: Abraham is a tent dweller, he moves with his flocks from pasture to pasture and from well to well. He does not live like a citizen of a great city; he lives the life of a typical nomad.

As we shall see, it was much farther to the north of the Fertile Crescent that the stories of the Biblical patriarchs emerged out of their mystical obscurity onto the plane of history.

CHAPTER 3 / Digging Up the Flood

The graves of the Sumerian kings—A puzzling layer of mud—Traces of the Flood under desert sands—A catastrophic flood about 4000 B.C.

AND THE LORD SAID UNTO NOAH, COME THOU AND ALL THY HOUSE INTO THE ARK. . . . FOR YET SEVEN DAYS, AND I WILL CAUSE IT TO RAIN UPON THE EARTH FORTY DAYS AND FORTY NIGHTS; AND EVERY LIVING SUBSTANCE THAT I HAVE MADE WILL I DESTROY FROM OFF THE FACE OF THE EARTH. . . . AND IT CAME TO PASS AFTER SEVEN DAYS THAT THE WATERS OF THE FLOOD WERE UPON THE EARTH. (Gen. 7:1, 4, 10)

When we hear the word "flood," almost immediately we think of the Bible and the story of Noah's Ark. This wonderful Old Testament story has traveled round the world with Christianity. But although this is the best known tradition of the flood, it is by no means the only one. Among people of all races there is a variety of traditions of a gigantic and catastrophic flood. The Greeks told a flood story and connected it with Deucalion; long before Columbus many stories told among the natives of the continent of America kept the memory of a great flood alive; in Australia, India, Polynesia, Tibet, Kashmir, and Lithuania tales of a flood have been handed down from generation to generation to the present day. Are they all fairy tales and legends? Are they all inventions?

It is highly probable that all flood stories reflect the same worldwide catastrophe. This frightful occurrence must, however, have taken place at a time when there were human beings on earth who could experience it, survive it, and then pass on an account of it. Geologists thought that they could solve this ancient mystery by pointing to the warm periods in the earth's history between the Ice Ages. They suggested that when the huge ice caps covering the continents, some of them

25

many thousand feet high, gradually began to melt, the level of the sea rose to four times its normal height all over the world. This great additional volume of water altered land contours, flooded low-lying coastal areas and plains, and annihilated their population, their animals, and their vegetation. But all these attempts at explanation ended in speculation and theory. Possible hypotheses satisfy the historian least of all. He constantly demands unambiguous factual evidence. But there was none; no scientist, whatever his line, could produce any. Actually it was by a coincidence, during research into something quite different, that unmistakable evidence of the Flood appeared, as it were, of its own accord. And that happened at a place with which we are already familiar—at the excavations at Ur.

For six years American and British archaeologists had been examining the ground at Tell al Muqayyar, which by that time looked like one vast building site. When the Baghdad railway stopped there for a moment, travelers looked with amazement at the soaring sandhills that had resulted from the diggings. Wagonloads of soil were removed, carefully searched, and put through the riddle. Rubbish thousands of years old was treated like precious cargo. Perseverance, conscientiousness, and painstaking effort had in six years yielded a handsome dividend. Discovery of the Sumerian temples with their warehouses, workshops, and law courts and of the villa type of dwellings was followed, between 1926 and 1928, by discoveries of such magnificence and splendor that everything uncovered thus far paled into insignificance.

"The graves of the kings of Ur"—so Woolley, in the exuberance of his delight at discovering them, had dubbed the tombs of Sumerian nobles whose truly regal splendor had been exposed when the spades of the archaeologists attacked a fifty-foot mound south of the temple and found a long row of superimposed graves. The stone vaults were veritable treasure chests, for they were filled with all the costly things that Ur in its heyday possessed. Golden drinking cups and goblets, wonderfully shaped jugs and vases, bronze tableware, mother of pearl mosaics, lapis lazuli, and silver surrounded these bodies which had moldered into dust. Harps and lyres rested against the walls. A young man, "Hero of the land of God," as an inscription described him, wore a golden helmet. A golden comb decorated with blossoms in lapis lazuli adorned the hair of the beautiful Sumerian Lady Shubad. Even the famous tombs of Nofretete and Tutankhamen contained no more beautiful objects. Moreover, "the graves of the kings of Ur" are 1000 years older at least.

The graves of the kings had, as well as these precious contents, another more grisly and depressing experience in store for the discoverers, enough to send a slight shiver down the spine. In the vaults were found teams of oxen with the skeletons still in harness, and each of the great wagons was laden with artistic household furniture. The whole retinue had clearly accompanied the nobleman in death, as could be gathered from the richly clad and ornamented skeletons with which they were surrounded. The tomb of the Lady Shubad had twenty such skeletons, other vaults had as many as seventy.

What can have happened here so long ago? There was not the slightest indication that they were victims of a violent death. In solemn procession, it would seem, the attendants with the ox-drawn treasure wagons accompanied the body to the tomb. And while the grave was being sealed outside they composed their dead master for his last rest within. Then they took some drug, gathered round him for the last time and died of their own free will in order to be able to serve him in his future existence.

For two centuries the citizens of Ur had buried their eminent men in these tombs. When they came to open the lowest and last tomb, the archaeologists of the twentieth century A.D. found themselves transported into the world of 2800 B.C.

As the summer of 1929 approached, the sixth season of digging at Tell al Muqayyar was drawing to a close. Woolley had put his native diggers once more onto the hill of "the graves of the kings." It left him no peace. He wanted to determine whether the ground

1. River Halys
2. Canish
3. Caspian Sea
4. Tarsus
5. Khalab (Aleppo)
6. Haran
7. Ugarit
8. Hamath
9. Tadmor
   (Oasis of Palmyra)
10. Great Plantations
    on the Euphrates
    and the Tigris
11. Sidon
12. Tyre
13. Hazor
14. Shechem
15. Egyptian
Coastal Vessels

NINEVEH

ASHUR

MARI

BABYLON

UR

"THE FERTILE CRESCENT"
About 2000 B.C.

16. Gerar
17. Mamre
18. Tanis
19. Road to the
Sinai Mines
20. Beersheba
21. Punon (Mines)

22. Sinai Mines with
Egyptian Temple
23. Nile
24. Red Sea
25. Tigris
26. Euphrates
27. Eshunna

28. Susa
29. Nomadic migrations
from South Arabia
30. Nippur
31. Erech
32. Persian Gulf

under the deepest royal grave had fresh discoveries in store for the next season's excavation.

After the foundations of the tomb had been removed, a few hundred thrusts of the spade made it quite plain that further layers of rubble lay below. How far into the past could these silent chronometers take them?

When had the very first human settlement arisen on virgin soil under this mound? Woolley had to know. To make certain he very slowly and carefully sank shafts and stood over them to examine the soil which came up from the underlying strata. "Almost at once," he wrote later in his diary, "discoveries were made which confirmed our suspicions. Directly under the floor of one of the tombs of the kings we found in a layer of charred wood ash numerous clay tablets, which were covered with characters of a much older type than the inscriptions on the graves. Judging by the nature of the writing the tablets could be assigned to about 3000 B.C. They were therefore two or three centuries earlier than the tombs."

The shafts went deeper and deeper. New strata, with fragments of jars, pots, and bowls, kept appearing. The experts noticed that the pottery remained surprisingly enough unchanged. It looked exactly like that which had been found in the graves of the kings. Therefore, it seemed that for centuries Sumerian civilization had undergone no radical change. They must, according to this conclusion, have reached a high level of development astonishingly early.

When after several days some of Woolley's workmen called out to him, "We are on ground level," he let himself down onto the floor of the shaft to satisfy himself. Traces of any kind of settlement did in fact break off abruptly in the shaft. The last fragments of household utensils lay on the smooth flat surface of the base of the pit. Here and there were charred remains. Woolley's first thought was, "This is it at last." He carefully prodded the ground on the floor of the shaft and stopped short. It was sand, pure sand of a kind that could only have been deposited by water. Mud in a place like that? Woolley tried to find an

Fig. 3. Traces of flood-clay about 4000 B.C. (a) River bed (Euphrates). (b) Layer of flood-clay. (c) Hill which projected above the flood.

explanation: it must be the accumulated silt of the Euphrates in bygone days. This stratum must have come into existence when the great river thrust its delta far out into the Persian Gulf, just as it still does, creating new land out of the sea at the river mouth at the rate of seventy-five feet a year. When Ur was in its heyday, the Euphrates flowed so close to it that the great staged tower was reflected in its waters and the Gulf was visible from the temple on its summit. The first buildings must therefore have sprung up on the mud flats of the delta.

Measurements of the adjacent area and more careful calculations, however, brought Woolley eventually to a quite different conclusion. "I saw that we were much too high up. It was most unlikely that the island on which the first settlement was built stood up so far out of the marsh."

The foot of the shaft, where the layer of mud began, was several yards above the river level. The mud, therefore, could not be river deposit. What then was the meaning of this remarkable stratum? Where did it come from? None of his associates could give him a satisfactory answer. They decided to dig on and make the shaft deeper. Woolley gazed intently as once more basket after basket came out of the trench and their contents were examined. Deeper and deeper went the spades into the ground: three feet, six feet—still pure mud. Suddenly, at nearly ten feet, the layer of mud stopped as abruptly as it had started. What would come now?

The next baskets that came to the surface gave an answer that none of the expedition would have dreamed of. They could hardly believe their eyes. They had expected pure virgin soil, but what now emerged into the glaring sunshine was rubble and more rubble, ancient rubbish, and countless potsherds. Under this clay deposit almost ten feet thick, they had struck fresh evidence of human habitation. The appearance and quality of the pottery had noticeably altered. Above the mud stratum were jars and bowls that had obviously been turned on a potter's wheel; here, on the contrary, they were handmade. No matter

Fig. 4. Pit showing flood stratum at Ur. 1. Graves of the Kings. 2. Sherds and vessels. 3. Bond of clay (10 feet). 4. Antediluvian vessels.

how carefully the contents of the baskets were sifted, amid increasing excitement, metal remains were nowhere to be found. The primitive implement that did emerge was made of hewn flint. It must belong to the Stone Age!

That day a telegram from Mesopotamia flashed what was perhaps the most extraordinary message that had ever stirred men's imaginations: "We have found the Flood." The incredible discovery at Ur made headline news in the United States and in Britain.

The Flood—that was the only possible explanation

of this great clay deposit beneath the hill at Ur, which quite clearly separated two epochs of settlement. The sea had left its unmistakable traces in the shape of remains of little marine organisms embedded in the mud. Woolley had to confirm his conclusions without delay; a chance coincidence—although the odds were against it—might conceivably have been making fools

Fig. 5. The extent of the Flood in Mesopotamia.

of them. Therefore, 300 yards from the first shaft he sank a second one.

The spades produced the same result: shards, mud, fragments of handmade pottery.

Finally, to remove all doubt, Woolley made his men dig a shaft through the rubble where the old settlement lay on a natural hill, that is to say, on a considerably higher level than the stratum of mud.

At just about the same level as in the two other shafts the shards of wheel-turned vessels ended suddenly. Immediately beneath them came handmade clay pots. It was exactly as Woolley had supposed and expected. Naturally the intermediate layer of mud was missing. "About sixteen feet below a brick pavement," noted Woolley, "which we could with reasonable certainty date about 2700 B.C., we were among the ruins of that Ur which had existed before the Flood."

How far did the layer of clay extend? What area was affected by the disaster? A proper hunt now started for traces of the Flood in other parts of Mesopotamia. Other archaeologists discovered a further important check point near Kish, northeast of Babylon, where the Euphrates and the Tigris flow in a great bend toward each other. There they found a similar band of clay, but only eighteen inches thick. Gradually, by a variety of tests, the limits of the Flood waters could be established. According to Woolley the disaster engulfed an area northwest of the Persian Gulf 400 miles long and 100 miles wide. Looking at the map today we should call it "a local occurrence," but for the inhabitants of the river plains it was, in those days, their whole world.

After endless inquiry and attempts at explanation, without achieving any concrete results, hope of solving the great riddle of the Flood had long since been given up. It seemed to lie in a dark and distant region of time which we could never hope to penetrate. Now Woolley and his associates had, through their tireless and patient efforts, made a discovery that shattered even the experts. A vast catastrophic inundation, resembling the Biblical Flood, which had regularly been described by skeptics as either a fairy tale or a legend, not only had taken place but was, moreover, an event within the compass of history.

At the foot of the old staged tower of the Sumerians, at Ur on the lower Euphrates, anyone could climb down a ladder into a narrow shaft and see and touch the remains of a gigantic and catastrophic flood which had deposited a layer of clay almost ten feet thick. Reckoning by the age of the strata containing traces of human habitation, and in this respect they are as reliable as a calendar, it can also be ascertained when the great Flood took place.

It happened about 4000 B.C.

*The Epic of Gilgamesh and the Bible—Twelve clay tablets
from Nineveh—An ancient epic from the library of Ashurbanipal—Utnapishtim, a Sumerian Noah?—The secret of
Mt. Ararat—A gigantic ship in a museum of ice—Expeditions in quest of the Ark*

AND GOD SAID UNTO NOAH, . . . MAKE THEE AN ARK
OF GOPHER WOOD; ROOMS SHALT THOU MAKE IN THE
ARK AND SHALT PITCH IT WITHIN AND WITHOUT
WITH PITCH. (Gen. 6:13-14)

About the turn of the century, long before Woolley discovered Ur, another find had aroused great interest
and given rise to lively discussions about the nature of
Holy Scripture.

From the dim recesses of the ancient East an old
and mysterious story came to light: a heroic epic, of
300 quatrains, inscribed on twelve large clay tablets,
which told of the wonderful experiences of the legendary king Gilgamesh. The text was astonishing. Gilgamesh told a tale exactly like that of the Bible—of a
man who was said to have lived before and after a
mighty and disastrous flood.

Where did this splendid and remarkable epic come
from?

During excavations in the eighteen-fifties British
archaeologists had found these twelve clay tablets, together with about 20,000 others, all in a good state of
preservation, among the ruins of the library at
Nineveh, which was reckoned to be the most famous
in the ancient world. In the seventh century B.C. King
Ashurbanipal had had it built high above the banks of
the Tigris in old Nineveh. Today on the other side of
the river the oil-derricks of Mosul tower into the sky.

A priceless treasure in packing cases started on its
long journey from Nineveh to the British Museum.
But not for several decades could they finally be de-

35

ciphered and the true value of the texts be revealed. At the time there was no one in the world who could read them. Despite every effort the tablets held their peace. Shortly before 1900 in the modest laboratories of the British Museum the old texts began, after an interval of twenty-five centuries, to unfold anew one of the finest narratives of the ancient East. Assyriologists heard for the first time the Epic of Gilgamesh. It is written in Akkadian, the language of the court and of diplomacy in the time of King Ashurbanipal. Its form, however, dates not from the time when it was placed in the library at Nineveh but from a thousand years earlier. It goes back as far as Hammurabi, the great king of Babylon, for a little later a second copy was discovered in his capital on the Euphrates. Further finds confirmed the view that the Gilgamesh Epic belonged to the rich heritage of all the great nations of the ancient East. Hittites and Egyptians translated it into their own tongues, and cuneiform tablets discovered by the Nile still show clearly the marks in red ink opposite those parts which the Egyptian scribes found difficult to translate.

At last a little clay fragment gave the clue to the origin of the Epic of Gilgamesh. The world owes its original composition to the Sumerians, the people whose capital stood on the site of Ur.

Gilgamesh, as the cuneiform writing on the eleventh tablet from the library at Nineveh tells us, decided to ensure his immortality and set out on a long adventurous journey to find his ancestor Utnapishtim, from whom he hoped to learn the secret of everlasting life which the gods had bestowed upon him. When Gilgamesh reached the island on which Utnapishtim lived, Gilgamesh asked of him the "Secret of Life." Utnapishtim related that he had once lived in Shuruppak and had been a true worshipper of the god Ea. When the gods decided to destroy mankind by a flood, Ea warned his devotee Utnapishtim and issued this command: "O man of Shuruppak, son of Ubar-Tutu, tear down thy house, build a ship; abandon wealth, seek after life; scorn possessions, save thy life. Bring up the seed of all kinds of living things into the ship:

the ship which thou shalt build. Let its dimensions be well measured."

We all know the wonderful story which follows. For what the Sumerian Utnapishtim is said to have experienced, the Bible tells us about Noah: "And God said unto Noah, . . . Make thee an ark of gopher wood. . . . And of every living thing of all flesh, two of every sort shalt thou bring into the ark, to keep them alive with thee; they shall be male and female." (Gen. 6:13ff.)

To make the comparison easier, let us set side by side what Utnapishtim says of his great experience and what the Bible tells us of Noah and the Flood.

In accordance with the command of the god Ea, Utnapishtim built the ship and says:

On the fifth day I decided upon its plan. The floor was 200 ft. square. The walls were 200 ft. high.	The length of the ark shall be three hundred cubits, the breadth of it fifty cubits, and the height of it thirty cubits. (Gen. 6:15)
I gave it six stories and divided the breadth seven times.	With lower, second, and third stories shalt thou make it. (Gen. 6:16)
Its interior I divided into nine.	. . . rooms shalt thou make in the ark. (Gen. 6:14)
6 sar of bitumen I poured into the kiln.	. . . and shalt pitch it within and without with pitch. (Gen. 6:14)

When Utnapishtim had finished building his ship, he arranged a sumptuous banquet. He provided venison and mutton for those who had helped with the work of building and dispensed "cider, beer, oil and wine to the people as if it were running water." Then he continues:

All that I had I loaded, of the seed of all living things.	And Noah went in, and his sons, and his wife, and his sons' wives, into the ark, be-

cause of the waters of the flood.

Of clean beasts, and of beasts that are not clean, and of fowls, and of every thing that creepeth upon the earth.

I brought into the ship my whole family and kinfolk.

There went in two and two unto Noah into the ark, the male and the female, as God had commanded Noah. (Gen. 7:7-9)

The cattle of the field, the beasts of the field, all craftsmen—I made them go up into it.

I went into the ship and closed my door.

And the Lord shut him in. (Gen. 7:16)

As soon as a gleam of dawn shone in the sky, came a black cloud from the foundation of heaven.

And it came to pass, after seven days, that the waters of the flood were upon the earth.

Inside it Adad thundered.

... the same day were all the fountains of the great deep broken up, and the windows of heaven were opened. (Gen. 7:10-11)

But the Flood raged on unceasing, as Gilgamesh learned:

Six days and nights. . . .	And the flood was forty days upon the earth; and the waters increased. . . .
Raged the wind, the flood, the cyclone devastated the land.	And the waters prevailed exceedingly upon the earth; and all the high hills, that were under the whole heaven, were covered. (Gen. 7: 17-19)
When the seventh day came, the cyclone, the flood, the battle was over.	And God remembered Noah . . . and God made a wind to pass over the earth, and the waters assuaged; (Gen. 8:1)
Which had battled like an army. The sea became calm, the cyclone died away, the flood ceased.	The fountains also of the deep and the windows of heaven were stopped, and the rain from heaven was restrained. And the waters returned from off the earth continually; and after the end of the hundred and fifty days the waters were abated. (Gen. 8:2, 3)
And all mankind had turned to clay. The ground was flat like a roof.	And all flesh died that moved upon the earth . . . and every man. (Gen. 7:21)

"And all mankind had turned to clay." Utnapishtim, the Sumerian Noah, was recording what he himself claimed to have lived through. Babylonians, Assyrians, Hittites, and Egyptians who translated or read aloud or narrated these words had no more notion that they were describing something that actually happened than did the modern Assyriologists who painfully deciphered them from the cuneiform tablets.

Today we know that line 134 on the eleventh tablet of the Epic of Gilgamesh must depend on an eyewitness account. Only someone who had himself seen the desolation caused by the catastrophe could have described it with such striking force.

The great layer of mud, which covered every living thing like a shroud and leveled the ground until it was as "flat as a roof," must have been seen with his own eyes by someone who had had a marvelous escape. The exact description of the great storm argues for this assumption. Utnapishtim expressly mentions a southern gale, which corresponds closely with the geographical situation. The Persian Gulf, whose waters were flung over the flat country by the gale, lies south of the estuary of the Tigris and Euphrates. To the last detail the weather conditions that he describes are characteristic of an unusual atmospheric disturbance: the appearance of black clouds and a roaring noise—sudden darkness in broad daylight—the howling of the southern gale as it drives the water in front of it. Any meteorologist recognizes at once that this is a description of a cyclone. Modern weather experts recognize that in tropical regions coastal areas, islands, but above all alluvial river flats are subject to a spiral type of tidal wave which leaves devastation and destruction in its wake, and which is often caused by cyclones, accompanied by earthquakes and torrential rain.

All along the coast of Florida, in the Gulf of Mexico, and on the Pacific there is today an up-to-date alarm system with all the latest equipment. But for southern Mesopotamia in 4000 B.C. not even a modern alarm system would have been of much use. Sometimes cyclones produce an effect which takes the shape of the Flood. There is an example in recent times. In 1876 a cyclone of this nature, accompanied by tremendous thunderstorms, swept across the Bay of Bengal and headed for the coast at the mouth of the Ganges. Up to 200 miles from its center ships at sea had their masts splintered. It was ebb tide along the coast. The receding water was seized by the broad high sweep of the cyclone, and a gigantic tidal wave reared up. It burst into the Ganges area, and sea water fifty feet high swept inland—141 square miles were buried and 215,000 people died.

Utnapishtim then told a horrified Gilgamesh what had happened when the disaster was over:

I opened the window and the light fell on my face.	And it came to pass at the end of forty days, that Noah opened the window of the ark which he had made: (Gen. 8:6)
The ship lay upon Mt. Nisir.	And the ark rested in the seventh month, on the seventeenth day of the month,
Mount Nisir held the ship and allowed it not to move.	enteenth day of the month, upon the mountains of Ararat. (Gen. 8:4)

Old Babylonian cuneiform texts describe with care where Mt. Nisir is to be found. It lies between the Tigris and the lower reaches of the river Zab, where the wild and rugged mountain ranges of Kurdistan rise sharply from the flat country bordering the Tigris. The alleged resting place corresponds perfectly with the last lap of the great catastrophe that burst inland from the south. We are told that Utnapishtim's home was in Shuruppak. It lay near the present-day Farah in the middle of the flat fenland where Tigris and Euphrates part company. A tidal wave from the Persian Gulf must have carried a ship from there right to the Kurdistan mountains.

Despite the precise descriptions in the Epic of Gilgamesh, Mt. Nisir has never tempted the curious to search for the remains of this giant ship. Instead, Mt. Ararat, which belongs to the Biblical tradition, has been the goal of a series of expeditions. Mt. Ararat lies in eastern Turkey, near the borders of Russia and Iran. Its snow-capped summit is over 16,000 feet high.

In the last century, before any archaeologist had turned a spadeful of Mesopotamian soil, the first expeditions were making their way to Mt. Ararat. A shepherd's story had started them off. At the foot of Ararat lies the little Armenian village of Bayazit, whose inhabitants have for generations recounted the remarkable experience of a mountain shepherd who was said to have seen one day on Ararat a great wooden ship. A report from a Turkish expedition in 1833 seemed to confirm the shepherd's story, since it mentioned a wooden bow of a ship which in the summer season stuck out of the south glacier.

The next person who claimed to have seen it was Dr. Nouri, Archdeacon of Jerusalem and Babylon. In 1892 this agile ecclesiastical dignitary undertook a journey to discover the sources of the Euphrates. On his return he told of the wreckage of a ship in the eternal ice: "The interior was full of snow: the outer wall was of a dark red color." In the First World War a Russian flying officer, by name Roskowitzki, an-

Fig. 6. Mount Ararat—where three countries meet: Turkey, Iran and U.S.S.R.

nounced that he had spotted from his plane "the remains of wreckage of a fair-sized ship" on the south flank of Ararat. Although it was the middle of the war, Czar Nicholas II dispatched a search party without delay. It is supposed not only to have seen the ship but even to have photographed it. All proof of this, however, perished, presumably in the Revolution.

From the Second World War there are likewise several cases of aerial observation. They come from a Russian pilot and from four American fliers. These latter reports brought into the field the American historian and missionary Dr. Aaron Smith, of Greensboro, an expert on the Flood. As a result of years of labor he has collected a complete history of the literature on Noah's Ark. There are 80,000 works in seventy-two languages about the Flood, of which

70,000 mention the legendary wreckage of the Ark. In 1951 Dr. Smith spent twelve days with forty companions to no purpose on the ice cap of Ararat. "Although we found no trace of Noah's Ark," he declared later, "my confidence in the Biblical description of the Flood is no whit the less. We shall go back."

Encouraged by Dr. Smith, the young French Greenland explorer Jean de Riquer climbed the volcanic peak in 1952. He too came back without accomplishing anything. Despite this, fresh expeditions are always getting ready for a further attempt on Mt. Ararat. The latest was in 1955. In that year, in the early morning of July 6th, Fernand Navarra from France, searching for the most famous ship in history, succeeded to his great surprise in salvaging three fragments of a wooden beam embedded in solid ice on top of the mountain. The timber was at least 5000 years old, although whether this was actually a relic of Noah's Ark it is of course impossible to say.

No tradition of the early days of Mesopotamia is in such close agreement with the Bible as the flood story in the Epic of Gilgamesh. In some places we find almost verbal correspondence. Yet, there is a significant and essential difference. The familiar story in Genesis knows of one God only. The oddly amusing and primitive conception of a heaven overcrowded with gods, many of whom bear all too human characteristics, who weep and wail, and who are afraid of one another and cower like dogs, has disappeared.

The Epic of Gilgamesh had its origin in the same great area, the Fertile Crescent, in which the Bible likewise had its birth. As a result of the discovery of the mud stratum at Ur, it is certain that the old Mesopotamian epic deals with a traditional event: the flood disaster about 4000 B.C. in southern Mesopotamia is vouched for by archaeology.

But is that Babylonian flood identical with the Flood of Biblical tradition?

This is the one great question that neither archaeology nor research has yet been able to answer.

A stone corpse—Lieutenant Cabane reports a find—A Syrian tell has important visitors—King Lamgi-Mari introduces himself—Professor Parrot discovers an unknown empire—A royal palace with 260 apartments and court yards —23,600 clay tablets have survived for 4000 years— Desert police report the "Benjamites"—Rebecca's home —A flourishing city

NOW THE LORD HAD SAID UNTO ABRAM, GET THEE OUT OF THY COUNTRY, AND FROM THY KINDRED, AND FROM THY FATHER'S HOUSE, UNTO A LAND THAT I WILL SHOW THEE. (Gen. 12:1)

The country of which the Bible is speaking in this case is Haran. Terah, his son Abram, his daughter-in-law Sarai, and his grandson Lot lived there. (Gen. 11:31)

What was actually meant by Haran was until recently almost entirely unknown. We knew nothing of its early history. All the old Babylonian documents were silent about the middle reaches of the Euphrates, Mespotamia, the land between the rivers, where Haran once stood.

A chance find led to excavations in 1933, which here also gave rise to a great and exciting discovery and added considerably to our knowledge. They brought the Haran of the Bible and the kind of life lived by the patriarchs quite unexpectedly into a historical context. On the line between Damascus and Mosul, where it cuts the Euphrates, lies the small unknown town of Abu Kemal. Since, as a result of the First World War, Syria was placed under a French mandate, there was a French garrison in the place.

Over the broad Euphrates plain in midsummer 1933 lay a brooding, paralyzing heat. Lieutenant Cabane, the station commander, expected, when he was called into the orderly room, that there was merely another

44

quarrel among the Arabs that he was supposed to settle. He had had more than enough of that already. But this time the excitement in the office seemed to be about something different. Eventually he managed to extract through the interpreter the following story: These people had been burying one of their relatives. They were digging the grave on a remote hillside, by name Tell Hariri, when out popped a stone corpse!

Perhaps, thought Lieutenant Cabane, this might be something that would interest the museum at Aleppo. At any rate, it was a pleasant change from the endless monotony of this Godforsaken post.

In the cool of the evening he drove out to Tell Hariri, which lay about seven miles to the north of Abu Kemal, near the Euphrates. The Arabs led him up the slope to the broken statue in a flat earthen trough which had so upset them the day before. Cabane was no expert, but he knew at once that the stone figure must be very old. Next day it was taken by French soldiers to Abu Kemal. The lights were on till long after midnight in the little command post. Cabane was writing a detailed report on the find to his superior officer, to Henry Seyrig, Director of Antiquities in Beirut, and to the museum at Aleppo.

Months went past and nothing happened. The whole thing seemed to be either unimportant or forgotten. Then at the end of November came a telegram from Paris, from the Louvre. Cabane could hardly believe his eyes and read the message again and again. In a few days important visitors from Paris would be arriving: Professor Parrot, the well-known archaeologist, accompanied by scientists, architects, assistants, and draughtsmen.

On the 14th of December Tell Hariri was buzzing like a beehive. The archaeologists had begun their detective work. First of all the whole mound was carefully measured and photographed in detail. Soundings were taken for echoes, specimens of soil were removed and submitted to expert opinion. December went by and the first weeks of the New Year. The 23rd of January 1934 was the decisive day.

As they were digging carefully through the outer

crust of the Tell there appeared out of the rubble a neat little figure which had some writing pricked out on the right shoulder. Everyone bent over it, fascinated. "I am Lamgi-Mari . . . king . . . of Mari . . . the great . . . Issakkv . . . who worships his statue . . . of Ishtar."

Slowly, word by word, this sentence rang in the ears of the silent circle as Professor Parrot translated it from the cuneiform. That was an unforgettable moment for him and his companions; an almost uncanny scene and probably unique in the history of archaeology with all its surprises and adventures.

The monarch had solemnly welcomed the strangers from distant Paris and introduced himself to them. It was as if he wanted politely to show them the road into his kingdom of long ago which lay in a deep sleep beneath him, and of whose pomp and power the Parisian scholars had as yet no conception.

Carved in stone, a marvelous piece of sculpture, King Lamgi-Mari stood before Parrot: a commanding broad-shouldered figure upon its base. But the face lacks that incredible arrogance which is so typical of the portraits of the other conquerors from the ancient East: the Assyrians, who without exception look fierce and bad-tempered. The king of Mari is smiling; he carries no weapons, and his hands are folded in an attitude of worship. His robe, which leaves one shoulder bare, like a toga, is richly decorated with fringes.

Seldom has an excavation been crowned with so much success from the first groping efforts, from the word go. Mari, the royal city, must be lying slumbering under this mound. Scholars had for a long time been familiar with the royal city of Mari which is featured in many old inscriptions from Babylonia and Assyria. One text maintained that Mari was the tenth city to be founded after the Flood. The great spade offensive against Tell Hariri began.

Broken by considerable intervals of inactivity, the digging went on from 1933 to 1939. For the greater part of the year the tropical heat made any activity impossible. Only in the cooler months of the rainy season, from the middle of December to the end of March, could anything be done.

The excavations at Tell Hariri brought a wealth of new discoveries to a chapter of the history of the ancient East that is still unwritten. No one yet knew how close a connection the finds at Mari would prove to have with quite familiar passages in the Bible.

Year by year reports of the expedition provided fresh surprises. In the winter of 1933-1934 a temple of Ishtar, the goddess of fertility, was exposed. Three of Ishtar's royal devotees have immortalized themselves as statues in the shrine which is inlaid with a mosaic of gleaming shells: Lamgi-Mari, Ebin-il, and Idi-Narum.

In the second season of digging the spades came upon the houses of a city. Mari had been found! However great was the satisfaction with their success, far more interest—indeed, astonishment—was aroused by the walls of a palace that must have been unusually large. Parrot reported: "We have unearthed 69 rooms and courts, and there are still more to come." Sixteen hundred cuneiform tablets carefully stacked in one of the rooms contained details of household management.

The record of the third campaign, in 1935-1936, noted that so far 138 rooms and courtyards had been found but that they had not yet reached the outer walls of the palace. And 13,000 clay tablets awaited deciphering. In the fourth winter a temple of the god Dagon was dug up and also a ziggurat, the typical Mesopotamian staged tower. In the palace 220 rooms and courtyards were now visible, and another 8000 clay tablets had been added to the existing collection.

At last in the fifth season, when a further forty rooms had been cleared of rubble, the palace of the kings of Mari lay in all its vast extent before Parrot and his assistants. This mammoth building of the third millennium B.C. covered nearly ten acres. Never before during any excavations had such an enormous building with such vast ramifications come to light.

Columns of lorries had to be commissioned to remove the cuneiform tablets from the palace archives alone. There were almost 25,000 documents. The great find of the tablets at Nineveh was put in the shade, since the famous library of the Assyrian king Ashurbanipal amounted to a mere 22,000 clay texts.

To get a proper picture of Mari palace, aerial photographs were taken. These pictures, taken from a low altitude over Tell Hariri, gave rise to almost incredulous amazement when they were published in France. This palace at Mari was, about 2000 B.C., one of the greatest sights of the world, the architectural gem of the ancient East. Travelers came from far and near to see it. "I have seen Mari," wrote an enthusiastic merchant from the Phoenician seaport of Ugarit.

The last king to live there was Zimri-Lim. The armies of the famous Hammurabi of Babylon subjugated the kingdom of Mari on the central reaches of the Euphrates and destroyed its mighty capital about 1700 B.C. Under the wreckage of roofs and walls were found the fire pans of the Babylonian warriors, the incendiary squad who set fire to the palace.

But they were not able to destroy it completely. Walls to a height of fifteen feet were left standing. "The installations in the palace kitchens and bathrooms," wrote Professor Parrot, "could still be put into commission without the need of any repair, four thousand years after its destruction." In the bathrooms they found the tubs, in the kitchens cake molds, even charcoal in the ovens.

The sight of these majestic ruins is an overwhelming experience. A single gate on the north side ensured easier control and better defense. After passing through a medley of courts and passages, one reaches the great inner courtyard and broad daylight. This was the center both of official life and of the administration of the kingdom. The monarch received his officials as well as couriers and ambassadors in the neighboring audience chamber, large enough to hold hundreds of people. Broad corridors led to the king's private apartments.

One wing of the palace was used exclusively for religious ceremonies. It contained also a throne room, approached by a marvelous staircase. A long processional way passed through several rooms to the palace chapel, in which stood the image of the mother-goddess of fertility. From a vessel in her hands flowed perpetually "the water of everlasting life."

The entire court lived under the king's roof. Ministers, administrators, secretaries, and scribes had their own roomy quarters. There was a Foreign Office and a Board of Trade in the great administrative palace of the kingdom of Mari. More than 100 officials were involved in dealing with the incoming and outgoing messages, which alone amounted to thousands of tablets.

Wonderful great frescoes added a decorative effect to the palace. Even to this day the colors have lost hardly any of their brilliance. They seem to have been laid on only yesterday, whereas, in fact, they are the oldest paintings in Mesopotamia—a thousand years older than the renowned colored frescoes in the splendid edifices of the Assyrian rulers at Khorsabad, Nineveh, and Nimrod.

The size and grandeur of this unique palace were not incongruous in the land that was governed from it. Through these many thousands of years the palace archives have preserved the record. Notices, public papers, decrees, accounts, scratched out on clay by the busy styli of well-paid scribes four thousand years ago, had to be brought to life again with tireless industry. In Paris, Professor Georges Dossin, of the University of Liége, and a host of Assyriologists are wrestling with the problem of deciphering and translating the tablets. It will be years before all the 23,600 documents are translated and published.

Each of the documents contains a little piece of the mosaic that makes up the true picture of the kingdom of Mari: Numerous orders for the construction of canals, locks, dams, and embankments make it plain that the prosperity of the country depended largely on the widespread system of irrigation, which was constantly under the supervision of government engineers who saw to its care and maintenance.

Two tablets contain a list of 2000 craftsmen, giving their full names and the names of their guilds.

The news service in Mari functioned so quickly and successfully that it would bear comparison with modern telegraphy. Important messages were sent by means of fire signals in a matter of a few hours from the frontier of Babylon to what is now Turkey, a distance of more than 300 miles.

Mari lay at the intersection of the great caravan routes from west to east and from north to south. It is not surprising, therefore, that the traffic in goods, which extended from Cyprus and Crete to Asia Minor and Mesopotamia, necessitated a lively correspondence on clay concerning imports and exports. But the tablets do not merely record everyday matters. They also give an impressive account of religious life, of New Year festivals in honor of Ishtar, auguries with the entrails of animals, and interpretation of dreams. Twenty-five gods made up the Mari pantheon. A list of sacrificial lambs, which Zimri-Lim presented, refers to these occupants of heaven by name.

From countless individual bits of evidence on these tablets we can form a picture of this masterpiece of organization and administration which constituted the kingdom of Mari in the eighteenth century B.C. What is most astonishing is that neither in their sculptures nor in their paintings is there any indication of warlike activity. The inhabitants of Mari were Amorites who had been settled there for a long time and who preferred peace. Their interests lay in religion and ceremonial, in

Fig. 7. This picture from Room 106 in the palace of Mari shows the investiture of Zimri-Lim by the goddess Ishtar.

trade and commerce. Conquest, heroism, and the clash of battle meant little to them. As we can still see from statues and pictures, their faces radiate a cheerful serenity.

That did not mean, however, that they were absolved from the necessity of defending and safeguarding their territory by force of arms. On their frontiers lived tribes of Semitic nomads, who found the lush pastures, market gardens, and cornfields of Mari a constant temptation. They were always crossing the border, grazing their cattle over wide stretches of the countryside, and disturbing the population. They had to be watched. Frontier posts were therefore established as a check on this danger, and any incident was immediately reported to Mari.

In Paris the Assyriologists were deciphering a clay tablet from the archives of Mari. They read with astonishment a report from Bannum, an officer of the desert police: "Say to my lord: This from Bannum, thy servant. Yesterday I left Mari and spent the night at Zuruban. All the Benjamites were sending fire signals. From Samanum to Ilum-Muluk, from Ilum-Muluk to Mishlan, all the Benjamite villages in the Terqa district replied with fire signals. I am not yet certain what these signals meant. I am trying to find out. I shall write to my lord whether or not I succeed. The city guards should be strengthened and my lord should not leave the gate."

In this police report from the central reaches of the Euphrates in the nineteenth century B.C. there appears the name of one of the tribes known to us from the Bible. It literally calls them Benjamites. There is frequent mention of these Benjamites. They seem to have given the ruler of Mari so many headaches and caused so much trouble that periods of a king's reign were even called after them.

In the Mari dynasties the years of each reign were not numbered but were identified with some notable event: for example, the building and consecration of new temples, the erection of great dams to improve irrigation, the strengthening of the banks of the Euphrates, or a national census. Three times the chronological tables mention the Benjamites: "The year in which Iahdulim went to Hen and laid hands upon the territory of the Benjamites" is referred to in the reign of King Iahdulim of Mari; "The Year that Zimri-Lim killed the Dawidum of the Benjamites"; and "The year after Zimri-Lim killed the Dawidum of the Benjamites. . . ." in the reign of the last monarch of Mari, Zimri-Lim.

An elaborate correspondence between governors, district commissioners, and administrators takes place over the single question: Dare we take a census of the Benjamites?

In the kingdom of Mari a census of the people was not uncommon. It provided a basis for taxation and for enlistment for military service. The population was summoned by districts and a nominal roll was made of every man liable for call-up. The proceedings lasted several days during which free beer and bread were distributed by government officials. The administration in the palace of Mari would have liked to include the Benjamites in this, but the district officers had doubts. They advised against it, since they understood only too well the temper of these roaming and rebellious tribes.

"Reference: the proposal to take a census of the Benjamites, about which you have written me," begins a letter from Samsi-Addu to Iasmah-Addu in Mari. "The Benjamites are not well disposed to the idea of a census. If you carry it out, their kinsmen, the Ra-ab-ay-yi, who live on the other bank of the river, will hear of it. They will be annoyed with them and will not return to their country. On no account should this census be taken!"

Thus the Benjamites lost their free beer and bread and also escaped paying taxes and military service.

Later, the children of Israel were to experience many times a census of this sort conducted exactly on the Mari pattern. The first time was on the command of Yahweh after Moses had led them out of Egypt. All men over twenty who were fit to fight were registered according to their families. (Num. 1-4) A generation later, after their sojourn in the desert, Moses took a second census with a view to dividing up the land of

Canaan. (Num. 26) During the monarchy David ordered a national census. What he had in mind on that occasion was the building up of an army and his commander in chief, Joab, was entrusted with the arrangements. (II Sam. 24) As the Bible depicts the incident, Yahweh had put the idea into the king's mind in order to punish the people. The Israelites loved their freedom above all else, and registration and the prospect of being called up were equally hateful to them. Even in A.D. 6 the census carried out by Governor Cyrenius almost led to open revolt.

It is worth noting that it is to peace-loving Mari that the world owes the original pattern of all recruiting campaigns. It was later followed by Babylonians and Assyrians, by Greeks and Romans, in exactly the same way, and, indeed, in later days by the nations of modern times. Thus Mari has given the lead to the whole world in this matter of taking a census for purposes of taxation and conscription for military service.

In Paris the mention of Benjamites gave rise to conjecture and anticipation along a particular line. And not without reason. On other clay tablets the Assyriologists dealing with these reports of governors and district commissioners of the Mari empire came across, one after another, a whole series of familiar sounding names from Biblical history—names like Peleg, and Serug, Nahor, and Terah and—Haran. "These are the generations of Shem," says Gen. 11. ". . . Peleg lived thirty years and begat Reu. . . . And Reu lived two and thirty years and begat Serug. . . . And Serug lived thirty years and begat Nahor. . . . And Nahor lived nine and twenty years and begat Terah. . . . And Terah lived seventy years and begat Abram, Nahor, and Haran."

Names of Abraham's forefathers emerge from these dark ages as names of cities in northwest Mesopotamia. They lie in Padan-Aram, the plain of Aram. In the center of it lies Haran which, according to its description, must have been a flourishing city in the nineteenth and eighteenth centuries B.C. Haran, the home of Abraham, father of the patriarchs, the birthplace of the Hebrew people, is here for the first time historically attested, for contemporary texts refer to it. Further up the same Balikh valley lay the city with an equally well-known Biblical name, Nahor, the home of Rebecca, wife of Isaac.

"And Abraham was old and well stricken in age: and the Lord had blessed Abraham in all things. And Abraham said unto his eldest servant of his house, that ruled over all that he had: Put, I pray thee, thy hand under my thigh: And I will make thee swear by the Lord, the God of heaven, and the God of the earth, that thou shalt not take a wife unto my son of the daughters of the Canaanites, among whom I dwell: But thou shalt go unto my country, and to my kindred, and take a wife unto my son Isaac. . . . And the servant took ten camels . . . and went to Mesopotamia, unto the city of Nahor." (Gen. 24:1-4, 10)

The Biblical city of Nahor is unexpectedly drawn into a recognizable historical setting. Abraham's servant set out for the land of the kings of Mari. The instructions of his master, according to the Biblical tradition, clearly indicate that Abraham must have known northern Mesopotamia, including Nahor, extremely well. How else could he have spoken of the city of Nahor?

If we follow the dates given in the Bible, we find that Abraham left his native place, Haran, 645 years before the Exodus of the people of Israel from Egypt. They wandered through the desert toward the Promised Land under the leadership of Moses in the thirteenth century B.C. This date is, as we shall see, assured by archaeology. Abraham must therefore have lived about 1900 B.C. The finds at Mari confirm the accuracy of the Biblical account. About 1900 B.C., according to the evidence of the palace archives, Haran and Nahor were both flourishing cities.

The documents from the kingdom of Mari produce startling proof again that the stories of the patriarchs in the Bible are not pious legends, as is often too readily assumed, but events that are described as happening in a historical period that can be precisely dated.

CHAPTER 6 / The Long Journey
to Canaan

*Six hundred miles by the caravan route—Nowadays four
visas are required—The land of purple—Punitive expeditions against "Sand dwellers"—Proud seaports with a
troublesome hinterland—An Egyptian best-seller about
Canaan—Sinuhe praises the Good Land—Jerusalem on
magic vases—Strongholds—Sellin finds Shechem—Abraham chooses the high road*

AND ABRAM TOOK SARAI HIS WIFE, AND LOT HIS
BROTHER'S SON, AND ALL THEIR SUBSTANCE THAT
THEY HAD GATHERED, AND THE SOULS THAT THEY
HAD GOTTEN IN HARAN; AND THEY WENT FORTH TO
GO INTO THE LAND OF CANAAN. . . . (Gen. 12:5)

The road from Haran, the home of the patriarchs,
to the land of Canaan runs south for more than 600
miles. It follows the River Balikh as far as the Euphrates, thence by a caravan route thousands of years old
via the oasis of Palmyra, the Tadmor of the Bible, to
Damascus, and from there in a southwesterly direction
to the Lake of Galilee. It is one of the great trade
routes that have always led from the Euphrates to Jordan, from the kingdoms of Mesopotamia to the
Phoenician seaports on the Mediterranean and the distant Nile lands in Egypt.

Anyone nowadays wanting to follow Abraham's
route requires four visas: one for Turkey, in which the
site of Haran lies; one for Syria, to cover the section
from the Euphrates via Damascus to the Jordan; and
one each for the states of Jordan and Israel which
occupy what was once Canaan. In the time of the father
of the patriarchs all this was much easier, for on his
long trek he had only to pass through one large stretch
of national territory, the kingdom of Mari, from which
he was in fact departing. The smaller city states between the Euphrates and the Nile could be by-passed.
The road to Canaan lay open.

The first city of any size that Abraham must have reached on his journey is still standing today—Damascus.

To go by car from Damascus to Palestine is, especially in springtime, an unforgettable experience.

The ancient city with its narrow streets and dark bazaar-filled alleys, with its mosques and its Roman remains, lies in the center of a wide and fertile plain.

Fig. 8. *The route taken by the Father of the Patriarchs from the Kingdom of Mari to Canaan.*

When the Arabs speak of Paradise they think of Damascus. What other Mediterranean city can compare with this place which every spring is decked with an incredible mantle of gay blossom? In all the gardens and in the hedgerows beyond the city walls apricots and almonds are a riot of pink. Flowering trees line the road that climbs gently as it heads for the southwest. Tilled fields alternate with olive groves and large mulberry plantings. High above, to the right of the road, rises the El Barada River, to which the land owes its fertility. Here mighty Hermon thrusts its steep slopes 10,000 feet into the heavens above the flat and verdant plain. From the side of this famous mountain ridge, to

the south, gushes the source of the Jordan. Towering
over both Syria and Palestine and visible from afar, it
seems to have been placed there by nature as a gigantic
boundary stone between them. Even in the blazing heat
of summer its peak remains covered with snow. The
effect becomes even more impressive as on the left of
the road the green fields disappear. Monotonous gray-
brown hills, streaked with dried-up river beds, pile up
toward the distant shimmering horizon where the
scorching Syrian Desert begins—the home of the Bedouins. The road climbs gradually for an hour and a
half. Fields and groves become rarer. The green is more
and more swallowed up by the sandy gray of the
desert. Then suddenly an enormous pipeline crosses the
road. The oil that flows through it has already come
quite a way. Its journey began in the oil wells of the
Bahrein Islands in the Persian Gulf, almost a thousand
miles distant, and will end in the port of Saïda on the
Mediterranean. Saïda is the old Sidon of the Bible.

Behind a ridge suddenly appear the hills of Galilee.
A few minutes later comes the frontier. Syria lies behind. The road crosses a small bridge. Under the arch
a fast-moving narrow current hurries on its way. It is
the Jordan: we are in Palestine, in the young state of
Israel.

After a few miles between dark basalt rocks the
bright blue of the Lake of Galilee sparkles up at us
from far below. It was on this lake, where time seems to
have stood still, that Jesus preached from a boat off
Capernaum. Here he told Peter to cast his nets and raise
the great draft of fishes. Two thousand years before
that the flocks of Abraham grazed on its shores; for the
road from Mesopotamia to Canaan went past the Lake
of Galilee.

Canaan is the narrow mountainous strip of land between the shores of the Mediterranean and the borders
of the desert, from Gaza in the south right up to
Hamath on the banks of the Orontes in the north.
Canaan means "Land of Purple." It owes its name to a
product of the country which was highly prized in the
olden days. From earliest times the inhabitants had extracted from a shellfish (Murex), which was native to

these parts, the most famous dye in the ancient world, purple. It was so uncommon, so difficult to obtain and therefore so expensive, that only the wealthy could afford it. Purple robes were throughout the ancient East a mark of high rank. The Greeks called the manufacturers of purple and the purple-dyers of the Mediterranean, Phoenicians. The country they called Phoenicia, which meant "purple" in their language.

The Land of Canaan is also the birthplace of two things which have radically affected the whole world: the word *Bible* and our alphabet. A Phoenician city was godparent to the Greek word for *book:* from Byblos, the Canaanite seaport, comes "Biblion" and, hence, later "Bible." In the ninth century B.C. the Greeks took over from Canaan the letters of our alphabet.

The part of the country which was to become the home of the Israelite people was named by the Romans after Israel's worst enemies. Palestine comes from Pelishtim, as the Philistines are called in the Old Testament. They lived on the southernmost part of the coast of Canaan. "All Israel, from Dan even to Beersheba" (I Sam. 3:20) is how the Bible describes the extent of the Promised Land, that is, from the sources of Jordan at the foot of Hermon to the hills west of the Dead Sea and to the Negeb in the south.

If we look at a globe of the world, Palestine is only a tiny spot on the earth's surface, a narrow streak. It is possible to drive comfortably in a single day round the borders of the old kingdom of Israel: 150 miles from North to South, 25 miles across at its narrowest point, 9500 square miles in all, its size was about that of the island of Sicily. Only for a few decades in its turbulent history was it any bigger. Under its renowned kings David and Solomon its territory reached to the arm of the Red Sea at Ezion-geber in the south, and far beyond Damascus into Syria on the north. The present state of Israel with its 8000 square miles is smaller by a fifth than the old kingdom.

There never flourished here crafts and industries whose products were sought after by the world at large. Traversed by hills and mountain chains whose summits rose to over 3000 feet, surrounded in the south and east by scrub and desert, in the north by the mountains of the Lebanon and Hermon, in the west by a flat coast with no natural harbors, it lay like a poverty-stricken island between the great kingdoms on the Nile and the Euphrates, on the frontier between two continents. East of the Nile delta, Africa stops. After a desolate stretch of 100 miles of desert Asia begins, and at its threshold lies Palestine.

When in the course of its eventful history it was constantly being dragged into the affairs of the wider world, it had its position to thank for it. Canaan is the link between Egypt and Asia. The most important trade route of the ancient world passes through this country. Merchants and caravans, migratory tribes and peoples, followed this road, which the armies of the great conquerors were later to make use of. Egyptians, Assyrians, Babylonians, Persians, Greeks, and Romans, one after another, made the land and its people the plaything of their economic, strategic, and political concerns.

It was in the interests of trade that the giant on the Nile in the third millennium B.C. was the first great power to stretch out its tenacles toward Canaan.

"We brought 40 ships, laden with cedar trunks. We built ships of cedarwood—one 'Pride of Two Lands,' a ship of 150 feet—and of meru wood, two ships 150 feet long. We made the doors of the king's palace of cedarwood." That is the substance of the world's oldest business record from a timber importer about 2700 B.C. The details of this cargo of timber in the reign of Pharaoh Snefru are scratched on a tablet of hard black diorite, which is carefully preserved in the museum at Palermo. Dense woods covered the slopes of Lebanon then. The excellent wood from its cedars and meru, a kind of conifer, was just what the Pharaohs needed for their building schemes.

Five hundred years before Abraham's day there was a flourishing import and export trade on the Canaanite coast. Egypt exchanged gold and spices from Nubia, copper and turquoise from the mines at Sinai, linen and ivory, for silver from the Taurus, leather goods from Byblos, painted vases from Crete. In the great

Phoenician dyeworks well-to-do Egyptians had their robes dyed purple. For their society women they bought a wonderful lapis lazuli blue—eyelids dyed blue were all the rage—and stibium, a cosmetic which was highly thought of by the ladies for touching up their eyelashes.

In the seaports of Ugarit (now Ras Shamra) and Tyre there were Egyptian consuls; the coastal fortress of Byblos became an Egyptian colony; monuments were erected to the Pharaohs, and Phoenician princes adopted Egyptian names.

If the coastal cities presented a picture of cosmopolitan life which was busy, prosperous, and even luxurious, a few miles inland lay a world which provided a glaring contrast. The Jordan mountains have always been a trouble spot. Bedouin attacks on the native population, insurrection, and feuds between towns were unending. Since they also endangered the caravan route along the Mediterranean coast Egyptian punitive expeditions had to bring the unruly elements to heel. The inscription on the tomb of the Egyptian Uni gives us a clear picture of how one of these expeditions was organized about 2350 B.C. Uni, an army commander, received orders from Pharaoh Phiops I to assemble a striking force agains Bedouins from Asia who were attacking Canaan. His report on the campaign reads as follows:

"His Majesty made war on the desert peoples and His Majesty gathered an army: In the south beyond Elephantine . . . all over the north . . . and among the Jertet-, Mazoi-, and Jenam-Nubians. I was entrusted with the whole campaign." The morale of this multicolored fighting force comes in for high praise, and in the course of it we learn what sort of attractions Canaan offered in those days in the way of loot: "None of them stole the sandals off anyone who came their way. . . . None of them stole food from any of the cities. . . . None of them stole any goats." Uni's war diary proudly announces a great victory and in passing gives us valuable information about the country: "The king's army returned in good order, after laying waste the country of the desert peoples, . . . after destroying their for-

tresses . . . after cutting down their fig-trees and vines
. . . and carrying off a large number into captivity.
His Majesty sent me five times to ravage the land of
the desert peoples with these troops every time they revolted."

Semites thus made their first entry into the land of
the Pharaohs as P.O.W.'s where they were contemptuously described as "sand-dwellers." Chu-Sebek, adju-
tant to King Sesostris III of Egypt, wrote in his war
diary five hundred years later the following account,
which has been preserved at Abydos on the Upper
Nile where it was chiseled out on a monument: "His
Majesty proceeded northward to crush the Asiatic
Bedouins. . . . His Majesty went as far as a place
called Sekmem. . . . Sekmem collapsed together with the
whole miserable country of Retenu."

The Egyptians then called Palestine and Syria together "Retenu." Sekmem is the Biblical town of
Shechem, the first town which Abraham struck on entering Canaan. (Gen. 12:6)

With the campaign of Sesostris III about 1850 B.C.
we are right in the middle of the patriarchal period.
Meantime Egypt had taken possession of the whole of
Canaan: the country now lay under the suzerainty of
the Pharaohs. Thanks to the archaeologists, we possess
a unique document from this epoch, a gem of ancient
literature. The author: a certain Sinuhe of Egypt.
Scene: Canaan. Time: between 1971 and 1928 B.C.
under Pharaoh Sesostris I. Sinuhe, a nobleman in at-
tendance at court, became involved in a political in-
trigue. He feared for his life and emigrated to Canaan:

"As I headed north I came to the Princes' Wall,
which was built to keep out the Bedouins and crush the
Sand ramblers.[1] I hid in a thicket in case the guard on
the wall, who was on patrol at the time, would see me.
I did not move out of it till the evening. When daylight
came . . . and I had reached the Bitter Lake[2] I col-

---

[1]"Sand ramblers" and "Wilderness wanderers" were the favorite
epithets that the Egyptians gave to their eastern and northeastern
neighbors, the nomads. This also included the tribes in Canaan and
Syria which had no fixed location.

[2]Still known as the "Bitter Lakes" on the Isthmus of Suez.

lapsed. I was parched with thirst, my throat was red-hot. I said to myself: This is the taste of death! But as I made another effort and pulled myself onto my feet, I heard the roaring of cattle and some Bedouins came in sight. Their leader, who had been in Egypt, recognized me. He gave me some water and boiled some milk, and I went with him to his tribe. They were very kind to me."

Sinuhe's escape had been successful. He had been able to slip unseen past the great barrier wall on the frontier of the kingdom of the Pharaohs which ran exactly along the line which is followed by the Suez Canal today. This "Princes' Wall" was even then several hundred years old. A priest mentions it as far back as 2650 B.C.: "The Princes' Walls are being built to prevent the Asiatics forcing their way into Egypt. They want water . . . to give to their cattle." Later on, the children of Israel were to pass this wall many times: there was no other way into Egypt. Abraham must have been the first of them to see it when he emigrated to the land of the Nile during a famine. (Gen. 12:10)

Sinuhe continues: "Each territory passed me on to the next. I went to Byblos,[1] and farther on reached Kedme[2] where I spent eighteen months. Ammi-Enschi,[3] the chief of Upper Retenu,[4] made me welcome. He said to me: 'You will be well treated and you can speak your own language here.' He said this of course because he knew who I was. Egyptians[5] who lived there had told him about me."

We are told in great detail of the day-to-day experiences of this Egyptian fugitive in north Palestine. "Ammi-Enschi said to me: 'Certainly, Egypt is a fine country, but you ought to stay here with me and what I shall do for you will be fine too.'

"He gave me precedence over all his own family

---

[1]Phoenician seaport north of present-day Beirut.
[2]Desert country east of Damascus.
[3]A western Semitic name; an Amorite.
[4]Name given to the hill country in the north of Palestine.
[5]Pharaoh's commissioners were at that time stationed all over Palestine and Syria.

and gave me his eldest daughter in marriage. He let me select from among his choicest estates, and I selected one which lay along the border of a neighboring territory. It was a fine place with the name of Jaa. There were figs and vines and more wine than water. There was plenty of honey and oil; every kind of fruit hung on its trees. It had corn and barley and all kinds of sheep and cattle. My popularity with the ruler was extremely profitable. He made me a chief of his tribe in the choicest part of his domains. I had bread and wine as my daily fare, boiled meat and roast goose. There were also desert animals which they caught in traps and brought to me, apart from what my hunting dogs collected. . . . There was milk in every shape and form. Thus many years went by. My children gew into strong men, each of them able to dominate his tribe.

"Any courier coming from Egypt or heading south to the royal court lived with me.[1] I gave hospitality to everyone. I gave water to the thirsty, put the wanderer on the right way, and protected the bereaved.

"When the Bedouins sallied forth to attack neighboring chiefs I drew up the plan of campaign. For the prince of Retenu for many years put me in command of his warriors and whichever country I marched into I made . . . and . . . of its pastures and its wells, I plundered its sheep and cattle, led its people captive and took over their stores. I killed its people with my sword and my bow,[2] thanks to my leadership and my clever plans."

Out of his many experiences among the "Asiatics," a life-and-death duel, which he describes in detail, seems to have made the deepest impression on Sinuhe. A "Strong man of Retenu" had jeered at him one day in his tent and called him out. He was sure he could kill Sinuhe and appropriate his flocks and herds and properties. But Sinuhe, like all Egyptians, was a practiced bowman from his earliest days and killed the "strong man," who was armed with shield, spear, and

---

[1] This points to a considerable traffic between Egypt and Palestine.
[2] The bow was the typical Egyptian weapon.

dagger, by putting an arrow through his throat. The spoils that came to him as a result of this combat made him even richer and more powerful.

At length in his old age he began to yearn for his homeland. A letter from his Pharaoh, Sesostris I, summoned him to return: ". . . Make ready to return to Egypt, that you may see once more the Court where you grew up, and kiss the ground at the two great gates. . . . Remember the day when you will have to be buried and men will do you honor. You will be anointed with oil before daybreak and wrapped in linen blessed by the goddess Tait.[1] You will be given an escort on the day of the funeral. The coffin will be of gold adorned with lapis lazuli, and you will be placed upon a bier. Oxen will pull it and a choir will precede you. They will dance the Dance of the Dwarfs at the mouth of your tomb. The sacrificial prayers will be recited for you and animals will be offered on your altar. The pillars of your tomb will be built of limestone among those of the royal family. You must not lie in a foreign land, with Asiatics to bury you, and wrap you in sheepskin."

Sinuhe's heart leapt for joy. He decided to return at once, made over his property to his children and installed his oldest son as "Chief of his tribe." This was customary with these Semitic nomads, as it was with Abraham and his progeny. It was the tribal law of the patriarchs, which later became the law of Israel. "My tribe and all my goods belonged to him only, my people and all my flocks, my fruit and all my sweet trees.[2] Then I headed for the south."

He was accompanied right to the frontier posts of Egypt by Bedouins, thence by representatives of the Pharaoh to the capital south of Memphis. The second stage was by boat.

What a contrast! From a tent to a royal palace, from a simple if dangerous life back to the security and luxury of a highly civilized metropolis. "I found His Majesty on the great throne in the Hall of Silver and Gold.

---

[1] Embalming.
[2] Date palms.

The king's family were brought in. His Majesty said to the Queen: 'See, here is Sinuhe, who returns as an Asiatic and has become a Bedouin.' She gave a loud shriek and the royal children screamed all at once. They said to His Majesty: 'Surely this is not really he, my lord King.' His Majesty replied: 'It is really he.'

"I was taken to a princely mansion," writes Sinuhe enthusiastically, "in which there were wonderful things and also a bathroom. . . . There were things from the royal treasure house, clothes of royal linen, myrrh and finest oil; favorite servants of the king were in every room, and every cook did his duty. The years that were past slipped from my body. I was shaved and my hair was combed. I shed my load of foreign soil[1] and the coarse clothing of the Sand ramblers. I was swathed in fine linen and anointed with the finest oil the country could provide. I slept once more in a bed. Thus I lived, honored by the king, until the time came for me to depart this life."

The Sinuhe story does not exist in one copy only. An astonishing number of copies has been found. It must have been a highly popular work and must have gone through several "editions." Not only in the Middle Kingdom but in the New Kingdom of Egypt it was read with pleasure, as the copies found indicate. One might call it a "best-seller," the first in the world.

The scholars who came across it again at the turn of the century were as delighted with it as Sinuhe's contemporaries had been 4000 years before. They regarded it, however, as a well-told story, exaggerated like all Egyptian writings and completely without foundation. The tale of Sinuhe became a mine of information for learned Egyptologists but not for historians. They were so busy disputing about the clarification of the text, the letters, the construction and connection of the sentences that the contents were forgotten.

Meantime Sinuhe came into his own. For we now know that the Egyptian had written a factual account of Canaan at about the time that Abraham migrated there. It is to hieroglyphic texts dealing with Egyptian

---

[1] I.e., the dirt that came off him.

campaigns that we owe the first evidence we possess
about Canaan. They agree with Sinuhe's description.
Similarly, the Egyptian nobleman's story shows in some
places almost literal correspondence with verses of the
Bible which are often quoted. "For the lord thy God
bringeth thee into a good land," says Deut. 8:7. "It was
a fine country," says Sinuhe. "A land," continues the
Bible, "of wheat and barley and vines and fig trees. . . ."
"Barley and wheat, figs and vines were there," Sinuhe
tells us. And where the Bible says, "A land of oil,
olive and honey, a land wherein thou shalt eat bread
without scarceness," the Egyptian text reads, "There
was plenty of honey and oil. I had bread as my daily
fare."

The description that Sinuhe gave of his way of life
among the Amorites, living in a tent, surrounded by
his flocks and herds, and involved in conflict with
presumptuous Bedouins whom he has to drive away
from his pastures and his wells, corresponds with the
Biblical picture of life in patriarchal times. Abraham
and his son Isaac have also to fight for their wells.
(Gen. 21:25, 26:15, 20)

The care and accuracy with which Biblical tradition
depicts the actual living conditions of those days is best
seen when we examine the results of sober investigation.
For the variety of recently discovered documents and
monuments makes it possible for us to reconstruct a
true picture of the conditions of life in Canaan at the
time when the patriarchs entered it.

About 1900 B.C. Canaan was but thinly populated.
Properly speaking it was No Man's Land. Here and
there in the midst of plowed fields a fortified keep could
be seen. Neighboring slopes would be planted with vines
or with fig trees and date palms. The inhabitants lived
in a state of constant readiness. For these widely scattered little townships, like veritable islands, were the
object of daring attacks by the desert nomads. Suddenly,
and when least expected, these nomads were upon them,
with indiscriminate butchery, carrying off their cattle
and their crops. Just as suddenly they would disappear
again into the vast recesses of the desert plains to the
south and east. There was endless war between the

settled farmers and cattle breeders and these plundering hordes who had no fixed abode, whose home was a goat's-hair tent somewhere out under the open skies of the desert. It was into this restless country that Abraham made his way with his wife Sarah, his nephew Lot, his kinsfolk and his flocks.

"And into the land of Canaan they came. And Abram passed through the land unto the place of Sichem, unto the plain of Moreh. . . . And the Lord appeared unto Abram and said: Unto thy seed will I give this land; and there builded he an altar unto the Lord, who appeared unto him. And he removed from thence unto a mountain on the east of Bethel, and pitched his tent having Bethel on the west, and Hai on the east: and there he builded an altar unto the Lord, and called upon the name of the Lord. And Abram journeyed, going on still toward the south." (Gen. 12:5-9)

In the twenties, remarkable shards were found on the Nile, the chief finds being at Thebes and Saqqara. Archaeologists in Berlin obtained some of them, others went to Brussels, and the rest went to the great museum at Cairo. Under the careful hands of experts the fragments were reassembled into vases and statuettes, but the most astonishing thing about them was the inscriptions. The writing is full of menacing curses and maledictions, such as "Death strike you at every wicked word and thought, every plot, angry quarrel and plan." These and other unpleasant wishes were generally addressed to Egyptian court officials and other eminent people, but also to rulers in Canaan and Syria.

In accordance with an old superstition it was believed that at the moment the vase or statuette was smashed the power of the person cursed would be broken. It was common to include within the spell the family, relatives, even the home town of the victim of the curse. The magical texts include names of cities, such as Jerusalem (Gen. 14:19), Ashkelon (Jud. 1:18), Tyre (Josh. 19:29), Hazor (Josh. 11:1), Bethshemesh (Josh. 15:10), Aphek (Josh. 12:18), Achshaph (Josh. 11:1), and Shechem (Sichem). Here is a convincing proof that these places mentioned in the Bible existed already in the nineteenth and eighteenth centuries B.C., since the vases and statuettes date from that time. Two of these towns were visited by Abraham. He calls on Melchizedek "King of Salem" (Gen. 14:18) at Jerusalem. Jerusalem is well enough known, but where was Sichem?

In the heart of Samaria lies a broad flat valley dominated by the high peaks of Gerizim and Ebal. Well-cultivated fields surround Ashkar, a small village in Jordan. Nearby at the foot of Gerizim in Tell el Balata the ruins of Sichem were discovered.

It was due to the work of the German theologian and archaeologist, Professor Ernst Sellin, that during excavations in 1913-1914 strata from very early times came to light. Sellin came across remains of walls dating back to the nineteenth century B.C. Bit by bit the picture emerged of a mighty surrounding wall with strong foundations, built entirely of rough boulders, some of them six feet in diameter. Archaeologists call this type a "cyclops wall." The wall was further strengthened by an escarpment. The builders of Sichem fortified the six-foot-thick wall with small turrets and provided an earth wall in addition.

The remains of a palace also emerged out of the ruins. The square, cramped courtyard, surrounded by a few rooms with solid walls, hardly deserved the name of palace. All the Canaanite towns whose names are so familiar, and which the Israelites feared so greatly in the early days, looked like Sichem. With few exceptions the notable building projects of that period are now known. Most of them have been excavated within the last thirty years. For thousands of years they have been buried deep in the ground; now they stand clearly before us. Among them are many towns whose walls the patriarchs had seen: Bethel and Mizpah, Gerar and Lachish, Gezer and Gath, Ashkelon and Jericho. Anyone who wanted to write the history of the building of fortresses and cities in Canaan would have no great difficulty in doing so in view of the wealth of material going back to the third millennium B.C.

The Canaanite towns were fortresses, places of refuge in time of danger, whether it was from sudden attack by nomadic tribes or civil war among the Canaanites themselves. Towering perimeter walls built of these great boulders invariably enclose a small area, not much bigger than St. Peter's Square in Rome. Each of these town-forts had a water supply, but they were not towns in which a large population could have made a permanent home. Compared with the palaces and great cities in Mesopotamia or on the Nile, they look tiny. Most of the towns in Canaan could have gone into the palace of the kings of Mari comfortably.

In Tell el-Hesi, probably the Eglon of the Bible, the ancient fortifications enclosed an area of just over an acre; in Tell es-Safi—formerly Gath—twelve acres; in Tell el-Mutesellim—formerly Megiddo—about the same amount; in Tell el-Zakariyah—the Biblical Azekah—less than ten acres: Gezer, on the road from Jerusalem to Jaffa, occupied just over twenty acres. Even in the more built-up area of Jericho, the inner fortified wall, the Acropolis proper enclosed a space of little more than five acres. Yet Jericho was one of the strongest fortresses in the country.

Bitter feuds between the tribal chiefs were the order of the day. There was no supreme authority. Every chieftain was master in his own territory. No one gave him orders and he did what he pleased. The Bible calls the tribal chieftains "kings." As far as power and independence were concerned that is what they were.

Between the tribal chiefs and their subjects the relationship was patriarchal. Inside the wall lived only the chief, the aristocracy, the Pharaoh's representatives, and wealthy merchants. Moreover, they alone lived in strong, solid, mostly one-story houses with four to six rooms built round an open courtyard. Upper-class homes with a second story were comparatively rare. The rest of the inhabitants—vassals, servants, and serfs—lived in simple mud or wattle huts outside the walls. They must have had a miserable life.

Since the days of the patriarchs two roads meet in the plain of Shechem. One goes down into the rich valley of the Jordan. The other climbs over the lonely hills southward to Bethel, on past Jerusalem, and down to the Negeb, or the Land of the South as the Bible calls it. Anyone following this road would encounter only a few inhabited areas in the central highlands of Samaria and Judah: Shechem, Bethel, Jerusalem, and Hebron. Anyone choosing the more comfortable road would find the larger towns and more important fortresses of the Canaanites in the lush valleys of the Plain of Jezreel, on the fertile coast of Judah, and amid the luxuriant vegetation of the Jordan Valley.

Abraham, as the Bible tells us, chose for his first exploration of Palestine the lonely and difficult road that points over the hills toward the south. For here the wooded hillsides offered refuge and concealment to a stranger in a foreign land, while the clearings provided pasture in plenty for his flocks and herds. Later on, he and his tribe and the other patriarchs as well went back and forth along this same wretched mountain track. However tempting were the fertile valleys of the plain, Abraham preferred to establish himself at first up in the hill country. For with his bows and slings he was in no condition to risk a clash with the Canaanites whose swords and spears were more than a match for him. Abraham was not yet ready to venture out of the highlands.

Abraham and Lot in the Land of Purple

Famine in Canaan—A family portrait of the patriarchal age—Permit of access to the Nile grazings—The mystery of Sodom and Gomorrah—Mr. Lynch investigates the Dead Sea—The great fissure—Submerged forests in the Dead Sea—The Vale of Siddim's headlong plunge—Pillars of salt at Jebel Usdum—At the terebinth of Abraham

AND THERE WAS A FAMINE IN THE LAND: AND ABRAM WENT DOWN INTO EGYPT TO SOJOURN THERE; FOR THE FAMINE WAS GRIEVOUS IN THE LAND. (Gen. 12:10)

We have to thank the dryness of the sands of the Egyptian desert for preserving a considerable variety of hieroglyphic texts, among which is to be found a wealth of written evidence of the immigration of Semitic families into the Nile Valley. The best and clearest proof is, however, a picture.

Halfway between the old cities of the Pharaohs, Memphis and Thebes, 200 miles south of Cairo, there lies on the banks of the Nile amid green fields and palm groves the little settlement of Beni-Hasan. Here in 1890 a British expert, Percy A. Newberry, was given an assignment by the Cairo authorities to investigate some old tombs. The expedition was financed by the Egyptian Exploration Fund.

The tombs were located at the outer end of a desert wadi, where the remains of old quarries and a large temple also lay in peaceful seclusion. Week after week nothing but debris, rubble, and the remnants of broken stone pillars streamed out of the rock face behind which the last resting place of the Egyptian nobleman Khnumhotep was concealed. Hieroglyphs in a small entrance hall indicated the name of the occupant. He was the ruler of this district of the Nile, which at one time was called Gazelle Province. Khnumhotep lived under Pharaoh Sesostris II about 1900 B.C.

After a great deal of time and effort had been expended, Newberry eventually reached a huge rock chamber. By the light of numerous torches he was able to see that there were three vaults and that the stumps of two rows of pillars protruded from the ground. The walls were bright with gorgeous colored paintings on a thin lime-washed plaster. These depicted scenes from the life of the nobleman telling of harvest, hunting, dancing, and sport. In one of the pictures on the north wall, immediately next to a more than life-size portrait of the nobleman, Newberry discovered foreign-looking figures. They were wearing a different type of clothing from that of the ordinary Egyptians, and they were fairer-skinned and had sharper features. Two Egyptian officials in the foreground were obviously introducing this group of foreigners to the nobleman. What sort of people were they?

Hieroglyphs on a written document in the hand of one of the Egyptians gave the explanation: they were "sand-dwellers," Semites. Their leader was called Abishai. With thirty-six men, women, and children of his tribe Abishai had come to Egypt. He had brought gifts for the nobleman, among which special mention was made of some costly stibium[1] for the nobleman's wife.

Abishai is a genuine Semitic name. After the conquest of Canaan by Joshua the name occurs in the Bible during the reign of the second king of Israel: "Then answered David and said to . . . Abishai the son of Zeruiah." (I Sam. 26:6) The Abishai of the Bible was the brother of King David's unpopular commander-in-chief Joab about 1000 B.C., when Israel was a large kingdom.

The artist whom Prince Khnumhotep entrusted with the decoration of his tomb has depicted the "sand-dwellers" with such care that the smallest detail is faithfully noted. This lifelike and unusually striking picture looks more like a colored photograph. It gives the impression that this family of Semites had just stopped for a second and that suddenly men, women,

---

[1] Coloring for eyelashes.

and children would start off again and continue their journey. Abishai at the head of the column makes a slight obeisance and salutes the nobleman with his right hand, while his left hand holds a short cord to which is attached a tame horned goat carrying between its horns a bent stick which is a shepherd's crook.

The shepherd's crook was so characteristic of the nomads that the Egyptians in their picture writing used it for the name of these foreigners.

The style and color of their clothing are faithfully reproduced. Square woolen blankets, reaching in the case of the men to the knee, in the case of the women to the calf, are caught up on one shoulder. They consist of highly colored striped material and serve as cloaks. Does that not remind us of the famous "coat of many colors" which Jacob, much to the annoyance of his other sons, bestowed upon his favorite son Joseph? (Gen. 37:3) The men's hair is trimmed into a pointed beard. The women's hair falls loosely over breast and shoulders. It is fastened by a narrow white ribbon round the forehead. The little curls in front of the ears seem to have been a concession to fashion. The men are wearing sandals; the women have dark-brown half-length boots. They carry their water ration in artistically embroidered containers made of animal skins. Bows and arrows, heavy throw sticks, and spears serve as their weapons. Even their favorite instrument has been brought with them on their long journey. One of the men is playing the eight-stringed lyre. According to the instructions given in the Bible, some of the Psalms of David were to be accompanied on this instrument: "To be sung to eight strings" is the heading of Psalms 6 and 12.

Since this picture dates from about 1900 B.C., which was the period of the patriarchs, we may imagine that Abraham and his family looked something like this. When he reached the Egyptian frontier, a similar scene must have taken place. For the procedure for admitting foreign visitors was exactly the same at all the other frontier posts as in the case of Prince Khnumhotep.

It was thus no different long ago from what it is now

to travel in a foreign country. Certainly there were no passports, but formalities and officialdom made life difficult for foreign visitors even then. Anyone entering Egypt had to state the number in his party, the reason for his journey, and the probable length of his stay. All the particulars were carefully noted down on papyrus by a scribe using red ink and then sent by messenger to the frontier officer who decided whether an entrance permit should be granted. This, however, was not left to his own judgment. Administrative officers at the court of Pharaoh issued from time to time precise directives, even to the point of specifying which grazings were to be put at the disposal of immigrant nomads.

In times of famine Egypt was for Canaanite nomads their place of refuge and often their only salvation. When the ground dried up in their own country, the land of the Pharaohs always afforded green pastures. The Nile with its regular annual flooding took care of that.

On the other hand the proverbial wealth of Egypt was often a temptation to theieving bands of daring nomads who were not interested in finding pasture but were much more concerned with the bursting granaries and sumptuous palaces. Often they could only be got rid of by force of arms. As a protection against these unwelcome invaders and to keep a closer check on the frontier, the erection of the great "Princes' Wall" was begun in the third millennium B.C. It consisted of a chain of forts, watchtowers, and strong points. It was only under cover of darkness that the Egyptian Sinuhe with his local knowledge was able to slip through unobserved. Six hundred and fifty years later, at the time

Fig. 9. A Semitic family at the time of the Patriarchs: from

of the Exodus from Egypt, the frontier was also strongly guarded. Moses knew only too well that escape from the country in defiance of Pharaoh's orders was impossible. The sentries would at once have sounded the alarm and summoned the guards. Any attempt to break through would have been nipped in the bud by sharpshooters and commandos in armored chariots and would have ended in bloodshed. That was the reason why the prophet, knowing the country, chose another, quite unusual route. Moses led the children of Israel southward, as far as the Red Sea, where there was no longer any wall.

After their return from Egypt, Abraham and Lot separated: "For their substance was great," says the Bible, "so that they could not dwell together. And there was a strife between the herdmen of Abram's cattle, and the herdmen of Lot's cattle. . . . And Abram said unto Lot, Let there be no strife, I pray thee, between me and thee, and between my herdmen and thy herdmen: for we be brethren. Is not the whole land before thee? Separate thyself, I pray thee, from me: if thou wilt take the left hand then I will go to the right: or if thou depart to the right hand, then I will go to the left." (Gen. 13:6-9)

Abraham left the choice to Lot, who, taking everything for granted, like so many young people, chose the best part, in the neighborhood of the Jordan. It was "well-watered everywhere . . . as thou comest unto Zoar" (Gen. 13:10) and blessed with luxuriant tropical vegetation "even as the garden of the Lord, like the land of Egypt." (Gen. 13:10)

From the wooded mountain chain in the heart of Palestine Lot made his way downhill to the east, wan-

a wall painting in the prince's tomb at Beni-Hasan on the Nile.

dered with his family and his flocks southward along
the Jordan Valley, and finally pitched his tent in
Sodom. South of the Dead Sea lay an extremely fertile
plain, the "Vale of Siddim, which is the salt sea."[1]
(Gen. 14:3) The Bible lists five towns in this valley,
"Sodom, Gomorrah, Admah, Zeboiim, and Zoar." (Gen.
14:2) It also knows of a warlike incident in the history of these five towns: "And it came to pass" that
four kings "made war with Bera, king of Sodom, and
with Birsha king of Gomorrah, and with Shinab king
of Admah and Shemeber king of Zeboiim and the king
of Bela, which is Zoar." (Gen. 14:2) For twelve years
the kings of the Vale of Siddim had paid tribute to
King Chedorlaomer. In the thirteenth year they rebelled. Chedorlaomer sought help from three royal allies; a punitive expedition would bring the rebels to
their senses. In the battle of the nine kings, the kings of
the five towns in the Vale of Siddim were defeated,
their lands ravaged and plundered.

Among the captives of the foreign kings was Lot.
He was set free again by his uncle Abraham (Gen.
14:12-16) who with his followers dogged the with-
drawal of the army of the victorious four kings like a
shadow. Abraham watched unobserved from safe
cover, made accurate reconnaissance, and bided his
time. Not until they reached Dan, on the northern
frontier of Palestine, did the opportunity arise for which
he had been waiting. Like lightning, under cover of
darkness, Abraham and his men fell on the rearguard,
and in the confusion that followed Lot was set free.
Only those who do not know the tactics of the Bedouins
will consider this an unlikely story.

Among the inhabitants of that stretch of country the
memory of that punitive expedition has remained alive
to this day. It is reflected in the name of a road which
runs eastward of the Dead Sea and parallel with it,
traversing what was in ancient times the land of Moab
and leading to the north. The nomads of Jordan know
it very well. Among the natives it is called, remarkably
enough, the "King's Way." We come across it in the

---

[1]Dead Sea.

Bible, where it is called "the king's high way" or "the high way." It was the road that the children of Israel wished to follow on their journey through Edom to the "Promised Land." (Num. 20:17, 19) In the Christian era the Romans used the "King's Way" and improved it. Parts of it now belong to the network of roads in the new state of Jordan. Clearly visible from the air, the ancient track shows up as a dark streak across the country.

"And the Lord said, Because the cry of Sodom and Gomorrah is great, and because their sin is very grievous. . . . Then the Lord rained upon Sodom and upon Gomorrah brimstone and fire from the Lord out of heaven; And he overthrew those cities, and all the plain, and all the inhabitants of the cities, and that which grew upon the ground. But his [Lot's] wife looked back from behind him, and she became a pillar of salt. . . . and, lo, the smoke of the country went up as the smoke of a furnace." (Gen. 18:20; 19:24-26, 28)

The calamity that is the subject of this powerful Biblical story of divine punishment for incorrigible sin has probably in all ages made a deep impression on men's minds. Sodom and Gomorrah have become synonymous for vice and godlessness. When men have talked in terms of utter annihilation, again the fate of these cities has always sprung to their minds. Their imaginations have constantly been kindled by this inexplicable and frightful disaster, as can well be seen from the many allusions to it in ancient times. Remarkable and quite incredible things are said to have happened there by the Dead Sea, the "Sea of Salt," where, according to the Bible, the catastrophe must have happened.

During the siege of Jerusalem in A.D. 70 it is said that the Roman army commander Titus sentenced certain slaves to death. He gave them short shrift, had them bound together by chains, and thrown into the sea at the foot of the mountains of Moab. But the condemned men did not drown. No matter how often they were thrown into the sea they always drifted back to the shore like corks. This inexplicable occurrence made such a deep impression upon Titus that he pardoned the unfortunate offenders. Flavius Josephus, the Jewish historian who lived latterly in Rome, repeatedly mentions a "Lake of Asphalt." Greeks lay stress on the presence of poisonous gases, which are reported as rising from all parts of this sea. The Arabs say that in olden times no bird was able to reach the opposite side. The creatures, as they flew across the water, would suddenly drop dead into it.

These and similar traditional stories were well enough known, but until a century ago we had no first-hand knowledge of this odd, mysterious sea in Palestine. No scientist had investigated it or even seen it. In 1848 the United States took the initiative and equipped an expedition to solve the riddle of the Dead Sea. One autumn day in that year the beach of the little coastal town of Acca, less than ten miles from present-day Haifa, was black with spectators who were engrossed in an unusual maneuver.

W. F. Lynch, a geologist and the leader of the expedition, had brought ashore from the ship lying at anchor two metal boats which he was now fastening on to large-wheel carts. Pulled by a long team of horses, the trek began. Three weeks later, after indescribable difficulties, they had succeeded in getting the wagons over the hills of southern Galilee. The two boats took the water again at Tiberias. When Lynch set up his theodolite at the Lake of Galilee, the result produced the first big surprise of the expedition. To begin with, he thought he had made an error in calculation, but a cross check confirmed the result. The surface of the lake, which played so notable a part in the life of Jesus, is 676 feet below the level of the Mediterranean. What then could be the height of the source of the Jordan, which flows through the lake?

Some days later W. F. Lynch stood on the slopes of snow-capped Hermon. Among remains of broken columns and gateways lies the little village of Baniya. Local Arabs led him through a thick clump of oleanders to a cave half-choked with rubble on the steep limestone flank of Hermon. Out of its darkness gushed a stream of pure water. This is one of the sources of the Jordan. The Arabs call the Jordan Sheri 'at el Kebire, the "Great River." This was the site of Panium where Herod built a temple of Pan in honor of Augustus. Shell-shaped niches are hewn out of the rock beside the Jordan cave. "Priest of Pan" is still clearly legible in Greek characters. In the time of Jesus the Greek pastoral god was worshiped at the source of the Jordan. There the goat-footed Pan raised his flute to his lips, as though he wanted to send the Jordan on its way with a tune. Only three miles west of this source lay Dan, which is frequently mentioned in the Bible as the most northerly point in the country. There, too, is another source of the Jordan where its clear waters spring out of the southern slopes of Hermon. A third stream pushes out of a wadi higher up. The bottom of the wadi, just above Dan, is 1500 feet above sea level.

Fig. 10. Diagram of the Jordan drop.

When the Jordan on its way south reaches little Lake Huleh twelve miles away, the river bed is only six feet above sea level. Then the river rushes down the next six miles to the Lake of Galilee. In the course of its descent from the slopes of Hermon to this point, a distance of only twenty-five miles, it has dropped 2275 feet.

From Tiberias the members of the American expedition in their two metal boats followed the endless windings of the Jordan downstream. Gradually the vegetation became sparser and the thick undergrowth extended no farther than the banks. Under the tropical sun an oasis came into view on their right—Jericho. Soon afterward they reached their goal. There before them, embedded between almost vertical precipices, lay the vast surface of the Dead Sea.

The first thing to do was to have a swim. But when they jumped in, they felt as if they were being thrown out again. It was like wearing life jackets. The old stories were therefore true. In this sea it is impossible to drown. The scorching sun dried the men's skins almost at once. The thin crust of salt which the water had deposited on their bodies made them look quite white. No fish of any kind, no seaweed, no coral—no fishing boat had ever rocked on this sea. Here was neither a harvest from the sea nor from the land, for the banks were equally bare and desolate. Huge

Fig. 11. Mediterranean and Jordan Basin.

deposits of coagulated salt made the beach and the rock face above it sparkle in the sun like diamonds. The air was filled with sharp acrid odors, a mixture of petroleum and sulphur. Oily patches of asphalt—the Bible calls it "slime" (Gen. 14:10)—float on the waves. Even the bright blue sky and the all-powerful sun could not breathe any life into this forbidding-looking landscape.

For twenty-two days the American boats went back and forth across the Dead Sea. They tested the water and analyzed it; they took innumerable soundings. The mouth of the Jordan, at the Dead Sea, lies 1280 feet below sea level. If there were any connection with the Mediterranean, the Jordan and the Sea of Galilee, sixty-five miles away, would be covered over and a vast inland sea would stretch almost up to the shores of Lake Huleh.

"When a storm sweeps up through this rocky basin," observed Lynch, "the waves strike the sides of the boats like blows from a hammer. But the weight of the water is such that a short time after the wind has died down the sea is calm again."

From the report of the expedition the world learned for the first time several astonishing facts. The Dead Sea is over 1200 feet in depth. The bottom of the sea is therefore about 2500 feet below the level of the Mediterranean. The water of the Dead Sea contains 30 per cent of solid ingredients, mostly sodium chloride, that is, cooking salt. The normal ocean has only 3.3 to 4 per cent salt. The Jordan and many smaller rivers empty themselves into this basin which is approximately 500 miles square and which has no outlet. Evaporation under the broiling sun takes place on the surface of the sea at a rate of over 280 million cubic feet per day. Chemical substances brought in by the small rivers remain deposited in this great basin.

It was only after the turn of the century that, keeping pace with excavations in other parts of Palestine, interest in Sodom and Gomorrah was also awakened. Archaeologists began their quest for the vanished cities that were said to have existed in the Vale of Siddim in Biblical times. At the furthermost southeast point of the Dead Sea remains of a large settlement were found. The place is still called Zoar by the Arabs. The scientists were delighted, for Zoar was one of the five wealthy cities in the Vale of Siddim, which had refused to pay tribute to the four foreign kings. But exploratory digging which was immediately undertaken proved a disappointment.

The date of the ruins that came to light showed it to be a town that had flourished there in the Middle Ages. There was no trace of the ancient Zoar of the King of Bela (Gen. 14:2) or of its neighbors. Nevertheless, there were plentiful indications in the environs of medieval Zoar that there had been a numerous population in the country in very early times.

We can say with certainty today that any future

search for Sodom and Gomorrah on the shores of the
Dead Sea will be in vain. For the riddle of the disappearance of the two cities has been solved.

On the eastern shore of the Dead Sea the peninsula
of el-Lisan protrudes like a tongue far into the water.
El-Lisan means "the tongue" in Arabic. The Bible
expressly mentions it when the country is being divided
up after the Conquest. The frontiers of the tribe of
Judah are being carefully outlined. In the course of
this Joshua gives an unusually illuminating description
of their southern limits: "And their south border was
from the shore of the Salt Sea, from the bay [lit.
'tongue'] that looketh southward." (Josh. 15:2)

Roman history has a story to tell of this tongue of
land, which has always been wrongly regarded with
considerable skepticism. Two deserters had fled to the
peninsula. The legionaries in pursuit combed the ground
for a long time in vain. When they eventually caught
sight of the men who had given them the slip, it was
too late. The deserters were clambering up the rocks
on the other side of the water—they had waded straight
across the sea.

Unseen from the land the ground falls away here
under the surface of the water at a prodigious angle,
dividing the sea into two parts. To the right of the
peninsula the ground slopes sharply down to a depth of
1200 feet. On the left of the peninsula the water remains remarkably shallow. Soundings taken in the last
few years established depths of only fifty to sixty feet.

If we take a row boat across the "Salt Sea" to the
southernmost point, we shall see, if the sun is shining
in the right direction, something quite fantastic: some
distance from the shore and clearly visible under the
surface of the water, are stretched the outlines of forests
which the extraordinarily high salt content of the Dead
Sea has kept in preservation.

The trunks and roots in the shimmering green depths
must be very ancient indeed. Once upon a time, when
they were in blossom and green foliage covered their
twigs and branches, perhaps the flocks of Lot grazed
under their shadow. That extraordinary shallow part of

the Dead Sea, from the peninsula el-Lisan to the southernmost tip, was the Vale of Siddim. The Bible itself is quite explicit: "All these [kings] were joined together in the Vale of Siddim, which is the salt sea." (Gen. 14:3)

Geologists added to these discoveries and observations a conclusive piece of evidence, which explains the occasion and the result of the Biblical story of the annihilation of Sodom and Gomorrah.

The American expedition under Lynch in 1848 produced the first information about the prodigious drop of the Jordan on its short course through Palestine.

Fig. 12. The Dead Sea (a) in 2000 B.C. before the end of Sodom and Gomorrah, (b) in 1900 B.C. after the disaster.

This plunging of the river bed until it is far below sea level is, as later investigation established, a unique geological phenomenon. "There may be something on the surface of another planet which is similar to the Jordan Valley, but on our planet there certainly is nothing," wrote the Glasgow Hebraist, George Adam Smith, in his *Historical Geography of the Holy Land*. "No other part of the globe, which is not under water, lies deeper than 300 feet below sea level."

The Jordan Valley is only part of a huge fracture in the earth's crust. The path of this crack has meanwhile been accurately traced. It begins far north, several hundred miles beyond the borders of Palestine, at the foot of the Taurus Mountains in Asia Minor. In the south it runs from the south shore of the Dead Sea through the wadi el-Arabah to the Gulf of Aqabah and only comes to an end beyond the Red Sea in Africa. At many points in this vast depression signs of intensive volcanic activity are obvious. In the Galilean mountains, in the highlands of Transjordan, on the banks of the Jabbok, a tributary of the Jordan, and on the Gulf of Aqabah are black basalt and lava.

Together with the base of this mighty fissure, which runs precisely through this area, the Vale of Siddim, including Sodom and Gomorrah, plunged one day into the abyss. The date of this event can be fairly accurately established by the geologists. It must have been soon after 2000 B.C.

"Probably it was about 1900 B.C. that the catastrophic destruction of Sodom and Gomorrah took place," wrote the American scholar Jack Finegan in 1951. "A careful examination of the literary, geological and archaeological evidence leads to the conclusion that the corrupt 'cities of the plain' (Gen. 19:29) lay in the area which is now submerged beneath the slowly rising waters of the southern section of the Dead Sea, and that their destruction came about through a great earthquake which was probably accompanied by explosions, lightning, issue of natural gas and general conflagration."

About 1900 B.C.—that is in the time of Abraham.

The subsidence released volcanic forces that had been lying dormant deep down along the whole length of the fracture. In the upper valley of the Jordan near Bashan there are still the towering craters of extinct volcanoes; great stretches of lava and deep layers of basalt have been deposited on the limestone surface. From time immemorial the area around this depression has been subject to earthquakes. There is repeated evidence of them and the Bible itself records them. As if in confirmation of the geological explanation of the disappearance of Sodom and Gomorrah, Sanchuniathon, the Phoenician priest, uses these words in his *Ancient History,* which has now been rediscovered: "The Vale of Sidimus[1] sank and became a lake, always evaporating and containing no fish, a symbol of vengeance and of death for the transgressor."

And Lot's wife "looked back from behind him and she became a pillar of salt." (Gen. 19:26) The nearer one gets to the south end of the Dead Sea the more wild and desolate it becomes. Landscape and mountain grow eerier and more forbidding. The hills stand there silent and everlasting. Their scarred slopes fall sheer and steep down to the sea; their lower reaches are crystal white. The unparalleled disaster which once took place here has left an imperishable and oppressive mark. Only occasionally is a band of nomads to be seen heading inland along one of the steep and rugged wadis.

Where the heavy oily water comes to an end in the south, the harsh rock face on either side breaks off abruptly and gives place to a salt-sodden swamp. The reddish soil is pierced by innumerable channels and can easily become dangerous for the unwary traveler. Sweeping southward the bogland merges into the desert wadi el-Arabah which continues down to the Red Sea.

To the west of the southern shore and in the direction of the Biblical "Land of the South," the Negeb, stretches a ridge of hills about 150 feet high and ten miles from north to south. Its slopes sparkle and glit-

---

[1] I.e., Siddim.

ter in the sunshine like diamonds. It is an odd phenomenon of nature. For the most part this little range of hills consists of pure rock salt. The Arabs call it Jebel Usdum, an ancient name, which preserves in it the word Sodom. Many blocks of salt have been worn away by the rain and have crashed downhill. They have odd shapes, and some of them stand on end, looking like statues. It is easy to imagine them suddenly seeming to come to life.

These strange statues in salt remind us vividly of the Biblical description of Lot's wife, who was turned into a pillar of salt. The sparkling salt hills lie very near the submerged Vale of Siddim. Anyone who escaped alive from the scene of the disaster might well be suffocated by the poisonous fumes which spread over the countryside. And everything in the neighborhood of the "Salt Sea" is even to this day quickly covered with a crust of salt.

"And Abram moved his tent and came and dwelt by the oaks (terebinths) of Mamre, which are in Hebron, and built there an altar unto the Lord." (Gen. 13:18 R.V.)

Not far from present-day Hebron, Abraham spent his last days in the little village of Mamre where he had built the altar. Here he gained possession of the first piece of land from the Hittites (Gen. 23) in order to provide a rock tomb for his wife Sarah as was the normal Semitic practice. He too was buried in the same sepulcher. (Gen. 25:9-10) Excavations appear to confirm these Biblical statements, too, about the father of the patriarchs.

About two miles north of Hebron the Arabs venerate a site which they call "Haram Ramet el-Khalil," that is, the sanctuary of the hill of the friend of God. "Friend of God" is the Mohammedan term for Abraham. Father A. E. Mader, the archaeologist, actually found nearby the stones of an altar from early times, which still bore clearly recognizable traces of burning. In 1927 Mader discovered traces of a large tree which must at one time have stood there. Traces of ancient roots were still easily discernible in the ground.

Abraham's grave is still exhibited today as a holy place much visited by pilgrims.

It is an apparently inexplicable thing that old oral traditions, handed down from father to son, are now receiving scientific confirmation.

II / In the Realm of the Pharaohs: From Joseph to Moses

CHAPTER 1 / Joseph in Egypt

*Had Potiphar a prototype?—The Orbiney Papyrus—
Hyksos rulers on the Nile—Joseph, official of an occupying power—Corn silos, an Egyptian patent—Evidence of
a seven-year famine—Assignments to Goshen—Bahr
Yusuf: Joseph's Canal—Jacob-Her on scarabs*

AND JOSEPH WAS BROUGHT DOWN TO EGYPT: AND
POTIPHAR, AN OFFICER OF PHARAOH, CAPTAIN OF
THE GUARD, AN EGYPTIAN, BOUGHT HIM OF THE
HANDS OF THE ISHMAELITES, WHICH HAD BROUGHT
HIM DOWN THITHER. (Gen. 39:1)

The tale of Joseph, who was sold by his brothers to
Egypt and later, as grand vizier, became reconciled to
them, is undoubtedly one of the finest stories in the
world's literature.

"And it came to pass after these things, that his
master's [Potiphar's] wife cast her eyes upon Joseph;
and she said, Lie with me. But he refused, and . . ."
(Gen. 39:7-8) When her husband came home, she
said: "The Hebrew servant, which thou hast brought
unto us, came in unto me to mock me." (Gen. 39:17)

"Nothing new under the sun," the Egyptologists repeated when they started work on the translation of
the Orbiney Papyrus. What they were deciphering
from hieroglyphics was a popular story about the
time of the XIXth Dynasty which bore the discreet
title *The Tale of the Two Brothers*. "Once upon a time
there were two brothers. . . . The name of the elder
one was Anubis, the younger was called Bata. Anubis
owned a house and a wife and his younger brother
lived with him as if he were his own son. He drove the
cattle out to the fields and brought them home at
night and slept with them in the cowshed. When plowing time came round, the two brothers were plowing
the land together. They had been a few days in the
fields when they ran out of corn. The elder brother
therefore sent the younger one off: 'Hurry and bring

91

us corn from the city.' The younger brother found his
elder brother's wife having her hair done. 'Up,' he said,
'and give me some corn, for I have to hurry back to
the field. My brother said, "Quick, don't waste any
time." ' He loaded up with corn and wheat and went
out with his burden. . . . Then said she to him: 'You
have so much energy! Every day I see how strong you
are. . . . Come! Let us lie down for an hour! It might
give you pleasure, and I shall also make you fine
clothes.' Then the young man was as angry as a southern panther at this wicked suggestion that had been
made to him. He said to her, 'What a disgraceful proposal you have just made. . . . Never do it again and I
shall say nothing to anyone.' So saying, he slung his
load on his back and went out to the fields. The wife
began to be frightened about what she had said. She
got hold of some grease paint and made herself up to
look like someone who had been violently assaulted.
Her husband . . . found his wife lying prostrate as a
result of the outrage. Her husband said to her, 'Who
has been with you?' She replied, 'No one . . . apart
from your young brother. When he came to fetch the
corn, he found me sitting alone and said to me:
"Come, let us lie down for an hour! Do up your
hair." But I paid no attention to him. "Am I not your
mother? and is your elder brother not like a father to
you?" I said to him. But he was afraid and struck me
to stop me telling you about it. If you leave him alive
now I shall die.' Then his brother grew as wild as a
southern panther. He sharpened his knife . . . to kill
his younger brother. . . ."

We can almost see Pharaoh's courtiers whispering
over it. They liked this story. Sex problems and the
psychology of women interested people even then.

Might this story of an adulteress in the heart of an
Egyptian tale be the prototype of the Biblical story of
Joseph? Scholars argued the pros and cons based on
the text of the Orbiney Papyrus long after the turn of
the century. On the debit side, there was not the
slightest trace of Israel's sojourn in Egypt apart from
the Bible itself. Historians and professors of theology
alike spoke of the "Legend of Joseph." Egypt was

just the kind of country from which one might hope for, and even expect, contemporary documentation about the events recorded in the Bible. At any rate this ought to be true as far as Joseph was concerned, for he was Pharaoh's grand vizier and therefore a most powerful man in Egyptian eyes.

No country in the ancient East has handed down its history so faithfully as Egypt. Right back to about 3000 B.C. we can trace the names of the Pharaohs practically without a break. We know the succession of dynasties in the Old, Middle, and New Kingdoms. No other people have recorded so meticulously their important events, the activities of their rulers, their campaigns, the erection of temples and palaces, as well as their literature and poetry.

But this time Egypt gave the scholars no answer. As if it were not enough that they found nothing about

Fig. 13.

Joseph, they discovered neither documents nor monuments out of this whole period. The records which showed hardly a break for centuries suddenly stopped about 1730 B.C. From then on for a long time an impenetrable darkness lay over Egypt. Not before 1580 B.C. did contemporary evidence appear once again. How could this absence of any information whatever over so long a period be explained, especially from such a highly developed people and civilization?

Something incredible and frightful befell the Nile country about 1730 B.C. Suddenly as a bolt from the blue, warriors in chariots drove into the country like arrows shot from a bow, endless columns of them in clouds of dust. Day and night horses' hooves thundered past the frontier posts, rang through city streets, temple squares and the majestic courts of Pharaoh's palaces. Even before the Egyptians realized it, it had happened; their country was taken by surprise, overrun and vanquished. The giant of the Nile, who never before in his history had seen foreign conquerors, lay bound and prostrate.

The rule of the victors began with a bloodbath. The Hyksos, Semitic tribes from Canaan and Syria, knew

Fig. 14. Installation of an Egyptian Vizier.

Fig. 15. Ceremonial chariot from Thebes.

no pity. With the fateful year 1730 B.C. the thirteen-hundred-year rule of the dynasties came to an abrupt end. The Middle Kingdom of the Pharaohs was shattered under the onslaught of these Asian peoples, the "rulers of foreign lands." That is the meaning of the name Hyksos. The memory of this political disaster remained alive among the Nile people, as a striking description by the Egyptian historian Manetho testified: "We had a king called Tutimaeus. In his reign, it happened. I do not know why God was displeased with us. Unexpectedly from the regions of the East, came men of unknown race. Confident of victory they marched against our land. By force they took it, easily, without a single battle. Having overpowered our rulers, they burned our cities without compassion, and destroyed the temples of the gods. All the natives were treated with great cruelty, for they slew some and carried off the wives and children of others into slavery. Finally they appointed one of themselves as king.

His name was Salitis and he lived in Memphis and made Upper and Lower Egypt pay tribute to him, and set up garrisons in places which would be most useful to him . . . and when he found a city in the province of Sais which suited his purpose (it lay east of the Bubastite branch of the Nile and was called Avaris) he rebuilt it and made it very strong by erecting walls and installing a force of 240,000 men to hold it. Salitis went there every summer partly to collect his corn and pay his men their wages, and partly to train his armed troops and terrify foreigners."

Avaris is a town that under another name plays an important role in Biblical history. Later called Pi-Ramses, it is one of the bond cities of Israel in Egypt. (Ex. 1:11)

The Biblical story of Joseph and the sojourn of the children of Israel in Egypt probably belong to this period of turbulent conditions on the Nile under the rule of the foreign Hyksos. It is therefore not surprising that no contemporary Egyptian information has come down to us. Nevertheless, there is indirect proof of the authenticity of the Joseph story. The Biblical description of the historical background is authentic; equally genuine is the colorful Egyptian detail. Egyptology confirms this from countless finds.

Spices and aromatic products were brought to Egypt by the Ishmaelites, the Arabian merchants who sold Joseph there. (Gen. 37:25) There was a heavy demand for these things in the Nile country. They were used in religious services, where the wonderfully fragrant herbs were burned as incense in the temples. The doctors found them indispensable for healing the sick, and priests required them for embalming the bodies of the nobility.

Potiphar was the name of the Egyptian to whom Joseph was sold. (Gen. 37:36) It is a thoroughly characteristic native name. In Egyptian it is "Pa-di-pa-ra," "the gift of the god Ra."

Joseph's elevation to viceroy of Egypt was reproduced in the Bible exactly according to protocol. He is invested with the insignia of his high office, he receives the ring, Pharaoh's seal, a costly linen vestment, and a golden chain. (Gen. 41:42) This is exactly how Egyptian artists depict this solemn ceremony on murals and reliefs.

As viceroy, Joseph rode in the Pharaoh's "second chariot."[1] (Gen. 41:43) That implies the time of the Hyksos. These "rulers of foreign lands" were the first to bring the swift war chariot to Egypt. We know too that the Hyksos rulers were the first to use a ceremonial chariot on public occasions in Egypt. Before their day this had not been the practice on the Nile. The ceremonial chariot harnessed to thoroughbred horses was in those days the Rolls-Royce of the governors. The first chariot belonged to the ruler, the "second chariot" was occupied by his chief minister.

Joseph in accordance with his rank married Asenath (Gen. 41:45) and thereby became the son-in-law of an influential man, Potipherah, the priest of Heliopolis. Heliopolis is the On of the Bible, and it lay on the right bank of the Nile a little to the north of present-day Cairo.

Joseph was thirty years of age when he "went out over all the land of Egypt." (Gen. 41:45) The Bible says no more about this, but there is a spot by the Nile which still bears his name.

The town of Medinet-el-Faiyûm, lying eighty miles south of Cairo in the middle of the fertile Faiyûm, was extolled as the "Venice of Egypt." In the lush gardens of this huge flourishing oasis grew oranges, mandarins, peaches, olives, pomegranates, and grapes. Faiyûm owed these delicious fruits to the artificial canal, over 200 miles long, which conveyed the water of the Nile and turned this district, which would otherwise have been desert, into a paradise. The ancient waterway is not only to this day called "Bahr Yusuf"—"Joseph's Canal"—by the fellahin, but is known by this name throughout Egypt. People say that it was the Joseph of the Bible, Pharaoh's "Grand Vizier," as Arab legends would describe him, who planned it.

The Bible depicts Joseph as an able administrator who as grand vizier guided the Egyptian people

---

[1] The chariot of the second person, i.e., the viceroy.

through difficult times by his counsel and actions, making provision in years of plenty for years of want. Thus he gathered in corn and laid it up in granaries against times of need.

"And the seven years of plenteousness that was in the land of Egypt were ended. And the seven years of dearth began to come . . . and the dearth was in all lands." (Gen. 41:53-54)

Years of drought, bad harvests, and famine are well attested in the lands of the Nile. In very early times, for example, at the beginning of the third millennium, there is said to have been a seven-year famine according to a rock inscription of the Ptolemies. King Zoser sent the following message to the governor of the great cataracts of the Nile at Elephantine. "I am very much concerned about the people in the palace. My heart is heavy over the calamitous failure of the Nile floods for the past seven years. There is little fruit; vegetables are in short supply; there is a shortage of food generally. Everybody robs his neighbor. . . . Children

Fig. 16. Selling corn to Semites from Canaan.

weep, young folk droop. The aged are depressed, they have no power in their legs, they sit on the ground. The court is at its wit's end. The storehouses have been opened, but everything that was in them has been consumed." Traces have been found of the granaries which existed even in the Old Kingdom. In many tombs there were little clay models of them. Apparently they were making provision for possible years of famine among the dead.

"Now when Jacob saw that there was corn in Egypt, Jacob said unto his sons, Why do ye look upon one another? And he said, Behold, I have heard that there is corn in Egypt: get you down thither and buy for us from thence: that we may live and not die. And Joseph's ten brethren went down to buy corn in Egypt." (Gen. 42:1-3)

This was the reason for the great journey which led to the reunion with the brother who had been sold as a slave and to the migration of the Israelites into Egypt. The viceroy brought his father, brothers, and other relatives into the country: ". . . all the souls of the house of Jacob, which came into Egypt, were there three score and ten . . . and they came into the land of Goshen." (Gen. 46:27-28) The viceroy had obtained permission from the highest authority for his family to cross the frontier, and what the Bible records corresponds perfectly with the administrative procedure of the government.

"And Pharaoh spake unto Joseph, saying, Thy father and thy brethren are come unto thee: The land of Egypt is before thee, in the best of the land make thy father and brethren to dwell: in the land of Goshen let them dwell." (Gen. 47:5-6)

A frontier official wrote to his superior on papyrus: "I have another matter to bring to the attention of my lord and it is this: We have permitted the transit of the Bedouin tribes from Edom via the Menephta fort in Zeku, to the fen-lands of the city of Per-Atum . . . so that they may preserve their own lives and the lives of their flocks on the estate of the king, the good Sun of every land. . . ."

Per-Atum, which crops up here in a hieroglyphic text, is the Biblical Pithom in the land of Goshen, later one of the bond cities of Israel in Egypt. (Ex. 1:11)

In cases of this sort the Egyptian frontier police, like the higher officials, were carefully graded in a chain of command right up to the court. The procedure to be followed was of a standard pattern: Petitioners for pasture land, refugees from famine-stricken countries, were accepted and almost always directed into the same area. It lay on the delta, on the right bank of the Nile in the Biblical land of Goshen. The seat of government of the Hyksos rulers was also in the delta.

The children of Israel must have appreciated life in

the land of Goshen. It was—exactly as the Bible describes it (Gen. 45:18; 46:32; 47:3)—extremely fertile and quite ideal for cattle breeding. When Jacob died at a ripe old age, something happened to him which was quite as unknown and uncommon in Canaan and Mesopotamia as among his own family, who considered it a very remarkable proceeding. His body was embalmed.

"And Joseph commanded his servants, the physicians, to embalm his father, and the physicians embalmed Israel.[1] And forty days were fulfilled for him; for so are fulfilled the days of those which are embalmed." (Gen. 50:2-3)

We can read in Herodotus, the globetrotter of the ancient world and best travel diarist, how closely this description corresponds with Egyptian practice. Later on Joseph was buried in the same way.

Under the Egyptian Pharaohs a sand-dweller could never have become viceroy. Nomads bred asses, sheep, and goats, and the Egyptians despised none so much as breeders of small cattle. "For every shepherd is an abomination unto the Egyptians." (Gen. 46:34) Only under the foreign overlords, the Hyksos, would an Asiatic have the chance to rise to the highest office in the state. Under the Hyksos we repeatedly find officials with Semitic names. On scarabs dating from the Hyksos period the name "Jacob-Her," has been clearly deciphered. "And it is not impossible," concludes the great American Egyptologist James Henry Breasted, "that a leader of the Israelite tribe of Jacob gained control for a time in the Nile valley in this obscure period. Such an occurrence would fit in surprisingly well with the migration to Egypt of Israelite tribes which in any case must have taken place about this time."

---

[1] Jacob received from Yahweh the name Israel. (Gen. 32:28) The nation was later called the "Children of Israel" after him.

CHAPTER 2 / Four Hundred Years of Silence

Reawakening on the Nile—Thebes instigates revolt—Rout of the Hyksos—Egypt becomes a world power—Indian civilization in Mitanni—A Horite settlement under the derricks of Kirkuk—Nofretete, an Indo-Aryan princess? —The "Sons of Heth" on the Halys—Pharaoh's widow in quest of a mate—The first nonaggression pact in the world —Hittite bridal procession through Canaan

AND ISRAEL DWELT IN THE LAND OF EGYPT IN THE COUNTRY OF GOSHEN: AND THEY HAD POSSESSIONS THEREIN, AND GREW AND MULTIPLIED EXCEEDINGLY. (Gen. 47:27)

For a space of four hundred years, during which, politically, the face of the Fertile Crescent was completely altered, the Bible is silent. In these four centuries there took place a vast rearrangement of the disposition of national groups. They interrupted the history of the Semitic kingdoms that for a thousand years had maintained their sway on the Euphrates and the Tigris. The great island of civilization in the Middle East was rudely dragged from its self-sufficient existence. Foreign peoples with foreign ways surged in from distant and hitherto unknown lands. For the first time it felt the clash with the outside world.

For a hundred and fifty years there is also silence in Egypt. The prelude to the reawakening of the giant of the Nile opens with a remarkable motif: the roaring of hippopotami.

A papyrus fragment[1] tells how the ambassador of the Hyksos king Apophis went from Avaris to the Prince of the City of the South. The City of the South was Thebes, and its prince was the Egyptian Sekenenrê, who paid tribute to the foreign overlords on the upper delta. The Prince in astonishment asked the emissary

---

[1] Papyrus Sallier I (British Museum).

of the Asiatic occupying power: "Why have you been sent to the City of the South? Why have you made this journey?" The messenger replied: "King Apophis —may he have long life, health, and prosperity!— bids me say to you: Get rid of the hippopotamus pool in the east end of your city. I cannot sleep for them. Night and day the noise of them rings in my ears." The Prince of the City of the South was thunderstruck because he did not know what answer to give to the ambassador of King Apophis—may he have long life, health, and prosperity! At last he said: "Very well, your master—may he have long life, health, and prosperity!—will hear about this pool in the east end of the City of the South."

The ambassador, however, was not to be so easily put off. He spoke more plainly: "This matter about which I have been sent must be dealt with." The Prince of the City of the South then tried in his own way to get round the determined ambassador. He was well aware of the ancient equivalent of the elaborate lunch as a means of creating an atmosphere of friendliness and goodwill. Accordingly he saw to it that the Hyksos commissioner was "supplied with good things, with meat and cakes." But his luck was out. For when the ambassador departed he had a promise from the prince in his saddle-bag, written on papyrus: "All that you have told me to do I shall do. Tell him that. Then the Prince of the City of the South summoned his highest officials and his leading officers and repeated to them the message that King Apophis—may he have long life, health, and prosperity!—had sent him. Then one and all remained silent for quite a while. . . ." At this point the papyrus text breaks off. The end of the story is unfortunately missing, but we can reconstruct the sequel from other contemporary evidence.

In the Cairo museum lies the mummy of Sekenenrê. When it was discovered at Deir-el-Bahri near Thebes, it attracted special attention from medical men, for there were five deep sword cuts in the head. Sekenenrê had lost his life in battle.

It sounds like a fairy tale, yet it is an attractive possibility that the roaring of hippopotami at Thebes should have unseated the Hyksos rulers up in the delta. The roaring of a hippopotamus is probably the most extraordinary *casus belli* in world history.[1]

Beginning at Thebes, the rebellion against the hated oppressor spread like wildfire throughout the country. Egyptian battalions marched once more down the Nile. They were accompanied by a well-equipped fleet of galleys which headed north down the sacred river. In 1580 B.C. after years of furious attacks, Avaris, the chief fortress of the Hyksos in the delta, fell amid bloody and savage fighting. Ahmose I, son of Sekenenrê, was the glorious liberator of Egypt. A namesake of his, Ahmose, an officer in the new Royal Egyptian Navy, has left us a record of this decisive battle on the walls of his tomb at El-Kab. After a detailed description of his education, he adds laconically: "Avaris was taken: I captured one man and three women, four people in all. His Majesty gave them to me as slaves."

This naval officer had also something to say about the military side of things: "Scharuhen was besieged for three years before his Majesty captured it." This was also a profitable occasion for Ahmose: "I collected two women and one laborer as my booty. I was given gold for my bravery, as well as prisoners for my slaves."

Scharuhen was, on account of its commanding position in the Negeb, an important strategic point south of the brown mountain chains of Judah. The small mound of rubble, Tell Far'a, is all that remains of it. Flinders Petrie, the famous British archaeologist, brought to light a thick wall here in 1928.

The multicolored army of mercenaries which the Egyptians controlled, consisting of Negroes, Asiatics, and Nubians, marched on northward through Canaan. The new Pharaohs had learned a lesson from the bitter experience of the past. Never again would their country be taken by a surprise attack. Egypt lost no time in creating a buffer state far in advance of its frontier posts. The remainder of the Hyksos empire was

---

[1]Apart from this literary tradition, an unpublished historical text from Karnak describes the beginning of the rebellion.

crushed, and Palestine became an Egyptian province. What had once been consular stations, trading posts, and messengers' quarters in Canaan and on the Phoenician coast became permanent garrisons, fortified strong points, and Egyptian fortresses in a subjugated land.

After a history of more than two thousand years the giant of the Nile stepped out of the shadows of his pyramids and sphinxes and claimed the right to take an active part in affairs beyond his own borders and to have some say in the outside world. Egypt matured more and more into a world power. Previously, all who lived outside of the Nile Valley were contemptuously described as "Asiatics," "Sand ramblers," "cattle breeders"—people not worthy of the attention of a Pharaoh. Now, however, the Egyptians became more affable. They began communications with other countries. Hitherto that had been unthinkable; among the diplomatic correspondence in the archives of the palace of Mari, there was not one single item from the Nile. Tempora mutantur—the times are changed.

The advance of the Egyptians brought them eventually to Syria, indeed, to the banks of the Euphrates. There, to their astonishment, they came up against people of whose existence they had no idea. The priests searched in vain through the ancient papyrus rolls in the temple archives and studied without result the records of the campaigns of earlier Pharaohs. Nowhere could they find even a hint about the unknown kingdom of Mitanni. Its foundation is attributed to an extremely active and creative people, the Horites, whose name is mentioned in the Bible about the time of Abraham. (Gen. 14:6, etc.)

In the neighborhood of the oil wells of Kirkuk in Iraq, where now American derricks draw immeasurable wealth from the earth, archaeologists from the United States and Iraq came across a large settlement, the old Horite city of Nuzu. Stacks of tablets which have been salvaged—and among these principally marriage contracts and wills—contained extremely interesting information: the Biblical Horites were not a Semitic people. Their home was among the mountains round the Black Sea. The names on many Horite documents indicate that at least the princely caste must be reckoned as Indo-Aryan. It is even certain that as far as their outward appearance was concerned they belonged to the brachycephalous type, such as present-day Armenians.

In the north of Mesopotamia these strangers had built up their powerful kingdom between the upper reaches of the Euphrates and the Tigris. Their kings had collected round them an aristocracy of warlike charioteers, and they bore Indo-Aryan names. The aristocracy of the country was called Marya, which is the equivalent of "Young Warriors." Marya is an old Indian word, and their temples were dedicated to old Indian gods. Magic incantations from the Rigveda were intoned in front of the images of Mithras, the victorious champion of light against darkness, of Indra, who ruled the storms, and of Varuna, who governed the eternal order of the universe. The old gods of the Semites had crashed from their pedestals.

The Mitanni were completely devoted to their horses, they were "horse crazy." They held the first races in the world along the banks of their great rivers. Advice on the breeding and care of stud animals, directions for the training of cavalry horses, instructions on the breaking in of young horses, regulations for feeding and training in racing stables fill veritable libraries of clay tablets. These are works on equitation that can bear comparison with any modern textbook on horse breeding. As far as the Marya, these aristocratic charioteers, were concerned, horses were of more account than human beings.

It was with this state of Mitanni that Egypt had now a common frontier; nevertheless, it was one on which there was to be no peace. Local feuds were unending. Raids on one side or the other constantly involved Egyptian archers in angry passages with the charioteers. In the course of these expeditions sometimes it was Egyptian striking forces, sometimes columns of Mitanni, who struck deep into the enemy's territory. The valleys of the Lebanon, the banks of the Orontes and the Euphrates were the scenes of endless battles and bloody melees. For almost a century the two great kingdoms were at each other's throats.

Shortly before 1400 B.C. the warlike Mitanni proposed a peaceful settlement with the Egyptians. The enemy became a friend. The kings of Mitanni turned their attention purposefully to dynastic politics. With great pomp and lavish gifts they sent their daughters down to the Nile and married their princesses to the Pharaohs. In three successive generations of rulers Indo-Aryan and Egyptian blood was mixed for the first time. Probably it was one of these princesses who became the most famous of all the wives of the Pharaohs, Nofretete, whose beauty still delights the world. Her husband, Amenophis IV, was the Egyptian sun king Akhnaton.

What was the reason for the unexpected desire for peace on the part of the warlike Mitanni?

The impulse came from outside. Their kingdom was suddenly threatened with war on two fronts. A second powerful opponent began to storm the frontiers with his armies from Asia Minor in the northwest. This was a nation about which scholars until this century knew hardly anything, but which plays a considerable part in the Old Testament—the Hittites.

It was among the "Sons of Heth" that Abraham pitched his tent near Hebron, south of the hills of Judah, and it was from them that he bought the land in which he laid his wife Sarah to rest. (Gen. 23:3ff.) Esau, much to the distress of his parents Isaac and Rebecca, married two Hittite women (Gen. 26:34), and King David himself took "the wife of Uriah, the Hittite." (II Sam. 11) We are told by the prophet Ezekiel that Hittites were partly responsible for founding Jerusalem: "Thy birth and thy nativity is of the land of Canaan: thy father was an Amorite, and thy mother a Hittite." (Ezek. 16:3, 45)

The rediscovery of the Hittite people who had sunk into complete oblivion took place in the heart of Turkey shortly after the turn of the century.

In the highlands east of Ankara, the capital, the River Halys makes a huge bend on its way to the

Black Sea. Almost exactly in the middle lies Boghaz-Keui: "Boghas" in Turkish means a gorge, and "Keui" is a village. Near this "Village in the gorge" the German Egyptologist Professor Hugo Winckler discovered in 1905 a number of cuneiform texts, among which was also a peculiar type of hieroglyphics. They aroused tremendous interest—and not only among scholars. The general public learned with amazement just what kind of people these Biblical "sons of Heth" were. The translations of the cuneiform writings brought to the notice of the world at large the hitherto unknown Indo-Germanic Hittites and their vanished empire.

Two years later a fresh expedition set out from Berlin for Boghaz-Keui. This time it was under the direction of the President of the Archaeological Institute of Berlin, Otto Puchstein. The great pile of ruins above the village was carefully examined. This was the site of royal Chattusas, the proud capital of the Hittite empire. What remained of it was a vast ruin of walls, temples, fortified gateways—the remnants of a great city. Its walls enclosed an area of 425 acres. Chattusas was almost as big as medieval Nuremberg. At the city gates were life-sized reliefs. It is to these effigies, carved out of black basalt as hard as iron, that we are indebted for our knowedge of the appearance of Hittite kings and warriors. Their long hair hung over their shoulders like a full-bottomed wig; on top sat a high-dented cap; their short aprons were fastened with a wide belt and their shoes had pointed toes.

When Subbiluliuma, King of the Hittites, marched southeast with a powerful army about 1370 B.C., the days of the kingdom of Mitanni were already numbered despite all their clever dynastic politics. Subbiluliuma crushed the kingdom of the warlike charioteers, compelled it to pay tribute, and then pressed on further to the mountains of the Lebanon in the north of Canaan. Overnight, as it were, Egypt had a new, equally powerful neighbor in Syria thirsting for victory.

A delightful document has come down to us from this period. Prince Mursilis, son of Subbiluliuma, tells

Fig. 17.

in his autobiography of an episode at the Hittite Court, which must have made such a lasting impression on him that he had it recorded.

Anches-en-Amun, the wife of Pharaoh Tutankhamun, had become a widow. She had very famous parents, Akhnaton and Nofretete. We know her from wonderful Egyptian representations as a slight young thing. But she must have been a woman who knew what she wanted and used all her natural charm to further the aims of her people in the realm of high politics. Using the inviting bed and throne of the Pharaohs as bait—and what attractive bait!—she tried to take the wind out of the sails of her powerful new neighbors by discouraging their warlike intentions. Hittite warriors had just made an attack on Amqa, the fertile country between Lebanon and Anti-Lebanon.

Mursilis dictated: "When the Egyptians heard of the attack on Amqa, they were alarmed. To make matters worse, their lord [Tutankhamun] had just died. But the widowed Queen of Egypt sent an ambassador to my father and wrote him the following letter: 'My husband is dead and I have no son. I am told that you have many sons. If you send me one of your sons, he could become my husband. I do not wish to take one of my servants and make a husband of him.' When my father heard this, he summoned his nobles to a council and said: 'I have never in all my life come across anything like this.' He dispatched his chamberlain Hattu-Zitis: 'Go and find out if this is true. Perhaps they are trying to deceive me. There may in fact be a prince. Bring me back reliable information.' The Egyptian ambassador, the honorable Hanis, came to my father. Since my father had instructed Hattu-Zitis before he left for Egypt, 'Perhaps they have a prince of their own: They may be trying to deceive us. They may not need one of my sons at all to occupy the throne,' the Queen of Egypt now replied to my father in a letter: 'Why do you say they may be trying to deceive me? If I had a son, would I write to a foreign country in a manner that is humiliating both for me and my people? You do not trust me; otherwise you would not say such a thing. He who was my husband is dead and I have no sons. Am I to take one of my servants and make him into my husband? I have written to no other country. I have only written to you. They tell me you have so many sons. Give me one of your sons and he shall be my husband and king over the land of Egypt.' Since my father was so fine a king, he complied with the lady's request and sent her the son she asked for."

Fate prevented the successful conclusion of this unusual offer of marriage. Both the royal throne and the bed of Anches-en-Amun remained empty, since the candidate was murdered on his way to Egypt.

Seventy-five years later another offer of marriage on this same Halys-Nile axis had a happy ending, al-

though the prelude to it, which was the din of battle
and the clash of weapons, pointed to a different conclusion. Ramesses II, who was called the "Great," set
out with his army for Palestine and Syria. He intended
to deal with the hated Hittites once and for all.

In the valley of the Orontes, where today fields of
cotton stretch far and wide and the old Crusader castle
"Krak des Chevaliers" keeps an eye on the fertile plain
of Bukea, there lay in those days the city of Kadesh,
a little to the south of the dark green of Lake Homs.
Before its walls four Egyptian armies threw themselves
on the swift war chariots and infantry of the Hittites.
The battle did not, as it happened, bring Ramesses II
the victory he had hoped for (he came, in fact, within
an ace of being captured himself), but it put an end
to these endless military incidents. In 1280 B.C. the
Hittites and the Egyptians concluded the first nonaggression and mutual defense pact in world history. The
good understanding was cemented at top level by the
marriage of Ramesses II to a Hittite princess. Many
lengthy inscriptions give in full and vivid detail the
colorful background of what was in the circumstances
an international event of the first order. Whether
found on the walls of the temples at Karnak, Elephantine, or Abu Simbel, or on the numerous monuments, they all tell the same story.

As far as self-advertisement and self-praise were concerned, Ramesses II put all his predecessors in the
shade. "Then came a messenger to inform His Majesty. He said: 'Behold, even the great Prince of Hatti!
[Hittites] His eldest daughter is on her way, and she
brings untold tribute of all kinds. . . . They have
reached His Majesty's frontiers. Let the army and the
dignitaries come to receive her!' Then His Majesty
was greatly delighted, and the palace was glad to hear
these unusual tidings, which were quite unheard of in
Egypt. He therefore sent forth the army and the dignitaries to receive her."

A large delegation was dispatched to the north of
Palestine to bring back the bride. Yesterday's enemies
became brothers: "So the daughter of the great Prince
of Hatti came to Egypt. While the infantry, charioteers,

and dignitaries of His Majesty accompanied them, they mingled with the infantry and charioteers from Hatti. The whole populace from the country of the Hittites was mixed up with the Egyptians. They ate and drank together; they were like blood-brothers. . . ."

The great bridal train proceeded from Palestine to the city of Pi-Ramses-Meri-Amun in the Nile delta: "Then they brought the daughter of the Great Prince of Hatti . . . before His Majesty. And His Majesty saw that she was fair of countenance like a goddess. . . . And he loved her more than anything else. . . ."

The children of Israel must have been eye witnesses of the ceremonial arrival of the bridal procession in the city of Pi-Ramses-Meri-Amun, which means "The House of Ramses the Beloved of the god Amun." As the Biblical description indicates, however, their presence in this city was by no means of their own accord. It is at this point also that the Bible resumes its narrative. Four hundred years which the children of Israel had spent as immigrants in the land of the Nile have been passed over in silence. A new and significant chapter of the history of the Biblical people now begins—but it begins with inauspicious tidings.

CHAPTER 3 / Forced Labor in Pithom and Raamses

Joseph had died a long time ago—A story in pictures from a prince's tomb—Pithom labor camp in Egyptian texts—The royal seat is transferred to the delta—A builder's enthusiasm and vanity lead to a fraud—Montet unearths the bond city of Raamses—Moses wrote his name "MS"—A Mesopotamian story about a baby in the bulrushes—Moses emigrates to Midian—Plagues are no strangers to Egypt

NOW THERE AROSE UP A NEW KING OVER EGYPT, WHICH KNEW NOT JOSEPH. THEREFORE THEY DID SET OVER THEM TASKMASTERS, TO AFFLICT THEM WITH THEIR BURDENS, AND THEY BUILT FOR PHARAOH TREASURE-CITIES [R.V.: store-cities], PITHOM AND RAAMSES. (Ex. 1:8-11)

The new king who "knew not Joseph" was most likely Ramesses II or one of his predecessors. His ignorance is understandable, for Joseph had lived centuries before him in the days of the Hyksos. The names of these Hyksos rulers who were so cordially detested by the Egyptians have hardly been recorded, much less the names of their dignitaries and officials. Even if this Pharaoh of the new dynasty, whether it was Ramesses II or a predecessor, had known of Joseph, that is as far as he would have wanted it to go. Joseph was bound to be an object of contempt to any nationally conscious Egyptian for two reasons: one, that he was an "Asiatic" and a miserable "Sand rambler," and, two, that he was the highest official of the hated occupying power. From the latter point of view any appeal to Joseph would hardly have been a recommendation for Israel in the eyes of a Pharaoh.

What forced labor meant in ancient Egypt and what the children of Israel experienced at the great building projects on the Nile can be gathered from a very old painting from the patriarchal period at Beni-

Hasan that Percy A. Newberry found in a rock tomb west of the royal city of Thebes.

On the walls of a spacious vault there is a series of paintings from the life of a great dignitary, the vizier Rekhmire, showing what he had done for the benefit of his country. One scene shows him in charge of

Fig. 18. Bricklaying with foreign labor in Egypt.

public works. The detail shows the manufacture of Egyptian bricks, the most notable feature being the light-skinned workmen, who are clad only in linen aprons. A comparison with the dark-skinned overseers shows that the fair-skinned men are probably Semites, but certainly not Egyptians. "He provides us with bread, beer and every good thing." Yet, despite these words of praise about the quality of the diet, there is no doubt about the fact that they are not working voluntarily but compulsorily. "The rod is in my hand," one of the Egyptian overseers is saying, according to the hieroglyphic inscription. "Be not idle."

The picture is an impressive illustration of the Biblical words: "And the Egyptians made the children of Israel to serve with rigor, and they made their lives bitter with hard bondage in mortar and in brick." (Ex. 1:13, 14) Israel was of shepherd stock, unused to work of any other kind, which made it therefore twice as hard for them. Building and brickmaking were forced labor.

The painting in the rock tomb shows a scene from the building of the Temple of Amun in Thebes. The classical bond cities of the children of Israel were, however, Pithom and Raamses. Both names appear in slightly different form in Egyptian inventories. "Pi-Tum"—"House of the god Tum"—is a town which was built by Ramesses II. Pi-Ramses-Meri-Amun, which has already been mentioned, is the Biblical Ra-amses. An inscription of the time of Ramesses II speaks of " 'PR, who hauled the stones for the great fortress of the city of Pi-Ramses-Meri-Amun." " 'PR" is Egyptian hieroglyphics for Semites.

The question of where these bond cities were situated remained unanswered. It was known that the rulers of the New Kingdom had moved their seat from ancient Thebes northward to Avaris, which was the place from which the Hyksos had also ruled the country. The new type of international power politics made it seem advisable to be nearer the center of things than was the case with Thebes, which lay much farther south. From the delta they could much more easily keep an eye on turbulent "Asia," their dominions in Canaan and Syria. Pharaoh Ramesses II gave his name to the new capital. Avaris became the city of Pi-Ramses-Meri-Amun.

After a fair amount of guesswork and supposition archaeologists' picks put an end to all differences of opinion about the site of one of the bond cities. Anyone who goes to Egypt can include a trip round its ruins in his program. It is sixty miles by car from Cairo. About halfway down the Suez Canal, where it goes through what was the Lake of Crocodiles,[1] a dried-up watercourse, known as Wadi Tumilat, stretches westward till it strikes the easternmost arm of the Nile. There two mounds of rubble lie about six miles apart. One is Tell er-Retaba, which was the Biblical Pithom, the other is Tell el-Maschuta, which was the Biblical Succoth. (Ex. 12:37; 13:20) Apart from remains of granaries, inscriptions have also been found which refer to storehouses.

If there had been patent laws 4000 years ago, the Egyptians could have claimed exclusive rights over granaries. The silos on Canadian and American wheat farms are still built on the same principle. Admitted-

---

[1]Lake Timsah.

ly, Egyptian silos did not reach the same gigantic proportions, but granaries, circular buildings about twenty-five feet in diameter with ramps leading up to the feeder, were not uncommon on the Nile. As grand vizier, Joseph built granaries (Gen. 41:48ff.), and as slave laborers his descendants built granaries in the land of Goshen.

The search for the other bond city, Raamses,[1] went on for a long time without success. Then, nearly thirty years after the discovery of Pithom, it was eventually found in 1930.

Ramesses II, the "Great," has given the archaeologists many a hard nut to crack. Apparently his vanity was even greater than his passion for building. He never hesitated to deck himself in borrowed plumes: posterity would marvel at the great builder Ramesses II. And, indeed, it did. The experts could hardly grasp

Fig. 19. Corn silos in Egypt.

at first how it come about that on so many temples and public buildings and in other places they came upon the cipher "Ramesses II." But when they examined the buildings a little more closely, the explanation was plain. Many of these buildings must have been built centuries before Ramesses II. To pander to his own vanity, however, Ramesses II decided to have his monogram carved on them all.

In the delta the search for the city of Pi-Ramses-

---

[1] I.e., Pi-Ramses-Meri-Amun, formerly Avaris.

Meri-Amun led from one mound to another. One excavated site after another throughout the Nile delta was thought to be the one they were looking for: Pithom, Heliopolis, Pelusium, and others. Guesswork came to an end only when the spade of Professor Pierre Montet of Strasbourg struck the ground near the present-day fishing village of San in 1929. Thirty miles southwest of Port Said, Montet unearthed between 1929 and 1932 an unusual number of statues, sphinxes, columns, and fragments of buildings, all of them stamped with the crest of Ramesses II. This time there was no doubt that it was the remains of Pi-Ramses-Meri-Amun, the Biblical bond city of Raamses. Just as in Pithom, they found here ruins of granaries and storehouses.

The Israelites became the victims, in the truest sense of the word, of Pharaoh's lust for building. The position of their immigration area made it easier for them to be dragooned into forced labor. The Goshen of the Bible, with its rich grazings, began just a few miles south of the new capital and stretched as far as Pithom. Nothing could be simpler than to drag these foreigners who lived, so to speak, on the doorstep of these great building projects away from their flocks and tents and force them into servitude.

The ruins at San no longer give any indication of the splendor of the former metropolis. What the columns of Israelite levies saw on their daily march to the building sites we can only gather from a contemporary papyrus letter. It is written by a schoolboy. Pai-Bes, to his teacher, Amen-em-Opet: "I have come to Pi-Ramses-the Beloved of Amun and find it wonderful. A splendid city without a rival. Ra, the same god who founded Thebes, founded this according to the same plan. To live here is to have a glorious life. The countryside provides a wealth of good things. Every day they get fresh provisions and meat. Their pools are full of fish, their lagoons are thick with birds, their meadows are covered with green grass, the fruit from their well-tilled fields has the taste of honey. Their storehouses are full of barley and corn and tower up to the sky. There are onions and chives to season the food, also pomegranates, apples, olives, and figs from the orchards. Sweet wine from Kenkeme, which tastes nicer than honey. The Shi-Hor branch of the Nile produces salt and saltpeter. Their ships come and go. Every day here there are fresh victuals and meat. People are glad to be able to live there and nobody cries, 'God help me!' Simple folk live like great folk. Come! Let us celebrate there the festivals of heaven and the beginning of the seasons."

Years later, life in the barren wilderness had blotted out the recollection of their forced labor from the minds of the children of Israel. All they remembered was the plentiful food of the delta: "Would to God we had died by the hand of the Lord in the land of Egypt, when we sat by the fleshpots and when we did eat bread to the full." (Ex. 16:3) "Who shall give us flesh to eat? We remember the fish which we did eat in Egypt freely: the cucumbers, and the melons, and the leeks, and the onions and the garlic." "Who shall give us flesh to eat, for it was well with us in Egypt." (Num. 11:4-5, 18)

Discoveries during excavations and contemporary texts, sometimes providing almost literal correspondence, confirm the Biblical picture. We must not think, however, that the academic dispute over the historicity of these events in the life of Israel is thereby settled.

Professor William Foxwell Albright of the United States has some sharp words to say on this subject. Since he is one of the few scholars with almost universal qualifications—as theologian, historian, philosopher, orientalist, archaeologist, and comparative philologist—they may well be cited as conclusive. "According to our present knowledge of topography of the eastern delta the account of the start of the Exodus, which is given in Ex. 12:37 and Ex. 13:20, is topographically absolutely correct. Further proofs of the essentially historical nature of the Exodus-story and the journey in the area of Sinai, Midian, and Kadesh can be supplied without great difficulty, thanks to our growing knowledge of topography and archaeology.

"We must content ourselves here with the assurance that the hypercritical attitude which previously obtained in respect of the earlier historical traditions of Israel has no longer any justification. Even the long-disputed date of the Exodus can now be fixed within reasonable limits. . . . If we put it at about 1290 B.C., we cannot go far wrong, since the first years of the reign of Ramesses II (1301-1234) were to a large extent occupied with building activities in the city to which he has given his name—the Raamses of Israelite tradition. The striking correspondence between this date and the length of their stay given by Ex. 12:40 as 430 years—'Now the sojourning of the children of Israel, who dwelt in Egypt, was 430 years' (Ex. 12:40) —may be purely coincidental but it is very remarkable. According to this the migration must have taken place about 1720 B.C."

The reign of Ramesses II is the time of the oppression and forced labor of Israel, but also the time at which Moses the great liberator of his people appears.

"And it came to pass in those days, when Moses was grown, that he went out unto his brethren, and looked on their burdens: and he spied an Egyptian smiting an Hebrew, one of his brethren. And he looked this way and that way, and when he saw that there was no man, he slew the Egyptian and hid him in the sand. Now when Pharaoh heard this thing, he sought to slay Moses. But Moses fled from the face of Pharaoh, and dwelt in the land of Midian: and he sat down by a well." (Ex. 2:11, 12, 15)

Moses was a Hebrew who was born in Egypt, brought up by Egyptians, and bore a typical Egyptian name. Moses is the name Mâose which is commonly found on the Nile. The Egyptian word "MS"[1] means simply "boy-son." A number of Pharaohs are called Ahmose, Amasis, Thutmose. And Thutmose was the name of the famous sculptor, among whose masterpieces the incomparably beautiful head of Nofretete is still the admiration of the world.

These are facts. Egyptologists know that. But the general public picks on the famous Biblical story of Moses in the bulrushes, and it is not difficult on the

---

[1]"MS" stands for Mosu. Egyptian hieroglyphics used no vowels.

basis of this charming story to produce an apparently valid argument against the authenticity of the figure of Moses. "It is simply the birth-legend of Sargon," they say. But they add mentally, "Plagiarism."

Cuneiform texts have this to say of King Sargon, the founder of the Semitic dynasty of Akkad in 2360 B.C.: "I am Sargon, the powerful king, the king of Akkad. My mother was a temple prostitute; I did not know any father. My mother conceived me and bore me in secret. She put me in a little box made of reeds, sealing its lid with pitch. She put me in the river. . . . The river carried me away and brought me to Akki the waterman. Akki the waterman adopted me and brought me up as his son. . . ."

The similarity with the Biblical story of Moses is in fact astounding: "And when she could no longer hide him, she took for him an ark of bulrushes, and daubed it with slime and with pitch and put the child therein: and she laid it in the flags by the river's brink." (Ex. 2:3ff.)

The basket story is a very old Semitic folk tale. It was handed down by word of mouth for many centuries. The Sargon legend of the third millennium B.C. is found on Neo-Babylonian cuneiform tablets of the first millennium B.C. It is nothing more than the frills with which posterity has always loved to adorn the lives of great men. Who would dream of doubting the historicity of the Emperor Barbarossa simply because he is said to be still sleeping under Kyffhäuser?

Officials everywhere and at all times enjoy the protection of the state. So it was in the time of the Pharaohs. So it is today. It was for this reason that Moses had no choice but to flee from certain punishment after he had in righteous indignation killed the guard in charge of the labor gangs.

Moses did what Sinuhe had done before him. He fled eastward to get out of Egyptian territory. Since Canaan was occupied by Egypt, Moses chose for his exile the mountains of Midian east of the Gulf of Aqabah, with which he had a remote connection. Ketura had been Abraham's second wife, after Sarah's death. (Gen. 25:1) One of her sons was called Midian. The tribe of Midian is often called Kenites in the Old Testament. (Num. 24:21) The name means "belonging to the coppersmiths." Qain in Arabic, Quainâya in Aramaic mean a smith. This designation connects up with the presence of metal in the neighborhood of the tribal territory. The mountain ranges east of the Gulf of Aqabah are rich in copper, as the latest investigations of Nelson Glueck, of the United States, have indicated.

No country will willingly part with a cheap supply of forced foreign labor. Israel had to learn that, too. Eventually, we are told that it was the occurrence of plagues that compelled the Egyptians to give way. Whether they raged exactly at the time of Moses can so far be neither affirmed nor denied, since no contemporary evidence on the subject has so far been found. But plagues are neither improbable nor unusual. Indeed, they are part of Egypt's local color. The water of the Nile "was turned to blood." "And the frogs came up and covered the land of Egypt." "Flies" appear, "lice," a "cattle murrain" and "boils"—finally, "hail," "locusts," and "darkness." (Ex. 7-10)

These things which the Bible describes are still experienced by the Egyptians, as, for example, the "red Nile." Deposits from the Abyssinian lakes often color the flood waters a dark reddish brown, especially in the Upper Nile. That might well be said to look like "blood." At the time of the floods "frogs" and also "flies" sometimes multiply so rapidly that they become regular plagues on the land. Under the heading of "lice" would come undoubtedly the dog-fly. These often attack whole areas in swarms, affecting eyes, nose, and ears, and can be very painful.

Cattle pest is known all over the world. The "boils," which attack human beings as well as animals, may be the so-called "Nile heat" or "Nile itch." This is an irritating and stinging rash that often develops into spreading ulcers. This horrible skin disease is also used as a threatened punishment by Moses in the course of the journey through the desert: "The Lord will smite thee with the botch of Egypt, and with the emerods and with the scab and with the itch whereof thou canst not be healed." (Deut. 28:27)

"Hailstorms" are extremely rare on the Nile, but they are not unknown. The season for them is January or February. "Swarms of locusts," on the other hand, are typical and disastrous phenomena in the countries of the Orient. The same is true of sudden "darkness." The khamsin, also called the simoon, is a blistering hot wind that whirls up vast masses of sand and drives them before it. They obscure the sun, give it a dull yellowish appearance, and turn daylight into darkness. Only the death of the "firstborn" is a plague for which there is no parallel. (Ex. 12) And it is indeed miraculous that these afflictions should have been visited upon the people of Egypt at the very time when the children of Israel were being so tormented by their oppressors, and that Moses was thereby enabled to help his people.

III/Forty Years in the Wilderness: From the Nile to the Jordan

CHAPTER 1 / On the Road to Sinai

*Departure from Raamses—Two possible sites for the
"miracle of the sea"—Traces of fords beside the Suez Canal
—Three days without water—Swarms of quails at the
migration season—An expedition clears up the mystery of
manna—Egyptian mining center in Sinai—The alphabet at
the Temple of Hathor*

AND THE CHILDREN OF ISRAEL JOURNEYED FROM
RAMESES TO SUCCOTH. (EX. 12:37) BUT GOD LED THE
PEOPLE ABOUT THROUGH THE WAY OF THE WILDER-
NESS OF THE RED SEA. (EX. 13:18) AND THEY TOOK
THEIR JOURNEY FROM SUCCOTH AND ENCAMPED IN
ETHAM, IN THE EDGE OF THE WILDERNESS. (EX.
13:20) BUT THE EGYPTIANS PURSUED AFTER THEM,
ALL THE HORSES AND CHARIOTS OF PHARAOH, AND
HIS HORSEMEN AND HIS ARMY, AND OVERTOOK THEM
ENCAMPING BY THE SEA, BESIDE PI-HAHIROTH BEFORE
BAAL-ZEPHON. (EX. 14:9)

The first section of the route followed by the fugitives
can easily be followed on the map. It is expressly noted
that they did not travel in the direction of the "way
of the land of the Philistines" (Ex. 13:17), which was
the preferred route from Egypt to Asia via Palestine.
This main highway for caravans and military expeditions ran almost parallel with the Mediterranean coast
and was the shortest and best route, but the one which
was most closely guarded. An army of soldiers and
officials in the frontier posts kept a sharp watch on
all traffic in both directions.

The main road was too risky. The Israelites therefore headed southward. From Pi-Ramses on the eastern branch of the delta, the first stage was Succoth
in Wadi Tumilat. After Etham the next stage was Pi-
Hahiroth. According to the Bible this place lay "between Migdol and the sea, over against Baal-Zephon."
(Ex. 14:2) "Miktol" appears also in Egyptian texts;
it means a "tower." A fort which stood there guarded

125

the caravan route to the Sinai area. All that remains of it has been excavated at Abu Hasan, fifteen miles north of Suez.

"And Moses stretched out his hand over the sea: and the Lord caused the sea to go back by a strong east wind all that night and made the sea dry land, and the waters were divided. And the children of Israel went into the midst of the sea upon the dry ground: and the waters were a wall unto them on their right hand and on their left." (Ex. 14:21-22)

A detachment of Egyptian chariots, which was attempting to recapture the Israelites, was swallowed up by the sea; the horses and their riders were drowned.

This "miracle of the sea" has perpetually exercised men's minds. The difficulty which faced science and research for a long time was not to shed light on the escape itself. The only dispute was about the scene of the event, and on this point it is only barely possible even yet to get a clear picture.

The first difficulty is one of translation. The Hebrew words "Yam Suph" are sometimes translated as the "Red Sea"; at other times as the "Reed Sea." The "Reed Sea" is frequently mentioned: "For we have heard how the Eternal dried up the water of the Reed Sea before you when you left Egypt." (Josh. 2:10— Moffatt's Translation) In the Old Testament up to Jeremiah it is called the "Reed Sea." The New Testament speaks only of the "Red Sea." (Acts 7:36; Hebrews 11:29)[1]

On the shores of the Red Sea there are no reeds. The Reed Sea proper lay farther north. A reliable reconstruction of the situation that existed then is hardly possible, and that is the second difficulty. The building of the Suez Canal in the last century has altered the appearance of the landscape to an extraordinary degree. According to those calculations which seem to

---

[1] Translator's Note: The German Bible uses two expressions: Ried-Meer=Reed Sea and Rotes Meer=Red Sea. The English Bible makes no distinction and uses "Red Sea" throughout. The Hebrew words "Yam Suph" mean "Reed Sea" or "Papyrus Marsh" as modern translations recognize.

have most probability, the so-called "miracle of the sea" must have taken place in that area. What was once Lake Balah, for example, which lay south of the "way of the land of the Philistines" disappeared when the canal was constructed and became marshland. In the time of Ramesses II the Gulf of Suez, in the south, was connected to the Bitter Lakes. Probably the connection extended up to Lake Timsah, the Lake of Crocodiles. In this area there was at one time a Sea of Reeds. The waterway to the Bitter Lakes could be forded at several points. Fords can actually be traced there. The flight from Egypt by way of the Sea of Reeds is therefore perfectly credible.

In early Christian times pilgrims surmised that the flight of Israel led them through the Red Sea. At that time they thought in terms of the northern end of the Gulf near the town of Es-Suwez, present-day Suez. The crossing could have taken place here too. Occasionally strong northwest winds drive the water at the northern extremity of the Gulf back so far that it is possible to wade across. In Egypt the prevailing wind is from the west. The east wind mentioned in the Bible is, on the other hand, typical of Palestine.

"So Moses brought Israel from the Red Sea: and they went out into the wilderness of Shur: and they went three days in the wilderness and found no water. And when they came to Marah they could not drink of the waters of Marah, for they were bitter." (Ex. 15:22-23) "And they came to Elim where were twelve wells of water and three-score and ten palm trees." (Ex. 15:27) "And they took their journey from Elim and all the congregation of the children of Israel came unto the wilderness of Sin, which is between Elim and Sinai. . . ." (Ex. 16:1)

The laborious journey began—a nomadic existence in a barren scrubland that was to last for forty years.

With donkeys, goats, and sheep, only short stretches of about twelve miles a day could be covered. The goal each day was invariably the next water hole. Forty long years the children of Israel wandered round the edge of the desert from well to well, from water hole to water hole. From the stopping places which the Bible mentions the most important stages of the journey can be marked out.

The route is realistically and convincingly described in Numbers, Chapter 33. As we should expect with a mixed company of human beings and animals, they never moved far from the oases and pastures of the Sinai peninsula and the Negeb.

From the Nile to the mountains of the Sinai peninsula stretches an ancient beaten track. It was the road followed by the countless labor gangs and slave gangs who had been digging for copper and turquoise in the Sinai mountains since 3000 B.C. More than once in the course of these millennia the mines had been forsaken and lapsed for centuries into oblivion. Ramesses II remembered the treasure that was lying dormant and started up the mines once more.

It was along this road to the mines that Moses led his people. The way began at Memphis, crossed the top of the Gulf, at what is now Suez, and then bent south along a waterless stretch of forty-five miles, without a single oasis or spring. The Bible expressly mentions that at the beginning of their journey they wandered for three days in the desert without water, then came to a well of undrinkable water after which they soon reached a particularly rich oasis with "twelve wells and seventy palm trees." This very exact Biblical description helped the experts to find the historical route of the Exodus.

A forty-five-mile trek with herds of cattle and a large contingent of people would take three days. Nomads can cope with the problem of thirst for a period of this length. They have always their "iron rations" for such an emergency—water in goatskin containers, like the patriarchal family in the mural painting at Beni-Hasan. Forty-five miles from the northern tip of the Red Sea there is still a spring called "Ain Hawarah" by the Bedouins. Nomads are very reluctant to stop here with their cattle. The water is not inviting for a long stay. It is salty and sulphurous, or "bitter," as the Bible calls it. This is Marah of olden times.

Fifteen miles further on to the south, exactly a day's

march, lies Wadi Gharandel. A fine oasis with shady
palms and plenty of water holes. That is the Biblical
Elim, the second stopping place. After Elim begins
the Wilderness of Sin, on the shore of the Red Sea,
now known as the Plain of El Kaa. The children of
Israel had come no great distance, but they were

Fig. 20. Catching quails on the Nile.

untrained and unused to privation after what was, despite its rigors, a well-fed and well-ordered life in
Egypt. It is no wonder that they gave tongue to their
disappointment and complaints. However, they were
able to augment their scanty diet with two unexpected
but most welcome items.

"And it came to pass, that at even the quails came
up, and covered the camp: and in the morning . . .
when the dew that lay was gone up, behold upon the
face of the wilderness there lay a small round thing,
as small as the hoar frost on the ground. And when
the children of Israel saw it, they said one to another,
it is manna [that is: What is this?], for they wist not
what it was. And Moses said unto them, This is the
bread which the Lord hath given you to eat." (Ex.
16:13-15)

Time and again more or less profound discussions

have taken place over this question of the quails and the manna. What a vast amount of disbelief they have occasioned. The Bible is telling us about things that seem miraculous and inexplicable but which are in themselves perfectly natural occurrences. We need only ask a naturalist or natives of these parts who can see the same thing happening today.

The Exodus of the Israelites began in the spring, the time of the great bird migrations. From Africa, which in summer becomes unbearably hot and dry, the birds have, from time immemorial, migrated to Europe along two routes. One route goes via the west coast of Africa to Spain; the other via the eastern Mediterranean to the Balkans. In the early months of the year, quails, together with other birds, fly across the Red Sea, which they must cross on the eastern route. Exhausted by their long flight, they alight on its flat shores to gather fresh strength for the next stage of their journey over the high mountains to the Mediterranean. Josephus (*Antiquities,* III:5) describes an experience of this kind, and even today the Bedouins of this area catch the exhausted quails in spring and autumn by hand.

As far as the famous manna is concerned, we have reliable information from the botanist. To anticipate: Anyone who is interested in manna will find it on the list of exports from the Sinai peninsula. Further, its supplier is registered in every botanical index of the Middle East; it is the *Tamarix Mannifera, Ehr.*

The general public has always regarded this Biblical bread from Heaven as a miracle beyond explanation. Indeed, this question of manna is a perfect example of how difficult it is to eradicate prejudices and misconceptions that have gone on for generations and how hard it is for the truth to penetrate some people's minds. It seems as though no one wants to believe that there is really such a thing as this "bread of Heaven." Yet, there is no lack of fully authenticated descriptions of its occurrence. The following eyewitness account is almost five hundred years old.

"In every valley throughout the whole region of Mt. Sinai there can still be found Bread of Heaven, which the monks and the Arabs gather, preserve and sell to pilgrims and strangers who pass that way." These words were written in 1483 by Breitenbach, Dean of Mainz, in an account of his pilgrimage to Sinai. "This same Bread of Heaven," he continues, "falls about daybreak like dew or hoarfrost and hangs in beads on grass, stones, and twigs. It is sweet like honey and sticks to the teeth. We bought a lot of it."

In 1823 the German botanist G. Ehrenburg published a paper[1] that even his colleagues received with incredulity. His explanation seemed indeed to ask people to believe too much, namely, that this notorious manna is nothing more than a secretion exuded by tamarisk trees and bushes when they are pierced by a certain type of shell-backed insect which is found in Sinai.

A hundred years later an organized manna expedition was under way. Friedrich Simon Bodenheimer and Iskar Theodor, botanical experts from the Hebrew University at Jerusalem, set out for the Sinai peninsula to clear up the disputed question of the existence of manna once and for all. For several months the two scientists investigated the dry water courses and oases in the whole area of Mt. Sinai. Their report caused a sensation. They not only brought back the first photographs of manna and fully confirmed the findings of Breitenbach and Ehrenburg but also established the factual truth of the Biblical description of the desert migration of the people of Israel.

Without the plant louse mentioned first by Ehrenburg there would, in fact, be no manna at all. These little insects live primarily off tamarisks, which are a type of acacia indigenous to Sinai. They exude a peculiar resinous secretion, which, according to Bodenheimer, is about the same shape and size as a coriander seed. When it falls to the ground, it is white in color, but after lying for some time it becomes yellowish brown. Naturally the two scientists did not fail to taste the manna. Bodenheimer's verdict was: "The taste of these crystallized grains of manna is peculiarly sweet.

---

[1] "Symbolae Physicae."

It is most of all like honey when it has been left for a long time to solidify." "And it was like coriander seed, white: and the taste of it was like wafers made with honey," says the Bible. (Ex. 16:31)

The findings of the expedition likewise confirmed the other features of the Biblical description of manna. "And they gathered it every morning, every man according to his eating: and when the sun waxed hot, it melted." (Ex. 16:21) Exactly in the same way today the Bedouins of the Sinai peninsula hasten to gather up their "Mann es-Samâ," the "manna from Heaven," as early as possible in the morning, for the ants are keen competitors. "They begin gathering when the ground temperature reaches 21 degrees Celsius," says the report of the expedition, "which is about 8:30 A.M. Until then the insects are inert." As soon as the ants become lively, the manna disappears. That must have been what the Biblical narrator meant when he said that it melted. The Bedouins prudently do not forget to seal the manna they have collected carefully in a pot; otherwise, the ants pounce on it. It was just the same in Moses' day during the sojourn in the desert: "But some of them left of it until the morning, and it bred worms. . . ." (Ex. 16:20)

The incidence of the manna depends on favorable winter rains and is different from year to year. In a good year the Bedouins of Sinai can today collect four pounds each in a morning, a considerable quantity, which is quite sufficient to satisfy a grown man. Thus Moses was able to order the children of Israel to "gather of it every man according to his eating." (Ex. 16:16)

The Bedouins knead the globules of manna into a purée which they consume as a welcome and nourishing addition to their often monotonous diet. Manna is indeed an exportable commodity, and if carefully preserved, it forms an ideal "iron ration," since it keeps indefinitely. "And Moses said unto Aaron: Take a pot and put an omer full of manna therein, and lay it up before the Lord, to be kept for your generations." (Ex. 16:33)

"And the children of Israel did eat manna forty years, until they came to a land inhabited: they did eat manna until they came unto the borders of the land of Canaan." (Ex. 16:35) Tamarisks with manna still grow in Sinai and along the Wadi el Arabah right up to the Dead Sea.

So much for natural science. However, having thus reached the limits of scientific investigation, we enter the realm of the unexplorable, the realm of the divine miracle. For there can be no doubt that the Bible relates this phenomenon not as something ordinary and normal, but as a miraculous occurrence, a gift sent by God to His people in their hour of need. And the same applies, *mutatis mutandis,* to the appearance of the quails.

"And they took their journey out of the wilderness of Sin, and encamped in Dophkah." (Num. 33:12)

Several hundred meters above the waters of the Red Sea lies the monotonous expanse of the Wilderness of Sin. On this torrid plateau the only things that break the bright yellow flatness of the sand are camel thorns and sparse brushwood. Not a breath of wind or a breeze fans the traveler's brow. Anyone following the ancient beaten track to the southeast encounters an unforgettable sight: directly ahead on the horizon a jagged mountain range rises abruptly from the plateau —the Sinai massif. At closer quarters geological formations of unusual and rare ranges of color meet the eye. Precipitous cliffs of pink and mauve granite thrust their way upward to the blue sky. Between them sparkle slopes and gorges of pale amber and fiery red streaked with lead-colored veins of porphyry and dark-green bands of feldspar. It is as if all the color and beauty of a garden had been poured into this wild serrated symphony in stone. At the margin of the Wilderness of Sin the beaten track ends abruptly and is lost in a wadi.

No one knew where to look for Dophkah until the turn of the century. The only clue was contained in the name of the place itself. "Dophkah," so the subtleties of philology inform us, is related in Hebrew to the word for "smelting operations." Smelting operations take place where there are mineral deposits.

In the spring of 1904 Flinders Petrie, who had made a name for himself in England as a pioneer of Biblical archaeology, set out from Suez with a long camel caravan. A veritable mass formation of scholars, thirty surveyors, Egyptologists, and assistants accompanied him. From the banks of the Suez Canal the expedition followed the line of the Egyptian beaten track into the wilds of Sinai. Through the Wilderness of Sin as far as the mountains it followed the same route as Israel.

Slowly the caravan made its way along a wadi and round a sharp bend in the hills. Suddenly time seemed to rush back three or four thousand years. The caravan was transported straight back into the world of the Pharaohs. Petrie ordered a halt. From a terrace in the rock face a temple projected into the valley. From the square columns at the gateway stared the face of a goddess with great cow's ears. A jumble of pillars, with one very tall one, seemed to be growing out of the ground. The yellow sand round a number of little stone altars showed unmistakable evidence of the ashes of burned offerings. Dark caverns yawned in the cliff face, and high above the wadi towered the solid massif of Sinai.

The cries of the drivers were silenced. The caravan stood motionless as if overpowered by the almost ghostly sight.

In the ruined temple Petrie found the name of the great Ramesses II carved on the walls. The expedition had reached Serabit el-Khadem, the ancient Egyptian mining and manufacturing center for copper and turquoise. In all probability this is where we should look for the Dophkah of the Bible.

For two long years a camp in front of the old temple brought new life into the valley. Representations of cultic acts and pictures of sacrifices on the walls of the temple indicated that this had been a center of worship of the goddess Hathor. An almost endless confusion of half-choked galleries in the neighboring wadis bore witness to the search for copper and turquoise. The marks of the workmen's tools were unmistakable. Tumbledown settlements that had housed the workers lay in the immediate neighborhood.

The pitiless sun beat down on this cauldron of a valley, filling it with unbearable heat and making the work of the expedition doubly difficult. A worker's life in these mines in the desert must have been—especially in summer—pure hell. An inscription from the reign of Amenemhet III, about 1800 B.C., told the party what it had been like. Hor-Ur-Re, bearer of the royal seal and "Minister of Labor" under Pharaoh, was addressing the miners and slaves. He was trying to cheer them on and encourage them: "Anyone should think himself lucky to work in the area." But the reply was: "Turquoise will always be in the mountain. But it is our skins we have to think about at this time of the year. We have already heard that ore has been quarried at this season. But, really, our skin is not made for that sort of thing at this time of year." Hor-Ur-Re assured them: "Whenever I have brought men out to these mines my one consideration has always been the honor of His Majesty. . . . I never lost heart at the sight of work. . . . There was no talk of 'O for a tough skin.' On the contrary, eyes sparkled. . . ."

While the excavations in the old mines, the dwelling houses, and the temple precincts were in full swing, only a few paces from the sanctuary of the goddess fragments of stone tablets were dug out of the sand together with a statue of a crouching figure. On both the tablets and the sculpture there were unusual markings. Neither Flinders Petrie nor the Egyptologists in the party could make anything of them. They were obviously written characters of a type never seen before. Although the inscriptions give a pictographic impression—they are reminiscent of Egyptian hieroglyphics—they can hardly be said to be a picture language. There are too few different signs for that.

When all the circumstances of the find had been carefully gone into, Flinders Petrie came to the following daring conclusion: "Workmen from Retenu, who were employed by the Egyptians and are often mentioned, had this system of linear writing. The inference that follows from that is extremely significant: namely, that about 1500 B.C. these simple workmen from Canaan were able to write and that the type of writing is independent both of hieroglyphics and cuneiform. Further, it invalidates once and for all the hypothesis that the Israelites who came through this area from Egypt were at that stage still illiterate!"

This explanation aroused considerable attention among antiquarians, paleographers, and historians. All existing theories about the origin and first use of writing in Canaan were at once out of date. It seemed incredible that the inhabitants of Canaan could have had their own type of script as far back as the middle of the second millennium B.C. Only from the text of the Sinai tablets could it be proved whether Petrie was actually right. Immediately on his return to England Petrie had the tablets copied.

Paleographers from all countries pounced upon these awkward-looking scratched-out characters. No one was able to make any sense of them. It was not till ten years later that Sir Alan Gardiner, the brilliant and tireless translator of Egyptian texts, lifted the veil. He it was who first succeeded in deciphering parts of the inscriptions.

The repeated appearance of the notched shepherd's crook helped him along. Eventually Gardiner conjectured that a combination of four or five signs which occurred several times represented ancient Hebrew words. The five characters l-B-'-l-t he interpreted as "(dedicated) to (the goddess) Baalath."

In the second millennium B.C. a female deity with the name of Baalath was venerated in the seaport of Byblos. It was to this same goddess that the temple at Serabit el-Khadem had been erected by the Egyptians. Only the Egyptians called her Hathor. Workmen from Canaan had dug for copper and turquoise beside her temple.

The chain of evidence was complete. The significance of the discovery at Sinai did not fully emerge until six years after Flinders Petrie's death, by which time there had been further exhaustive research and study.

Gardiner had been able to decipher only part of the strange characters. Thirty years later in 1948 a team of archaeologists from the University of Los Angeles found the key which made it possible to give a literal translation of all the characters on the Sinai tablets. Without a doubt, the inscriptions had their origin about 1500 B.C. and are written in a Canaanite dialect.

What Flinders Petrie wrested from the burning sands in Sinai in 1905 nowadays meets the eye everywhere in a different form in newspapers, magazines, books— and on the keys of a typewriter. For these stones in Serabit el-Khadem are the ancestors of our alphabet. The two primary modes of expression in the Fertile Crescent, namely, hieroglyphics and cuneiform, were already quite ancient when a third fundamental way of expressing men's thoughts was born in the second millennium B.C. Possibly stimulated by the picture

	SINAI 1500. B.C.	CANAAN 1000 B.C.	PHOENICIAN 750 B.C.	OLD GREEK B.C.	PRESENT DAY
OX-HEAD					A
FENCE					H
WATER					M
MAN'S HEAD					R
BOW					S

Fig. 21. Development of our alphabet.

language of their Egyptian comrades, these Semitic workmen in Sinai devised their own peculiar and quite different type of script.

The famous Sinai inscriptions are the first stage of the north-Semitic alphabet, which is the direct ancestor of our present alphabet. It was used in Palestine, in Canaan, in the Phoenician Republics on the coast. About the end of the ninth century B.C. the Greeks adopted it. From Greece it spread to Rome and from there went round the globe.

1. Mediterranean
2. Way of the Land of the Philistines
3. Egyptian frontier forts (Princes' wall)
4. Sea of Reeds (15)
5. Pithom (12)
6. Route of Mineworkers
7. Nile Inset (small circle A-B-5)
8. Mediterranean (1)
9. Raamses (A)
10. East branch of the Nile
11. Grazing land
12. Pithom (5)
13. Wadi Tumilat
14. Succoth (B)
15. Sea of Reeds (4)
16. Flight of quails
17. Gulf of Suez
18. Red Sea

Route of the
Exodus

A. Raamses (9)
B. Succoth (14)
C. Migdal
D. Marah
E. Elim
F. Dophkah
G. Rephidim
H. Mount of Moses
I. Hazeroth
J. Ezion-Geber
K. Desert route
L. Kadesh
M. Miracle of water
N. Punon
O. Oboth
P. Mt. Nebo

Israel's Exodus from Egypt
and Journey through
the Desert

9. Gulf of Aqabah
10. Flight of quails
**11. Edomite frontier
ortress**
**12. The "River of
gypt"**
**13. The route of
he spies**

24. Valley of grapes
25. Gaza
26. Lachish
27. Askelon
28. Ashdod
29. Hebron
30. Dead Sea

**31. Moabite frontier
fortress**
32. River Arnon
33. Wadi Sered
**34. Edomite frontier
fortress**
**35. The King's
Highway**

"And the Lord said unto Moses, Write this for a memorial in a book . . ." (Ex. 17:14) The first time that the word "write" is mentioned in the Old Testament is when Israel reaches the next stopping place after Dophkah. Previously the word is never used. The deciphering of the Sinai tablets places this Biblical passage in a completely new light as a historical statement, because we now know that three hundred years before Moses led his people out of Egypt to Sinai, men from Canaan had already been "writing" in this area in a language which was closely related to that of Israel.

*The "Pearl of Sinai"—Israel was 6000 strong—Striking
water from rock—Practical experience in desert life—Was
the burning bush a gas plant?—The valley of the monks
and hermits—The great miracle*

AND ALL THE CONGREGATION OF THE CHILDREN OF
ISRAEL JOURNEYED FROM THE WILDERNESS OF SIN,
AFTER THEIR JOURNEYS, ACCORDING TO THE COM-
MANDMENT OF THE LORD, AND PITCHED IN REPHI-
DIM: . . . (Ex. 17:1) THEN CAME AMALEK AND
FOUGHT WITH ISRAEL IN REPHIDIM. (Ex. 17:8)

Rephidim is now Feiran, extolled by the Arabs as
the "Pearl of Sinai." Protected by the lonely but colorful rock barrier which surrounds it, this miniature
paradise has presented the same appearance for thousands of years. A small grove of palm trees provides
welcome shade. As they have always done since the
days of their remote ancestors, the nomads bring their
flocks here to drink and rest on the tiny grass carpet.

From the main camp Flinders Petrie organized par-
ties to investigate the neighboring territory. By dint of
exhausting and difficult journeys he got to know the
wadis and mountains right down to the shores of the
Red Sea. He established that Feiran is the only oasis in
the whole southern part of the massif. For the nomads
who lived, and still live, here, it is essential for existence
and is their most precious possession. The Amalekites
must have been trying to defend Wadi Feiran from
the foreign invaders, reflected Flinders Petrie. His next
thought was: If the climate has not changed—and the
proof of that lies in the fact that the sandstone pillars
in Serabit el-Khadem show no sign of erosion despite
the thousands of years of their existence—the population must also be numerically the same. Today at a
rough estimate 5000 to 7000 nomads live with their
flocks on the Sinai peninsula. Israel must therefore have

been about 6000 strong, since the battle with the Amalekites appears to have been indecisive. "And it came to pass, when Moses held up his hand, that Israel prevailed: and when he let down his hand Amalek prevailed." (Ex. 17:11)

Bitter fighting continued all day "until the going down of the sun" when at length Joshua won a decisive victory for Israel. Thereafter the way was open to the water supply in the oasis of Rephidim. Before that, "there was no water for the people to drink." (Ex. 17:1) In this emergency Moses is said to have taken his rod and produced water by striking a rock (Ex. 17:6), an action that has been regarded, and not only by skeptics, as quite incomprehensible, although the Bible is merely once more recording a perfectly natural occurrence.

Major C. S. Jarvis, who was British Governor of Sinai in the thirties, has seen it happen himself. He writes: "Moses striking the rock at Rephidim and the water gushing out sounds like a genuine miracle, but the writer has actually seen this happen. Several men of the Sinai Camel Corps had halted in a dry wadi and were in process of digging about in the rough sand that had accumulated at the foot of a rock face. They were trying to get at the water that was trickling slowly out of the limestone rock. The men were taking their time about it and Bash Shawish, the colored sergeant, said: 'Here, give it to me!' He took the spade of one of the men and began digging furiously in the manner of N.C.O.'s the world over who want to show their men how to do things but have no intention of keeping it up for more than a couple of minutes. One of his violent blows hit the rock by mistake. The smooth hard crust which always forms on weathered limestone split open and fell away. The soft stone underneath was thereby exposed and out of its apertures shot a powerful stream of water. The Sudanese, who are well up in the activities of the prophets but do not treat them with a vast amount of respect, overwhelmed their sergeant with cries of: 'Look at him! The prophet Moses!' This is a very illuminating explanation of what happened when Moses struck the rock at Rephidim."

C. S. Jarvis had witnessed a pure coincidence. For the men of the Camel Corps were Sudanese and not in any sense natives of Sinai, who might be expected to be familiar with the technique of producing water in this way. On the journey from Kadesh to Edom, Moses employed this method of striking water once more. "And Moses lifted up his hand and with his rod he smote the rock twice," as we are told in Num. 20:11. "And the water came out abundantly and the congregation drank and their beasts also." He had obviously discovered this highly unusual method of finding water during his exile among the Midianites.

At the beginning of the Christian era many monks and hermits settled in Feiran, where Israel had had to cope with its first hostile attack under Moses. In the gullies and on the cliffs they built their tiny cells. A church was founded in Feiran and twenty-five miles south of the oasis a little chapel was erected at the foot of Jebel Musa. The barbaric tribes of nomads, however, gave the hermits and monks of Sinai no peace. Many of them lost their lives in these repeated attacks. St. Helena, eighty-year-old mother of Constantine, the first Christian emperor, during a visit to Jerusalem in A.D. 327, learned of the plight of the monks of Sinai and founded a tower of refuge which was erected at the foot of the mountain of Moses.

In A.D. 530 the Byzantine Emperor Justinian caused a strong defensive wall to be built round the little chapel at the mountain of Moses. Right up to the Middle Ages this fortified church at Jebel Musa was the goal of devout pilgrims who came to Sinai from every land. This notable spot is today called St. Catherine's Monastery. Napoleon was instrumental in saving the masonry of this isolated early Christian fortress from collapse.

In 1859 the German theologian Constantine von Tischendorf discovered in the Monastery of St. Catherine at Sinai in a good state of preservation one of the precious parchment manuscripts of the Bible, the famous Codex Sinaiticus. It dates from the fourth century of the Christian era and contains the New Testament and parts of the Old Testament.

The Czar accepted it as a gift, giving the monastery 9000 rubles for it. Then this priceless possession found its way into the library at St. Petersburg. Finally, in 1933 the British Museum bought the Codex Sinaiticus from the Soviet for £100,000.

The little chapel at the foot of Jebel Musa was built on the site where Moses, according to the Bible, encountered the burning bush: "And he looked and behold the bush burned with fire, and the bush was not consumed." (Ex. 3:2)

Different attempts have been made to find a scientific explanation of this remarkable phenomenon. An expert on the botany of the Bible, Dr. Harold N. Moldenke, Director and Curator of the Botanical Garden in New York, has this to say: ". . . Among the commentators who think that a natural explanation can be found, some think that the phenomenon of the bush that 'burned with fire' and yet 'was not consumed' can be explained as a variety of the gas plant or Fraxinella, the Dictamnus Albus L. This is a plant with a strong growth about three feet in height with clusters of purple blossom. The whole bush is covered with tiny oil-glands. This oil is so volatile that it is constantly escaping and if approached with a naked light bursts suddenly into flames. . . . The most logical explanation seems to be that suggested by Smith. He puts forward the theory that the 'flames' may have been the crimson blossoms of mistletoe twigs (Loranthus Acaciae) which grow on various prickly acacia bushes and acacia trees throughout the Holy Land and in Sinai. When this mistletoe is in full bloom the bush becomes a mass of brilliant flaming color and looks as if it is on fire."

"For they were departed from Rephidim, and were come to the desert of Sinai, and had pitched in the wilderness: and there Israel camped before the mount. And Moses went up unto God. . . ." (Ex. 19:2-3) "So Moses went down unto the people and spake unto them. And God spake all these words saying, I am the Lord thy God. . . . Thou shalt have no other gods before me." (Ex. 19:25; 20:1-3)

At Sinai something happened that is unique in the history of mankind. Here lie both the roots and the greatness of a faith without precedent or prototype which was strong enough to affect the entire globe.

Moses, this child of a world which believed in a host of deities and in gods of all shapes and forms, proclaimed his faith in one God alone. Moses was the prophet of monotheism; that is the true greatness of this incomprehensible miracle of Sinai. Moses—this unknown son and grandson of desert nomads, brought up in a foreign land—"went down unto the people and spake unto them." Nomads in their goat's-hair tents, camping in the desert under the open sky, were the first to hear this astounding message, to accept it, and to transmit it. First of all, for thirty-nine years, in the solitude of the desert, by gurgling springs, beside the still waters of shady oases, and facing the biting wind which sweeps across the sullen landscape, as they fed their sheep, their goats, and their donkeys, they spoke among themselves of the one great God YHWH.

So begins the wonderful story of this world-embracing faith. Simple shepherds, inured to hardship, carried the great new idea, the new faith, to their homeland, whence the message was one day to go out into the whole world and to all the peoples of the earth. The great nations and mighty empires of these far-off days have long since disappeared into the dark recesses of the past. But the descendants of those shepherds who were the first to pledge their faith in a sole omnipotent God are still alive today.

"I am the Lord thy God. . . . Thou shalt have no other gods before me." That was a word heard for the first time since men inhabited this planet. There was no pattern for this faith, little hint of it from other nations.

We can make this assertion with confidence, thanks to archaeological discoveries in Egypt, the land in which Moses grew up and received his education, as well as in other lands of the ancient East. Both the sun worship of Akhnaton and the appearance in Mesopotamia of a blending of many deities into one god, Ninurta, god of war, are but vague preludes to monotheism. In all these conceptions what is lacking is the concentrated power and redemptive moral purpose that are rooted in the Ten Commandments, which Moses brought down from the lonely heights of Mt. Sinai into the hearts and minds of men.

It is only among the people of Israel out of the whole of the Fertile Crsecent that there is this awakening of the new idea of God in all its clarity and purity, untainted by magic, free from a variegated and grotesque imagery, and conceived as something other than a materialistic preparation for perpetuating the self beyond the grave. Without precedent and prototype likewise is the clear imperative of the Ten Commandments. The Israelites are bidden not to sin because they are under the obedience of Yahweh!

CHAPTER 3 / Under Desert Skies

Sinai—150 miles to Kadesh—Two springs at the chief halting place—Scouts sent out to Hebron—The bunch of grapes was a vine—Foreign races—Peasant woman finds the Amarna tablets—Letters from Indo-Aryan Canaanite princes—Scouts' report leads to a new decision—The "wilderness" of the Bible was a steppe

AND THE CHILDREN OF ISRAEL TOOK THEIR JOURNEYS OUT OF THE WILDERNESS OF SINAI. (Num. 10:12)

Israel had pledged itself to believe in one God and His laws. The portable palladium that they had constructed for Him—the Ark of the Covenant—had been made out of acacia wood (Ex. 25:10) which is still indigenous to Sinai and widely used.

For almost a year they had lingered at Mt. Sinai. Now they set out again, heading north for Canaan. Kadesh, the next stage, which is a landmark in the long desert wanderings of the children of Israel, lies 150 miles from Sinai as the crow flies.

Fig. 22. The Ark of the Covenant with Cherubim and carrying-poles (Reconstruction).

This stretch, too, can be accurately traced on the basis of the very precise topographical details given in the Bible. The route lies along the west side of the

147

Gulf of Aqabah to the "Wilderness of Paran" (Num. 12:16)—now Badiet et-Tin, that is, "Wilderness of Loneliness"—and then continues along its eastern edge. Among the halts made on this journey (Num. 33:16-36), Hazeroth and Ezion-geber can be identified with certainty. Hazeroth is the present-day Ain Huderah, which lies near the Gulf. Ezion-geber lies at the topmost point of the Gulf of Aqabah and is the place which was later to become a center for shipping and industry in the days of King Solomon. (I Kings 9:26)

As they made their way along the shores of the Gulf, the "miracle" of the quails was repeated. Once more it was springtime, the time of bird migration, and again the description is true to nature: "And there went forth a wind from the Lord, and brought quails from the sea, and let them fall by the camp." (Num. 11:31)

"And they removed from Ezion-gaber, and pitched in the wilderness of Zin which is Kadesh." (Num. 33:36) Below Hebron the hill country of Judah falls away into a fairly flat plain, the southern part of which, toward the frequently mentioned "river of Egypt," which is a ramification of wadis, always very poorly supplied with water. (Num. 34:5; Josh. 15:4; I Kings 8:65) This is the Negeb, the Biblical "Land of the South." (Num. 13:17) Amid innumerable wadis—dried-up river beds that run with water only in the rainy season during the winter months—lies Kadesh. The old name Kadesh is preserved in the name of the little spring, Ain Qedeis, from which passing Bedouins water their cattle. But this trickle of spring water can hardly have been sufficient to provide for 6000 Israelites and their flocks for any length of time. Only about five miles to the northwest of Kadesh, however, lies the most ample supply of water in the whole area, "Ain el-Qudeirât." Wadi Qudeirât has this to thank for its fertility. It was from here that the children of Israel saw in the distance the land that had been promised to them, of which as yet they had been able to form no clear picture. It may be that their hasty departure from Egypt had prevented them

from finding out about it before they left. Palestine
was so well known to the inhabitants of the Nile country that anyone who was lacking in detailed knowledge
of it was reckoned to be lacking in proper education. Aman-Appa, a "commissioned scribe of the army"
under Ramesses II, was even ridiculed for his ignorance about Palestine. Hori, an officer of the royal
stables, replies to a letter from him in an extremely
satirical vein and puts his geographical knowledge to
the test:

"Your letter is overloaded with big words. You have
asked for it and you shall have it—and more than you
bargained for. What we say is: If what you say is true,
come and let us test you. We shall harness a horse for
you which will bring you as fast as any jackal can
run. Let us see what you can do. Have you not seen the
country of Upe near Damascus? Don't you know its
peculiarities, or those of its river? Have you not been
to Kadesh? Have you never found your way to the
Lebanon where the sky is dark in broad daylight? It is
overgrown with cypresses, oaks and cedars which rise
sky-high. I shall also mention a mysterious city, Byblos by name. What does it look like? Tell me too
about Sidon and Sarepta. They talk about another city
that lies in the sea, the port of Tyre is its name. Water
is carried to it by ship. If you go to Jaffa you will find
that the fields are green. Go . . . and look for the pretty
girl who is in charge of the vineyards. She will accept
you as her mate and grant you her favours. . . . You
will be drowsy and indolent. They will steal . . . your
bow, your knife, your quiver. Your reins will be
slashed in the darkness . . . your chariot will be
smashed to pieces. But you will say: Bring me food
and drink, I am happy here! They will pretend they
are deaf and pay no attention. Come with me south to
the region of Accho. Where is the hill of Shechem?
Can this clever scribe tell me how to get to Hazor?
What is special about its river? Now let me ask you
about some other towns. Tell me what Kjn near
Megiddo looks like, describe Rehob to me, give me a
picture of Bethshan and Kiriath-El. Let me know how
to get past Megiddo. How does one cross the Jordan?

You see," concludes Hori, officer of the royal stables, "I have taken you through the whole of Palestine, . . . have a good look at it, so that in future you will be able to describe it properly, and . . . you will . . . be made a councillor."

Government officials, soldiers, merchants had at least some clear notion of Palestine. Moses, who belonged to a poor shepherd folk, had first to find out about this country. He sent out scouts.

"And Moses sent them to spy out the land of Canaan, and said unto them, Get you up this way southward, and go up into the mountain: and see the land what it is; and the people that dwelleth therein, whether they be strong or weak, few or many." (Num. 13:17-18)

Among the twelve scouts was Joshua, a man with great gifts as a strategist, as later became plain during the conquest of Canaan. They chose as the best spot to spy out the land the country round Hebron in the south of Judah. Forty days later the men reported back to Moses. As proof that they had done their job they brought fruit from the area they had scrutinized: figs and pomegranates. Incredulous astonishment greeted one gigantic bunch of grapes, cut at the "Brook of Eshcol," for "they bare it between two upon a staff." (Num. 13:23) Posterity is equally skeptical because the narrative speaks of only one cluster. Surely it must have been a whole vine with all its fruit. The spies could have cut it down with the grapes on it to keep them fresher. At all events the place of their origin according to the Bible is reliable. "Brook of Eshcol" means "Valley of Grapes"; it lies southwest of Hebron and even today this district is rich in vines. Fine heavy bunches of from ten to twelve pounds are no rarity. The scouts made their report and, like Sinuhe 650 years earlier, described Canaan as a land that "floweth with milk and honey" only, "the people be strong that dwell in the land, and the cities are walled and very great." (Num. 13:27, 28; Deut. 1:28)

In their recital of the different inhabitants of the country they mention some we already know, Hittites, Amorites, Jebusites in and around Jerusalem, Canaanites and Amalekites with whom Israel had already come into conflict in Sinai. They also mention the "children of Anak" which is supposed to mean the "children of the giants." (Num. 13:22, 28, 33) "Anak" might mean "long-necked," and that is as much as the experts can tell us. It has been surmised that these "giants" are possibly survivals of ancient pre-Semitic elements in the population, but there is no certainty in the matter.

Actually there were people from other countries living in Canaan at that time who must have been quite unknown to Israelites coming from Egypt. Whose "children" they were they intimated to posterity themselves on clay tablets which were accidentally discovered by a peasant woman at Tell el-Amarna[1] in 1887. Further investigation produced eventually a collection of 377 documents in all. These are cuneiform letters from the royal archives of Amenophis III and his son Akhnaton who built himself a new capital at el-Amarna on the Nile. The tablets contain correspondence from the princes of Palestine, Phoenicia, and Southern Syria to the Foreign Office of both Pharaohs. They are written in Akkadian, the diplomatic language of the second millennium B.C. Most of the writings are full of typically Canaanite words; some of them are in fact written almost exclusively in this dialect. This priceless find threw light for the first time on conditions in Palestine in the fifteenth and fourteenth centuries B.C.

One of the letters runs: "To the King, my Lord, my Sun, my God, say: Thus (says) Suwardata, thy servant, the servant of the King and the dust under his feet, the ground on which thou dost tread: At the feet of the King, my Lord, the Sun of Heaven, seven times, seven times I prostrated myself, on my belly and on my back. . . ."

This is only the introduction. Nor is it in any way extravagant. On the contrary it is extremely formal, in accordance with contemporary protocol. Suwardata then comes to the matter in hand: "The King, my

---

[1] Middle Egypt.

Lord, should know that the Hapiru have risen in the lands which the God of the King, my Lord, has given me, and that I have beaten them, and the King, my Lord, should know that all my brothers have left me; and that I and Abdu-Kheba alone are left to fight against the leader of the Hapiru. And Zurata, Prince of Accho [Jud. 1:31], and Indaruta, Prince of Achsaph [Josh. 11:1], were the ones who hastened to my help in return for fifty chariots, of which I have now been deprived. But behold, (now) they have been fighting against me and may it please the King, my Lord, to send the Janhamu, so that we can wage a proper war and restore the land of the King, my Lord, to its old frontiers. . . ."

This letter from a prince of Canaan paints a picture which faithfully reflects the times. In these few sentences we can recognize unmistakably the intrigues and endless feuds both among the princes themselves and among the warlike nomadic tribes. The most interesting point about the letter, apart from the style and contents, is its author, Prince Suwardata. His name shows clearly that he was of Indo-Aryan descent. Prince Indaruta, whom he mentions, is also an Indo-Aryan. Though it may sound extraordinary, a third of these princely correspondents from Canaan have Indo-Aryan ancestry. Biryawaza of Damascus, Biridiya of Megiddo, Widia of Askelon, Birashshena of Shechem in Samaria all have Indo-Aryan names. Indaruta, the name of the Prince of Achsaph, is in fact identical with names from the Vedas and other early Sanskrit writings. Abdu-Kheba of Jerusalem, who has been mentioned, belongs to a people often referred to in the Bible as Horites.

The reliability of this tradition has recently been illumined by the discovery of Egyptian papyri of the fifteenth century B.C., in which the land of Canaan is repeatedly called "Khuru" after the Horites of the Bible. According to this the Horites must for a time at least have been widespread throughout the whole country.

"And all the congregation lifted up their voice, and cried: and the people wept that night . . . wherefore

hath the Lord brought us into this land, to fall by the
sword, that our wives and our children should be a
prey?" (Num. 14:1-3)

The reports that the spies brought back telling of
the strongly fortified cities of Canaan, "great and walled
up to heaven" (Deut. 1:28), and of their superbly
armed inhabitants were not exaggerated. Turreted fortresses were to the children of Israel an unaccustomed
and menacing sight. In the land of Goshen, which for
many generations had been their home, there was only
one fortified town, Raamses. In Canaan the fortresses
were practically cheek by jowl. The country was plas-
tered with them. Numerous strong points stared down
from hilltops and mountain peaks, which made them
look even more powerful and terrifying. Little wonder
that the report of the scouts was shattering in its effect.

Israel was quite unskilled in the use and manufacture of implements of war. They had at their disposal
only the most primitive weapons—bows, javelins,
swords, knives—but certainly no horse-drawn chariots
which the Canaanites possessed in vast numbers. Israel
was still spoiled by the "fleshpots of Egypt," for which
especially the older people among them were continually sighing and bemoaning their present lot. Despite
their new faith and the experiences of the Exodus
which they had shared together, they were not yet
welded into a community which would be prepared to
risk a clash with superior forces.

In view of these facts Moses wisely resolved not to
carry out his original intention of marching upon
Canaan from the south. Neither time nor the people
were ripe for the great moment. They must begin
their roaming afresh; the time of testing and proving
their mettle must be prolonged in order to allow these
refugees and land-hungry wanderers to develop into a
tough and compact national group schooled to bear
any privation. A new generation must first emerge.

We know very little about the obscure period which
now follows: Forty years—almost a generation, and
time enough to mold a nation. This was the duration of
their sojourn in the "wilderness." Frequently associated with the "miracles" of the quails and the manna,

this section of Biblical chronology and topography sounds highly improbable. And with good reason, as would appear from systematic investigations, though on different grounds from those generally supposed. Actually there never was a "sojourn in the wilderness" in the proper sense of the words.

Although the Biblical data for this period are very scanty, we can obtain a sufficiently clear picture from the few places that can be scientifically established. According to this the children of Israel with their flocks spent a long time in the Negeb, near the two sources of water at Kadesh. Once they went back again to the Gulf of Aqabah into the area of Midian and the Sinai peninsula. Compared with the deadly stretches of African sand dunes in the Sahara, this tract of land has never been a proper desert. Examination of the terrain has established the fact that since neither the irrigation nor the rainfall has altered greatly, the "wilderness" must have had at least the character of steppe country with water holes and possibilities for grazing.

The archaeological activities of the American, Nelson Glueck, in the last few years have enhanced our knowledge of the general conditions in that period. According to him these regions were inhabited about the thirteenth century B.C. by seminomadic tribes who had brisk and flourishing trading and commercial relations with both Canaan and Egypt. Among them we should include the Midianites, with whom Moses lived during his exile and one of whom, Zippora, he married. (Ex. 2:21)

*Rise of a new generation—Change of plan—Transit permit
for Edom—Pressing on through Transjordan—King Og's
"iron bedstead"—Dolmen discovered near Amman—Moab
sends its daughters—Baal worship in Canaan—Moses sees
the Promised Land—Camping opposite Jericho*

AND HE MADE THEM WANDER IN THE WILDERNESS
FORTY YEARS, UNTIL ALL THE GENERATION THAT
HAD DONE EVIL IN THE SIGHT OF THE LORD WAS
CONSUMED. (Num. 32:13)

Not until the long years of their wanderings were approaching an end does the Bible take up again the thread of the story of the children of Israel. A new generation has sprung up and is ready to cross the threshold of the Promised Land. None of the men who led the Exodus out of Egypt will, according to the Bible, set foot in the land of promise—not even Moses himself.

The new plan of campaign is to conquer Canaan from the east, that is, the territory east of the Jordan. Nevertheless, the road to Upper Transjordan from Kadesh is blocked by five kingdoms, which occupy the broad strip of land between the Jordan Valley and the Arabian desert: in the north, beginning at the spurs of Hermon is the kingdom of Bashan, then the Amorite kingdom of Sihon, next the kingdom of Ammon, then the kingdom of Moab, on the east side of the Dead Sea, and, right in the south, Edom.

Edom is therefore the first kingdom that has to be negotiated on the way to Upper Transjordan. The children of Israel asked permission to pass through: "And Moses sent messengers from Kadesh unto the king of Edom, . . . Let us pass, I pray thee, through thy country." (Num. 20:14, 17)

Main roads are the quickest roads to anywhere. In those days what corresponded to our twentieth-century main routes and highways was a road that ran right through the middle of Edom. This was the old "King's Highway," which dated back to Abraham's time. "Let us pass, I pray thee, through thy country," they asked, "we will go by the king's highway." (Num. 20:17)

The settled population of the East has always distrusted nomads, then as much as now, even though Israel's emissaries declared expressly: "We will not pass through the fields, or through the vineyards . . . we will not turn to the right hand nor to the left, until we have passed thy borders . . . and if I and my cattle drink of thy water, then I will pay for it." (Num. 20:17, 19)

In the course of an expedition which lasted several years Nelson Glueck confirmed the aptness of the Biblical description of Edom. In the southern part of Transjordan, in the territories that had once belonged to Edom and Moab, he came across numerous traces of a settlement that dated from the beginning of the thirteenth century. Signs of cultivated ground, which were also discovered, suggested well-stocked fields. It is therefore understandable that in spite of all assurances Edom refused the children of Israel permission to use the road and pass through their country.

Their hostility compelled Israel to go a long way round. They trekked northward along the western edge of Edom toward the Dead Sea. Phunon, now called Kirbet-Phenan, an old copper mine, and Oboth were visited for the sake of their water supplies. Then the Israelites followed the little river Sered, which marked the frontier between Edom and Moab, and reached Transjordan. They made a wide circle round Moab on the southeast side of the Dead Sea. By this time they had reached the River Arnon and the southern frontier of the kingdom of the Amorites. (Num. 21:13) Once more the Israelites asked for permission to use the "King's Highway." (Num. 21:22) Once more it was refused, this time by Sihon, king of the Amorites. A battle began and the process of conquest by force of arms had started.

By defeating the Amorites, the Israelites collected their first laurels. Conscious of their strength, they pushed northward over the River Jabbok and conquered the kingdom of Bashan in addition. Thus by their first determined attack they became masters of Transjordan from the River Arnon to the banks of the Lake of Galilee.

Into the matter-of-fact description of this military offensive in Transjordan there has crept a reference to the "iron bed" of a giant, King Og of Bashan (Deut. 3:11), which may have puzzled many people. This mysterious and improbable-sounding passage in the Bible has, however, a very natural and at the same time striking explanation. The Bible is preserving here in all faithfulness a memory that takes us back to Canaan's dim and distant past.

When the scholars were searching the Jordan country for evidence that would tie up with Biblical history, they came upon remarkable structures such as archaeologists had already encountered in other countries as well. These consisted of tall stones, built in oval formation and every now and then roofed over with a heavy transverse block—the famous great stone graves. They are also called megalithic graves or dolmens and were once used for burying the dead. In Europe—they are found in north Germany, Denmark, England, and northwest France—they are called locally "giants' beds." Since these massive monuments are also found in India, East Asia, and even the South Sea Islands they are ascribed to a great mass migration in early times.

In 1918 Gustav Dalman, a German scholar, discovered in the neighborhood of Amman, the modern capital of Jordan, a dolmen that aroused unusual interest because it seemed to shed light on a factual Biblical reference in quite an astonishing way. Amman stands precisely on the old site of Rabbath-Ammon. The Bible says about this giant King Og: "Behold his bedstead was a bedstead of iron; is it not in Rabbath of the children of Ammon [Rabbath-Ammon]? nine cubits was the length thereof, and four cubits the breadth of it, after the cubit of a man." (Deut. 3:11) The size of the dolmen discovered by Dalman corresponded approximately to these measurements. The "bed" consisted of basalt, an extremely hard, gray-black stone. The appearance of such a burying place may have given rise to the Biblical description of the "iron bed" of the giant king. Further investigations have proved that dolmens are common in Palestine, principally in Transjordan above the River Jabbok, that is, in present-day Ajlun. Well over a thousand of these ancient monuments are to be found among the coarse grass of the highlands. The country above the Jabbok, so the Bible tells us, is the kingdom over which King Og of Bashan is said to have reigned, Og who alone "remained of the remnant of giants." (Deut. 3:11) Bashan, which was conquered by Israel, was also called "the land of giants." (Deut. 3:13)

West of the Jordan the only dolmens to be found are in the neighborhood of Hebron. The scouts, whom Moses sent out from Kadesh, "ascended by the south, and came unto Hebron . . . and there we saw the giants, the sons of Anak." (Num. 13:22, 33) They must have seen the stone graves that have now been discovered at Hebron in the vicinity of the Valley of Grapes.

Who the "giants" really were is still quite unknown. Possibly they were a people who were much taller than the old established population around the Jordan. Clearly, there was some racial memory of a taller type of man, which was enough to make a deep impression, and perhaps this is the reason why it appears in the Bible too.

These huge stone graves and the stories about giants once again bear witness to the colorful and varied history of the land of Canaan, that narrow strip of land on the Mediterranean coast, into which from earliest times waves of alien peoples surged incessantly and left their mark behind them.

The news that Israel had conquered the whole of Jordan put King Balak of Moab into a panic. He was afraid that his own people too would be no match in physique or military skill for these tough sons of the desert. He convened "the elders of Midian" and incited them against the children of Israel. (Num. 22:4) They resolved to employ other than military measures. They would attempt to impose a check on Israel by means

of magic. Incantations and curses, in the efficacy of
which the peoples of the ancient East firmly believed,
would assuredly smash Israel's power. Balaam was summoned in haste from Pethor in Babylonia, where these
black arts flourished. But Balaam, the great sorcerer
and magician, failed. As soon as he tried to utter a
curse, a blessing upon Israel came out instead. (Num.
23) Then the King of Moab threw the most dangerous trump card in existence into the balance, a wicked
card that was to have a lasting effect on the lives of
the children of Israel.

The Bible passage that contains a description of the
abominable stratagem of King Balak is felt by theologians to be embarrassing and therefore they prefer to
gloss it over. The real question is, however, why such
a scandalous affair appears in the Bible at all. The
answer is simple: The event was one which was of
the deepest and most fateful significance for the people
of Israel. That is the reason why the narrator does not
maintain a modest silence but gives a frank and candid
account of what actually happened.

It was in the thirties that French archaeologists working at the Mediterranean port of Ras Shamra—the
"White Haven" on the coast of Phoenicia—under the
direction of Professor Claude Schaeffer of Strasbourg
brought to light some evidence of Canaanite religious
practices. Only then was it possible to estimate and understand the nature of the disaster that is recorded in
Numbers, Chapter 25.

"And Israel abode in Shittim, and the people began
to commit whoredom with the daughters of Moab. And
they called the people unto the sacrifices of their gods."
(Num. 25:1-2)

It is not the attractions of vice that the children of
Israel are faced with. That is something that is and always has been universal. It was not professional prostitutes who led Israel astray. It was the daughters of the
Moabites and the Medianites, their own wives and
sweethearts. They enticed and seduced the men of Israel
to take part in the rites of Baal, the fertility cult
of Canaan. What Israel encountered, while still on the
other side of Jordan, was the voluptuous worship of

the Phoenician gods, in face of which in the centuries that lay ahead Israel had to test and prove the strength of its ethical principles.

But the Moabites and Midianites hoped in vain that they would make these young and unsophisticated nomads the slaves of the sensual temptations of their religious practices, and in this way sap the strength of the sons of Israel. Even at this first encounter it was plain that there could never be any compromise between Yahweh and Baal. The leaders of Israel struck swiftly and struck hard. They did not even spare their own men. Offenders were slaughtered and hanged. Phinehas, grandnephew of Moses, who saw an Israelite taking a Midianite woman into his tent, took a javelin "and thrust both of them through, the man of Israel, and the woman through her belly." (Num. 25:8) The people of Moab were spared, since they were related to Israel—Lot, Abraham's nephew, was regarded as their ancestor. (Gen. 19:37) But against the Midianites a war of extermination was let loose, the classical "herem," or ban, as it is laid down in the Law. (Deut. 7:2ff., 20:13ff.) "Now therefore kill every male among the little ones and kill every woman that hath known man by lying with him," ordered Moses. Only the young girls were spared; everyone else was killed. (Num. 31:7, 17, 18)

"And Moses went up from the plains of Moab unto the mountain of Nebo, to the top of Pisgah, that is over against Jericho. And the Lord showed him all the land." (Deut. 34:1)

Moses had now fulfilled his heavy task. From the bond cities of Egypt, through the years of hardship and privation in the steppes, right up to that moment he had had to travel a long and bitterly hard road. He had nominated as his successor Joshua, a tried and trusted man and an unusually gifted strategist, which was what Israel was most in need of. Moses had finished the course and could take his leave of the world. He was not allowed to set foot himself on the soil of the Promised Land. But he was allowed to glimpse it from afar, from Mt. Nebo.

To visit this Biblical mountain means a journey of

about eighteen miles from Amman, center and seat of government of the present kingdom of Jordan. The trip takes rather more than half an hour in a jeep, crossing the hill country on the edge of the Arabian desert, through wadis and sometimes past plowed fields, heading straight for the southeast in the direction of the Dead Sea.

After a short climb over bare rocks we reach a broad barren plateau, 2500 feet above sea level. On the western edge the cliffs drop sharply down to the Jordan basin. A fresh breeze blows on the summit. Under the clear blue skies there stretches into the distance a unique panorama.

To the south lie the broad waters of the "Salt Sea" with their silvery sheen. On the far bank rises a dreary desolate scene of stone humps and hillocks. Behind it towers the long chain of brownish-white limestone mountains of the land of Judah. Just where the mountains begin, rising sharply out of the Negeb, lies Hebron. In the west, towards the Mediterranean, two tiny dots can be distinguished with the naked eye from the mountain range that stands out against the horizon —the towers of Bethlehem and Jerusalem. The eye wanders northward over the highlands of Samaria, past Galilee to the snow-capped peaks of Hermon in the shimmering distance.

At the foot of Nebo narrow gorges drop downward, their sides brilliant with the green pomegranate trees and their orange-colored fruit. Then the ground sinks abruptly into the desolate steppe of the Jordan basin. A landscape of dazzling white chalk hills almost as ghostly as the mountains of the moon and without a single blade of grass flanks the mere thirty-foot width of the River Jordan. The only comfort to the eye is a small green patch in front of the mountains that rise steeply on the west side of the Jordan—the oasis of Jericho.

This view from Nebo into Palestine was the last thing that Moses saw.

But beneath him on the broad steppe of Moab thin columns of smoke were rising heavenward. Day and night campfires were burning among the mass of black goat's-hair tents. Joined to the hum of voices of all these men, women, and children, the wind also carried over to the Jordan Valley the bleating of grazing flocks. It was a peaceful scene. But it was only a moment of respite before the long-yearned-for day, the great calm before the storm, which was decisively to affect the destiny of Israel and of the land of Canaan.

IV / The Battle for the Promised Land: From Joshua to Saul

CHAPTER 1 / Israel Invades

The world about 1200 B.C.—The weakness of Canaan—The first iron merchants—The ford across the Jordan—The stronghold of Jericho, the oldest city in the world—Scholars quarrel over broken walls—A trail of fire—Pharaoh mentions "Israel" by name for the first time—Excavations at Hazor—Graves at the village of Joshua

NOW AFTER THE DEATH OF MOSES THE SERVANT OF THE LORD IT CAME TO PASS, THAT THE LORD SPAKE UNTO JOSHUA, THE SON OF NUN, MOSES' MINISTER, SAYING: MOSES MY SERVANT IS DEAD; NOW THEREFORE ARISE, GO OVER THIS JORDAN, THOU, AND ALL THIS PEOPLE, UNTO THE LAND WHICH I DO GIVE TO THEM, EVEN TO THE CHILDREN OF ISRAEL. (Josh. 1:1-2)

About the same time as Israel was standing by the Jordan ready to march into the Promised Land, fate was advancing upon Mediterranean Troy, and the days of the proud stronghold of King Priam were numbered. Soon the Homeric heroes of Greece—Achilles, Agamemnon, and Odysseus—would be arming for the fray. The hands of the timepiece of history were moving toward 1200 B.C. Israel could have chosen no better time for invasion. No danger threatened them from Egypt. The land of the Nile had become weak, its great days were over. Two thousand years had drained its strength. After the ineffective policies of the sun king, Akhnaton, the power of Egypt was obviously on the wane. Egyptian suzerainty over Canaan was greatly weakened. Torn by internal feuds between the innumerable petty kingdoms and principalities of its city-states and sucked dry by the corrupt politics of Egyptian occupation, Canaan itself had shot its bolt.

Ever since the expulsion of the Hyksos about 1550 B.C., Palestine had been an Egyptian province. Under the Hyksos a feudal system had broken up the old patriarchal social structure as it had existed in the towns

165

of Abraham's day. Under an aristocratic ruling class, which was self-centered and despotic, the people were reduced to the level of subjects without rights and became mere plebeians. Egypt left this feudal system in Palestine unaltered. Native princes could do as they pleased; they had their own armies, which consisted of patrician charioteers and plebeian infantry. Bloody warfare between the city-states did not worry the Egyptians. All they were interested in was the payment of tribute, which was supervised by strict and inflexible Egyptian inspectors. Garrisons and defense posts tacitly lent their activities the necessary weight. Gaza and Joppa housed the most important Egyptian administrative centers. By means of labor levies supplied by the feudal lords, roads were built and maintained, the royal estates on the fertile plain of Jezreel south of Nazareth were managed, and the glorious cedar forests of Lebanon were felled. The commissioners of the Pharaohs were corrupt. Often the troops' pay and rations were misappropriated; whereupon they took the law into their own hands, and mercenaries from Egypt and Crete, Bedouins, and Nubians plundered defenseless villages.

Under Egyptian rule the land of Canaan bled to death. The population shrank. Patrician houses of the thirteenth century B.C. are more primitive than they had been in earlier times, as is shown by excavations. Objets d'art and jewelry of any value are rarer, and gifts deposited with the dead in their tombs are of poorer quality. Fortress walls have lost their old solidity.

Only on the coast of Syria, protected on the landward side by the mountain ridges of the Lebanon and less affected by the quarrels of the princes, life in the maritime republics pursued its untroubled way. Whatever else happens, seaports are always places where men can exchange what they have for what they want. About 1200 B.C. an entirely new metal—as valuable to begin with as gold or silver—appeared on the price lists: iron. Since it came from the Hittite country the Phoenicians were the first to deal in this metal, which was to give its name to one of the ages of man's history. The Egyptians had known about iron for nearly two thousand years and valued it as an extremely unusual and rare commodity. The iron they knew, however, did not come from our planet at all but from meteors. And the few weapons that they managed to produce in this way were very properly called "daggers from Heaven."

With the appearance of this new metal a new epoch, the Iron Age, made its entrance. The Bronze Age with its unique civilizing achievements died away, and a great epoch of the ancient world came to an end.

At the end of the thirteenth century B.C. a great new wave of foreign peoples surged down from the northern Aegean. By land and water these "sea peoples" flowed over Asia Minor. They were the fringes of a great movement of population to which the Dorian migration to Greece also belonged. The impetus of these foreigners—they were Indo-Germanic—was directed to Canaan and Egypt. For the time being, Israel, waiting poised by the Jordan, had nothing to fear from them. And the Canaanites were divided and weak. Israel's hour had come. The Biblical trumpets of Jericho gave the signal ". . . and they removed from Shittim and came to Jordan . . . and all the Israelites passed over on dry ground, until all the people were passed clear over Jordan . . . and encamped in Gilgal, in the east border of Jericho." (Josh. 3:1, 17; 4:19)

Today there is a bridge over the river at this point. The Jordan is very narrow and has always been fordable in many places. The natives know exactly where these fords are. In the dry season the dirty yellow water at Jericho is only about thirty feet wide.

When Israel reached the Jordan they found it in full spate, "for Jordan overfloweth all his banks all the time of harvest." (Josh. 3:15) As happened every year, the snow on Hermon had begun to melt. ". . . the waters which came down from above stood and rose up upon an heap [that is, were dammed] very far from the city Adam . . . and all the Israelites passed over on dry ground, until all the people were passed clear over Jordan." (Josh. 3:16, 17) A much frequented ford on the middle reaches of the Jordan, El-Damiyah, recalls the "city Adam." Should there be a sudden spate it can quite easily be damned at such a place for a short time, and while it is blocked the lower part of the river is almost dried up.

Considerable damming of the Jordan has, however, often been attributed to the action of earthquakes. The last occurrence of this kind was in 1927. As a result of a severe quake the river banks caved in, tons of soil crashed down into the river bed from the low hills that follow the Jordan's winding course. The flow of water was completely stopped for twenty-one hours. In 1924 the same thing happened. In 1906 the Jordan became so choked up with debris as the result of an earthquake that the river bed on the lower reaches near Jericho was completely dry for twenty-four hours. Arab records mention a similar occurrence in A.D. 1267.

It is easy to see from the air why this part of the Jordan Valley was so important thousands of years ago. To the east, between the river and the Arabian desert, stretches the hilly plateau of Jordan which has always been the home of countless tribes of nomads and from which they have always been able to look across to the fertile pastures and plowed fields of Canaan. It is a natural line of attack—the principal ford across the Jordan, easily negotiated by man and beast. But anyone trying to force his way in from the east had to face the first serious obstacle soon after crossing the river—Jericho, the strategic key to the conquest of Canaan.

"And it came to pass, when the people heard the sound of the trumpet, and the people shouted with a great shout, that the wall fell down flat, so that the people went up into the city, every man straight before him, and they took the city. . . . And they burnt the city with fire and all that was therein." (Josh. 6:20, 24)

Joshua's battle for this city has made it famous. Today, a battle rages round it, but it is between experts armed with spades, picks, and chronological tables. According to the Bible it took Joshua seven days to subdue Jericho. The battle of the archaeologists over what is left of it has lasted—with intervals—for more than fifty years now and is by no means settled.

The exciting and dramatic excavations at Jericho are rife with remarkable finds and unexpected discoveries, with surprises and disappointments, with assertions and counter assertions, with disputes over interpretation and chronology.

The Jordan basin has a tropical climate. The village of Eriha, the modern successor of Jericho, gives the impression of being an oasis on the edge of a barren waste of chalk. Even palm trees grow here, although they are seldom found anywhere else in Palestine, except to the south of Gaza. The Bible too calls Jericho "the city of palm trees." (Jud. 3:13) Golden-red clusters of dates shimmer among the green foliage. From ancient times the spring called "Ain es-Sultan" has produced, as if by magic, this lush patch of vegetation. North of present-day Jericho a mound of ruins is named after it, Tell es-Sultan. This is the battleground of the archaeologists. Anyone wanting to examine it must buy a ticket. The site of the excavations lies behind a barbed-wire fence.

The remains of Jericho have made Tell es-Sultan one of the most extraordinary scenes of discovery in the world, for it has long since been not merely a matter of investigating the fortress of Biblical times. In this mound, under the strata of the Bronze Age, lie traces of the Stone Age that take us back to the earliest times of all, to the days when man first built himself settled habitations. The oldest of Jericho's houses are 7000 years old and, with their round walls, resemble Bedouins' tents. But the art of pottery was as yet unknown among their inhabitants. In 1953 a British expedition conducted excavations here, and the director of the enterprise, Dr. Kathleen M. Kenyon, declared, "Jericho can lay claim to being by far the oldest city in the world."

Shortly after the turn of the century archaeologists directed their attention to this lonely mound of Tell es-Sultan. From 1907 to 1909 picks and spades carefully felt their way through layer after layer of this massive mound of ruins. When the two leaders of the German-Austrian expedition, Professor Ernst Sellin and Professor Karl Watzinger, made known what they had discovered, they caused genuine amazement. Two concentric rings of fortification were exposed, the inner ring surrounding the ridge of the hill. Is is a masterpiece of military defense made of sun-dried bricks in

Fig. 23. The walls of the old Canaanite fortress of Jericho (Reconstructed).

the form of two parallel walls about ten or twelve feet apart. The inner wall, which is particularly massive, is about twelve feet thick throughout. The outer ring of fortification runs along the foot of the hill and consists of a six-foot brick wall about twenty-five to thirty feet high with strong foundations. These are the famous walls of Jericho. The two lines of fortification, their exact historical placing, the dates of their erection and destruction have given rise to a vehement dispute among the experts who advance the pros and cons in a welter of opinions, hypotheses, and arguments. It began with the first announcement by Sellin and Watzinger and has continued ever since.

Both discoverers arrived themselves at what they called a "considerable modification" of their first conclusion. They issued a joint statement in which they maintained that the outer wall "fell about 1200 B.C., and therefore must be the city wall which Joshua destroyed." To shed new light on the whole business a British expedition set out for Tell es-Sultan in 1930. After six years' digging, further portions of the fortifications were exposed. Professor John Garstang as leader of the expedition noted every detail with the utmost precision. He described graphically the violence with which the inner circle of parallel fortifications had been destroyed: "The space between the two walls is filled with fragments and rubble. There are clear traces of a tremendous fire, compact masses of blackened bricks, cracked stones, charred wood, and ashes. Along the walls the houses have been burned to the ground and their roofs have crashed on top of them."

After Garstang had consulted the best informed experts, the outcome of the second archaeological battle was that the inner ring was the more recent, therefore the one which must have been destroyed by the Israelites. But that did not settle the matter. The wrangle about the walls of Jericho continues. Garstang dates the destruction of the inner ring about 1400 B.C. Father Hugues Vincent, a leading archaeologist and one of the most successful investigators into Jerusalem's ancient past, also studied the evidence and dated the destruction of the walls between 1250 and 1200 B.C. Despite all opposition he still holds to this dating. Jericho has given the archaeologists a hard nut to crack, for the important factor is missing, namely, fragments of pottery. The shattered houses are empty. We must leave the final solution of the date to the keen detective work of the experts. At all events the walls of Jericho were once standing, and they still bear traces of a mighty conflagration: "And they burnt the city with fire and all that was therein."

But what was it that brought down the walls? "And they blew with the trumpets," says the famous and frequently quoted passage, "and the wall fell down flat." As he was examining the ruined walls Garstang made a remarkable discovery. The stones of the outer ring had fallen outward and downhill, but the inner wall along the crest of the hill had fallen the opposite way, namely, inward. It had buried the buildings which lay behind it. Moreover, the walls showed evidence of several large cracks and fissures.

According to Garstang, these observations could

lead to only one conclusion: that an earthquake must have shattered the city. Physical geography tells us that Jericho lies in an earthquake zone which runs obliquely across Asia and over the Himalayas into Tibet.

Jericho was the first strong point to be overcome on the way to the Promised Land. Archaeologists have been able on other sites to follow the further progress of the children of Israel toward their conquest of Canaan.

About twelve miles southwest of Hebron lay the Debir of the Bible. Defended by a strong enclosing wall, it dominated the Negeb. Excavations by W. F. Albright and M. G. Kyle of the United States in Tell Beit Mirsim since 1926 disclosed a layer of ashes and considerable destruction. The stratum of ashes contained shards which undoubtedly date from the end of the thirteenth century B.C. Immediately above the burned layer are traces of a new settlement by Israel. "And Joshua returned, and all Israel with him, to Debir, and fought against it." (Josh. 10:38)

Thirty miles southwest of Jerusalem the Lachish of the Bible can be identified. It must have been an extraordinarily strong fortress for Canaan. In the thirties at Tell ed-Duweir a British expedition under James Lesley Starkey measured out an area of twenty-four acres which had at one time been built up and surrounded by a strong wall. This city also fell victim to a conflagration which destroyed everything. A bowl that was salvaged from the ruins bears an inscription giving its date as the fourth year of Pharaoh Merenptah. That corresponds to the year 1230 B.C. "And the Lord delivered Lachish into the hand of Israel." (Josh. 10:32)

In the Cairo Museum there is a monument from a mortuary temple near Thebes, on which the victory of Pharaoh Merenptah[1] over the Libyans is commemorated and celebrated. In order to augment his triumph, other notable victories that this ruler is said to

---

[1]Acceded to the throne in 1234 B.C

have achieved are also mentioned. The end of the hymn of praise runs as follows: "Canaan is despoiled and all its evil with it. Askelon is taken captive, Gezer is conquered, Yanoam is blotted out. The people of Israel is desolate, it has no offspring. Palestine has become a widow for Egypt."

This triumphal hymn, written in 1229 B.C., is in more than one respect valuable and illuminating. Here for the first time in human history the name "Israel" is immortalized, and that by a foreigner and a contemporary. Israel is expressly described as a "people," and, moreover, a people connected with Palestinian place names. This is surely a proof for the most hardened skeptic that Israel was already properly settled

Fig. 24.

in Canaan in 1229 B.C. and no longer completely unknown.

Shortly before 1200 B.C. Israel had reached the goal that had for so long been the object of its aspirations. It is now in Canaan, but it is not yet in full control of the country. A trail of burned-out cities marks its path and indicates an extremely shrewd strategic plan. Joshua avoided the strongest fortresses, such as Gezer and Jerusalem. Obviously he followed the line of least resistance. The fertile plains and river valleys were likewise still in the hands of the Canaanites and would remain so for many generations to come. Israel had neither the armor to resist the dreaded chariots nor the technique and experience required to war against strongly fortified cities. But it had secured a foothold in the more sparsely populated areas; the hill country on both sides of the Jordan was in its hands. About ten miles north of the Lake of Galilee the mighty stronghold of Hazor falls before it; Joshua "took Hazor, and smote the king thereof with the sword: for Hazor beforetime was the head of all those kingdoms." (Josh. 11:10)

The rediscovery of this royal city can be counted as one of the most surprising pieces of good fortune in recent Biblical archaeology. John Garstang, the English archaeologist, had already identified as the site of old Hazor the extensive mound of rubble Tell el-Qedah, which stands out prominently to the west of the Jordan between Lake Huleh and the Lake of Galilee. But it was not until excavations, begun in 1953 under the auspices of the Hebrew University of Jerusalem and directed by Yigael Yadin of the James A. de Roth-schild expedition, had continued over several seasons that the hitherto undisturbed Tell could be awakened from its dreams and induced to part with its closely guarded secrets. Bit by bit its layers began to tell the experts the long and exciting story of the checkered fortunes of Hazor.

No fewer than twenty-one stages of development can be distinguished: twenty-one cities growing up on top of one another, each built on the rubble of past generations and each in its turn leveled to the ground, destroyed by war or fire or the force of nature. Surmounted by its citadel and fortified area the city spread its lower reaches far out into the plain. An ingenious drainage system consisting of clay pipes looked after public sanitation.

What has been discovered confirms in a striking way what the Bible has to say about the powerful role that Hazor played in Canaan at the time of the Israelite conquest. Hazor was in fact not only one of the largest settlements of the country but also one of the strongest fortresses. In the thirteenth century B.C. it was destroyed, as the book of Joshua records. A layer of burnt rubble indicates a great conflagration about that time —Joshua's army had done its work.

With these victories and the promised occupation of Canaan, Joshua's great assignment has been fulfilled. At a ripe old age he dies and is buried "in Timnath-Serah which is in mount Ephraim, on the north side of the hill of Gaash." (Josh. 24:30) The Greek text (LXX, 24:30b) adds a very significant remark: "There they put with him into the tomb in which they buried him, the knives of stone with which he circumcised the children of Israel in Gilgal." In Gilgal, on the way from the Jordan to Jericho, the rite of circumcision was carried out on the men of Israel according to tradition "with stone knives." "Now all the people that came out were circumcised: but all the people that were born in the wilderness by the way as they came forth out of Egypt, them they had not circumcised." (Josh. 5:5) Ten miles northwest of Bethel lies Kefr Ishu'a, the "Village of Joshua." In the neighboring hillside are some rock tombs. In 1870 in one of these sepulchers a number of stone knives was found. . . .

CHAPTER 2 / Under Deborah and Gideon

Israel settles down—Pioneering in the mountains—Peasants' huts instead of palaces—Deborah incites to revolt—Clash in the plain of Jezreel—Victory over the "chariots of iron"—Israelite crockery at Megiddo—Marauders from the desert—Traces of Abimelech's destruction of Shechem—Gideon's successful tactics—First battle in history against a camel corps—A new breed of long-distance carriers

AND THE LORD GAVE UNTO ISRAEL ALL THE LAND WHICH HE SWARE TO GIVE UNTO THEIR FATHERS: AND THEY POSSESSED IT AND DWELT THEREIN. (Josh. 21:43)

Immediately after the conquest an astonishing thing happened: the tribes of Israel dug their toes into the ground they had won. They can therefore no longer

Fig. 25. Israelite storing-jar.

have been a typical nomadic people. Canaan had experienced invasions of nomads from time immemorial but they had always been merely episodes. The tribes would graze their flocks and then one day they would disappear as suddenly as they had come. Israel, on the other hand, settled, cultivating fields and clearing forests. . . . "if thou be a great people, then get thee up to the wood country and cut down for thyself there." (Josh. 17:15) They gave up their tents and built themselves huts: they settled down among the ruins of the houses in the towns they had conquered. In Debir, Bethshemesh, and Bethel remains of their primitive and poverty-stricken furnishings were found on top of the strata which were deposited when the towns were burned down.

This break with the past is clearly recognizable from the excavations. Where previously patrician houses and palaces of the long-established feudal barons had been standing, there now arose peasants' huts and fences. The massive defense walls show signs of having had necessary repairs done to them. But what the men of Israel replaced was of the thinnest masonry. The construction of a new system of strong defensive walls would have entailed forced labor, and there was nothing the Israelites hated more. They regarded themselves as freemen, as independent farmers. "But every man did that which was right in his own eyes." (Jud. 17:6) Even the word generally used in Canaan meaning a "bondsman" was used by the Israelites in exactly the opposite sense to mean a "freeman." In the feudal system under the princes of the city-states all the drudgery was done by slaves. In the case of Israel the work of the farm was done by the freeborn sons of the family. At their head stood the father, the patriarch. Countless new settlements sprang into being. Archaeologists have found traces of them throughout the highlands. But there is very little of them left. For the first building material they used was sun-dried mud bricks, and the buildings they put up in this way did not last.

Real pioneer work was done by the Israelites in the mountains. Uninhabitable areas, districts without springs or streams were opened up. Although it sounds unbelievable, what remains of a technique invented by their ancestors has been partly taken over and put into commission again by the new state of Israel. They dug cisterns in the ground to collect the rainfall, and lined the insides with a type of limestone plaster which was hitherto unknown. These fixtures were so solidly built that they have been able to withstand the ravages of time for thousands of years.

As the Book of Judges tells us, and investigation confirms, the Israelites put down roots in their new home as settlers and farmers. In continuous fighting with their neighbors and feuds among themselves they gradually gained in military power and experience. The Bible mentions disputes with Moabites, Ammonites, and Aramaean tribes from the Syrian desert. It speaks of bloody civil war, when the tribes fought against Benjamin. (Jud. 20) Bethel lay in the territory of Benjamin, and Albright, digging there, found strata that showed that the place had been destroyed four times between 1200 and 1000 B.C.

It was around this time too that "Abimelech fought against the city all that day: and he took the city and slew the people that was therein, and beat down the city, and sowed it with salt." (Jud. 9:45) So runs the description in the Book of Judges of the conquest of Shechem by Abimelech, the ambitious and vindictive son of Gideon who murdered all his brothers.

In 1959 at Tell el Balata, on the site of this Biblical city which had been the first place Abraham encountered on his arrival in Canaan, excavations by American archaeologists from Drew University and McCormick Theological Seminary led by Professor G. Ernest Wright, who was following the earlier investigations of Professor Ernst Sellin of Germany, were able to confirm what the Bible has to say about the fate of Shechem. Fragments of clay jars which were scattered among the ruins and could be identified as typical Israelite pottery put the date of the destruction of Shechem toward the end of the twelfth century B.C., that is, about the period of Abimelech. At the same time the remains of the "tower of Shechem" were identified, as well as the "hold of the house of the god Berith" and the "house of Millo" which are mentioned in Jud. 9:20, 46. It does seem, however, that all of these were part of a single building which towered above the city wall and which had been built upon the ruins of an earlier Hyksos temple.

These troubled years of the first colonists have

found an imperishable memorial in three narratives of the Book of Judges: in the song of Deborah, in the story of Gideon, and in the doughty deeds of Samson.

The background of these "pious tales" is made up of facts, contemporary events which as a result of the latest research can be dated with considerable accuracy. When Israel entered Canaan about 1230 B.C., it had to be content with the mountains, for it "could

Fig. 26. Canaanite Prince from Megiddo seen on his throne, with harpist and war-chariot (1200 B.C.).

not drive out the inhabitants of the valley, because they had chariots of iron." (Jud. 1:19) It was not until a century later that the tide turned. It would seem that among the mountains of Galilee, tribes which had settled there had to render bond service to the Canaanites. Among them was the tribe of Issachar, which is ridiculed in the Bible as "a strong ass couching down between two burdens," and who became a "servant unto tribute." (Gen. 49:14, 15)

Revolt broke out in Galilee in protest against this oppression. The impetus was supplied by a woman, Deborah. She summoned the tribes of Israel to fight for their freedom. It is from her that that wonderful song, which she sang to the assembled throng, has come down to us.

Barak, one of the tribe of Issachar, became the leader. Other tribes joined in, and a great army was formed. Then Barak took a decisive step. He dared to do what Israel had never previously risked: he came to grips with the dreaded enemy on the plain. "So Barak went down from mount Tabor, and ten thousand men after him." (Jud. 4:14) The scene of the encounter was the broad and fertile plain of Jezreel between the mountains of Galilee in the north and Samaria in the south—absolute and sovereign domain of the Canaanite city princes and feudal barons. Here they awaited the dangerous fighting forces of the Canaanites. ". . . then fought the kings of Canaan in Taanach by the waters of Megiddo." (Jud. 5:19) The incredible happened—Israel won. For the first time they had succeeded in smashing and routing a force of chariots in open battle. The spell had been broken. Israel had shown that it had the measure of the military technique of the Canaanites and could beat them at their own game.

Two mounds of rubble lying about five miles apart in the plain of Jezreel preserve all that is left of Taanach and Megiddo. The cities alternated several times in importance. About 1450 B.C. Taanach was a large city-state while Megiddo was only a small Egyptian garrison. About 1150 B.C. Megiddo was destroyed and deserted by its inhabitants. For a long time it lay in ruins and was not rebuilt and inhabited until 1100 B.C. The pottery of the new settlers there is striking. It consists of large clay preserving jars of exactly the same type as were used at this time by the Israelites. Archaeologists found them in all the other settlements in the mountains of Samaria and Judaea. Taanach is specifically mentioned in the song of Deborah as the site of the battle. The reference to its being "by the waters of Megiddo" is presumably a more precise description of its situation. Megiddo itself, whose "water" is the River Kishon, cannot at that time have been in existence.

Archaeological discoveries and Biblical references make it possible to date the first battle against the Canaanite chariots in the period between the destruction and rebuilding of Megiddo, about 1125 B.C.

The Gideon story tells of the second triumph of Israel. Suddenly out of the East came a new, unfamiliar, and sinister threat to Israel's safety. Hordes of Midianite nomads, mounted on camels, attacked the country, plundering, burning, and massacring. ". . . for both they and their camels were without number: and

they entered into the land to destroy it." (Jud. 6:5)
For years Israel was at the mercy of these Midianite
attacks. Then Gideon appeared as their deliverer. He
adopted successfully, as the Bible describes in detail
(Jud. 7:20ff.), a new kind of surprise tactics which
routed the Midianites and apparently persuaded them
to leave the Israelites in peace from then on.

It is often the lot of peaceful inventions to be used
first of all in time of war. The "invention" that made
it possible for the Midianites to terrorize Israel was—
the taming of the camel!

Tame camels are likely to have been something
quite new in the ancient world. The people of the
Bronze Age probably did not use them. Egyptian texts
never mention them. Even in Mari, next door to the
great Arabian desert, there is no single reference to
them in any of that vast collection of documents. We
must eliminate the camel from our conception of life
in the ancient world of the Orient. References to them
in the book of Genesis must have crept in at a later
date. The attractive scene, for example, where we meet
Rebecca for the first time in her native city of Nahor
must make do with a change of stage props. The
"camels" belonging to her future father-in-law, Abraham, which she watered at the well were—donkeys.
(Gen. 24:10ff.) Similarly it was donkeys that for
thousands of years carried on their backs all kinds of
burdens and costly merchandise along the great trade
routes of the ancient world until the tame camel saved
them.

It is not quite certain exactly when the taming of the
camel took place, but there are some facts that point to
a general conclusion. In the eleventh century B.C. the
camel appears in cuneiform texts and reliefs and from
then on is more and more frequently mentioned. This
must be about the time of the Gideon story. Doubtless such marauding attacks with animals that had until then been regarded as wild must have come as a
frightful shock.

The third challenge held the greatest and deadliest
danger for Israel and threatened its very existence—
the clash with the Philistines.

CHAPTER 3 / The Warriors from Caphtor

Invasion by the "Sea Peoples"—The great trek from the Aegean—Triumphal progress with ox wagons and ships—The Hittite empire disappears—Seaports in flames on the coast of Canaan—General mobilization on the Nile—Pharaoh Ramesses III saves Egypt—The great land and sea engagement—Interrogation in P.O.W. camps—Life-sized portraits of the Philistines

HAVE NOT I BROUGHT UP ISRAEL OUT OF THE LAND OF EGYPT? AND THE PHILISTINES FROM CAPHTOR . . . ? (Amos 9:7)

The fabulous tales of the redoubtable Samson, that great bear of a man full of enormous energy, herald the beginning of the great tussle.

Philistines! This name has become part of our language. Who does not know the tragic love story of Samson and Delilah, the woman who betrayed him to the Philistines? Who does not remember the super-human strength of Samson, who could strangle lions with his bare hands, who slew a thousand Philistines with the jawbone of an ass, and in the end, blind and deserted by the woman he loved, brought a Philistine temple crashing down about his head in the fury of his anger? Yet we have never really known many facts about these Philistines who played a decisive role in the life of Israel. It is only quite recently that it has been possible to find out something about them. Bit by bit, as a result of careful examination of the fruits of scientific research, the picture has become clearer. Fragments of pottery, inscriptions in temples, and traces of burned-out cities give us a mosaic depicting the first appearance of these Philistines, which is unrivaled in its dramatic effect.

Terrifying reports heralded the approach of these alien people. Messengers brought evil tidings of these unknown strangers who appeared on the edge of the civilized ancient world, on the coast of Greece. Ox wagons, heavy carts with solid wheels, drawn by hump-backed bullocks, piled high with household utensils and furniture, accompanied by women and children, made their steady advance. In front marched armed men. They carried round shields and bronze swords. A thick cloud of dust enveloped them, for there were masses of them. Nobody knew where they came from. The enormous trek was first sighted at the Sea of Marmora. From there it made its way southward along the Mediterranean coast. On its green waters sailed a proud fleet in the same direction, a host of ships with high prows and a cargo of armed men.

Wherever this terrifying procession halted, it left behind burning houses, ruined cities, and devastated crops. No man could stop these foreigners; they smashed all resistance. In Asia Minor towns and settlements fell before them. The mighty fortress of Chattusas on the Halys was destroyed. The magnificent stud horses of Cilicia were seized as plunder. The treasures of the silver mines of Tarsus were looted. The carefully guarded secret of the manufacture of iron, the most valuable metal of the times, was wrested from the foundries beside the ore deposits. Under the impact of these shocks one of the three great powers of the second millennium B.C. collapsed. The Hittite empire was obliterated.

A fleet of the foreign conquerors arrived off Cyprus and occupied the island. By land the trek continued: it pressed on into northern Syria, reached Carchemish on the Euphrates, and moved on up the valley of the Orontes. Caught in a pincer movement from sea and land, the rich seaports of the Phoenicians fell before them. First Ugarit, then Byblos, Tyre, and Sidon. Flames leapt from the cities of the fertile coastal plain of Palestine. The Israelites must have seen this wave of destruction, as they looked down from their highland fields and pastures, although the Bible tells us nothing about it. For Israel was not affected. What went up in flames down there in the plains were the strongholds of the hated Canaanites.

On and on rolled this human avalanche by water

and by land, forcing its way all the time toward the Nile, toward Egypt. . . .

In Medinet Habu west of Thebes on the Nile stands the imposing ruin of the splendid temple of Amun dating from the reign of Ramesses III (1195-1164 B.C.). Its turreted gateway, its lofty columns, and the walls of its halls and courts are crammed with carved reliefs and inscriptions, thousands upon thousands of square feet filled with historical documents carved in stone. The temple is one of vast literary and pictorial record of the campaigns of the Pharaohs and is the principal witness to events on the Nile at that time.

It is more than plain from these records that Egypt was then in a state of acute panic and only too conscious of the danger in which it stood. One of the texts rings with a note of anxious foreboding: "In the eighth year of the reign of Ramesses III. . . . No country has been able to withstand their might. The land of the Hittites, Kode,[1] Carchemish, . . . and Cyprus have been destroyed at one stroke. . . . They have crushed their peoples, and their lands are as if they had never been. They marched against Egypt. . . . They laid hands on every land to the farthest ends of the earth. Their hearts were high and their confidence in themselves was supreme: 'Our plans will succeed.' "

Ramesses III made feverish preparations for battle and decreed a general mobilization: "I manned my borders . . . and drew up my armies before them: princes, garrison commanders, and warriors. I turned the river mouths into a strong defensive wall, with warships, galleys and coastal vessels . . . fully manned from stem to stern with brave warriors armed to the teeth. The troops were the best that Egypt could muster. They were as ready for battle as lions roaring on the mountains. The chariot detachments consisted of the swiftest runners, and every first-class charioteer available. The horses flew like the wind ready to crush foreign lands under their feet. . . ."

With an enormous fighting force and every able-

---

[1] The coastal area of Cilicia and Northern Syria.

bodied warrior that Egypt could call on, Ramesses III advanced to engage in a great battle on land against the foreign hordes. The inscriptions have nothing very

Fig. 27. The battle between Pharaoh Ramesses III and the Philistines.

definite to say about this battle. As usual, the Egyptian war reports confine themselves in this case to singing the praises of the victor. "His troops," it is recorded of Ramesses III, "were like bulls ready for battle: his horses were like falcons amid a flock of tiny birds. . . ." But a huge relief still portrays this terrible battle after 3000 years: The Egyptian chariot commandos have scurried in among the armed enemy trekkers. Fearful slaughter rages among the ponderous ox wagons carrying the women and children. Under the hooves of the bullocks and horses the bodies of the slain lie in heaps. Victory seems to have been won already, since Egyptian soldiers are seen plundering the ox wagons.

Egypt had won a battle of prime significance in world history. The enemy land forces had been annihilated. Ramesses III hastened to the coast in a swift chariot since "they had entered the mouths of the river" with their ships.

This great naval battle is likewise perpetuated on a stone relief in the temple at Medinet Habu: The fleets of the two opposing forces have approached each other. Shortly before their encounter the wind must have suddenly died down, since the sails are reefed. That meant a severe handicap for the foreigners. Their ships could no longer be maneuvered. The war-

Fig. 28. Examination of Philistine

riors stood there ready for the fray but helpless. Their swords and spears were useless except in hand-to-hand fighting when the ships were close enough together. The calm let the Egyptians have it all their own way. Their vessels, manned by oarsmen, approach the enemy ships at a safe distance, then the archers are given the order to fire. A murderous hail of arrows pours down upon the foreigners who provide a mass target and fall overboard in vast numbers. The bodies of badly wounded and dead men cover the water. When the enemy had been decimated and was in complete disorder, the Egyptians rowed toward them and capsized their boats. Those who escaped death by the hail of arrows or by drowning were killed or captured by Egyptian soldiers on the nearby shore.

Ramesses III had been able to ward off this deadly threat to Egypt on land and sea in these two decisive battles. There had been no victory like it in all the past history of the Nile.

After the victory a gruesome reckoning was made of dead and wounded by hacking off their hands and piling them in heaps. This was the method of counting the numbers of a defeated enemy. About what happened to the women and children of the foreigners the inscriptions tell us nothing.

The reliefs show the first P.O.W. camps in history. The defeated soldiers are herded together. The treatment that the mass of prisoners received was in principle the same as that of today. Drawn up in rank and file, they squat on the ground awaiting checking. Even the much maligned questionnaire was included: Egyptian officers dictate to scribes the statements made by *prisoners by Egyptian officers.*

the prisoners. Only one matter was differently dealt with in those days. Nowadays prisoners of war have P.O.W. or K.G. painted on their tunics; the Egyptians branded Pharaoh's name on their prisoners' skins. It lasted longer.

It is to the hieroglyphics of these, the oldest questionnaires in the world, that we owe the first historical information about the famous Philistines in the Bible.

Among these "Sea Peoples," as the Egyptians called the foreign invaders, one racial group assumed special importance, the Peleste or PRST. These are the Philistines of the Old Testament.

Egyptian artists were masters at depicting the physiognomy of foreign races and had an extraordinary ability to distinguish characteristic features. The reliefs at Medinet Habu indicate with this wonted accuracy the faces of the Biblical Philistines. They look like photographs carved in stone 3000 years ago. The tall, slim figures are about a head higher than the Egyptians. We can recognize the special type of dress, and weapons, and their tactics in battle. If we substitute the men of Israel for the Egyptian mercenaries, we have a true-to-life picture of the battles which took place years later in Palestine and which reached the height of their fury in the reigns of Saul and David about 1000 B.C.

CHAPTER 4 / Under the Yoke of
the Philistines

*Philistines on the coast—Swan pattern pottery—Beer mugs
with filters—Carefully guarded iron monopoly—Philistines
occupy the highlands—Traces of the burning of Shiloh—
Choosing a king from dire necessity—Allenby successfully
uses Saul's tactics—Surprising the Turks—Albright finds
Saul's castle—Two temples in Beth-Shan—The end of Saul*

AND THE CHILDREN OF ISRAEL DID EVIL IN THE
SIGHT OF THE LORD AND THE LORD DELIVERED THEM
INTO THE HANDS OF THE PHILISTINES FORTY YEARS.
(Jud. 13:1)

It was in 1188 B.C. that the Philistines suffered their
severe defeat at the hands of Ramesses III. Thirteen
years later they were firmly settled on the coastal plain
of southern Canaan, the fertile brown plain between
the mountains of Judah and the sea. The Bible lists the
five cities which they possessed: Ashkelon, Ashdod,
Ekron, Gaza, and Gath. (I Sam. 6:17) East of these
cities and the land adjoining, which was cultivated by
soldiers under the command of paid leaders, was ruled
over by a "lord" who was independent and free. For
all political and military purposes, however, the five
city rulers always worked hand in hand. In contrast
to the tribes of Israel the Philistines acted as a unit in
all matters of importance. That was what made them
so strong.

The Biblical narrator tells of other groups of these
"Peoples of the Sea" who had arrived with the Philistines and had settled down on the coast of Canaan:
"Behold I will stretch out mine hand upon the Philistines, and I will cut off the Cherethims [Cretans] and
destroy the remnant of the sea coast." (Ezek. 25:16)
Crete is an island in the Mediterranean which lies far
removed from Israel. Since we have learned of the
historical attack of the "Sea Peoples" on Canaan, the

otherwise obscure meaning of these words has become clear. They fit exactly the situation at that time.

When the Philistines appeared in Canaan a new and distinctive type of pottery also made its appearance. It is easily recognizable as different from the pottery which had previously been in use both in the cities of the Canaanites and in the hill settlements of the Israelites. Throughout the area occupied by the five Philistine cities—and only there—excavations have unearthed this type of ceramic ware. The Philistines must therefore have produced their own pottery.

The first find of this Philistine crockery astonished the archaeologists. They had seen these shapes and

Fig. 29. Philistine jar with swan pattern.

colors and patterns before. The leather-colored drinking cups and jars, with red and black geometrical designs and swans cleaning their feathers, were already known as coming from Mycenae. From 1400 B.C. onward the wonderful pottery made by Mycenaean manufacturers was greatly sought after in the ancient world, and their export trade had flooded every country with them. Shortly before 1200 B.C., with the destruction of Mycenae this import from Greece suddenly stopped. The Philistines must have come by way of Mycenae and must have started in Canaan the manufacture of this type of ware with which they were familiar. "Have not I brought up Israel out of the land of Egypt? and the Philistines from Caphtor?"

(Amos 9:7) Caphtor is Crete, the great island that lies close to Greece.

But Philistine pottery illustrates another interesting fact, which is also hinted at in the Bible. Many of their handsome mugs are fitted with a filter, and there can be no doubt about what it was used for. They are typical beer mugs. The filter served to keep back the barley husks which floated about in the home-brewed ale and would tend to lodge in the throat. Large numbers of wine cups and beer mugs have been found in the Philistine settlements. They must have been powerful drinkers. Carouses are mentioned in the Samson stories (Jud. 14:10; 16:25), where the fact is emphasized that the strong man himself drank no alcohol.

Beer, however, is no Philistine invention. The first great breweries flourished in the ancient East. In the hostelries of Babylon there were, in fact, five kinds of beer: mild, bitter, fresh, lager, and a special mixed beer for export and for carrying which was also called "honey beer." This was a condensed extract of roots which would keep for a long time. All that had to be done was to mix it with water and the beer was ready—an ancient prototype of our modern dry beer for use in tropical countries.

But another discovery was much more important. The Philistines were the first people in Canaan to process iron, and they made the most of it. Their graves contain armor, implements, and ornaments made of this rare and costly metal, as it then was. As in the case of the Mycenaean jars, they likewise manufactured their own iron. The first iron foundries in Canaan must have been built in Philistine territory. The secret of smelting iron was brought back as part of their booty as they drove through Asia Minor, where the Hittites had been the first iron founders in the world until 1200 B.C.

This formula which they had acquired was guarded by the Philistine princes as a state secret. It was their monopoly and they traded in it. Israel during this first period of settlement up on the mountains was far too poor to be able to afford iron. The lack of iron farm implements, of iron nails for building houses, and of iron weapons was a severe handicap. When the Philistines had occupied the mountains as well as the plains, they tried to prevent the making of new weapons by prohibiting the trade of smiths. "Now there was no smith found throughout the land of Israel: for the Philistines said, Lest the Hebrews make them swords or spears. But all the Israelites went down to the Philistines, to sharpen every man his share and his coulter and his axe and his mattock." (I Sam. 13:19-20)

Equipped with the most up-to-date weapons, tested and tried in their long experience of military campaigns, organized into a first-class political system, there stood the Philistines about 1200 B.C., on the west coast hungry for conquest. They had their eye on the same goal as Israel: Canaan.

Samson's prowess and his mighty deeds are legendary tales. (Jud. 14-16) But there are hard facts behind them. The Philistines were beginning to push forward and extend their territory eastward.

Separated from one another by long valleys, lines of hills sweep up from the coastal plain to the mountains of Judah. One of these long valleys is the valley of Sorek. Samson lived in Zorah (Jud. 13:2), and in Timnath, not far from it, he married a "daughter of the Philistines." (Jud. 14:1) Delilah, too, lived there. (Jud. 16:4) It was along this valley that the Philistines later on sent back the Ark of the Covenant which they had captured. (I Sam. 6:12ff.) This penetration of the Philistines into the hill country below the mountains of Judah was only the prelude to the great clash with Israel which followed years later.

"Now Israel went out against the Philistines to battle, and pitched beside Eben-Ezer; and the Philistines pitched in Aphek." (I Sam. 4:1)

Aphek lay on the northern rim of the Philistine domains. A mound of ruins, Tell el-Muchmar, conceals all that is left of this place which lay on the upper reaches of a river which flows into the sea to the north of Jaffa. From a strategic point of view Aphek was extremely favorably situated. Eastward lay the road to the mountains of central Palestine where Israel had settled. On the edge of the mountain range lay Eben-Ezer, where the opposing forces met. At the first encounter the Philistines were victorious. The Israelites in dire straits sent to Shiloh for the Ark of the Covenant, their sacred talisman. In a second encounter they were completely beaten by the vastly superior force of the Philistines. The Israelite army was routed and the victors carried off the sacred Ark as the spoils of war. (I Sam. 4:2-11)

The hill country was occupied, Israel was disarmed, and garrisons were located in the tribal territories. At their first assault the Philistines had achieved their purpose; central Palestine was in their hands.

This advance of the Philistines must have gone hard with Israel, as can be judged from the contemporary evidence that has been discovered. The temple at Shiloh which Israel had built for the Ark of the Covenant was burned to the ground. Fifteen miles south of Shechem lies Seilun which was once the flourishing town of Shiloh. On a neighboring hill lay the sacred precincts, Israel's sanctuary and place of pilgrimage. (Josh. 18:1; Jud. 21:19ff.; I Sam. 3:21) After the Old Testament period, early Christian and Mohammedan memorials were erected on the site.

Between 1926 and 1929 a Danish expedition carried out excavations at this spot, under the direction of H. Kjaers. The remains of Shiloh clearly indicate that the city was destroyed about 1050 B.C. at the time of the Philistine victory over Israel. Shiloh must have stood in ruins for a long time. For four hundred years after its fall the prophet Jeremiah refers to it: "But go ye now unto my place which was in Shiloh, where I set my name at the first, and see what I did to it for the wickedness of my people Israel." (Jer. 7:12) Other places in the mountains of Judah shared the same fate as Shiloh. Archaeologists found telltale traces of ashes in Tell Beit Mirsim near Hebron, the Debir of the Bible, and in Beth-Zur, south of Jerusalem.

About 1050 B.C. Israel's very existence was threatened. It saw itself to be on the point of losing all the fruits of its conquests and all its work of colonization, which had gone on almost two hundred years. It was on the verge of falling under the yoke of the Philistines and facing an existence of hopeless slavery. The only way to meet this frightful peril would be to amalgamate the loosely federated tribes and form a solid united front. It was in the face of this pressure from without that Israel became a nation. In those days there was only one possible form of government, a monarchy. The choice fell upon Saul, a Benjamite, a man renowned for his bravery and his great height. (I Sam. 9:2) It was a wise choice, for Saul belonged to the weakest tribe (I Sam. 9:21), and the remaining tribes would therefore have no cause to be jealous.

Saul constituted his native town Gibeah as the capital (I Sam. 10:26; 11:4), collected round him a small standing army, and began guerrilla warfare. (I Sam. 13:1ff.) By surprise attacks he hunted the Philistine occupation troops out of the tribal territory.

That Saul was a tactician of a high order has recently, after 3000 years, been demonstrated anew. One example, unique in its way, shows how accurate the Bible is even in the smallest details and how reliable are its dates and information.

We owe to Major Vivian Gilbert, a British Army officer, this description of a truly remarkable occurrence. Writing in his reminiscences,[1] he says: "In the First World War a brigade major in Allenby's army in Palestine was on one occasion searching his Bible with the light of a candle, looking for a certain name. His brigade had received orders to take a village that stood on a rocky prominence on the other side of a deep valley. It was called Michmash and the name seemed somehow familiar. Eventually he found it in I Samuel 13 and read there: 'And Saul, and Jonathan his son, and the people that were present with them, abode in Gibeah of Benjamin, but the Philistines encamped in Michmash.' It then went on to tell how Jonathan and his armor-bearer crossed over during the night 'to the Philistines' garrison' on the other side, and how they passed two sharp rocks: 'there was

---

[1] *The Romance of the Last Crusade.*

a sharp rock on the one side, and a sharp rock on the other side: and the name of the one was Bozez and the name of the other Seneh.' [I Sam. 14:4] They clambered up the cliff and overpowered the garrison 'within as it were an half acre of land, which a yoke of oxen might plough.' The main body of the enemy awakened by the mêlée thought they were surrounded by Saul's troops and 'melted away and they went on beating down one another.' [I Sam. 14:14-16]" Thereupon Saul attacked with his whole force and beat the enemy, "So the Lord saved Israel that day."

The brigade major reflected that there must still be this narrow passage through the rocks, between the two spurs, and at the end of it the "half acre of land." He woke the commander and they read the passage through together once more. Patrols were sent out. They found the pass, which was thinly held by the Turks, and which led past two jagged rocks—obviously Bozez and Seneh. Up on top, beside Michmash they could see by the light of the moon a small flat field. The brigadier altered his plan of attack. Instead of deploying the whole brigade, he sent one company through the pass under cover of darkness. The few Turks whom they met were overpowered without a sound, the cliffs were scaled, and shortly before daybreak the company had taken up a position on "the half acre of land."

The Turks woke up and took to their heels in disorder since they thought that they were being surrounded by Allenby's army. They were all killed or taken prisoner.

"And so," concludes Major Gilbert, "after thousands of years British troops successfully copied the tactics of Saul and Jonathan."

Saul's successes gave Israel new heart. The pressure of the occupying power on the highlands had certainly been eased, but it was only a short respite. In the following spring the Philistines launched their counter attack.

Toward the end of the winter rainy season they gathered their fighting forces once again in Aphek.

(I Sam. 29:1) But this time they had a different plan of action. They avoided an engagement in the mountains, since Israel knew that country far too well. The Philistine princes chose rather to advance northward across the coastal plain to the Plain of Jezreel (I Sam. 29:11), the scene of Deborah's battle "at Taanach by the waters of Megiddo," and then eastward almost to the banks of the Jordan.

"By a fountain which is in Jezreel" (I Sam. 29:1) —the spring of Harod at the foot of the mountains of Gilboa—King Saul and his army ventured to meet the Philistines on the plain. The result was fatal. At the very first attack the army was scattered, the retreating troops were pursued and struck down. Saul himself committed suicide after his own sons had been killed.

The triumph of the Philistines was complete. The whole of Israel was now occupied: the central uplands, Galilee, and Transjordan. (I Sam. 31:7) Saul's body and the bodies of his sons were impaled and exposed on the city walls of Beth-Shan, not far from the battlefield. "And they put his armour in the house of Ashtaroth" (I Sam. 31:10), the goddess of fertility. Israel's last hour seemed to have struck. It seemed doomed to extinction. The first kingdom which began so hopefully had come to a fearful end. A free people had sunk into slavery, and its Promised Land had fallen into the hands of foreigners.

The spades of the archaeologists have unearthed from among the masses of heavy black rubble silent evidence of this fateful period. The wind sweeps over the broken and crumbling masonry of the walls which saw the success and the tragedy of Israel, ruins that witnessed Saul's happiest hours as a young king and also his shameful end.

A few miles north of Jerusalem, near the ancient road that leads to Samaria, lies Tell el-Ful, which means, literally, "hill of beans." This was once Gibeah.

In 1922 a team from the American Schools of Oriental Research began digging there. Professor W. F. Albright, who promoted the expedition, directed the operations. Remnants of walls came to light. After a long interval Albright continued his work at Tell el-Ful in 1933. A log-shaped corner turret was exposed, and then three more. They are joined by a double wall. An open courtyard forms the interior. The total area is about 40 by 25 yards. The uncouth-looking structure of dressed stone gives an impression of rustic defiance.

Albright examined the clay shards which were scattered among the ruins. They came from jars that had been in use about 1020 to 1000 B.C. Albright had discovered Saul's citadel, the first royal castle in Israel, where "the king sat upon his seat, as at other times, even upon a seat by the wall." (I Sam. 20:25) It was here that Saul reigned as king, surrounded by his closest friends, with Jonathan his son, with Abner his cousin and commander of his army, and with David, his young armor-bearer. Here he forged his plan to set Israel free, and from here he led his partisans against the hated Philistines.

The other place where King Saul's destiny was fulfilled and which research has brought once more to the light of day lies about forty-five miles farther north.

On the edge of the Plain of Jezreel rises the great mound of rubble called Tell el-Husn, which is visible far beyond the Jordan Valley. This is the site of the ancient Beth-Shan. On the north and south slopes the strong foundation walls of two temple buildings emerge out of the piles of cleared debris.

Archaeologists of the University of Pennsylvania led by Clarence S. Fisher, Alan Rowe, and G. M. Fitzgerald excavated them in 1921 and 1933 almost at the same time as King Saul's castle was rediscovered at Gibeah.

Religious objects found among the ruins, principally medallions and little shrines with a serpent motif, indicate that these temples were dedicated to Astarte, the Canaanite goddess of fertility, and to Dagon, the chief god of the Philistines, who was half fish, half human. Their walls witnessed what the Philistines did to Saul, as the Bible records: "And they put his armour in the house of Ashtaroth; and they fastened his body to the wall of Beth-Shan." (I Sam. 31:10) The house of

Ashtaroth is the temple ruin on the south side. ". . . and [they] fastened his head in the temple of Dagon." (I Chron. 10:10) That is the temple which has been excavated on the north slope.

V / When Israel Was an Empire: From David to Solomon

CHAPTER 1 / David, a Great King

A man of genius—Poet, composer, and musician—From armor-bearer to monarch—Unintentional military aid for Assyria—From the Orontes to Ezion-geber—Revenge at Beth-Shan—New buildings with casemated walls—Finding of the pool of Gibeon—Jerusalem fell by a stratagem—Warren discovers a shaft leading to the city—The Sopher kept the "Imperial Annals"—Was David called David?—Ink as a novelty—Palestine's climate is unpropitious for keeping records

SO ALL THE ELDERS OF ISRAEL CAME TO THE KING TO HEBRON: AND KING DAVID MADE A LEAGUE WITH THEM IN HEBRON BEFORE THE LORD. AND THEY ANOINTED DAVID KING OVER ISRAEL . . . AND HE REIGNED FORTY YEARS. (II Sam. 5:3, 4)

The new king was so versatile that it is difficult to decide which of his qualities deserves most admiration. It would be just as difficult to find as gifted and rounded a personality within the last few centuries of our own time. Where is the man who could claim equal fame as soldier, statesman, poet, and musician? For his poetry alone a modern David would have been a Nobel prize winner. Yet, like the medieval troubadours, he was poet, composer, and musician rolled in one.

These last accomplishments were not then unusual. No people were more devoted to music than the inhabitants of Canaan. Palestine and Syria were renowned for their music, as we learn from Egyptian and Mediterranean sources. Part of the essential goods and chattels that the patriarchal group, depicted in the wall painting at Beni-Hasan, took with them on their journey to Egypt was musical instruments. The ordinary household instrument was the eight-stringed lyre.

David's sixth and twelfth Psalms are prefaced by the instruction "a psalm for eight strings." The lyre traveled from Canaan to Egypt and Greece.

In the New Kingdom of Egypt (1580–1085 B.C.)

201

inscriptions and reliefs deal with a series of themes connected with Canaanite musicians and instruments. Canaan was an inexhaustible treasure house of musicians, from which court chamberlains and seneschals obtained singers and even orchestras to provide entertainment for their masters on the Nile, the Euphrates, and the Tigris. Above all ladies' bands and dancers were in great demand. Artists with international engagements were by no means a rarity. And King Hezekiah of Judah knew very well what he was doing

Fig. 30. Captive musicians from Judah.

when, in 701 B.C., he sent men and women singers to Sennacherib, the formidable king of Assyria.

From the depths of despair, from their hopeless situation under the yoke of the Philistines, Israel within a few decades climbed to a position of power, esteem, and greatness. All of that was the work of David, the poet and singer of psalms. He first appeared, completely unknown, as Saul's armor-bearer, became a mercenary, then a fierce guerrilla fighter at war with the Philistines, and ended up as an old man seated on the throne of a people that had become a great power.

As happened two centuries earlier at the time of the conquest of Canaan under Joshua, David's efforts were assisted by favorable external circumstances. Just after the beginning of the last millennium B.C., there was no state in Mesopotamia or Asia Minor, Syria or Egypt, which was in a position to stop an expansion of Canaanite territory.

After the death of Ramesses XI, the last of the Ramessid dynasty, in 1085 B.C. Egypt fell into the greedy hands of a priestly clique who ruled the land from Thebes. Vast wealth had come into the possession of the temple.

A hundred years earlier, as the Harris Papyrus informs us, 2 per cent of the population was employed as temple slaves, and 15 per cent of agricultural land was temple property. Their herds of cattle amounted to half a million head. The priests had at their disposal a fleet of eighty-eight vessels, fifty-three workshops and wharves, 169 villages and towns. The pomp with which the daily ritual of the great deities was carried out beggared all description. To make the temple scales alone, on which the sacrifices at Heliopolis were weighed, 212 pounds of gold and 461 pounds of silver were used. To look after the luxury gardens of Amun, in the old royal city of Pi-Raamses in the delta, 8000 slaves were employed.

We get some idea of Egypt's status in the eyes of the outside world during this priestly regime from a unique document, the travel diary of Wen-Amun, an Egyptian envoy, dating from 1080 B.C. Wen-Amun's mission was to get cedar wood from Phoenicia for the sacred barge of the god Amun in Thebes. Herihor, the high priest, furnished him with only a small amount of gold and silver but with a picture of Amun, which he obviously expected to be more effective.

The frightful experiences that Wen-Amun had to go through on his journey have left their mark in his report. In the seaports he was treated like a beggar and an outlaw, robbed, insulted, and almost murdered

—he, an ambassador of Egypt, whose predecessors had always been received with the greatest pomp and the utmost deference.

At last Wen-Amun, having had his money stolen on the way, reached the end of his journey. "I came to the port of Byblos. The prince of Byblos sent to me to tell me: 'Get out of my harbor.' "

This went on for nineteen days. Wen-Amun in desperation was on the point of returning to Egypt "when the harbor master came to me and said: 'The prince will see you tomorrow!' When tomorrow came, he sent for me and I was brought into his presence. . . . I found him seated in his upper room, with his back leaning against a window. . . . He said to me: 'What have you come here for?' I replied: 'I have come to get timber for the splendid great barge of Amun-Re, the king of the gods. Your father gave it, your grandfather gave it, and you must also give it.' He said to me: 'It is true that they gave it. . . . Yes, my family supplied this material, but then Pharaoh sent six ships here laden with the produce of Egypt. . . . As far as I am concerned I am not your servant, nor the servant of him who sent you, . . . what kind of beggar's journey is this that you have been sent on!' I replied: 'Don't talk nonsense! This is no beggar's errand on which I have been sent.' "

In vain Wen-Amun insisted on Egypt's power and fame and tried to beat down the prince's price for the timber. For lack of hard cash he had to bargain with oracles and a picture of the god, which was supposed to guarantee long life and good health. It was only when a messenger sent by Wen-Amun arrived from Egypt with silver and gold vessels, fine linen, rolls of papyrus, cow hides, and ropes, as well as twenty sacks of lentils and thirty baskets of fish, that the prince permitted the required quantity of cedars to be felled.

"In the third month of summer they dragged them down to the seashore. The prince came out and said to me: 'Now, there is the last of your timber and it is all ready for you. Be so good as to get it loaded up and that will not really take very long. See that you get on your way and do not make the bad time of year an excuse for remaining here.' "

David had nothing to fear from a country whose ambassador had to put up with disrespect of this sort. He advanced far into the south and conquered the kingdom of Edom, which had once refused Moses permission to pass through it on the "King's Highway." (II Sam. 8:14) This meant for David an accession of territory of considerable economic significance. The Arabah desert, which stretches from the south end of the Dead Sea to the Gulf of Aqabah, is rich in copper and iron, and what David needed most of all was iron ore. His most dangerous opponents, the Philistines, had a monopoly of iron in their clutches. (I Sam. 3:19-20) Whoever controlled Edom could break the Philistine monopoly. David wasted no time: "And David prepared iron in abundance for the nails for the doors of the gates, and for the joinings: and brass in abundance without weight." (I Chron. 22:3)

The most important caravan route from South Arabia, the famous "Incense Road," likewise terminated in the south of Edom. By pressing forward to the shores of the Gulf of Aqabah, the sea route lay open to him across the Red Sea to the remote shores of South Arabia and East Africa.

The situation was also favorable for a northward advance.

In the broad plains at the foot of Hermon and in the fertile valleys that lay in front of Anti-Lebanon, Arab desert tribes had settled down and become static. They belonged to a race which was destined to play an important role in Israel's life, the Aramaeans, called simply Syrians in our Bible. They had founded city-states and smallish kingdoms as far down as the river Yarmuk, south of the Lake of Galilee over in Transjordan.

About 1000 B.C. they were in the process of reaching out eastward into Mesopotamia. In the course of it they came up against the Assyrians who within the next few centuries were to become the strongest power in the ancient world. After the downfall of Babylonia, the Assyrians had subjugated Mesopotamia as far as the upper reaches of the Euphrates. Cuneiform texts recovered from palaces on the Tigris and dating from this period mention Assyria as being threatened by danger from the west. These were the Aramaeans whose thrusting attacks were made with ever-increasing force.

In the face of this situation David pushed north through Transjordan right up to the Orontes. The Bible says, "And David smote Hadarezer king of Zobah unto Hamath, as he went to stablish his dominion by the river Euphrates." (I Chron. 18:3) Reference to contemporary Assyrian texts shows how accurately these words in the Bible describe the historical situation. King David attacked the Aramaean king as he was on his way to conquer Assyrian territory on the Euphrates.

Without being aware of it, David was aiding those same Assyrians who later wiped out the kingdom of Israel.

The frontier posts of Israel were moved forward by David to the fertile valley of the Orontes. His most northerly sentries patrolled Lake Homs at the foot of the Lebanon, where now petroleum gurgles through the great pipe lines from distant Kirkuk. From this point it was 400 miles as the crow flies to Ezion-geber on the Red Sea, the most southerly point in the kingdom.

Excavations have revealed plenty of traces of the acquisitions and expansion of the kingdom under David. There is a clear trail of evidence which accompanies his advance, including the burning of the cities of the Plain of Jezreel. Not much later than 1000 B.C., Beth-Shan, together with its pagan sanctuaries, was leveled to the ground. Archaeologists from the University of Pennsylvania dug up on these sites of ruthless fighting, shattered temples, deep layers of ashes on top of ruined walls, ritual objects and pottery belonging to the Philistines. David's vengeance administered a crushing blow to the city that had compassed the shameful end of the first king of Israel, a blow from which it did not recover for many years to come. There is no indication above the layer of ashes of any habitation having existed there during the centuries immediately following.

Various building projects dating from the earlier years of David's reign remain in some state of preservation, principally fortresses in Judah, which had been erected for defense against the Philistines. The structures clearly reflect the pattern of Saul's stronghold in Gibeah. They have the same rough-hewn casemated walls.

Seven miles north of Jerusalem, American excavations in 1956 brought to light not only traces of the walls of the town of Gibeah, which is so frequently mentioned in the Bible, but also uncovered the scene of a bloody encounter in these olden days. As we are told in II Samuel, once upon a time on this spot there took place a murderous hand-to-hand combat between supporters of the rival generals Joab and Abner— twelve on each side, the one lot on the side of David. the other owing allegiance to the surviving son of Saul. According to II Sam. 2:13, they "met together by the pool of Gibeon." Beneath a field of tomatoes in el-Jib, as the place is now called, Professor J. B. Pritchard, of Columbia University, discovered the "Pool of Gibeon," apparently in its day a well-known spot. He found a circular shaft, over thirty feet in diameter and thirty feet deep, which had been driven vertically into bed rock. A spiral path led down a ramp cut into the inside wall. Below that a winding staircase, with two openings for light and air, descended for a further forty-five feet to the reservoir itself, chiseled out of solid limestone. When the rubble which covered the whole layout had been cleared away, the great cistern began to fill sowly again with water from the fissures in the rock as it had done 3000 years ago. This Biblical "Pool of Gibeon" had also provided the town with an ample supply of fresh drinking water during an emergency or in time of siege.

Valuable evidence as to the celebrated wealth of the place—"because Gibeon was a great city, as one of the royal cities" (Josh. 10:2)—was collected by the American scholars from among the rubble of the vast cistern. It is now clear that the source of Gibeon's prosperity was a flourishing and well-organized wine trade. Sixty handles belonging to clay wine pitchers, together with the appropriate clay stoppers and fillers, were stamped in ancient Hebrew characters with firms' trade marks—among them vintners with genuine Biblical names. Repeatedly the stamp of "Gibeon" cropped up and a word that probably means "walled vineyard" and might indicate a wine of special quality. Other handles again bore the names of towns in Judah, like Jericho, Succoth, and Ziph (Josh. 15:24) to which the various consignments were to be delivered.

Quite near the reservoir, further diggings in the winter season of 1959-60 led to the discovery of extensive wine cellars. Sixty-six almost circular cavities about six feet deep and the same in diameter had been carved out of the rock and sealed with round stone bungs. Some of these cellars had obviously been used as wine presses for trampling out the grapes; other cavities, protected by a waterproof cover, could be identified as fermentation vats. The total storage capacity so far discovered approaches 50,000 gallons.

In view of this new evidence of what was at one time a flourishing wine industry at Gibeon, a hitherto apparently insignificant point in the Biblical narrative acquires fresh significance. It concerns an incident which took place while the Israelites were bent on the conquest of Canaan. We are told in Josh. 9:3-5 that "when the inhabitants of Gibeon heard what Joshua had done unto Jericho and to Ai they did work wilily . . . and took . . . wine bottles, old and rent and bound up . . . and old garments upon them." In this guise they appeared before Joshua and succeeded in hiding from him both where they came from and what a prosperous place it was.

Finally, in Jerusalem, later David's capital, the foundations of a tower and large sections of the revetment certainly point to David as the builder. "So David dwelt in the fort and called it the city of David. And David built round about. . . ."

The romantic manner in which the stoutly guarded stronghold of Jerusalem fell into David's hands was brought to light last century partly by chance and partly by the scouting proclivities of a British Army captain.

On the east side of Jerusalem, where the rock slopes down into the Kidron Valley, lies the "Ain Sitti Maryam," the "Fountain of the Virgin Mary." In the Old Testament it is called "Gihon," that is, "bubbler," and it has always been the main water supply for the inhabitants of the city. The road to it goes past the remains of a small mosque and into a vault. Thirty steps lead down to a little basin in which the pure water from the heart of the rock is gathered.

In 1867 Captain Warren, in company with a crowd of pilgrims, visited the famous spring, which, according to legend, is the place where Mary washed the swaddling clothes of her little son. Despite the semidarkness, Warren noticed on this visit a dark cavity in the roof, a few yards above the spot where the water flowed out of the rock. Apparently no one had ever noticed this before, because, when Warren asked about it, nobody could tell him anything.

Filled with curiosity, he went back to the Virgin's Fountain next day equipped with a ladder and a long rope. He had no idea that an adventurous and somewhat perilous quest lay ahead of him.

Behind the spring a narrow shaft led off at first horizontally and then straight up into the rock. Warren was an alpine expert and well acquainted with this type of chimney climbing. Carefully, hand over hand, he made his way upward. After about forty feet, the shaft suddenly came to an end. Feeling his way in the darkness Warren eventually found a narrow passage. Crawling on all fours, he followed it. A number of steps had been cut in the rock. After some time he saw ahead of him a glimmering of light. He reached a vaulted chamber which contained nothing but old jars and glass bottles covered with dust. He forced himself through a chink in the rock and found himself in broad daylight in the middle of the city, with the Fountain of the Virgin lying far below him.

Closer investigation by Parker who, in 1910, went from the United Kingdom under the auspices of the Palestine Exploration Fund, showed that this remark-

able arrangement dated from the second millennium
B.C. The inhabitants of old Jerusalem had been at pains
to cut a corridor through the rock in order that in time
of siege they could reach in safety the spring that
meant life or death to them.

Warren's curiosity had discovered the way which,
3000 years earlier, David had used to take the fortress
of Jerusalem by surprise. David's scouts must have
known about this secret passage, as we can now see
from a Biblical reference that was previously obscure.
David says, "Whosoever getteth up to the gutter and
smiteth the Jebusites. . . ." (II Sam. 5:8) The Authorized Version translated as "gutter" the Hebrew word
"sinnor," which means a "shaft" or "channel."

It was in David's reign that the exact recording of
Old Testament history began. "We must regard the
David-narratives as largely historical," writes Martin
Noth, who is a critical theologian.

The increasing clarity and lucidity of contemporary
records is closely associated with the gradual creation
of a political system which was David's great achievement and something new for Israel. A loose federation
of clans had become a nation: a settlers' colony grew
into an empire that filled Palestine and Syria.

For this extensive territory David created a Civil
Service, at the head of which, next to the Chancellor,
stood the Sopher. "Sopher" means "writer of chronicles" (II Sam. 8:16, 17), a writer in the second
highest position in the state.

In the face of the millions of secretaries and typists
in the modern world, and the thousands of tons of
paper that they put into their machines and cover
with type every day, the legendary glory of the "scribe"
has long since departed. Not even the enviable post of
chief secretary to an oil magnate can be compared
with that of her ancient colleague in either salary or,
more important, in influence. It was only on the stage
of the ancient Orient that the scribes played the role
of their profession incomparably and uniquely. And
little wonder, considering how much depended on
them! Mighty conquerors and rulers of great empires

were their employers who, themselves, could neither read nor write.

This can clearly be seen from the style of the letters. It is not the person to whom the letter or message is sent who is addressed in the first instance. Greetings and good wishes from scribe to scribe take precedence.

Fig. 31. A Government office on the Nile.

There is also a request to read out the contents of the letter distinctly and, most important, correctly and under no circumstances to suppress any of it. How things were managed within this scribal sphere of authority is indicated by a vivid scene in the Foreign Office of Pharaoh Merenptah. The scribes' department is divided into three sections. In each of the two side aisles about ten secretaries sit tightly packed toether. Some of them have one foot on a stool; great rolls of papyrus lie across their knees. The spacious middle section is reserved for the chief. A zealous slave keeps the troublesome flies off him with a fan. At the entrance stand two commissionaires. One is telling the other, "Spray some water and keep the office cool. The chief is busy writing."

No doubt the administrative office at the court of Jerusalem was considerably less impressive. The young state of Israel was still too rustic and too poor for that. Yet David's "recorder" must have been an important and awe-inspiring official. It was his job to compile the "Imperial Annals," which doubtless were the basis of all the factual Biblical references to the administrative

system and social structure under David. Among these
are the great national census conducted on the approved
Mariplan (II Sam. 24), as well as the information
about his bodyguard of "Cherethites and Pelethites,"
a kind of Swiss guard, which consisted of Cretans and
Philistines. (II Sam. 8:18; 15:18; 20:7)

Undoubtedly the "Sopher" would also be the first
to write down the new name of his sovereign. For in all
probability David was not called David at all. This
was a surprising discovery made recently by scholars
who were puzzled by the wording of certain texts
from the palace of Mari on the Euphrates. The word
"Dâvìdum" cropped up repeatedly in them. It means
"commander" or "general"; it is therefore not a proper
name, but a title.

The proper name "Caesar" later became a title, and
from Caesar we get "Kaiser" and "Czar." In David's
case it appears to have worked the other way round.
His military title, which probably dated back to his
days as a wandering soldier, was turned into a proper
name for him. "Dâvìdum" became David and has
stuck to him down to the present day.

This question of "writing" conjures up one of the
arguments leveled by critics of the Bible. In Egypt,
wagonloads of papyrus have been found, similarly in
Babylonia and Assyria mountains of cuneiform tablets.
Where then are the literary documents of Palestine?

Archaeologists and meteorologists may be permitted
to answer this question.

About the beginning of the last millennium B.C.,
Canaan deserted its angular cuneiform writing and the
use of clumsy clay tablets in favor of a less cumber-
some method of writing. Until then the text of the
document had to be scratched in soft clay with a stylus.
The clay had then to be baked or dried in the sun, a
time-wasting procedure, before the bulky letters were
ready for dispatch. A new type of writing, with wavy
lines, became more and more fashionable. This was the
alphabet that we have already encountered in the attempts at writing made by the Semitic miners at Sinai.
Stylus and clay were clearly unsuited for these new
smoothly rounded letters. So they looked for new writ-

ing utensils and found them in their baked clay tablets, inkpot and ink. Archaeologists call these little tablets with their flowing script "Ostraca." They were replaced in special cases by papyrus, the most elegant writing material of the ancient world. The Wen-Amun report shows how greatly this Egyptian export was in demand. The prince of Byblos received in return for his cedars 500 rolls of it: well over a mile of writing paper.

Palestine has a damp climate in winter on account of its rainfall. In such a climate ink is very quickly washed off hard clay, and papyrus soon disintegrates. Greatly to the distress of archaeologists, scientists, and historians, all of them thirsting for knowledge, practically the sum total of Canaan's records and documents has been lost to posterity for this reason. The fact that the archaeologists were able to produce such an impressive haul from Egypt is simply due to its proximity to the desert and the unusually dry climate.

CHAPTER 2 / Solomon the Copper King

Expedition to the Gulf of Aqabah—Iron ore and malachite —Glueck discovers Ezion-geber—Desert storms used as bellows—The Pittsburgh of old Israel—Shipyards on the Red Sea—Hiram brought the timber—Ships' captains from Tyre—The mysterious land of Ophir—An Egyptian portrait of the queen of Punt—American archaeologists buy a Tell—A model dig at Megiddo—The fateful plain of Jezreel—Royal stables with 450 stalls

SO KING SOLOMON WAS KING OVER ALL ISRAEL. (I Kings 4:1) . . . AND SOLOMON HAD 40,000 STALLS OF HORSES FOR HIS CHARIOTS, AND 12,000 HORSE-MEN. (I Kings 4:26)

AND SOLOMON BUILT . . . ALL THE CITIES OF STORE . . . AND CITIES FOR HIS CHARIOTS AND CITIES FOR HIS HORSEMEN. . . . (I Kings 9:17, 19)

AND KING SOLOMON MADE A NAVY OF SHIPS IN EZION-GEBER WHICH IS BESIDE ELOTH. . . . AND THEY CAME TO OPHIR . . . (I Kings 9:26, 28)

AND ALL KING SOLOMON'S DRINKING VESSELS WERE OF GOLD . . . NONE WERE OF SILVER: IT WAS NOTHING ACCOUNTED OF IN THE DAYS OF SOLOMON. FOR THE KING HAD AT SEA A NAVY . . . BRINGING GOLD AND SILVER, IVORY AND APES, AND PEACOCKS. (I Kings 10:21, 22)

AND THE HOUSE WHICH KING SOLOMON BUILT FOR THE LORD . . . WAS . . . OVERLAID WITH GOLD. (I Kings 6:2, 22)

AND SOLOMON HAD HORSES BROUGHT OUT OF EGYPT AND LINEN YARN . . . AND SO FOR ALL THE KINGS OF THE HITTITES, AND FOR THE KINGS OF SYRIA, DID THEY BRING THEM OUT BY THEIR MEANS. (I Kings 10:28, 29)

214

NOW THE WEIGHT OF GOLD THAT CAME TO SOLOMON
IN ONE YEAR WAS SIX HUNDRED THREESCORE AND
SIX TALENTS OF GOLD. (I Kings 10:14)

Doesn't it sound like a fairy tale?

Any man, even a king, about whom so much is
told, is hard put to it to escape the charge of boasting.
And any chronicler, telling such a story, easily gets a
reputation for exaggeration. There are certainly stories
in the Bible which are regarded by scholars as legends,
such as the tale of Balaam the sorcerer and his talking
ass (Num. 22) and the tale of Samson, whose long
hair gave him strength (Jud. 13-16). But this most
fabulous of all stories is really no fairy tale at all.

The archaeologists dug their way to the heart of the
trust-worthiness of these Solomon stories—and, lo and
behold, Solomon became their unique showpiece.

When the "fairy tale" of King Solomon, as many still
believe it to be, has been stripped of its frills, there
remains a framework of sober historical facts. That is
one of the most exciting discoveries of very recent
times. It was only in 1937 that a wealth of surprising
finds during excavations by two American expeditions
produced proof of the truth of this Biblical story.

Packed high with the latest equipment, with drills,
spades, and picks, and accompanied by geologists, historians, architects, excavators, and the photographer
who is now indispensable on a modern expedition,
a caravan of camels left Jerusalem. Its leader was Nelson Glueck who, like the others, is a member of the
famous American Schools of Oriental Research.

Soon they left the brown mountains of Judah behind. They headed south through the dreary Negeb.
Then the caravan entered Wadi el-Arabah, the "Valley of the Desert." The men felt as though they had
been transported into some scene from a primeval
world, where some titanic power out of the depths had
left its mark when it formed the earth. The "Valley of
the Desert" is part of the mighty fissure which begins
in Asia Minor and ends in Africa.

The scientists paid their respects to this impressive

*Fig. 32. Life in a harem. "Solomon had 700
wives . . ." (1 Kings 11:3)*

vista and then turned to their task. Their questing eyes
roamed over the steep rock face. Light and shade
varied with the sun, and here and there the stone was
hacked away and dented. They found that it consisted
of muddy-yellow feldspar, silvery-white mica, and,
where the stone showed up reddish black, iron ore and
a green mineral—malachite, copper spar.

Along the whole length of the wadi the American
scientists came upon deposits of iron ore and copper.
Wherever their tests indicated the presence of ore,
they found galleries let into the rock, all that remained
of mines long since deserted.

At last the caravan reached the shores of the Gulf.
However invitingly the white houses of Aqabah, the
Eloth of the Bible, seemed to beckon them in the glaring sun, however tempting were the sounds of this busy
eastern seaport after their trek through the desolate
wadi, nevertheless, the scientists turned their backs on
this intersection of three worlds.[1] Their goal was "Tell
el-Kheleifeh." This lonely mound, which seems no
more than a pile of rubble, rises inland out of the
shadeless plain.

---

[1] Africa, Arabia, and Palestine-Syria.

Careful probing with spades prefaced the first stage of the excavation and produced unexpectedly quick results. Fishhooks came out; they were made of copper. Then came tiles and remnants of walls. Some coarse-looking lumps of material in the vicinity of the Tell showed traces of green; they turned out to be slag. Everywhere around them the scientists met this sandstone with the distinctive green color.

In his tent one evening Glueck reflected on the results of the work up to date. It had produced nothing remarkable. Meanwhile, the whole of Transjordan was still on the program. Glueck wanted to track down the past in Edom, Moab, Ammon, even as far as Damascus. Looking through his notes, he stopped and pondered. Iron ore and melachite in the Arabah and, in this mound of debris in front of his tent, the remains of walls, slag, and copper fishhooks—and all of it in the immediate neighborhood of the Gulf which the Bible calls the "Red Sea." Thoughtfully Glueck turned up the Bible passage that mentions the Red Sea in connection with a great king: "And king Solomon made a navy of ships in Ezion-geber, which is beside Eloth, on the shore of the Red Sea, in the land of Edom." (I Kings 9:26) In Biblical times Edom came right down to the gulf of the Red Sea. Could this mound be . . . ?

It was decided to make a thorough investigation of Tell el-Kheleifeh next day. As they dug up the material from the test shafts, they found that at several points they came upon wall foundations at the same level. Below that was virgin soil. Shards gave them an indication of the date of construction of the masonry. It was within the period of Solomon's reign, after 1000 B.C.

The time factor compelled Glueck to stop operations. This particular expedition had other tasks ahead. But in the following years the Americans continued the excavations in three stages, which ended in 1940 and confirmed Glueck's theory. It appeared that the first ruins that came to light had once been workers' dwellings. Then came ramparts of the casemated type, the unmistakable building style of the first Iron Age. After that, remains of an extensive settlement were excavated. The most interesting things were casting molds and a vast quantity of copper slag.

Casting molds and copper slag in the middle of the scorching, pitilessly hot plain?

Glueck tried to find an explanation for this strange fact. Why did the workshops have to be located right in the path of the sandstorms which almost incessantly sweep down the wadi from the north? Why were they not a few hundred yards further on in the shelter of the hills where there were also fresh-water springs? The astonishing answer to these questions was not forthcoming until the last excavation period.

In the middle of a square, walled enclosure an extensive building came into view. The green discoloration on the walls left no doubt as to the purpose of the building. It was a blast furnace. The mud-brick walls had two rows of openings. They were flues; a skillful system of air passages was included in the construction. The whole thing was a proper, up-to-date blast furnace built in accordance with a principle that celebrated its resurrection in modern industry a century ago as the Bessemer system. Flues and chimneys both lay along a north-to-south axis. For the incessant winds and storms from the Wadi el-Arabah had to take over the role of bellows. That was 3000 years ago. Today compressed air is forced through the forge.

One question alone still remained unanswered: How was the copper refined in this ancient apparatus? Smelting experts of today cannot solve the mystery.

Earthenware smelting pots still lie about in the vicinity. Many of them have the remarkable capacity of 14 cubic feet. In the surrounding hill slopes the multiplicity of caves hewn out of the rock indicate the entrances to the galleries. Fragments of copper sulphate testify to the busy hands that worked these mines thousands of years ago. In the course of factfinding excursions into the surrounding country, the members of the expedition succeeded in identifying numerous copper and iron mines in the wadis of the Arabah desert.

Eventually Nelson Glueck discovered in the case-

mated wall of the mound of rubble a stout gateway
with a triple lockfast entrance. He was no longer in any
doubt. Tell el-Kheleifeh was once Ezion-geber, the long
sought vanished seaport of King Solomon: "And king
Solomon made a navy of ships in Ezion-geber which is
beside Eloth. . . ."

Ezion-geber, however, was not only a seaport. In its
dockyards ships for ocean travel were also built. But
above all Ezion-geber was the center of the copper
industry. Nowhere else in the Fertile Crescent, neither
in Babylonia nor in Egypt, was such a great furnace
to be found. Ezion-geber had therefore the best smelting facilities in the ancient Orient. It produced the
metal for the ritual furnishings of the Temple at Jerusalem—for the "altar of brass," the "sea," as a great
copper basin was called, for the "ten bases of brass,"

*Fig. 33. Brass laver from Solomon's Temple (I Kings
7:27ff.; II Chron. 4:6) (Reconstructed).*

for the "pots, shovels, basins" and for the two great pillars "Jachin and Boaz" in the porch of the Temple. (I Kings 7:15ff.; II Chron. 4) For "in the plain of Jordan did the king cast them in the clay ground between Succoth and Zarthan . . ." (I Kings 7:46). One of the most recent finds in Biblical archaeology fell to the lot of a Dutch expedition which has now established the site of the former of these two places. At Tell deir Alla in Transjordan, where the river Jabbok leaves the hills six miles before it joins the Jordan, the expedition discovered traces of Succoth, the Israelite city dating from the days of Joshua.

Glueck's delight at these unparalleled finds can still be detected in the official report which gathered together the results of the researches at the Gulf of Aqabah: "Ezion-geber was the result of careful planning and was built as a model installation with remarkable architectural and technical skill. In fact practically the whole town of Ezion-geber, taking into consideration place and time, was a phenomenal industrial site, without anything to compare with it in the entire history of the ancient Orient. Ezion-geber was the Pittsburgh of old Palestine and at the same time its most important seaport."

King Solomon, whom Glueck describes as the "great copper king," must probably be reckoned among the greatest exporters of copper in the ancient world. Research on other sites completes the picture of Palestine's economy under King Solomon. South of the old Philistine city of Gaza, Flinders Petrie dug up iron-smelting installations in Wadi Ghazze. The furnaces are like those at Tell el-Kheleifeh, but smaller. David had disputed the Philistines' right to their monopoly of iron, and he had extracted their secret smelting process as one of the prices of their defeat. Then under Solomon the iron and copper deposits were mined on a large scale and smelted.

Twenty years after Professor Glueck's first discovery of the presence of copper and slag heaps, an amateur archaeologist, Benno Rothenberg, made a striking find in the same Wadi el-Arabah of a large copper mine dating from the same time. In the spring of 1959, twenty miles north of Ezion-geber in Wadi Timna, Rothenberg's expedition came across extensive workings where the stone had been cut out of the rocks in thick slices and then subjected to the first process of removing the slag in basalt smelting vats.

"For the Lord thy God bringeth thee into a good land . . . a land whose stones are iron and out of whose hills thou mayest dig brass." (Deut. 8:7-9) So runs part of the detailed description of the Promised Land which Moses gave the children of Israel. Copper and iron in Palestine? The work of the archaeologists has now produced evidence showing how true is this description that the Bible gives and introduces a new factor into our picture of old Palestine which we shall in future have to take into account, namely, its remarkable industrial development.

Solomon was a thoroughly progressive ruler. He had a flair for exploiting foreign brains and foreign skill and turning them to his own advantage. That is the secret, otherwise scarcely understandable, of how what began as the simple peasant regime of his father David developed by leaps and bounds into a first-class economic organism. Here also is to be found the secret of his wealth which the Bible emphasizes. Solomon imported smelting technicians from Phoenicia. Huram-Abhi,[1] a craftsman from Tyre, was entrusted with the casting of the Temple furnishings. (I Kings 7:13, 14) In Eziongeber Solomon founded an important enterprise for overseas trade. The Israelites had never been sailors and knew nothing about shipbuilding, but the Phoenicians had behind them practical experience accumulated over many centuries. Solomon therefore sent to Tyre for specialists for his dockyards and sailors for his ships: "And Hiram[2] sent in the navy his servants, shipmen that had knowledge of the sea. . . ." (I Kings 9:27)

The construction of the harbor on the Red Sea is actually also mentioned in Phoenician sources. The priest Sanchuniathon described the course of events.

---

[1] A.V.=Hiram.
[2] The king of Tyre.

Hiram of Tyre offered "to deliver to the prince of the Judaeans building materials for a new palace, if he would concede him a port on the Ethiopian Sea." Solomon "gave him the town and port of Eilotha."[1] King Solomon built himself a palace, his famous "House of the forest of Lebanon." (I Kings 7:1ff.) ". . . now Hiram the king of Tyre had furnished Solomon with cedar trees, and fir trees, and with gold according to all his desire." (I Kings 9:11) The Biblical reference is supplemented in an illuminating way by the following interesting quotation from the same Sanchuniathon dealing with the building of the ships.

"Although there were great palm forests in the neighborhood of this place, there was no timber suitable for building purposes, so Joram[2] had to transport the timber there on 8000 camels. A fleet of ten ships was built from it." Even the names of the Phoenician captains who commanded the fleet were known to Sanchuniathon. The "shipmen that had knowledge of the sea" were Kedarus, Jaminus, and Kotilus.

Ezion-geber was the well-equipped and heavily defended export center for the new foreign trade. From Ezion-geber the ships set sail on their mysterious voyages to distant and unfamiliar shores. Ophir? Where was the legendary land of Ophir, the "warehouse" in which the ancient Orient purchased the costliest and choicest commodities?

Many a scholarly quarrel has broken out about Ophir. Someone was always claiming to have found it. Carl Mauch, of Germany, came upon the ruins of a temple city on the borders of Southern Rhodesia and Mozambique in East Africa in 1864. Fifteen years later, J. Steinberg, of South Africa, dug up, a few miles to the south, pre-Christian mining installations which were thought to be connected with the temple city. Rock tests were supposed to show that gold and silver had at one time been quarried there. In 1910 the famous African explorer Dr. Karl Peters, of Germany, photographed carvings on this site in which experts

---

[1] I.e., Eloth.
[2] I.e., Hiram.

claimed that they detected odd Phoenician characteristics.

This mysterious land of Ophir has, however, so far eluded the grasp of the scientists. Many indications nevertheless point to East Africa. Experts such as Professor Albright suggest that it was located in Somaliland. That would tie up very well with what the Bible says about the length of time it took to get there.

"Once in three years came the navy. . . ." (I Kings 10:22) "The fleet may have sailed from Ezion-geber in November or December of the first year," suggested Albright, "and returned in May or June of the third year. In this way the hot weather in summer would be avoided as much as possible. The journey in this case need have taken no more than eighteen months." Further, the nature of the merchandise—"gold, silver, ivory and apes" (I Kings 10:22)—points to Africa as the obvious place of origin.

The Egyptians were well informed about Punt, which may be identifiable with Ophir. They must have been on the spot and kept their eyes open. How, otherwise, could these impressive pictorial representations of Punt have originated, which light up the walls of the terraced temple of Deir el-Bahri? Wonderful colored reliefs adorn this temple on the west side of Thebes, lending splendor and charm to a dusky lady—the queen of Punt—and her retinue. As usual, the Egyptians have here, too, lavished devoted attention to the details of the costumes, the round huts, the animals, and plants of Punt. Anyone looking at them has a clear picture in his mind's eye of what this legendary Ophir looked like.

Inscriptions adjoining the reliefs give an account of the sensational expedition that a woman ordered to be equipped and to set out for Punt in 1500 B.C. On the throne of the Pharaohs at that time, as coregent of Tutmose III, sat the famous Queen Hatshepsut, "the first great woman in history," as Breasted, the Egyptologist, calls her. In response to an oracle of the god Amun, which enjoined that the routes to Punt should be explored and that trade relations with the Red Sea ports which had been interrupted by the Hyksos wars should be resumed, the queen sent out a flotilla of five seagoing vessels in the ninth year of her reign. They were to bring back myrrh trees for the temple terraces. The fleet sailed from the Nile along a canal in the eastern part of the delta into the Red Sea and "arrived safely in Punt," where it exchanged Egyptian produce for a precious cargo of myrrh trees, ebony,

Fig. 34. One of Queen Hatshepsut's ships returning from Punt (Ophir) with a cargo of myrrh and apes.

and gold, as well as all sorts of sweet-smelling wood and other exotic articles, such as sandalwood, panther skins, and apes.

A display such as they had never seen before met the gaze of the Thebans as, at the close of a successful trip, the strange collection of dark-skinned natives of Punt made their way to the queen's palace with the marvelous products of their country. "I have made his garden into another Punt, as he commanded me . . . ," says Hatshepsut exultingly, referring to the myrrh trees on the temple terraces. Egyptologists found dried-up roots of myrrh in the hot yellow sand in front of the temple of Deir el-Bahri.

Like the Thebans, men and women of Israel must also have stood in wonder and amazement on the quayside of Ezion-geber when their King Solomon's fleet returned from distant Ophir and discharged its cargo of sandalwood "and precious stones, gold, silver, ivory, apes and peacocks." (I Kings 10:11, 22)

Archaeological work can normally be started only

when permission to excavate has been given by the landowner or by the government of the country. This is not always easy to obtain, quite apart from the fact that in the course of the operations protests or restrictions can make life difficult for the investigators. In 1925 the Americans hit upon an unusual way of ensuring that they would be left in peace to get on with the work. They bought without a moment's hesitation the mound of rubble called Tell el-Mutesellim in the Plain of Jezreel from ninety native proprietors, peasants, and shepherds, lock, stock, and barrel. For the Oriental Institute of the University of Chicago had in mind a model excavation for the whole of the Middle East, the most comprehensive, most painstaking, and most accurate investigation that had ever been started in Palestine.

Tell el-Mutesellim covers the site of the Megiddo of the Bible. This discovery is based on the first large-scale excavation that was undertaken on this spot by the German Oriental Society, under Dr. J. Schumacher, between 1903 and 1905.

Like a small edition of Table Mountain, Tell el-Mutesellim lies in the heart of a unique scenic setting. Looking down from the plateau is like looking down on a vast green lake. Into the far distance stretches the great plain, the "valley of Jezreel" (Josh. 17:16), in which the green meadows of the fenland and well-stocked fields of grain alternate with one another. Flocks of cranes and storks frequent the spot. Where the plain ends, the wooded hump of Carmel stands guard over the Mediterranean shore. To the north the hills of Galilee, with the little village of Nazareth, sweep upward, tinted a delicate blue, and far to the right the somber summit of Mount Tabor bars the view into the deep cleft of the Jordan Valley.

Nothing in this fertile triangle, this friendly countryside surrounded by gentle lines of hills, suggests that this narrow tip of land was for many thousands of years the scene of mighty battles and of momentous and decisive history.

About 1500 B.C. Pharaoh Tutmose III, riding in a "golden chariot," led his army through a narrow pass into the plain and attacked the Canaanites, who fled in terror and complete disorder to Megiddo. On the same plain the Israelites, incited by the heroic Deborah, smashed the supremacy of the Canaanite charioteers; Gideon surprised the plundering camel-borne nomads from Midian; Saul lost the battle against the Philistines; and King Josiah of Judah died about 600 B.C., as he and his men threw themselves in vain against the armed might of Egypt under Pharaoh Necho. Ruins mark the site of the Frankish castle of Faba, which the Knights of St. John and the Templars occupied during the Crusades until Saladin drove them off the plain after a frightful massacre. On April 16, 1799, there was a battle here between the Turks and the French. With only 1500 men, Kleber, the French general, held 25,000 of the enemy at bay. The French fought like heroes from sunrise till noon. Then, over a ridge, to the rescue charged a troop of 600 mounted men. The officer at their head was called Napoleon Bonaparte. After the victorious Battle of Tabor, Napoleon rode up into the hills of Galilee and ate his supper in Nazareth. In 1918 British cavalry under Lord Allenby swept through the same pass as Tutmose III and destroyed the Turkish army which was encamped on the plain.

A silent witness of all these events was Tell el-Mutesellim, where Clarence S. Fisher began operations on the model excavation in the spring of 1925. The hill was literally cut into slices inch by inch, like cutting a cake, except that the slices were horizontal. The centuries flashed past like a kaleidoscope. Every layer that was removed signified a chapter of world history from the fourth to the tenth century B.C.

Of the four top layers, Stratum I contained ruins from the time of the Persian and Babylonian empires. Cyrus, King of Persia, destroyed the power of Babylon in 539 B.C. King Nebuchadnezzar of Babylon had conquered Syria and Palestine fifty years earlier, in 597 B.C. The walls of an unusually solidly built palace still remain from that period. Stratum II provided evidence of Assyrian rule, with ruins of a palace dating from the eighth century B.C. Tiglath-Pileser III subdued Palestine in 733 B.C. Stratum III and Stratum IV incorporated the Israelite period.

The most important find in this case was two seals with old Hebrew letters on them. One of them bore the inscription "Shema, servant of Jeroboam." Jeroboam I was the first ruler of Israel after the kingdom had been divided (926-907 B.C.). A stone preserved another familiar name: Pharaoh Sheshonk I, of Egypt. The Bible calls him Pharaoh Shishak. In 922 B.C., the fifth year of King Jeroboam's reign, he attacked Palestine.

After almost ten years of toil, picks, and spades had reached the layers dating from the time of King Solomon, who had died four years before the attack of Sheshonk in 926 B.C. The lowest level of rubble in Stratum IV then produced sensational surprises from King Solomon's time for the archaeologists, Gordon Loud and P. L. O. Guy, as well as for posterity.

In Solomon's day a new method of construction was adopted in the case of public buildings, defense walls, etc. Instead of the previous style of building, this new type involved the introduction of smooth-dressed stones at the corners and at intervals along the walls. On the lowest level of the rubble of Stratum IV ruins of a palace were exposed that displayed this characteristic feature. They are enclosed by a square wall whose sides are about sixty yards long. Additional protection was afforded by the handsome entrance gateway flanked by three pairs of close-set pillars. Archaeologists came across similar town gates with this threefold security in Ezion-geber and in Lachish. A building with massive walls that was excavated almost at the same time turned out to be a granary, one of the "cities of store that Solomon had." (I Kings 9:19) Storehouses of this kind were also found at Beth-Shan and Lachish. Megiddo was the administrative center of the Fifth District in the Israel of Solomon's day. Solomon's representative in the palace, who was also responsible for the deliveries of taxes in kind to the "city of store," was "Baana, the son of Ahilud, to him pertained Taanach and Megiddo." (I Kings 4:12)

Although these finds were remarkable, they were not sensational. The sensation was still lying untouched in the heart of Tell el-Mutesellim, as though the old mound had been keeping the best to the last. In the course of the excavations there appeared among the rubble on the edge of the Tell a flat stone surface, studded with stone stumps, ranged one behind the other in long rows and square in shape.

Loud and Guy had at first no idea what it could have been. There seemed to be no end to this remarkable series of flat surfaces which emerged yard by yard out of the rubble. It occurred to Guy that they might be the remains of stables. Did the Bible not speak of the untold horses of King Solomon?

Amid the generally monotonous sameness of a dig that had lasted several years, with its daily stint of carrying away, emptying out, sifting, and arranging every fragment worth considering, Guy's idea gave at once a new fillip to the excavations, which even the digging gangs shared.

The archaeologists' astonishment grew with every new structure that came to light. They found that several large stables were always grouped round a courtyard, which was laid with beaten limestone mortar. A ten-foot-wide passage ran down the middle of each stable. It was roughly paved to prevent the horses from slipping. On each side, behind the stone stumps, lay roomy stalls, each of which was exactly ten feet wide. Many of them had still remains of feeding troughs, and parts of the watering arrangements were still recognizable. Even for present-day circumstances they were veritable luxury stables. Judging by the extraordinary care which had been lavished on buildings and services, horses in those days were at a premium. At all events, they were better looked after than were human beings.

When the whole establishment was uncovered, Guy counted single stalls for at least 450 horses and sheds for 150 chariots. A gigantic royal stable, indeed. "And this is the reason of the levy which king Solomon raised: for to build . . . the wall of Jerusalem and Hazor and Megiddo. . . ." (I Kings 9:15) "And Solomon gathered together chariots and horsemen: and he had a thousand and four hundred chariots and twelve thousand horsemen, whom he bestowed in the cities for chariots. . . ." (I Kings 10:26) In view of the size of the royal stable at Megiddo and the stables and chariot sheds of similar type which have been found at Tell el-Hesi, at Taanach, and also at Jerusalem, the Biblical references must be regarded as mere hints at the reality. These tremendous results of the excavations give us a clear conception of the lavishness to which old Israel was accustomed in its imperial days.

Megiddo was, after all, only one of the garrisons for Solomon's new chariot corps, which formed part of the king's standing army.

In one of the ancient stable buildings that were cut deep into the rock under the high walls of the city of Jerusalem, the Crusaders tethered their horses after the conquest of the Holy City by Godfrey of Boulogne almost 2000 years after Solomon.

Horses and chariots alike were considered in Solomon's day to be worthwhile trading commodities. Israel had, indeed, in this matter a complete monopoly. (I Kings 10:28, 29)

All the important caravan routes between Egypt, Syria, and Asia Minor went through Solomon's kingdom. Egypt was the chief exporter of war chariots. ". . . the king's merchants received the linen yarn at a price. And a chariot came up and went out of Egypt for six hundred shekels of silver. . . ." Egyptian wheelwrights were unsurpassed craftsmen in building swift two-wheeled chariots for war and hunting. The hardwood for them had to be imported from Syria. This explains the high rate of exchange. According to the Bible, one chariot was worth four horses. (I Kings 10:29)

The horses came from Egypt, "and from Koa" as another tradition tells us. "Koa" was the name of a state in Cilicia which lay in the fertile plain between the Taurus Mountains and the Mediterranean. After the destruction of the kingdom of Mitanni by the Hittites, Cilicia became the land of horse breeders and the livery stables of the ancient world. Herodotus mentions that later on the Persians fetched the best horses for their Imperial Messenger Service from Cilicia.

Israel's trading partners in the North were the "Kings of Syria" and the "Kings of the Hittites." (I Kings 10:29) This too is historically accurate. The kingdom of the Hittites had long been extinct by Solomon's day but some smaller successor states had taken its place. One of them was discovered in 1945 by Professor H. T. Bossart of Germany. This was the royal castle in the forest of Mount Karatepe, not far from Adana in the Southeast of Turkey. Asitawanda, who built it in the ninth century B.C., was one of these "Kings of the Hittites."

Fig. 35. "And a chariot came . . . out of Egypt for six hundred shekels of silver." (I Kings 10:29)

as a Business Partner

"Arabia Felix," the mysterious land—Death march of 10,000 Romans—Number one exporter of spices—First news of Marib—Halévy and Glaser have a dangerous adventure—When the great dam burst—An American expedition to Yemen—The temple of the moon in Sheba—Camels, the new long-distance transport—Export talks with Solomon

AND WHEN THE QUEEN OF SHEBA HEARD OF THE FAME OF SOLOMON, SHE CAME TO PROVE SOLOMON WITH HARD QUESTIONS AT JERUSALEM, WITH A VERY GREAT COMPANY, AND CAMELS THAT BARE SPICES, AND GOLD IN ABUNDANCE AND PRECIOUS STONES. (II Chron. 9:1)

For thousands of years richly laden caravans have made their way from "fortunate Arabia" to the north. They were well known in Egypt, in Greece, and in the Roman Empire. With them came tales of fabulous cities, of tombs filled with gold, tales which persisted through the centuries. The Roman Emperor Augustus determined to find out the truth about what camel drivers continually extolled in their remote country. He instructed Aelius Gallus to fit out a military expedition and to satisfy himself on the spot as to the truth of these incredible tales about south Arabia. With an army of ten thousand Roman soldiers, Gallus marched south from Egypt and proceeded along the desolate shores of the Red Sea. Marib, the legendary capital city, was his goal. But he was never to reach it, for in the pitiless heat of the desert, after endless clashes with wild tribes, his army, decimated by treacherous diseases, went to pieces. The few survivors who reached their native land again had no reliable, factual details to add to the legendary stories of "Arabia Felix."

"In fortunate Arabia," writes Dionysius the Greek, about A.D. 90, "you can always smell the sweet per-

fume of marvelous spices, whether it be incense or
wonderful myrrh. Its inhabitants have great flocks of
sheep in the meadows, and birds fly in from distant
isles bringing leaves of pure cinnamon."

South Arabia was even in the ancient world the
principal export country for spices, and it is still so
today. Yet it seemed to be shrouded in dark mystery.
No Western man had ever seen it with his own eyes.
"Arabia Felix" remained a book with seven seals. The
first European in recent times to embark upon this
dangerous adventure was Carsten Niebuhr, a German, who led a Danish expedition to south Arabia in
the eighteenth century. Even he got only as far as
San'a. He was still sixty miles from the ruined city of
Marib when he had to turn back.

A Frenchman, J. Halévy, and an Austrian, Dr.
Eduard Glaser, were the first white men actually to
reach this ancient goal about a century ago. Since no
foreigner, far less a European, was allowed to cross
the frontier of Yemen, and no permit could be obtained, Halévy and Glaser embarked on an enterprise
that might have cost them their lives. They chartered a
sailing boat and disguised as Bedouins landed secretly
in the Gulf of Aden. After an arduous journey of over
200 miles through parched and desolate mountain
country, they eventually reached Marib. Greatly impressed by what they saw, they threw caution to the
winds and clambered around the ruins.

Suspicious natives came toward them. The two
scholars knew that it would cost them their lives if
their disguise was discovered and took to their heels.
At last, after many adventures, they reached Aden by
a circuitous route. However, they had been able to
smuggle out copies and rubbings of inscriptions, concealed under their burnooses, on the strength of which
they were able to prove that Marib really existed.

Traveling merchants likewise brought inscriptions
with them later on. Up to the present day their number reaches the sizable total of 4000. Scholars have
examined and sifted the material. The script is alpha-
betic and therefore originated in Palestine. Dedicatory
inscriptions give us information about gods, tribes, and

MIRACLES, MYSTERIES AND WONDERS OF THE ANCIENT WORLD FROM THE BIBLE AS HISTORY

"I am Lamgi-Mari . . . King of Mari." With
these words, engraved on his right shoulder, the ruler
of the Kingdom of Mari, on the central reaches
of the Euphrates, introduced himself to
archaeologists from Paris on January 23, 1934.

In a corner of Room 78 stood some large damaged clay jars. In 1750 B.C. the ceilings fell on top of them when King Hammurabi's commandos set fire to the palace of Mari.

The mummy of Ramesses II lies in the Cairo Museum in a perfect state of preservation. It was in his reign that Moses led the children of Israel out of Egypt.

Young Najococci with
manna excretion.

The first and so far the only photograph of manna.
The light-colored glassy formations on the branch of a
tamarisk which is occupied by Najococci (plant lice) are drops
of manna. Manna is still available commercially as Mannite.

The Monastery of St. Catherine
at the foot of Mt. Sinai.

This group of prisoners, the work of
Egyptian artists in the Temple of Medinet-Habu, is
an accurate portrayal of racial characteristics.
A Libyan (left) is followed by a Semite from
Palestine/Syria, a Hittite, a Philistine and another Semite.

"King Solomon's Pillars" near Ezion-Geber
on the Gulf of Aqabah,
center of the copper industry in the ancient East.

View of the model excavation at Tell El-Mutesellim.
A chain of laborers is passing up baskets filled with rubble. They are
standing (from top to bottom) on ruins of Persian, Babylonian,
Assyrian and Israelite times. It was in Stratum IV that the royal stables,
chariot sheds and the palace built for the local Governor,
Baana, at Megiddo (I Kings 4, 12) were discovered.

In the land of the Queen of Sheba an
American expedition in 1951 dug the imposing
Temple of the Moon near ancient Marib
in Yemen out of sand dunes as high as houses.

A Gezer schoolboy, practicing writing in 925 B.C.
scratched out on limestone these regulations for peasants.
Item 4 of this oldest piece of writing in Palestine
directed Israel to take up the cultivation of flax at Gezer.

Ivory relief of the bare-breasted fertility goddess of
Canaan: from a vault in the harbor area at Ugarit.

Figures of wild bulls and griffins adorn the Ishtar Gate
in Babylon, excavated by Professor Koldewey.

Rows of tall columns, the remains of a Forum, have been preserved on the site of Gerasa, on the upper reaches of the river Jabbok in Transjordan. In the lifetime of Christ many cities on both sides of the Jordan had their temples, theaters and circuses on the normal Greek pattern.

Professor G. Lankester Harding seen in
Jerusalem sorting out fragments
of the Old Testament, dating from the time of
Christ, which were discovered in a cave
by the Dead Sea in 1949.

On the "Via Dolorosa," the "Way of Sorrows," the Ecce-Homo Arch bridges the narrow alley at the point where Pilate is supposed to have pointed to Jesus and said: "Behold the man!" (John 19, 5) Beneath this arch Father L. H. Vincent actually found the Roman "Pavement" mentioned by St. John (19, 13).

cities of a million inhabitants. And the names of four countries—"The Spice Kingdoms"—which are mentioned are: Minaea, Kataban, Hadhramaut, and— Sheba.

The kingdom of Minaea lay in the northern part of Yemen and is referred to up to the twelfth century B.C. Writings of the ninth century B.C. mention its southern neighbor, the land of the Shebans. Assyrian documents of the eighth century B.C. likewise speak of Sheba and of close trade relations with this country whose kings were called "Mukarrib," that is, "priest-princes."

Gradually, with the discovery of documentary evidence, this fairytale country of Sheba began to take definite shape.

A gigantic dam blocked the River Adhanat in Sheba, collecting the rainfall from a wide area. The water was then led off in canals for irrigation purposes, which was what gave the land its fertility. Remains of this technical marvel in the shape of walls over sixty feet high still defy the sand dunes of the desert. Just as Holland is in modern times the Land of Tulips, so Sheba was then the Land of Spices, one vast fairy-like scented garden of the costliest spices in the world. In the midst of it lay the capital, which was called Marib. For 1500 years this garden of spices bloomed around Marib. That was until 542 B.C. Then the dam burst. The importunate desert crept over the fertile lands and destroyed them. "The people of Sheba," says the Koran, "had beautiful gardens in which the most costly fruits ripened." But then the people turned their backs upon God, wherefor he punished them by causing the dam to burst. Thereafter nothing but bitter fruit grew in the gardens of Sheba.

In 1928 the German scholars Carl Rathjens and H. von Wissmann uncovered the site of a temple near San'a which had been first seen by their countryman Niebuhr. It was a significant start, but almost another quarter of a century was to elapse before the greatest team of experts so far set out on an expedition at the end of 1951 to solve the archaeological riddle of Sheba, The American Foundation for the Study of Man provided the expedition with unusually large financial resources. The organizer of the enterprise was an extremely versatile paleontologist from the University of California, Wendell Phillips, then only twenty-nine years old. After long-drawn-out negotiations, they succeeded in getting permission from King Imam Achmed to excavate at Marib. Marib lies at the southern tip of the Arabian peninsula about 6000 feet up on the eastern spurs of the mountain range that skirts the Red Sea. The archaeologists started with high expectations.

A long column of jeeps and trucks rolled northward in a cloud of dust through barren mountain country with neither roads nor paths. Suddenly, like a phantom out of the shimmering yellow sand dunes, there appeared before them massive ruins and columns—Haram Bilqis. It was the ancient Almaqah temple of Aum, a center of worship wrapped in legend, in the neighborhood of Marib, the capital of the old Arabian kingdom of Sheba. Although partly covered by sand dunes as high as houses the lines of this oval-shaped temple, over 300 feet long, were clearly recognizable. The sanctuary was of the same type as the ruins of Mozambique in the East African jungle that were discovered during the quest for Ophir. The ground plans of the two temples were remarkably alike.

Fig. 36. *In Marib an American expedition discovered the Temple of the Moon in the Kingdom of Sheba in 1951.*

According to an inscription on the wall, Ilumquh, god of the moon, was worshiped at Haram Bilqis. Masses of sand covered the temple, which stood in the middle of the oval. Digging therefore began on the entrance to the great circle. The archaeologists wanted to try to approach the temple gradually from that point.

Under a broiling sun a gatehouse of surprising splendor and beauty was exposed amid understandable excitement. Wide steps covered with bronze led inside. The inner court was surrounded by a pillared hall. Stone columns fifteen feet high once bore a roof that shielded it from the sun. Flanked by pillars on each side, the processional way led from this point to the sanctuary of the moon-god. An unusual ornamental fixture caused astonishment. From a height of fifteen feet, glittering fountains of water must in those days have played into this quiet courtyard. As it descended, the water was caught in a narrow channel which then wound its way through the whole pillared court.

What must have been the feelings of pilgrims who made their way past these plashing, sparkling fountains, fanned by the drowsy fragrance of incense and myrrh, through the pillared courts of this most marvelous edifice in old Arabia.

The digging went steadily forward until they were within a few yards of the temple. The archaeologists could see in front of them the wonderful temple gate, flanked by two slender columns, but at this point the excavation had to be precipitately abandoned. The hostility of the governor of Marib, which had been growing for weeks, had now reached a dangerous point, and the expedition was no longer sure of its safety. They had to rise and run, leaving everything behind them. Fortunately they had some photographs among the few things they had been able to salvage in their hasty escape from the site.

Nearby in Hadhramaut, three digs were carried out in the following few years which were crowned with more success.

Soon after the experts had begun to evaluate the results of these four brief and somewhat dramatic expeditions, Professor W. F. Albright could say: "They are in process of revolutionizing our knowledge of southern Arabia's cultural history and chronology. Up to now the results to hand demonstrate the political and cultural primacy of Sheba in the first centuries after 1000 B.C."

Just as King Solomon's ships made long sea voyages through the Red Sea to Arabia and Africa, so long-distance travel began on the Red Sea coastal route through the southern Sea of Sand. The new form of transport called, not unjustly, "ships of the desert," consisted of camels. They were able to compass distances that were hitherto reckoned impossible. An unsuspected development both in trade and transport through these vast desolate territories took place about 1000 B.C., thanks to the taming and training of these desert animals. South Arabia, which had for so long been almost as far away as the clouds, was suddenly brought into the Mediterranean world and into closer contact with the other kingdoms of the Old World. Just as with the introduction of long-range aircraft America was suddenly brought closer to Europe in transatlantic services, so was it also, even if on a different scale, with south Arabia and the Old World.

Previously it was by the employment of donkeys, plodding endlessly and painfully, month after month, each short day's journey governed by the distance from water hole to water hole, and always in danger of attack, that the treasures of Arabia trickled northward along the ancient Incense Road through 1250 miles of desert. With the arrival of the new type of long-distance transport, however, a wide range of goods began to flow out of "fortunate Arabia." The new method was quicker, almost independent of water holes and therefore not tied to the old traffic routes which zigzagged from well to well. It had also a greater capacity. The camel could carry many times the burden that an ass could carry.

The terminus of the Incense Road was Israel. Solomon's official agents, the "king's merchants," took delivery of the costly wares. Whether the caravans would be allowed to proceed on their journey through Solo-

Fig. 37.

mon's kingdom to Egypt, Phoenicia, and Syria also depended on these officials.

No wonder that "the fame of Solomon" came to the
knowledge of the Queen of Sheba. (I Kings 10:1)
Bearing all this in mind, if we read carefully the
tenth chapter of the First Book of Kings, we shall
think of it no longer in terms of a "pious story" or of
the Queen of Sheba as a character in a fairy tale. On
the contrary, the whole passage rings true and is com-

pletely intelligible. "And she [that is, the Queen of Sheba] came to Jerusalem . . . and when she was come to Solomon, she communed with him of all that was in her heart." (I Kings 10:2) The Queen of Sheba had assuredly quite a number of things she wanted to talk about. The head of a state whose chief export trade could only be with and through Israel, and that for unavoidable geographical reasons, would certainly have plenty to discuss with the king of that country. Today we should describe the affair more concretely as trade talks and should send experts minus crowns to other countries for discussions. They, too, would carry with them in their diplomatic bags presents that would show the respect due to the head of the state, just as the Queen of Sheba did.

Israel's love of ornamentation—Secrets of the boudoirs of Palestine—Sleeping with myrrh and aloes—The Balsam gardens of Jericho—Mastic, a favorite chewing gum— Perfumes of Canaan—The Egyptians invented the bed—An ostracon describes a cloak being taken in pledge—Noisy flour mills

Amid the revelations of Egyptian, Babylonian, or Assyrian splendor to which archaeology has borne witness, we have been inclined to forget until now the gray and apparently monotonous daily life of Israel. Certainly there has been nothing to record which could compare with the golden treasure of Troy: no Tutankhamun, no charming Nofretete. But was the daily life of Israel really so drab, with no color and no sparkle?

Israel loved bright colors. They colored their dress, the walls of their houses, and the faces of their women. Even in the days of the patriarchs, their delight in color was apparent: "Now Israel loved Joseph more than all his children and he made him a coat of many colors." (Gen. 37:3) One of the pictures in the tomb at Beni-Hasan shows this type of coat with a wonderful red and blue pattern. Red and blue were the colors for men's wear; green seems to have been reserved for women. During the desert days, mention is made of "blue and purple and scarlet." (Ex. 25:4) "Ye daughters of Israel, weep over Saul, who clothed you in scarlet . . ." (II Sam. 1:24), cries David, in his grief after the death of the first king. "And she had a garment of divers colours upon her," it is recorded of Tamar, daughter of David, "for with such robes were the king's daughters that were virgins apparelled." (II Sam. 13:18)

Nature had given the land of Canaan one of the most wonderful painters' palettes. The children of Israel needed only to stretch out their hands. Pomegranates and saffron yielded a lovely yellow; madder root and safflower, a fiery red; woad, a heavenly blue;

239

there was also ocher and red chalk. The sea donated the queen of all dye merchants, the murex snail. Its soft colorless body turned purple in the sunlight. That was its undoing. Vast mountains of empty snail shells have been found at Tyre and Sidon, which lead us to the conclusion that this was the center for the extraction of purple. The Phoenicians were the first to create a proper industry for the extraction of purple in their seaports, but later Palestine, too, devoted itself to the profitable business of snail catching.

The textile town of Beth-Asbea, in south Judah, was famous for byssus, the finest kind of bleached linen: "10 shirts of byssus" are actually mentioned in an inscription of Esar-haddon the mighty king of Assyria. Hebron and Kirjath-Sepher had the reputation of being important centers of the dye industry. Great stone basins and things such as cauldrons with inflow and outflow pipes, which were dug up in these places, turned out to be dyeing vats. In Tell Beit Mirsim, the ancient Debir, they were familiar even with the technique of cold dyes. "That saith, I will build me a wide house," says Jeremiah (22:14), ". . . and it is cieled with cedar and painted with vermilion." Walls were varnished, mosaic chips and fabrics, leather and wood were dyed, as also were the lips, cheeks, and eyelids of beautiful women. "Thy lips are like a thread of scarlet . . . ; thy temples are like a piece of pomegranate . . ."; ". . . the hair of thy head like purple . . ."; ". . . how much better . . . the smell of thine ointments than all spices" (Song of Solomon 4:3; 7:5; 4:10), sings King Solomon himself in his Song of Songs, one of the most beautiful love songs in the world.

In highly poetic language it refers to Israel's delight in adornment and discreetly deals with the secrets of the beauty parlor. These perfumes and paints, ointments and hair dyes, choice and expensive, manufactured with the best ingredients that the world could provide would still do credit to the much-lauded cosmetics industry of Europe and America.

Sweet-smelling perfumes have always been highly

prized; aromatic resins were not only primarily esteemed as incense in the ritual of the Temple, but they had also their place in everyday life, in the home, in clothing, on the hair, and in divans and beds.

"I have decked my bed with coverings of tapestry . . . of Egypt. I have perfumed my bed with myrrh, aloes and cinnamon" (Prov. 7:16ff.), runs the warning against the artful wiles of the adulteress. "All thy garments smell of myrrh, and aloes and cassia, out of the ivory palaces, whereby they have made thee glad" is the song of praise in Psalms 45:8.

Botanists have investigated these stories that often sound like fairy tales, and have hunted up the ingredients of perfumes and the suppliers of dyes. They found them among delicate flowers and herbs, in the sap of shrubs and blossoms. Many came from foreign lands, but many still grow in Palestine today.

Fig. 38. Stone dyeing plant in ancient Israel.

From India came cassia (cinnamomum cassia), a tree with a cinnamon-like bark, and calamus (andropogon aromaticus), also called ginger grass. They came across the Indian Ocean in the course of foreign trade to the packing stations for spices in south Arabia and made their way from there by caravan to the Mediterranean countries.

Cinnamon had a world tour behind it. Originally it came from China; then on to Persia; thence, to India, where it became indigenous and was exported to Arabia.

Incense was obtained from the Boswellia bush. Its home is in Arabia and Somaliland, like the Commiphora Myrrha, the myrrh tree. The cradle of the aloe is the island of Socotra at the lower end of the Red Sea, whence comes its name Aloe Succotrina.

There was many a dispute about the origin of balsam. The Bible seemed to be really in error, for botanists know very well that the balsam bush (Commiphora Opobalsamum) grows only in Arabia. How could Ezekiel (27:17) claim that Judah and Israel had sent to Tyre "Wax, honey, oil and balsam." (Moffatt)

The botanists and Ezekiel are both right. The botanists had merely forgotten to look up Josephus, the great Jewish historian, where he tells us that there has been balsam in Palestine since the time of Solomon. The bushes were cultivated principally in the neighborhood of Jericho. Josephus also answers the question as to how they got there. They were reared from seeds which had been found among the spices which the Queen of Sheba brought as gifts.

That seems a daring assertion.

But there is a further bit of evidence. When the Romans entered Palestine, they actually found balsam plantations in the plain of Jericho. The conquerors prized the rare shrub so highly that they sent twigs of it to Rome as a sign of their victory over the Jews. In A.D. 70 Titus Vespasian put an imperial guard in charge of the plantings to protect them from destruction. A thousand years later, the Crusaders found no trace of the precious bushes. The Turks had neglected them and allowed them to die.

Mastic, which Ezekiel also mentions, is still found in Palestine. These are the yellowish-white transparent globules from a pistachio bush (Pistacia Lentiscus). They are greatly valued for their perfume and are used medicinally. Children gladly surrender their last baksheesh for a few bits of this native chewing gum, which was wisely extolled in ancient times as being good for teeth and gums.

In the Promised Land the following aromatic resins are indigenous: Galbanum from a parsley-shaped plant (Ex. 30:34), stacte from the Storax bush (Ex. 30:34), Ladanum from the rock rose, and Tragacanth (Gen.

37:25) from a shrub of the clover family. Botanists found all the Biblical spices.

The receptacles for these often expensive items have been found by archaeologists under the debris of walls, among the ruins of patrician houses, and in royal palaces. Bowls of limestone, ivory, and sometimes of costly alabaster, with little pestles, were used for mixing the aromatic ingredients of the finest unguents. The recipes of experts in ointments were greatly sought after. Tiny bottles of burned clay were used for keeping perfumes. In larger jars and jugs the scented spices were replaced with olive oil. Oil was well known for keeping hair and skin in good condition. Even poor folk rubbed it into their hair and skin, without the scented and generally very expensive ingredients. They got plenty of oil from their olive groves.

Washing in water was a daily necessity and was done as a matter of course. They washed before and after meals, washed the feet of their guests, and washed themselves each evening. Stone basins, foot baths, and clay bowls found throughout the whole country

Fig. 39. Stone footbath, with heel-rest, handles and waste-pipe.

during excavations confirm the numerous Biblical references to this practice. (Gen. 18:4; 19:2; 24:32; Song of Solomon 5:3; Job 9:30; Luke 7:44; Mark 7:3; etc.) Lyes from plants and minerals provided lotions and soap. (Jer. 2:22; Job. 9:30)

"A bundle of myrrh is my well beloved unto me: he shall lie all night betwixt my breasts." (Song of Solomon 1:13) This is a transference of ideas referring to the discreet practice whereby women carried a small bag containing myrrh under their dresses. Neither curling pins, nor hair pins, nor mirrors—brightly polished metal discs—failed to find a place on the dressing table. These important items of beauty culture counted as luxury imports from the Nile, where they had been regarded as indispensable by the wives of the Pharaohs for many dynasties.

However much the prophets railed against it they were never able to drive the ancient equivalents of rouge and mascara completely out of the boudoirs of the wealthy.

Women were fond of decorating their hair with delicate yellow sprays of the lovely loosestrife bush. But they were even more fond of a yellowish-red powder that was extracted from the bark and the leaves of the same shrub. The Arabs call it henna. With this henna they dyed their hair, their toenails, and their fingernails. Astonished archaeologists found nail varnish of this bright red hue on the hands and feet of Egyptian mummies. Cosmetic laboratories and factories still use henna, despite all recent developments. Eyebrows and eyelashes were tinted with galena; powdered lapis lazuli gave the desired shadows on the eyelids. Dried insects provided, as in the modern lipstick, the necessary carmine for a seductive mouth.

In view of the dainty perfume flasks, the ivory ointment boxes, the mixing jars and rouge pots, which have been salvaged from the ruins of Israelite cities, we can well imagine how harsh the threats of the prophet Isaiah sounded in this world which cared so much for color cosmetics and perfume: "And it shall come to pass, that instead of sweet smell there shall be stink; and instead of a girdle, a rent; and instead of well-set hair, baldness; and instead of a stomacher a girding of sackcloth; and burning instead of beauty." (Isa. 3:24)

In the Old Testament there is certainly mention of sitting at table on couches, but no one goes to bed in our sense. The bed is a rare, de luxe item of furniture.

The Pharaohs and the "upper crust" of their court dignitaries were the first to be lucky enough to have a bed to sleep in. It was on the Nile that the earliest

Fig. 40. Spice mill (left) and stone grater for grinding corn.

model was thought up of that piece of furniture that we should be least willing to dispense with. With great delight Sinuhe on his return observes, "I slept on a bed once more." But even five hundred years later a bed was still a novelty. For when the Princess of Mitanni, Taduchepa, presumably afterward Queen Nofretete, was married into the Egyptian royal family, she brought bedspreads as her dowry, admittedly expensively woven, but only bedspreads. The royal palace in her home country did not know what a bed was—everyone slept on the floor.

In Israel, too, only court circles and the well-to-do possessed so expensive an item. The plain man's bed was his cloak. At night he wrapped himself in it (Ex. 22:27) The law made allowance for this in that, while it declared that a man's "bed" could be taken in pledge, that was only permissible during the day. At night he had to have it back again. (Ex. 22:26) A lucky chance led to the discovery in 1959 among the ruins of Yavne Yam, eight miles south of Tel Aviv, of a unique document which records an actual case of a cloak being taken in pledge. In a letter of the seventh century B.C., the text of which is clearly written in ink on a fragment of pottery, an "ostracon," a peasant from whom such a cloak had been taken in pledge, defends himself against the charge of being in debt. The archaeologists could make out distinctly ". . . And he took thy servant's cloak after I had brought in the harvest . . . and all my brothers will testify truthfully on my behalf that I am not in his debt." The "cloak" was in reality only a woolen cover and seems to have been designed for any emergency. As well as keeping out the

1. Cyprus
2. Hamath
3. Mountains of
   Lebanon
4. Kadesh
5. Caravan route to
   the Euphrates
6. Palmyra
7. Hazor-Enan
8. Byblos
9. King's Highway
10. Helbon
11. Sidon
12. Damascus
13. Tyre
14. Mt. Hermon
15. Hazor
16. Akka
17. Dor
18. Megiddo
19. Beth-Shan
20. Ramoth-Gilead
21. Taanach
22. Joppa

THE KINGDOM OF SOLOMON
965-926 B.C.

23. Rabbath-Ammon
24. Jerusalem
25. Ashdod
26. Askelon
27. Jericho
28. Heshbon
29. Gaza
30. Gath
31. Hebron
32. Dibon
33. "The Way of the Land of the Philistines" (caravan route to Egypt)
34. Eglon
35. Lachish
36. Debir
37. Punon
38. Sela (Petra)
39. Ezion-Geber and Elath
40. Red Sea
41. Caravan route to S. Arabia (incense route)

cold in our sense and serving as a bed, it was also used as a carpet (II Kings 9:13; Matt. 21:7, 8)

The bed was never regarded as the ideal place to rest either in Israel or in the ancient East in general. It was a foreign institution and always remained so. Its cousin,

Fig. 41. Simple oil lamp and seven-pointed candlestick.

the divan, however, likewise a product of the Fertile Crescent, became famous for its comfort and its cushions. With its arrangement of pillows during the day, which were spread out at night, it was the prototype of our modern variety. What even bombed-out Central Europe and the smallest twentieth-century households have been able to afford was the last word in furniture 3000 years ago. The divan was also known in Israel. "And satest upon a stately bed, and a table prepared before it. . . ." (Ezek. 23:41)

We are prone to thunder against the nerve-shattering noise of our machine age and often wish the good old days of peace and quiet would come back again. Was Israel any better off?

Instead of the blaring of loud-speakers, from daybreak onward, houses and tents echoed to the sound of stone hand mills. At crack of dawn began the grinding of the corn and the pounding of it into flour. This was as much the woman's job as grinding coffee today. Only grinding flour was incomparably harder and heavier work. It often took two of them to turn the heavy stone.

The threat of a thorough-going antinoise campaign, which is often talked about nowadays, would have meant something frightful in those circumstances. If the noise of the mill stopped, hunger crept over the land. Jeremiah had a vision of this as he foretold what would happen during the exile in Babylon: "Moreover I will take from thee the voice of mirth . . . the sound of the millstones and the light of the candle, and this whole land shall be a desolation. . . ." (Jer. 25:10, 11)

VI/Two Kings—Two Kingdoms: From Rehoboam to Jehoiachin

CHAPTER 1 / The Shadow of a New World Power

The Empire splits—Frontier posts between Israel and Judah—Napoleon reads Shishak's report on Palestine—Samaria, the northern capital—Traces of Ahab's "ivory palace"—A mysterious "third man"—Arabs blow up victory monument in Moab—Mesha the mutton king's song of triumph—Assyria steps in—The black obelisk from Nimrud—King Jehu's portrait in Assyria—Consignments of wine for Jeroboam II—Uzziah's palace—The prophet Amos warns in vain—The walls of Samaria are strengthened to 30 feet

SO ISRAEL REBELLED AGAINST THE HOUSE OF DAVID UNTO THIS DAY. . . . THERE WAS NONE THAT FOLLOWED THE HOUSE OF DAVID, BUT THE TRIBE OF JUDAH. (I Kings 12:19, 20)

Solomon the Great died in 926 B.C. The dream of Israel as a great power was buried with him forever. Under the leadership of two unusually gifted men—David and Solomon—this ambitious dream had been built up stone by stone for two generations. But at the very moment of Solomon's passing, the old tribal dissensions broke out again and the empire of Syria and Palestine was shattered as the inevitable end of the quarrel. Two kingdoms took its place—the kingdom of Israel in the north and the kingdom of Judah in the south. A new chapter in the history of the people of the Bible had begun.

It was the Israelite people itself that gnawed away its own foundations and destroyed its empire. It became only too plain what road they proposed to follow slowly until the bitter end when the inhabitants of Israel fell a prey to the Assyrian and the inhabitants of Judah a prey to the Babylonians. Divided among themselves, what happened to them was worse than simply sinking back into obscurity. They were caught between the millstones of the great powers which were in the

253

following centuries to dominate the world stage. Israel and Judah collapsed amid a welter of dispute, and barely 350 years after Solomon's death both kingdoms were no more.

Solomon's last wish was certainly carried out: his son Rehoboam sat on the throne at Jerusalem for a short spell as ruler of all the tribes. The endless quarreling of the tribes among themselves hastened the end of the empire, since this resulted in civil war. Ten tribes in the north seceded. Jeroboam, who had lost no time in returning from exile in Egypt, assumed the crown in 926 B.C. and became king of Israel in the north. The remainder stayed faithful to Rehoboam and formed Judah in the south with its capital at Jerusalem (I Kings 12:19, 20)

There was no harmony between Judah and Israel. They shed each other's blood in feud after feud. Time and again fighting broke out over the question of frontiers. "And there was war between Rehoboam and Jeroboam all their days." (I Kings 14:30) It was no different under their successors. "And there was war between Asa and Baasha king of Israel all their days." (I Kings 15:16) Judah built the fortress of Mizpah on the main strategic route from Jerusalem to the north; further to the east they strengthened Geba ". . . and king Asa built with them Geba of Benjamin and Mizpah." (I Kings 15:22) That was the final frontier.

From 1927 to 1935 an American expedition from the Pacific School of Religion, under the direction of William Frederick Bade, excavated abnormally massive stonework at Tell en-Nasbe, seven miles north of Jerusalem. It was the remains of the old frontier fortress of Mizpah. The enclosing wall was twenty-six feet thick. This tremendous defensive wall shows how hard and bitter was the civil war that raged between north and south.

Israel was hemmed in on both sides: by Judah on the south, who even summoned the hated Philistines to help to keep Israel in check, and in the north, by the kingdom of the Aramaeans, whose powerful aid had been secured by Judah through an alliance. (I Kings 15:18ff.)

Centuries passed, centuries of endless conflict with this vastly superior power which was the deadly enemy. The continuous sequence of wars did not end until the new world power, Assyria, had crushed the Aramaeans. But with the emergence of Assyria, Israel's days—indeed, the days of both kingdoms—were numbered.

Over and above all this, just after the civil war had started, the country suffered unexpectedly the first foreign invasion in generations. Shishak[1] of Egypt attacked with his armies and marched through the country

Fig. 42. Border stronghold of Mizpah between Judah and Israel (Reconstruction).

plundering as he went. His greatest haul was from the old capital Jerusalem: ". . . and he took away the treasures of the house of the Lord, and the treasures of the king's house; he even took away all: and he took away all the shields of gold which Solomon had made." (I Kings 14:25, 26) The Temple and the House of Lebanon, as the Bible calls the royal palace, had been standing scarcely twenty years, and already these proud tokens of Solomon's greatness were robbed of their glory. In place of the golden shields that had been plundered "king Rehoboam made in their stead brazen shields." (I Kings 14:27) It was an ill-omened act.

---

[1]Pharaoh Sheshonk I.

The first European of note to stand in front of a large document of the Pharaoh whom the Bible calls Shishak was Napoleon Bonaparte. He was not aware of it, however, since at that time no one had as yet deciphered hieroglyphics. It was in 1799 that he wandered, deeply impressed, with a company of French scholars, through a vast Egyptian temple area at Karnak on the east side of Thebes. In the middle of this, the greatest temple area ever constructed by human hands, 134 columns up to 75 feet high support the roof of a colossal court. On the outer wall of this, on the south side, an imposing relief, which perpetuates the marauding expedition of this Pharaoh, stands out boldly in the bright sunshine of the Nile.

The god Amun, holding in his right hand a sickle-shaped sword, brings to Pharaoh Sheshonk I, 156 manacled Palestinian prisoners who are attached by cords to his left hand. Every prisoner represents a city or a village. Some of them have Biblical names such as "the Feather of Arad" (Josh. 12:14; Jud. 1:16) and "the Field of Abraham." The fortified city of Megiddo is among those represented, and in the ruins of Megiddo the name of Sheshonk I has been found.

Sheshonk's campaign was the last for a long time. Not for more than three hundred years was Egypt once more in a position to enforce its ancient claim to the suzerainty of the Syrian-Palestine territories.

The deadly danger that faced Israel came from the north—Assyria. During the reign of King Omri (882-871 B.C.), Assyria prepared to pounce. As if in a practice maneuver for the real thing, it tried a thrust westward from Mesopotamia.

"From Aleppo I launched the attack and crossed the Orontes." This sentence from a cuneiform inscription of Ashurnasirpal II rings out like an opening fanfare of trumpets. It had taken Assyria more than 200 years to dispose of its enemies inside and outside Mesopotamia. From the ancient city of Ashur on the Tigris, which bore the name of its chief god, the Semitic race of Assyrians, eager for conquest and skilled in administration, had extended their dominion over all the peoples of Mesopotamia. Now their eyes were fixed on the conquest of the world. The prelude to that had to be the possession of the narrow coastal strip of Syria and Palestine which barred the way to the Mediterranean, as well as the occupation of the important seaports, the control of the chief caravan routes and of the only military road into Egypt.

When Assyria set itself this target the fate of Syria and Palestine was sealed.

The report of Ashurnasirpal indicates briefly what was also in store for Israel and Judah. "I marched from the Orontes, . . . I conquered the cities. . . . I caused great slaughter, I destroyed, I demolished, I burned. I

Fig. 43. Victory relief of Pharaoh Sheshonk I (the "Shishak" of the Bible) in the Temple at Karnak.

took their warriors prisoner and impaled them on stakes before their cities. I settled Assyrians in their place. . . . I washed my weapons in the Great Sea."

As unexpectedly as the Assyrians had appeared, so with equal abruptness they departed, laden with "silver, gold, lead, copper," the tribute of the Phoenician cities of Tyre, Sidon, and Byblos.

King Omri of Israel heard of all this with dark foreboding. This former army officer, however, still showed his outstanding flair for soldiering now that he had become king. In the heart of the Samarian highlands he bought a hill on which he built a new capital for Israel, the stronghold of Samaria. (I Kings 16:24) He was certain that Israel would need it and need it badly.

The choice of a site revealed the expert who was guided by strategic considerations. Samaria lies on a solitary hill, about 300 feet high, which rises gently out of a broad and fertile valley and is surrounded by a semicircle of higher mountains. A local spring makes the place ideal for defense. The view westward from the summit extends as far as the Mediterranean.

King Omri made an impression on the Assyrians. A century after his dynasty had crashed, Israel was still officially called "The House of Omri" in cuneiform texts.

Eighteen years after Omri's death what they had dreaded actually happened. Shalmaneser III fell upon Carchemish on the Euphrates and then was on his way to Palestine.[1]

Ahab, Omri's son who succeeded him on the throne, guessed what a violent clash with the rising world power of Assyria would mean and did the only proper thing in the circumstances. He had recently beaten his old enemy Benhadad of Damascus, King of the Aramaeans. Instead of letting him taste to the full the victor's power, he handled him with unwonted magnanimity; he "caused him to come up into the chariot," called him "my brother," made "a covenant with him and sent him away." (I Kings 20:33, 32, 34) So he made an ally out of an enemy. His people misunderstood his

---

[1] 853 B.C.

policy, and one of the prophets took him to task. Only the future would show how well he had known what he was doing. War on two fronts had been avoided.

"In sheepskin boats I crossed the Euphrates in flood," runs the cuneiform report of Shalmaneser III, King of Assyria. His sappers knew how to make a pontoon bridge out of inflated animal skins.

In Syria he was met by an opposing coalition from Syria and Palestine, and he took careful note of how the army was made up. Apart from the troops of the Biblical Benhadad of Damascus and another Syrian prince, there were "2000 chariots and 10,000 horses belonging to Ahabbu the Sirilaean." Ahabbu the Sirilaean, who provided the third strongest army, was king Ahab of Israel.

The alliance between Israel and Damascus did not last long. Hardly had the Assyrians left the country when the old enmities broke out again and Ahab lost his life fighting the Aramaeans.

The Bible devotes six chapters to the life of this king. Much of it has been dismissed as legend, such as "the ivory house which he made" (I Kings 22:39); or his marriage to a Phoenician princess, who brought with her a strange religion: ". . . he took to wife Jezebel the daughter of Ethbaal king of the Zidonians, and went and served Baal and worshipped him . . . and made the Asherah. . . ." (I Kings 16:31, 33—R.V.); or the great drought in the land: "And Elijah . . . said unto Ahab: As the Lord, the God of Israel liveth, before whom I stand, there shall not be dew nor rain these years, but according to my word." (I Kings 17:1)

Nonetheless they are historical facts.

Two great assaults have been made on the old ruined mound of Samaria. The first campaign was led by George A. Reisner, Clarence S. Fisher, and D. G. Lyon, of Harvard University, from 1908 to 1910, the second excavation by an Anglo-American team under the British archaeologist J. W. Crowfoot from 1931 to 1935.

The foundations of Israel's capital rest on virgin soil. Omri had in fact acquired new land.

During the six years when he reigned there, this otherwise peaceful and lonely hill must have been one great bustling building site. The huge blocks of the strong fortifications make the strategic intention of the builder plain. The walls are fifteen feet thick. On the

Fig. 44. 1. "Cyclops" wall at Jericho (patriarchal age). 2. Wall of Saul's royal earth at Gibeah (1020 B.C.). 3. Wall of Solomon's "chariot city" of Megiddo (950 B.C.). 4. Wall of King Ahab's palace in Samaria (850 B.C.).

acropolis on the west side of the hill, foundations and walls of a building were exposed. This enclosed a wide courtyard and was the royal palace of the northern kingdom of Israel.

After Omri, Ahab his son, the new king, lived there. He continued building in accordance with his father's plans. The construction was carried out with remarkable skill, nothing but these huge, carefully dressed limestone blocks being used.

As the rubble was being carted off, the diggers very quickly noticed the innumerable splinters of ivory that it contained. Finds of ivory itself are nothing unusual in Palestinian excavation. On almost every site this expensive material is encountered, but always in isolated pieces; yet in Samaria the ground is literally covered with them. At every step, every square yard, they came across these yellowish-brown chips and flakes, as well as fragments that still showed the marvelous craftsmanship of these elegant reliefs carved by Phoenician masters.

There was only one explanation of these finds: this palace was the famous "ivory house" of King Ahab. (I Kings 22:39)

Obviously this monarch did not build his entire palace of ivory. Since this has, however, generally been assumed, the veracity of the Biblical passage has been questioned. It is now quite clear what happened: Ahab had the rooms of the palace decorated with this wonderful material and filled them with ivory furniture.

The proofs of the historical basis for the drought and for Ahab's father-in-law, Ethbaal of Sidon, were provided by Menander of Ephesus, a Phoenician historian. The Ethbaal of the Bible was called Ittobaal by the Phoenicians, and in Ahab's day he was king of the port of Tyre.[1] Meander records the catastrophic drought that set in throughout Palestine and Syria during the reign of Ittobaal and lasted a whole year.

Under King Jehoram, Ahab's son, Israel suffered an invasion which had terrible consequences and resulted in a considerable loss of territory.

The Aramaeans attacked them and besieged Samaria. A frightful famine racked the inhabitants. Jehoram, who held the prophet Elisha responsible for it, wanted to have him put to death. Elisha, however, prophesied that the famine would end on the following day. As the Bible records, "a lord, on whose hand

---

[1]The Biblical historians often used the term Sidonian to mean Phoenicians generally.

the king leaned" (II Kings 7:2) doubted this prophecy.

This "lord" has given rise to great discussions. His function appeared to be extremely mysterious. Nothing was known of any office of this sort. Biblical commentators sought in vain for some explanation. Eventually philologists found a slight clue. The Hebrew word "shlish," which has been translated as "lord," comes from the word for "three." But there was never a third-class officer. When Assyrian reliefs were examined more closely, the true explanation was found.

Every chariot was manned by three men: the driver, the fighter, and a man who stood behind them. With outstretched arms he held on to two short straps which were fastened to the right and left sides of the chariot. In this way he protected the warrior and the driver in the rear and prevented them from being thrown out during those furious sallies in battle when the open car passed over dead and wounded men. This then was the "third man." The inexplicable "lord, on whose hand the king leaned" was the strap hanger in King Jehoram's chariot.

Under Jehoram, Israel lost a large slice of territory east of the Jordan. Moab in Transjordan was a tributary state of Israel. There is a detailed account of a campaign against Mesha, the rebellious "mutton king": "And Mesha, king of Moab, was a sheepmaster, and rendered unto the king of Israel a hundred thousand lambs, and a hundred thousand rams, with the wool. But it came to pass, when Ahab was dead, that the king of Moab rebelled against the king of Israel." (II Kings 3:4, 5) Israel summoned to her aid the southern kingdom Judah and the land of Edom.

They decided to make a joint attack on Moab from the south. This meant going round the Dead Sea. Relying on the prophecy, "Ye shall not see wind, neither shall ye see rain: yet that valley shall be filled with water, that ye may drink, both ye, and your cattle and your beasts" (II Kings 3:17), the allies ventured to march through that desolate country. "And they fetched a compass of seven days' journey: and there was no water for the host, and for the cattle that followed them." On the advice of the prophet Elisha they made the valley "full of ditches." "And it came to pass in the morning, . . . behold, there came water by the way of Edom, and the country was filled with water." This was seen by spies from Moab, who "saw the water on the other side as red as blood" (II Kings 3:9, 16, 20, 22) and thought that the enemy were fighting among themselves.

The allied force was successful in Moab; they laid waste the land, "they beat down the cities, and on every good piece of land cast every man his stone, and filled it: and they stopped all the wells of water, and felled all the good trees: only in Kir-Haraseth left they the stones thereof." (II Kings 3:25)

Oddly enough the end of this successful campaign was "that they departed from him and returned to their own land." (II Kings 3:27)

It seemed impossible to check up on the accuracy of this Biblical story.

In 1868, F. A. Klein, a missionary from Alsace, was visiting Biblical sites in Palestine. The route he followed took him through Transjordan, through Edom, and eventually to Moab. As he was riding in the neighborhood of Diban, the ancient Dibon on the middle reaches of the Arnon, his attention was particularly aroused by a large smooth stone. The yellow sand had almost completely drifted over it. Klein jumped from his horse and bent over the stone curiously. It was unmistakably ancient Hebrew writing. He could hardly believe his eyes. It was as much as he could do in the heat of the midday sun to stand the heavy basalt stone upright. It was three feet high and rounded on top. Klein cleaned it carefully with a knife and a handkerchief. Thirty-four lines of writing appeared.

He would have preferred to take the stone document away with him, then and there, but it was far too heavy. Besides, in no time a mob of armed Arabs was on the spot. With wild gesticulations they surrounded the missionary, maintaining that the stone was their property and demanding from him a fantastic price for it.

Klein guessed that his discovery was an important

Fig. 45.

one and was in despair. Missionaries never have much money. He tried in vain to make the natives change their minds. There was nothing for it but to mark the site carefully on his map. He then gave up the idea of continuing his journey, hurried back to Jerusalem and from there straight home to Germany to try to collect the necessary money for the Arabs.

But in the meantime other people got busy, which was a good thing; otherwise, an extremely valuable piece of evidence for Biblical history might well have been lost forever.

A French scholar, Clermont-Ganneau, who was working in Jerusalem, had heard of the German missionary's discovery and had at once set out for Diban. It needed all his powers of persuasion to get the suspicious Arabs even to allow him to examine the writing on the basalt stone. Surrounded by the hostile eyes of the natives, Clermont-Ganneau took a squeeze of the surface. Months later when Parisian scholars had translated the text, the French government sanctioned the purchase without hesitation. But judge the Frenchman's disappointment when he reached Diban, equipped with a caravan and the necessary sum of money, and found that the stone had disappeared. Only a patch of soot indicated the spot where it had been. The Arabs had blown it to pieces with gunpowder— from avarice. They hoped to do a more profitable trade with Europeans whose obsession with antiquity would make them willing to buy the individual pieces.

What could Clermont-Ganneau do but set out on the trail of the individual pieces of the valuable document. After a great deal of trouble and searching, and after endless haggling, he was successful in retrieving some of the broken fragments. Two larger blocks and eighteen smaller pieces were reassembled and completed in accordance with the squeeze, and before Klein had even collected the necessary money, the impressive stone from Diban was standing among the valuable recent acquisitions in the Louvre in Paris.

This is what it says: "I am Mesha, son of Chemosh, king of Moab. . . . My father was king of Moab for thirty years and I became king after my father: and I built this sanctuary to Chemosh[1] in Qerihoh,[2] a sanctuary of refuge: for he saved me from all my op-

---

[1]God of Moab, worshiped also in Jerusalem among other foreign deities in the time of Solomon.

[2]The capital of Moab, the Kir-Haraseth of the Bible. (II Kings 3:25)

pressors and gave me dominion over all my enemies. Omri was king of Israel and oppressed Moab many days, for Chemosh was angry with his land. And his son succeeded him and he also said, I will oppress Moab. In my days he said this: but I got the upper-hand of him and his house: and Israel perished for ever. . . . I have had the ditches of Qerihoh dug by Israelite prisoners. . . ."

This Moabite victory message aroused considerable interest in learned circles. Many scholars did not conceal their suspicion that it was a forgery. International experts scrutinized the stone and its inscription. All the tests made it plain beyond doubt that this was in fact a historical document, a contemporary record of the King Mesha of Moab who is mentioned in the Bible.

It is also Palestine's oldest written document, dating from about 840 B.C., in Moabite dialect, which is closely related to Biblical Hebrew. That caused a real sensation.

Audiatur et altera pars: there are always two sides to a story.

If we want an objective picture, it is always advisable to study the war diaries of both opponents. There is then more likelihood of getting a clearer picture of the real situation. In this particular case, as it happens, the Biblical description and the Moabite text supplement each other admirably. The Mesha stele[1] adds the necessary color to the Biblical narrative and illumines its obscurity. The stele and the Bible agree on the decisive point, namely, that the campaign ended with the defeat of the Israelite king. The Bible describes at length the initial success of Israel, which King Mesha passes over in silence. The unfortunate outcome of the campaign is only briefly hinted at in the Bible, wheras the Moabite king revels in his victory. Both are telling the truth.

As far as the "bloody water" is concerned, which saved the Israelites from dying of thirst on their march through this barren country, a geologist found a nat-

---

[1] A "stele" in archaeology is an independent upright column or pillar; also a tombstone.

ural explanation. If trenches are dug in the tufa beside the Dead Sea, they fill up at once with water, which seeps through from the high plateau and owes its reddish color to the character of the soil. To this day shepherds in Transjordan often manufacture water holes in exactly the same manner.

"And Israel perished for ever," says the Mesha stele triumphantly. By this is meant the bloody extirpation of the dynasty of Omri from the throne of Israel. Jehoram was killed. Not one member was spared of the ruling house which had propagated the hated worship of Baal in Israel through King Ahab's marriage to the Phoenician princess Jezebel. (II Kings 9:24ff.; 10:11ff.)

Information about King Jehu's reign is scanty: "In those days the Lord began to cut Israel short: and Hazael smote them in all the coasts of Israel." (II Kings 10:32) The total extent of the losses in men and material first becomes plain in a passage about the reign of Jehoahaz, son of Jehu:[1] "Neither did he leave of the people to Jehoahaz but fifty horsemen, and ten chariots, and ten thousand footmen: for the king of Syria had destroyed them and had made them like the dust by threshing." (II Kings 13:7) Ahab's proud chariot corps was reduced from 2000 to 10. How could that have happened?

A young Englishman, Henry Layard, a lawyer by profession and attaché-elect at Constantinople, had an incredible stroke of luck as a novice in archaeology in 1845. With literally only £50 in his pocket, he had set out to excavate an old mound on the Tigris, Tell Nimrud. On the third day he came upon remains of a palace. He dug a trench, but nothing but masses and masses of sand came out of it. When the trench was twenty feet deep, Layard, to his great disappointment, had to stop work, as his money had run out.

He was feeling depressed as he loaded his few tools onto the pack mules, when excited cries from the natives made him pause. One of them ran up to him and got him to go and look at the end of the trench where

---

[1] 818-802 B.C.

something dark was showing up against the golden-yellow sand. Digging was hastily resumed and produced a huge pure-black stone in the shape of an obelisk. Layard tenderly cleaned the ancient dust and dirt off his find. And now he could see reliefs, pictures, and inscriptions in cuneiform writing on all four sides.

Well wrapped up and guarded like the apple of his eye the black stone sailed up the Tigris in one of the fragile riverboats to be presented to the more than somewhat astonished officials of the British Embassy in Constantinople. A meager £50 had produced unexpected dividends indeed. Never again in the history of archaeology would such a valuable find result from such a small investment.

Proudly the technicians cleared a fitting site for the stone in the British Museum. Thousands of Londoners and European scholars marveled at this ancient piece of evidence from the distant East. The tip of the six-foot obelisk of black basalt is in the shape of a three-tiered temple tower. Visitors gazed in astonishment at the wonderful reliefs displayed in five rows round the column.

Magnificently attired royal personages are chiseled out as in real life. Some of them prostrate themselves with their faces to the ground in front of a commanding figure. Long columns of bearers are laden with costly treasures, such as ivory tusks, bales of fringed fabrics borne on poles, pitchers and baskets full to the brim. Among the animals included can be observed an elephant with remarkably small ears: there are camels with two humps, apes, antelopes, even a wild bull and a mysterious unicorn.

Anyone trying to interpret the meaning of the reliefs was thrown back on pure conjecture, for at that time no one in the world could read cuneiform script. The stone remained mute. Even the scholars learned no more about the Assyrians than the Bible told them. At the beginning of the nineteenth century even the names Sumerian and Akkadian meant nothing. "One box, not more than three feet square," wrote Layard, "fitted with little inscribed cylinders, seals and textual

fragments, which could not even be systematically arranged, were at that time all that London knew of the
early period of Mesopotamian history."

It was only later, when the text had been translated,
that it transpired that the black obelisk was a victory
monument by the Assyrian king Shalmaneser III,[1] contemporary and adversary of King Ahab of Israel. It
celebrates an endless succession of bloody campaigns.
The enumeration of them contains an extremely interesting cross-reference to the Biblical tradition dealing with the period.

Three times, in the sixth, eleventh, and fourteenth
years of his reign, the Assyrian came up against a
coalition of kings of Syria and Palestine during his
victorious incursions into the West. In the campaign
in the eighteenth year of his reign, however, only one

Fig. 46. Tribute of King Jahu to Shalmaneser III.

king opposed him in this territory. The Assyrian texts
name as the adversary only King Hazael of Damascus
whom the Bible also mentions.

But the victory monument gives ample information
about the former ally of the King of Damascus, Jehu
of Israel.

The second row of the relief shows a long queue of
heavily laden envoys in richly ornamented tunics and

_____
[1]858-824 B.C.

peaked caps. The relevant text reads: "Tribute of Jaua of Bit-Humri: Silver, gold, a golden bowl, golden goblets, a golden beaker, pitchers of gold, lead, sceptres for the king and balsam-wood I received from him."

"Jaua of Bit-Humri" is none other than King Jehu of Israel. The Assyrians called Israel "Bit-Humri" which means "House of Omri."

This hint from the royal palace on the Tigris provides the key to our understanding of the losses that the northern kingdom of Israel sustained during the reign of Jehu.

Tribute is paid only by those who voluntarily surrender; a vanquished enemy supplies loot. Jehu had been disloyal to Damascus and had brought gifts to the Assyrians. For his faithlessness toward his old ally, for deserting Damascus, Jehu and his son Jehoahaz and most of all the people of Israel had to pay a bitter price. Hardly had the Assyrians turned their backs on Syria than Hazael of Damascus began to make a destructive onslaught on Israel in revenge. The result of it is described in the Bible: "In those days the Lord began to cut Israel short: and Hazael smote them in all the coasts of Israel . . . and made them like the dust by threshing."

"That lie upon beds of ivory, and stretch themselves upon their couches, and eat the lambs out of the flock, and the calves out of the midst of the stall: that chant to the sound of the viol, and invent to themselves instruments of music, like David; that drink wine in bowls and anoint themselves with the chief ointments . . . ." (Amos 6:4-6)

The fact that Assyria had, after Shalmaneser III, a succession of weak kings, allowed both kingdoms, Israel and Judah, another respite, which, however, meant only a postponement. Since Assyria was occupied with unrest in its own territory, Israel and Judah were able to enjoy a spell of peace from 825 to 745 B.C.

For forty years Uzziah, the leper, reigned as king of Judah. Israel was governed by Jeroboam II.[1] Under his

---

[1] 787-747 B.C.

long rule Israel flourished again, became rich, and wallowed in luxury; and the aristocracy lived for themselves and for the moment, effete, corrupt, and vicious. The prophet Amos raised his voice in warning. He lashed out at their unbridled love of pleasure.

Archaeological reports and dry accounts of expeditions shed a powerful light upon these prophetic warnings. In Israel, in and around the old mound of ruins that represented ancient Samaria, evidence that would indicate this materialism and luxury was lying dormant in the soil strata from the decades following 800 B.C. in the reign of Jeroboam II. The royal palace of Samaria contained a considerable number of elegant clay tablets inscribed with ink and paint. On sixty-three of these invoices for wine and oil that had been delivered at the Court, the senders are the managers of the crown lands of Jeroboam II, farmers and their employees, whose handwriting is extremely good.

From the same period come a number of beautifully carved ivories, some of which are expensively embellished with gold and semiprecious stones and ornamented with colorful powdered glass. They show mythological motifs borrowed from Egypt, such as Harpocrates on the lotus flower or figures of gods, like Isis and Horus, or cherubs. At that time all over Israel granaries and storehouses were being built to hold goods of all descriptions whose supply exceeded demand.

What was the reason for this sudden change? To what did they owe their new-found riches?

A few decades previously things had looked black for Israel. A sentence from the record of the forty-one-year reign of Jeroboam II contains the clue to the problem: "He restored the coast of Israel from the entering of Hamath unto the sea of the plain." (II Kings 14:25) The "sea of the plain" is the Dead Sea. Once again the kingdom stretched into Transjordan and, as in David's and Solomon's time, up to Syria.

About 800 B.C. the conquest of Damascus by the Assyrians had broken the power of the Aramaeans and thereby—it sounds as though fate were being ironical—cleared Israel's arch enemy out of the way.

Fig. 47. Nobleman's house at Megiddo during the monarchy (Reconstruction).

Israel seized the opportunity to reconquer long-lost territory and exploited the situation to its own advantage. The tribute exacted from Transjordan proved a source of new wealth for Israel.

Evidence of a similar period of peace and prosperity in the southern kingdom of Judah has recently come to hand. Professor Michael Evenari, vice president of the Hebrew University, discovered in 1958 traces of several Judaean farms equipped with cisterns, irrigation systems, and fortifications, far south in the arid Negeb near Mizpeh Ramon. The finds date from the reign of Uzziah, king of Judah. We are specifically told in II Chron. 26:10 that this king "built towers in the desert and digged many wells; for he had much cattle . . ."

In 1959 Professor Aharoni of the Hebrew University was the first to discover a Judaean palace two miles south of Jerusalem. On Rachel's hill on the road to Bethlehem, at the spot where, according to tradition, Mary and Joseph on their way to Bethlehem "to be taxed" refreshed themselves at the spring, the site of a large castle was excavated, 250 feet by 150 feet square, and dating from the eighth century B.C. It had been surrounded by a casemated wall like that of King Ahab in Samaria and had a triple gate in the style of Solomon's day. Three sides of the courtyard were surrounded by buildings, two sides residential and the third for stores. When the excavators asked themselves the question as to who could have been the builder and the first tenant of this lordly rural demesne they were given only one hint: "And Uzziah the king was a leper unto the day of his death, and dwelt in a several house, being a leper; for he was cut off from the house of the Lord." (II Chron. 26:21)

Individual items removed from the palace rubble indicate how right the prophets were in their condemnation. Several symbols of Astarte witness to the "idolatry" that went on in this princely home. (II Kings 15:4)

Harsh and full of foreboding in these days of pseudo prosperity ring out the prophetic words of Amos: "Woe . . . to them, that trust in the mountain of Samaria, . . . ye that put far away the evil day and cause the seal of violence to come near: . . . Therefore now shall they go captive with the first that go captive and the banquet of them that stretched themselves shall be removed." (Amos 6:1, 3, 7) But in vain. They fall upon deaf ears. Only King Jeroboam cannot have had much faith in the peace, perhaps because the words of the prophet found an echo in his heart. At all events he feverishly set about strengthening the defenses of the royal city of Samaria, which were in any case sufficiently forbidding.

J. W. Crowfoot, the English archaeologist, found what Jeroboam in his wisdom and foresight had achieved. Samaria had been surrounded with a double wall, and the existing walls, which were already massive, had been further strengthened. In the northern section of the acropolis, where Samaria must have been most vulnerable, Crowfoot exposed a titanesque bastion. He measured it and was certain he must have made a mistake. He measured it carefully once more. No doubt about it, the wall—solid stone through and through—was thirty feet thick.

*Pul the soldier becomes Tiglath-Pileser III—King Pekah
mentioned at Hazor—Assyrian governors over Israel—
Samaria's three-year defiance—Consul Botta looks for
Nineveh—The bourgeois king opens the first Assyrian
museum—Searching for evidence by moonlight—The library of Ashurbanipal—Deportation of a people*

AND PUL THE KING OF ASSYRIA CAME AGAINST THE
LAND. (II Kings 15:19)

Concise, sober, and dispassionate, these words an-
nounce the end of the northern kingdom. The death
of Jeroboam II introduced the last act. In the same year,
747 B.C., the leprous King Uzziah of Judah also died.
In the short intervening period during which anarchy
reigned Menahem made himself king at Samaria. In
745 B.C. a former soldier, by name Pul, had ascended
the throne of Assyria and from then on was known
as Tiglath-Pileser III.[1] He was the first of a succession
of brutal tyrants who conquered what was so far
the greatest empire of the ancient East. Their goal was
Syria, Palestine, and the last cornerstone of the old
world, Egypt. That meant that both Israel and Judah
were caught between the pitiless millstones of a military
state, for which the word peace had a contemptible
sound, whose despots and cohorts had only three values:
marching, conquering, oppressing.

From North Syria Tiglath-Pileser III swept through
the Mediterranean countries and forced independent
peoples to become provinces and tributaries of the
Assyrian Empire. Israel at first submitted voluntarily:
"And Menahem gave Pul[2] a thousand talents of silver,
that his hand might be with him, to confirm the kingdom in his hand. And Menahem exacted the money

[1]745-727 B.C.
[2]Tiglath-Pileser III.

of Israel, even of all the mighty men of wealth, of each man fifty shekels of silver, to give to the king of Assyria so the king of Assyria turned back, and stayed not there in the land." (II Kings 15:19, 20) "I received tribute from Menahem of Samaria," noted Tiglath-Pileser III in his annals.

One thousand talents correspond to 6 million gold sovereigns; 50 shekels per head from the "men of wealth" amounted to 100 gold sovereigns each. Economists and statisticians will gather that there must have been 60,000 well-to-do people in Israel.

King Menahem entertained the illusion that a pact with the tyrant and voluntary tribute would be the lesser of two evils. But the result was bad blood among his own people. Anger at the Assyrian taxes found an outlet in conspiracy and murder. Pekah, an army officer, murdered Menahem's son and heir and ascended the throne. From then on, the anti-Assyrian party was the determining factor in the policy of the northern kingdom.

Rezin, King of Damascus, powerfully grasped the initiative. Under his leadership the defensive league of

Fig. 48. Tiglath-Pileser III (with bow and sword) be-sieging a fortress. Battering rams pound the walls. Impaled victims in background.

the Aramaean states against Assyria came to life again. Phoenician and Arabian states, Philistine cities, and Edomites joined the alliance. Israel, too, took its place in the federation. Only King Ahaz of Judah remained obstinately outside. Rezin and Pekah tried to force Judah into the league violently. "Then Rezin, king of Syria, and Pekah son of Remaliah king of Israel, came up to Jerusalem to war: and they besieged Ahaz, but could not overcome him." (II Kings 16:5)

In dire straits the King of Judah sent out an SOS. "So Ahaz sent messengers to Tiglath-Pileser king of Assyria, saying, I am thy servant, and thy son: come up and save me out of the hand of the king of Syria, and out of the hand of the king of Israel, which rise up against me. And Ahaz took the silver and gold that was found in the house of the Lord, and in the treasures of the king's house, and sent it for a present to the king of Assyria." (II Kings 16:7, 8) "I received tribute from Jauhazi (Ahaz) of Judah," observed the Assyrian once more.

Now events took their disastrous course. For our knowledge of further developments we are indebted to two great historical records: first, the Bible, and second, the cuneiform tablets of stone and clay on which, over 600 miles from where the terrible events took place, the military developments were officially recorded. For more than two and a half millennia these documents lay in the magnificent palaces on the Tigris until scholars ran them to earth and translated them into our tongue. They make it plain once more in quite a unique way how true to history are the contents of these Biblical stories.

The Bible and the Assyrian monuments are in entire agreement in their description of these events which were fatal for the northern kingdom. The Old Testament historian notes down the facts soberly, the Assyrian chronicler records every brutal detail:

Second Book of Kings	Cuneiform Text of Tiglath-Pileser III
"The king of Assyria went up against Damascus, and took	"His noblemen I impaled alive and displayed this ex-

it, and carried the people of it captive to Kir, and slew Rezin." (II Kings 16:9)

hibition to his land. All his gardens and fruit orchards I destroyed. I besieged and captured the native city of Reson (Rezin) of Damascus. Eight hundred people with their belongings I led away. Towns in sixteen districts of Damascus I laid waste like mounds after the Flood." (From: Western Campaign, 734-733 B.C.)

"In the days of Pekah king of Israel came Tiglath-Pileser king of Assyria and took . . . Hazor and Gilead and Galilee, all the land of Naphtali, and carried them captive to Assyria." (II Kings 15:29)

"Bet-Omri (Israel) all of whose cities I had added to my territories on my former campaigns, and had left out only the city of Samaria. . . . The whole of Naphtali I took for Assyria. I put my officials over them as governors. The land of Bet-Omri, all its people and their possessions I took away to Assyria." (From: Western Campaign and Gaza-Damascus Campaign, 734-733 B.C.)

"And Hoshea . . . made a conspiracy against Pekah . . . and slew him and reigned in his stead." (II Kings 15:30)

"They overthrew Pekah their king and I made Hoshea to be king over them." (From: Gaza-Damascus Campaign.)

Somber evidence of the capture of Hazor by Tiglath-Pileser III, king of Assyria (II Kings 15:29), has been supplied by a layer of rubble at Tell el-Qedah in Israel. In the course of the most recent excavations by archaeologists from the Hebrew University, traces came to light of the shattered Israelite fortress which had been rebuilt during the monarchy for defense purposes by Solomon and Ahab on the site of the old Canaanite fort which had been conquered by Joshua. The strength of the keep with its six-foot-thick walls was such that it was only surpassed by the famous royal palace at Samaria, now likewise rediscovered.

The apartments in the castle at Hazor were covered by a layer of ashes three feet thick, the stones were blackened with smoke, charred beams and fragments of what had been at one time paneled ceilings lay scattered about the ground. By exercising the utmost care the archaeologists were able to salvage from the piles of rubble some precious examples of the arts and crafts of northern Israel: a statuette of a well-groomed young woman and a marble incense-spoon. The greatest thrill was to find among the fragments of broken pottery the name of king Pekah himself, written in old Semitic script. This was the first written evidence of an Israelite king in Galilee.

When the armed hordes of Assyrians withdrew from Palestine they left Israel mortally wounded, smashed to the ground, decimated by deportation, beaten back into a tiny corner of the northern kingdom. With the exception of Samaria, all its cities had been annexed, and the country had been divided into provinces over which Assyrian governors and officials exercised strict control.

All that was left of Israel was a dwarf state, a tiny pinpoint on the map: the mountain of Ephraim with the royal city of Samaria. There lived King Hoshea.

The southern kingdom of Judah still remained free from foreign domination—for the time being. But it had to pay tribute to Tiglath-Phileser III.

The warlike Assyrian colossus had enclosed in his mighty grip the whole of the Fertile Crescent, from the shores of the Persian Gulf, from the mountains of Persia to Asia Minor, from the Mesopotamian plain through Lebanon and Anti-Lebanon as far as Palestine. Alone, away to the southwest, the twenty-acre royal city of Samaria, with its few square miles of hinterland, which provided it with corn and barley, was unsubdued.

From this corner a gauntlet of defiance flew through the air to land at Assyria's feet.

After the death of Tiglath-Pileser III, Hoshea conspired with Egypt. He refused to pay his annual tribute to Assyria. Shalmaneser V,[1] the successor of Tiglath-Pileser III, at once struck back, for when he "found conspiracy in Hoshea: for he had sent messengers to So[2] king of Eygpt, and brought no present to the king of Assyria, as he had done year by year: therefore the king of Assyria shut him up and bound him in prison." (II Kings 17:4) Part of the organization of the hated reign of terror, even in those days, was a widespread net of informers and spies.

With the fall of Samaria the last remnant of the northern kingdom of Israel suffered the fate of Damascus. ". . . in the ninth year of Hoshea the king of Assyria took Samaria and carried Israel away into Assyria." (II Kings 17:6)

For three years the little mountain fortress withstood the deadly pressure of superior forces with the courage of a lion. (II Kings 17:5)

Cuneiform texts record that Shalmaneser V died unexpectedly during the siege of Samaria. His successor, Sargon II,[3] nevertheless continued the attack. "In the first year of my reign," boasted Sargon in his annals, "I besieged and conquered Samaria. . . . I led away into captivity 27,290 people who lived there."

The discovery of the Sargon inscriptions over a hundred years ago is like a romantic tale from the fabulous land of the caliphs. Nonetheless it is a milestone in our knowledge of the ancient world, for it marked the birth of Assyriology, which by its sensational discoveries has for the first time given many Biblical narratives a genuine historical content.

The motor car had not been invented; electric light was still unknown; no steel frames of derricks towered out of the sand flats by the Tigris; Mosul still wore the colorful variegated garb of a city from the *Arabian Nights*. Bazaars, harems, and a real live caliph were all there. It was the heart of the ancient Orient

---

[1] 727-722 B.C.
[2] So=Sewe, ruler of Egypt, called Sib'e by the Assyrians.
[3] 721-705 B.C.

and the year was 1840. Summer lay like a red-hot breath over the city with its elegant white minarets and its narrow, dirty, muddy alleyways.

For a European the heat was enervating and unbearable. Paul-Émile Botta, the New French consular agent, escaped from the incubator as often as he could to take a ride by the Tigris and breathe fresher air. But soon certain desolate mounds on the other side of the river began to fascinate him more. Admittedly they had nothing to do with the routine duties of a consular agent, but M. Botta was a scholar. He had been carefully following an academic dispute which had broken out over the Biblical name Nineveh. No one could say with any certainty where this city lay in olden times. It was a case of one surmise being as good as another. One suggestion pointed in the direction of Mosul. In the coarse of his wanderings among the yellow-brown sand hills on the far side of the river, Botta had repeatedly noticed fragments of bricks. They were only plain-looking, uncommunicative fragments. Nevertheless, he mentioned them in a letter to Paris. In reply came a letter from M. Mohl, Secretary to the Société Asiatique. It encouraged him to examine the terrain a little more closely.

Out of his own pocket Botta hired a gang of natives. In the typical round Tigris boats, they headed upriver toward the mounds and prepared to excavate. This first attempt of a modern European to come to grips with ancient Nineveh and wrest its secrets from it failed to achieve the desired result. Botta ordered digging to begin on several slopes. Several weeks passed as the work went busily on. But the result was precisely nothing. Botta saw his money being expended to no purpose and brought his private expedition, which had been started with such enthusiasm, to a disappointing end.

Perhaps he might have kept his hands off any further researches in this area except that he heard something which spurred him to new activity. In the village of Khorsabad, seven miles to the north, Arabs working in the fields were said to have found great pillars. In the early part of March, 1842, Botta and his workers were on the spot. They began to excavate, and on the same day they struck stone work, apparently the inner walls of a large building.

Botta was highly delighted, although at that moment he had no idea that he was responsible for an historic event of the greatest importance for scholarship. The stonework was part of the first of the gigantic Assyrian palaces that, after lying dormant for thousands of years, were now to come to light. It was the birth of Assyriology. And the first thing that this new science got involved in was, as we shall see in a moment, an erroneous idea.

Once again French scholarship displayed in this case sound judgment. The Académie des Inscriptions, which Botta informed at once, saw to it that the government placed funds at his disposal. It was, to begin with, no vast amount of money, but gold francs were still worth something in the East. The sultan gave the required permission for excavation.

But on the site itself Botta had to endure unimaginable difficulties arising from the extremely underhanded dealings of the local authorities in Mosul. At one moment the trenches came under suspicion as be-

Fig. 49. Ruins of the royal homes of Assyrian monarchs on the Tigris.

ing military defenses; at another the primitive shelters of the members of the excavations were suspected of being army bivouacs. It seemed that by every possible means the great excavation was to be thwarted. More than once Botta had to send an SOS to Paris and to invoke the aid of the French diplomatic service.

Despite all this, sections of a huge palace were liberated from the sand at Khorsabad.

Eugène N. Flandin, a well-known Paris artist, who specialized in antiquities, had been given the assignment by the Louvre which nowadays falls on the official photographer of any expedition. His pencil reproduced accurately on paper all that the ground yielded up. The drawings were collected into a handsome folio, and the large volume was adorned with the proud title *Le Monument de Ninive*. For Botta was convinced that he had found the Biblical city of Nineveh at Khorsabad. And that was where he was wrong.

If he had only dug a few inches deeper into the mounds opposite Mosul, where two years earlier he had given up the apparently hopeless task in disgust, he would in fact have made the discovery of his life. As it happened the credit for discovering Nineveh went to Henry Layard, who at the instigation of the British government commenced digging in 1845 at the very spot where Botta had given up. At the first spadeful, so to speak, he came upon the walls of one of the great palaces of Nineveh.

What Botta had excavated at Khorsabad was the great castle of Sargon, the home of Sargon II, King of Assyria. But that did not emerge until later. If Botta had been able to read the tablets that were salvaged at Khorsabad, he would never have made his mistake. "Dur-Sharrukin," Castle of Sargon, was written there in cuneiform, which at that time, 1842, had not yet been completely deciphered. The key to its translation was not agreed on until fifteen years later.

In 1857 Rawlinson and Hincks in England and Oppert in France independently of each other produced translations of a piece of text that corresponded exactly.

With that the correct interpretation of Assyrian script was assured.

In October, 1844, the tablets salvaged by Botta containing reliefs and historical texts, as well as statues and sections of pillars, started out on an adventurous journey. From Khorsabad the precious cargo rocked its way down the Tigris on skiffs and rafts. At Basra on the Persian Gulf the valuable freight was transferred to the "Cormoran," which conveyed it to Europe. It made a great sensation in Paris and evoked as lively an interest among the general public as among the scholars.

On May 1, 1847, in the splendid galleries of the Louvre designed by Percier and Fontaine, Louis Philippe, the bourgeois king, handed over to the public with impressive ceremony this collection which contained the earliest evidence from the realm of Biblical story. With that the first Assyrian museum in the world had been founded.

The mounds of old Nineveh, however, provided the modern world with its most extensive collection of information about ancient times. The story of this discovery left a bitter taste in French mouths. When the British began their diggings, the French had also staked a claim on a section of the mounds.

In the British excavation area a vast palace had come to light which had been identified as the historic Nineveh of the Bible. But what might still be lying hidden over there in the French sector? Rassam, one of the members of the British party, decided to take time by the forelock. He took advantage of the absence of his chief, Rawlinson, leader of the expedition, and of the presence of a full moon to make a purposeful excursion into the French reservation. At the first stroke he came upon the palace of Ashurbanipal with the famous library belonging to that monarch, which was, indeed, the most famous in the whole of the ancient Orient. Thus, 22,000 cuneiform tablets found their way into the British Museum.

They contained the essential material for understanding the historical and intellectual background of

Mesopotamia, its peoples, its kingdoms with their arts and crafts, cultures and religions. Among them were the Sumerian flood story and the epic of Gilgamesh.

What had been until then a mysterious, sealed chapter of our world's history was suddenly opened, and page after page was turned over. Rulers, cities, wars, and stories that people had only heard about through the Old Testament revealed themselves as real facts.

We must include among these the city of Erech which is described in the tenth chapter of Genesis as part of the kingdom of Nimrod, the "mighty hunter before the Lord." About fifty miles to the northwest of Ur of the Chaldees, Professor H. J. Lenzen has been directing excavations which have continued from 1928 to the present day. From a pile of ruins, which the Arabs call Warka, he has produced impressive evidence of the ancient city of Uruk, as Erech is styled in the cuneiform texts, including written tablets which go back to the fourth and third millennium B.C. In the course of his investigations the German archaeologist came across the remains of walls which could be credited to the legendary king Gilgamesh. Over five miles in length they afforded their protection to this ancient Biblical city.

Meanwhile, the original starting point of all these exciting investigations and discoveries had long been forgotten. But if it had not been for the Bible perhaps the quest would never have begun.

About the middle of the last century, Nineveh, Sargon's castle, and, at Tell Nimrud, the Calah of Genesis which Nimrod built (Gen. 10:11) were all discovered. But it was several decades before the enormous quantity of cuneiform texts was deciphered, translated, and made available to a wider circle. It was not until the turn of the century that several comprehensive scholarly works appeared, containing translations of some of the texts, including the annals of Assyrian rulers well known to readers of the Old Testament, Tiglath-Pileser or Pul, Sargon, Sennacherib, and Esarhaddon.

Since then these works have become essential features of all national libraries, as well as of universities and colleges, a unique mine of information eagerly studied and used by historians, Assyriologists, and theological students—all of them people with a professional interest. But who else reads them or knows about them? Yet they could easily, even taking the reliefs alone, provide a large, clearly illustrated commentary on the Bible.

The Assyrian documents contain a wealth of interesting and informative details which corroborate the historical truth of the Bible. Botta found in Sargon's castle at Khorsabad his reports on his campaigns in Syria and Palestine and his capture of Samaria in Israel.

". . . in the first year of my reign I besieged and conquered Samaria." Sargon II reigned from 721 to 705 B.C. According to that the northern kingdom of Israel collapsed in 721 B.C. (II Kings 17:6)

"People of the lands, prisoners my hand had captured, I settled there. My officials I placed over them as governors. I imposed tribute and tax upon them, as upon the Assyrians." So reads the account of the conquest of Samaria in the annals. The Old Testament describes the uprooting tactics employed in this case, too, by ruthless dictators, the first large-scale experiment of its kind in the world made by the Assyrians: "And the king of Assyria brought men from Babylon, and from Cuthah, and from Ava, and from Hamath, and from Sepharvaim, and placed them in the cities of Samaria, instead of the children of Israel: and they possessed Samaria, and dwelt in the cities thereof." (II Kings 17:24)

Tens of thousands of human beings were violently driven from their homeland, deported to foreign lands, and their places filled by others dragged from different areas. The aim of this was clear. National consciousness, and with it the will to resist, was to be broken. The Fertile Crescent was plowed up, its peoples tossed about hither and thither. Instead of a varied range of races and religions existing side by side, the result was a jumble.

Samaria shared this fate. Its motley collection of inhabitants became known as "Samaritans." "Samaritans" became a term of abuse, an expression of abhorrence. They were despised not only on religious grounds but also as individuals: "For the Jews have no dealings with the Samaritans." (John 4:9) It was only when Jesus told the story of the good Samaritan that he turned this term of abuse into a byword for practical Christian charity. (Luke 10:30ff.)

The people of the northern kingdom and their kings with them disappeared, were absorbed into the population of these foreign lands, and never emerged again in history. All investigation into what became of the ten tribes who had their home there has so far come to nothing.

CHAPTER 3 / Judah Under the Yoke
of Assyria

*Hopes aroused by Sargon's death—A fig poultice cures
King Hezekiah—A well-tried ancient eastern remedy—
Merodach-Baladan, gardener and rebel—Secret armaments
in Judah—Aqueduct through the rocks of Jerusalem—
Inscription describes Hezekiah's tunnel—The fate of
Lachish in stone relief—Traces of Assyrian battering rams
in the ruins—A puzzling retreat—Herodotus' story of the
king with the mouse—Starkey finds a plague grave—Sennacherib describes the siege of Jerusalem*

THEREFORE I WILL WAIL AND HOWL, I WILL GO
STRIPPED AND NAKED: I WILL MAKE A WAILING LIKE
THE DRAGONS, AND MOURNING AS THE OWLS. FOR
HER [THAT IS, SAMARIA'S] WOUND IS INCURABLE: FOR
IT IS COME UNTO JUDAH: HE IS COME UNTO THE
GATE OF MY PEOPLE, EVEN TO JERUSALEM. (Micah
1:8-9)

In Judah there may have been some who rejoiced at
the downfall of their hostile brother. The prophet
Micah, however, was overwhelmed with grief and
filled with deep anxiety at the news. He guessed that
the blow that had crushed Samaria would one day
strike the people of Judah and the city of Jerusalem.
At that time Hezekiah was King of Judah,[1] "and he did
that which was right in the sight of the Lord." (II
Kings 18:3) Since the father of Hezekiah had voluntarily submitted to Tiglath-Pileser III in 733 B.C.,
Judah had been a dependent vassal state, whose deliveries of tribute were carefully noted in Nineveh.
Hezekiah was not prepared to follow in his father's
footsteps. The reaction set in when he came to the
throne. "He rebelled against the king of Assyria." (II
Kings 18:7)
Hezekiah was no hothead, but a clever, cool, cal-

[1]725-697 B.C.

Fig. 50.

culating, and farsighted man. He knew very well that what he was about was a highly dangerous and risky business for himself and his people. Only thirty miles from Jerusalem the Assyrian governor of Samaria was sitting eyeing him with suspicion. One careless step, a nod to Nineveh, and Hezekiah would find himself off his throne and clapped in irons. He merely held the throne in fee. Hezekiah proceeded with the utmost caution, "and he prospered, whithersoever he went forth." (II Kings 18:7)

In the Philistine city-state of Ashdod which was oppressed in the same way, anti-Assyrian riots broke out. That brought into being a league against the tyrant on the Tigris.[1] Hezekiah saw a chance to further his plan.

[1] 713 B.C.

He showed his sympathy but remained officially aloof and intrigued behind the scenes.

Jerusalem had at this time visitors from overseas, tall personages from "beyond the rivers of Ethiopia." (Isa. 18:1) These were Ethiopian envoys. The King of Egypt at that point was Shabaka, a Pharaoh from Ethiopia. The Assyrians replied to the riots in Ashdod with armed force. A "turtanu," a field marshal, appeared on the scene with an army. "In the year that Tartan came unto Ashdod (when Sargon the king of Assyria sent him) and fought against Ashdod and took it. . . ." (Isa. 20:1)

On the walls of Sargon's castle the court chroniclers describe the carrying out of this punitive expedition as follows: "Ashdod . . . I besieged and conquered. . . . its gods, its women, its sons, its daughters, its goods and chattels, the treasures of its palace, and all the people of its territory I counted as plunder. I settled those cities anew. . . ."

Fig. 51. King Sargon II of Assyria with his Tartan (relief from Khorsabad).

The anti-Assyrian league had gone to pieces on the approach of the Assyrians. Ashdod's territory became an Assyrian province.

Nothing happened to Hezekiah, although his name was on the black list. Assyrian informers had seen through his game and had given Sargon II full details of Hezekiah's secret dealings with Egypt, as can be seen from the text of a fragment of a prism: "Philistia, Judah, Edom and Moab, who planned hostilities, infamies without number . . . who, in order to prejudice him against me and make him my enemy, brought gifts in homage to Pharaoh, king of the land of Egypt . . . and begged him to form an alliance. . . ."

In 705 B.C. news spread like wildfire raising at once fresh hopes of liberation from the Assyrian yoke— Sargon had been murdered! All over the Fertile Crescent, in the Assyrian provinces and in the vassal states, conspiracies, discussions, and intrigues began.

"In those days was Hezekiah sick unto death." (II Kings 20:1) Happening precisely at this moment of feverish political activity, it was a grave handicap. For many states in Syria and Palestine were looking expectantly to the able king of Judah.

How could Hezekiah be cured of his serious illness? "And Isaiah said, Take a lump of figs, And they took and laid it on the boil, and he recovered." (II Kings 20:7)

The course of histoy is often rich in remarkable parallels and associations. So it is in the case of this Biblical therapy.

In the north Syrian harbor of Ras Shamra, French excavators in 1939, digging among the ruins of the Phoenician seaport of Ugarit, came upon fragments of an old book of veterinary science, which contained prescriptions for the treatment of sick and ailing horses. The captain of the household cavalry of the King of Ugarit had, about 1500 B.C., entered in it tried remedies of this sort: "If a horse has a sore nose, prepare a salve from figs and raisins, mixed with oatmeal and liquid. The mixture should be poured into the horses's nostrils."

For every kind of sickness there is a very detailed prescription. The chief medicaments are plants and fruit, such as mustard and liquorice juice. Advice is even given on how to deal with horses that bite and neigh too much. Does any modern breeder or owner of horses know how to cure that? In those days a neighing horse could in certain circumstances be fatal. Horses were used exclusively for fighting and hunting. A troop of chariots, however well hidden in an ambush, could be betrayed by a sudden loud neighing. It was the same in hunting.

These recognized cures have been tried out succesfully from time immemorial by the people of the ancient Orient. They are nature's remedies which can also be profitably used in the case of human beings. One of them, which is particularly recommended in the veterinary manual, is "Debelah," a sort of poultice of compressed figs. It was a "Debelah" that the prophet prescribed for Hezekiah's abscess. It worked, and he was all right again in three days.

Many of these tried remedies dating back to Biblical times and largely consisting of ingredients supplied by Mother Nature have been either lost or forgotten in the whirligig of time. Many of them on the other hand have been quietly passed on from generation to generation. This prescription for figs is one of them. Swiss doctors still prescribe finely chopped figs steamed in milk for certain kinds of abscesses. An Arabic remedy reminds us of the "Debelah": a thick sticky liquid made from grapejuice is called "Dibis" in the native tongue.

"At that time Berodach-Baladan,[1] the son of Baladan king of Babylon, sent letters and a present unto Hezekiah: for he had heard that Hezekiah had been sick." (II Kings 20:12) This was the traditional practice in court circles and was part of the royal etiquette in the ancient East. Presents were sent and enquiries and made about the health of "our brother." The clay tablets of El-Amarna mention the habit frequently.

Merodach-Baladan,[2] however, found Hezekiah's illness a convenient pretext for making contact with him. The real reason for his polite courtesies lay in the field of high-level politics.

"Merodach-Baladan, king of Babylon," was for a long time a mysterious personage both to readers of the Bible and to scholars. It is now quite certain that

---

[1] Here wrongly spelled Berodach-Baladan. Isaiah (39:1) spells it correctly Merodach-Baladan.

[2] Marduk-Aplaiddin in Babylonian.

he was in his own day an extremely important person. We even know something about his private habits. He was, for example, a great gardener, not in the sense of being keen to lay out handsome royal parks, but with a real down-to-earth interest in the vegetables and fruits of Mesopotamia, whether it was endives, beetroot, cucumbers, thyme, coriander, saffron, peaches, or medlars. He described the various types of plants and how to cultivate them and was in fact the author of a practical handbook on vegetable gardens, as archaeologists discovered with no little astonishment.

Apart from his private hobby of gardening, Merodach-Baladan both as a king and as a Babylonian was the most bitter and determined opponent of Nineveh. No other monarch in the Fertile Crescent attacked the Assyrians so vigorously over many years, engaged them in so many heated battles, or intrigued so unremittingly against the tyrants of the Tigris, as he did.

The assassination of Sargon brought Merodach-Baladan into the field. It was at this point that his ambassadors visited Hezekiah. What was in fact discussed on the occasion of the official visit during the convalescence of Hezekiah can be read between the lines: "And Hezekiah hearkened unto them, and showed them all the house of his precious things . . . and all the house of his armour." (II Kings 20:13) Judah's arsenal. Secret armaments and feverish preparations for D-day, the great showdown with Assyria which they saw to be imminent, were in full swing. "Also . . . he built up all the wall that was broken, and raised it up to the towers, and another wall without, and repaired Millo in the city of David, and made darts and shields in abundance." (II Chron. 32:5)

Jerusalem's defenses were overhauled and strengthened for a long siege; the old perimeter wall was renewed, breaches repaired, and turrets erected. On the north side of the city, its most vulnerable point, a second outer wall was added. Hezekiah even pulled down houses to make room for it. (Isa. 22:10) But that did not exhaust his precautions. "And the rest of the acts of Hezekiah, and all his might, and how he

Fig. 52. King Hezekiah's great tunnel of Siloam in Jerusalem.

made a pool, and a conduit, and brought water into the city, are they not written in the book of the Chronicles of the kings of Judah?" (II Kings 20:20) The chronicler completes the story: "The same Hezekiah also stopped the upper water course of Gihon, and brought it straight down to the west side of the city of David. . . ." (II Chron. 32:30)

Jerusalem, the old city of David, has many mysterious corners. Pilgrims from all over the world, travelers of three faiths, Christians, Jews, Mohammedans, come to pay homage at its holy places. Seldom does one of this endless stream of visitors stumble upon the dark depressing spot outside the walls, far below the noisy streets of the city, which bears eloquent testimony to one of the most dire moments in its ancient story, to a time fraught with fear and menace. This spot had sunk into oblivion. In 1880 it was discovered by a fluke. It still bears as plain as day all the marks of feverish haste.

Outside the city, where its southeastern slopes sweep gently down to the Valley of the Kidron, lies a small still sheet of water, enclosed by walls, the Pool of Siloam. Two Arab boys were playing there—one of them fell in. Paddling for all he was worth, he landed on the other side, where a rock wall rose above the pool. Suddenly it was pitch black all round him. He groped about anxiously and discovered a small passage.

The name of the Arab boy was forgotten but not his story. It was followed up and a long underground tunnel was discovered. A narrow passage about two feet wide and barely five feet high had been cut through the limestone. It can be negotiated only with rubber boots and a slight stoop. For about 500 yards the passage winds imperceptibly uphill. It ends at the Virgin's Fountain, Jerusalem's water supply since ancient times. In Biblical days it was called the Fountain of Gihon.

As experts were examining the passage, they noticed by the light of their torches old Hebrew letters on the wall. The inscription, which was scratched on the rock only a few paces from the entrance at the Pool of Siloam, reads as follows: "The boring through is completed. And this is the story of the boring: while yet they plied the pick, each toward his fellow, and while yet there were three cubits to be bored through, there was heard the voice of one calling to the other that there was a hole in the rock on the right hand and on the left hand. And on the day of the boring through the workers in the tunnel struck each to meet his fellow, pick upon pick. Then the water poured from the source to the pool twelve hundred cubits, and a hundred cubits was the height of the rock above the heads of the workers in the tunnel."

The Turkish government had the inscription prized out before the First World War. It is now exhibited in the museum at Istanbul.

It was Hezekiah's aqueduct.

During a siege the first problem is that of providing drinking water. The founders of Jerusalem, the Jebusites, had sunk a shaft down through the rock to the fountain of Gihon. Hezekiah directed its water, which would otherwise have flowed into the Kidron Valley, through the mountain to the west side of the city. The Pool of Siloam lies inside the second perimeter wall which he constructed.

There was no time to lose. Assyrian troops could be at the gates of Jerusalem overnight. The workmen therefore tackled the tunnel from both ends. The marks of the pickaxes point toward each other, as the inscription describes.

𐤀𐤒𐤏𐤂 · 𐤀𐤂𐤒𐤉𐤀 · 𐤒𐤂𐤀 · 𐤀𐤓𐤀𐤀𐤄𐤟𐤉 · 𐤀𐤂𐤒𐤉𐤀

Fig. 53. ". . . the boring through. And this is the story of the boring through: while yet . . ." (Beginning of the Siloam inscription.)

Oddly enough the canal takes an S-shaped course through the rock. Why did the workmen not dig this underground tunnel the shortest way to meet each other, that is, in a straight line? The wretched job would have been finished quicker, and 700 feet of hard work would have been saved out of the total 1700 feet.

Locally, there is an old story which has been handed down which claims to explain why they had to go the long way around. Deep in the rock, between the spring and the pool are supposed to lie the graves of David and Solomon. Archaeologists took this remarkable piece of folklore seriously and systematically tapped the walls of the narrow, damp tunnel. They sank shafts into the rock from the summit. But they found nothing.

"Now in the fourteenth[1] year of king Hezekiah did Sennacherib king of Assyria come up against all the fenced cities of Judah and took them." (II Kings 18: 13)

The states of Syria and Palestine took defensive measures. The Assyrian governors were expelled. A strong league was formed. The kings of Askelon and Ekron joined up with Hezekiah, and Egypt promised help in case of military developments.

Naturally the new Assyrian ruler Sennacherib[2] was

---

[1] Biblical chronology is out here by ten years; it was the twenty-fourth year.

[2] 705-681 B.C.

not unaware of all this. But his hands were tied. After the assassination of his predecessor, Sargon, the eastern part of his empire revolted. The leading spirit in this was Merodach-Baladan. As soon as Sennacherib was once more in control of the situation in Mesopotamia, by the end of the year 702 B.C., he set out for the west and smashed the rebellious little countries in one single campaign. A similar fate overtook the Egyptian army which Pharaoh Shabaka had sent under the command of his nephew Taharka against the Assyrians. The Second Book of Kings and the Book of Isaiah confer upon the latter, a future pharaoh, who was also related to the Ethiopian dynasty, distinction which was still to come, in that they describe him even in those troubled times as "Tirhakah, king of Ethiopia." (II Kings 19:9; Isa. 37:9) The whole of Judah was occupied by Sennacherib's troops, and Hezekiah was shut up in Jerusalem. Among the frontier fortresses Lachish alone still offered resistance. Sennacherib deployed his storm troopers against this unusually strongly fortified city.

Anyone who wishes to relive the frightful battle of Lachish, vividly and dramatically to the smallest detail, must pay a visit to the British Museum. It is here that the massive reliefs, which eyewitnesses created on the orders of Sennacherib 2650 years ago, have found a resting place. Sir Henry Layard salvaged this precious object from the ruins of Nineveh.

On the turrets and breastwork of the stronghold of Lachish with its stout high walls the Judahite defenders fought with clenched teeth. They showered a hail of arrows on the attackers, hurled stones down upon them, threw burning torches—the fire bombs of the ancient world—among the enemy. The faces, curly hair, and short beards are easily recognizable. Only a few wear any protection for head or body.

At the foot of the wall the Assyrians were attacking with the utmost violence and with every type of weapons. Sennacherib had deployed the whole range of approved assault tactics. Every Assyrian was armed to the teeth; each one wore shield and helmet. Their pioneers had built sloping ramps of earth, stones, and felled trees. Siege engines, the first tanks in history, pushed forward up the ramps against the walls. They were equipped in front with a battering ram which stuck out like the barrel of a cannon. The crew consisted of three men. The archer shot his arrows from behind a sheltering canopy. A warrior guided the ram, and under its violent blow stones and bricks crashed down from the walls. The third man doused the tanks with ladlefuls of water, extinguishing the smoldering fire bombs. Several "tanks" were attacking at the same time. Tunnels were being driven into the

Fig. 54. Assyrians storming Lachish 701 B.C.

rock beneath the foundations of the walls. Behind the tanks came the infantry, that is, bowmen, some of them kneeling, some stooping, each protected by a shield bearer. The first captives, men and women, were being led off. Lifeless bodies were hanging on pointed stakes—impaled.

James Lesley Starkey, a British archaeologist, dug up the ruins of the walls of the fortress of Lachish. The holes and breaches made by the Assyrian "tanks" can be seen to this day.

Amid the confusion of the battle and the din of the siege around the frontier fortress of Judah, an order went out from Sennacherib: "And the king of Assyria sent Tartan, and Rabsaris and Rab-Shakeh from Lachish to king Hezekiah with a great host again Jerusalem." (II Kings 18:17)

That meant—attack on Jerusalem.

The historians of the Assyrian king have preserved a record of what happened next. An hexagonal prism from the rubble heaps of Nineveh says: "And Hezekiah of Judah who had not submitted to my yoke . . . him I shut up in Jerusalem his royal city like a caged bird. Earthworks I threw up against him, and anyone coming out of his city gate I made to pay for his crime. His cities which I had plundered I cut off from his land. . . ."

Surely now must come the announcement of the fall of Jerusalem and the seizing of the capital. But the text continues: "As for Hezekiah, the splendour of my majesty overwhelmed him . . . 30 gold talents . . . valuable treasures as well as his daughters, the women of his harem, singers both men and women, he caused to be brought after me to Nineveh. To pay his tribute and to do me homage he sent his envoys."

It is simply a bragging account of the payment of tribute—nothing more.

"And the king of Assyria appointed unto Hezekiah king of Judah three hundred talents of silver and thirty talents of gold." (II Kings 18:14)

The Assyrian texts pass on immediately from the description of the battle of Jerusalem to the payment of Hezekiah's tribute. Just at the moment when the whole country had been subjugated and the siege of Jerusalem, the last point of resistance, was in full swing, the unexpected happened: Sennacherib broke off the attack at five minutes to twelve. Only something quite extraordinary could have induced him to stop the fighting. What might it have been?

While the Assyrian records are enveloped in a veil of silence, the Bible says: "And it came to pass that night, that the angel of the Lord went out, and smote in the camp of the Assyrians an hundred fourscore and five thousand: and when they arose early in the morning, behold, they were all dead corpses. So Sennacherib, king of Assyria departed, and went and returned, and dwelt at Nineveh." (II Kings 19:35, 36)

Herodotus of Halicarnassus, the most famous traveler in the ancient world, historian, and author of an early Baedeker, helped to solve the puzzle. This friend of Pericles and Sophocles who was born about 500 B.C. had a definite flair for finding out strange facts about people and nations. Like a personified questionnaire, he extracted from his contemporaries on his

Fig. 55. King Sennacherib seated on his throne in front of the vanquished city of Lachish. (Detail of a campaign relief.)

travels through the ancient East information on all sorts of things that he thought were worth knowing or were unknown to him. In Egypt he had a long conversation with a temple priest who imparted a strange story to the inquisitive Greek.

It happened that at the very time that Sennacherib the Assyrian marched against Egypt with a large armed force, there was a priest-king on the throne of Egypt who treated the army as a contemptible profession. The Egyptian warriors, who had been so disdainfully dealt with, refused to take the field. Thereupon the priest-king hurried to the temple in deep despair. There he was told that the god would help him. Relying upon this the king, who had actually no soldiers behind him but only shopkeepers, tradesmen, and market folk, went to meet Sennacherib. At the narrow entrances into the country "an army of field-mice

Fig. 56. Assyrian encampment in Sennacherib's day—a relief from Nineveh.

swarmed over their opponents in the night . . . gnawed through their quivers and their bows, and the handles of their shields, so that on the following day they fled minus their arms and a great number of them fell. Hence," concluded Herodotus' story, "this king still stands in Hephaestus' temple with a mouse in his hand, and with the following inscription: 'Look on me and live in safety.' "

However obscure the meaning of this religious legend may be, its core is historical. For the peoples of the ancient world—as also for the Bible (I Sam.

6:4)—the mouse was what the rat was for the people of the Middle Ages. It was the symbol of plague.

On the edge of the city of Lachish, the archaeologist Starkey found shocking proof of the story in 1938: A mass grave in the rock with 2000 human skeletons, unmistakably thrown in with the utmost haste. The epidemic must have raged with frightful destruction among the Assyrian warriors.

The drama of the campaign had been unfolded, and once more Jerusalem had escaped. But all round it the land of Judah presented a pitiable spectacle: "The daughter of Zion is left as a cottage in a vineyard," laments the prophet Isaiah, "as a lodge in a garden of cucumbers." The "country is desolate," the "cities are burned with fire . . . and it is desolate as over-thrown by strangers." (Isa. 1:8, 7)

Only the thought of the marvelous deliverance of the city of David gave the sorely tried people new hope and courage. Undaunted, they bent all their energies to rebuilding, which, without interference from Nineveh, went quickly forward. Sennacherib never came back. For the next twenty years the tyrant de-voted himself to campaigns and battles in Mesopotamia. Then Sennacherib, like his father Sargon, was felled by an assassin's hand. "And it came to pass, as he was worshipping in the house of Nisroch his god, that Adrammelech and Sharezer his sons smote him with the sword: and they escaped into the land of Armenia. And Esarhaddon his son reigned in his stead." (II Kings 19:37) So runs the brief account of the event in the Bible.

Esarhaddon himself, the successor to the throne, describes in vivid detail these turbulent days in Nineveh: "Disloyal thoughts inspired my brothers. . . . They rebelled. In order to exercise royal authority they killed Sennacherib. I became a raging lion, my mind was in a fury. . . ."

Despite the intense cold and amid snow and ice, he set out without delay to destroy his enemies in the eleventh month of the year 681 B.C. "These usurpers . . . fled to an unknown land. I reached the quay on the Tigris, sent my troops across the broad river as if it were a canal. In Addar[1] . . . I reached Nineveh well pleased. I ascended my father's throne with joy. The south wind was blowing . . . whose breezes are propitious for royal authority. . . . I am Esarhaddon king of the world, king of Assyria, . . . son of Sennacherib."

---

[1] Twelfth month.

CHAPTER 4 / The Seductive Religions
of Canaan

*The "abominations of the heathen"—Harsh words from
the prophets—Philo of Byblos, a witness—Eusebius, the
Christian Father, finds no one to believe him—A plowman
stumbles upon Ugarit—A powerful seaport disappears—
Schaeffer digs at the "Head of Fennel"—The library in the
priest's house—Three scholars decipher an unknown alphabet*

MANASSEH WAS TWELVE YEARS OLD WHEN HE BEGAN
TO REIGN, AND REIGNED FIFTY AND FIVE YEARS IN
JERUSALEM. . . . AND HE DID THAT WHICH WAS EVIL
IN THE SIGHT OF THE LORD, AFTER THE ABOMINA-
TIONS OF THE HEATHEN, WHOM THE LORD CAST OUT
BEFORE THE CHILDREN OF ISRAEL. (II Kings 21:1, 2)

"Abominations of the Heathen," said the official report.
Isaiah, the great prophet, who was contemporary with
King Manasseh,[1] put it more plainly when he com-
plained bitterly, "How is the faithful city become a
harlot." (Isa. 1:21)

All the other prophets through the centuries constantly utter the same harsh and unambiguous ac-
cusation, which seems so monstrous to readers of the
Bible. The charge runs like a red thread through many
books of the Old Testament, accompanying the chances
and changes of Israel's history.

It rings out from the time when Israel after its long
desert wanderings reached the Jordan about 1230 B.C.
(Num. 25:1, 3) We hear it in the time of the
Judges. (I Sam. 2:22) It echoes through the two kingdoms, Judah (I Kings 14:23, 24) as well as Israel
(Hosea 4:13, 14). Even in the years of captivity by
the waters of Babylon in the sixth century B.C. it is
not silent. (Ezek. 16:15ff.)

For fifteen hundred years after the books of the

---

[1]696-642 B.C.

Bible had made their way into Europe, their contents were communicated to the people exclusively by priests and monks, for they were written in Greek, Latin, and Hebrew. It was only at the Reformation, when the first translations had been printed and could be obtained by everyone, that as more and more people came to read the Bible for themselves they came across passages that startled them. The Bible spoke about harlots. It is understandable that people whose houses and dwellings lay close in the shadow and protection of cathedrals and churches, which pointed them heavenward, found difficulty in comprehending this fact.

What did the European, for whom God was "a safe stronghold," know about the religions of the land in which the Bible was first written. The prophets and chroniclers tended to be thought of as men who in their zeal for Yahweh and their anger against foreign religions had probably gone too far. This objection has been leveled at the Bible right up to the present day.

There is secular evidence for what the Bible calls "the abominations of the heathen." Philo of Byblos, a Phoenician scholar who lived a hundred years before Christ, had collected abundant material from his native land and had written a history of Phoenicia, the *Phoinikika*. It dealt with historical events in the seaports and maritime republics of Canaan from earliest times and described the Phoenician gods, mythologies, and religious practices. As a reliable source for his work Philo of Byblos cited the Phoenician priest Sanchuniathon, who lived in the sixth or seventh century B.C. and has been already referred to. When, as the result of an earthquake, the inscribed pillars in the temple of Melkart at Tyre crashed to the ground, Sanchuniathon was said to have copied the ancient inscriptions.

Bishop Eusebius of Caesarea in Palestine discovered the writings of Philo of Byblos in A.D. 314 and gave an account of them. Much of what they recorded, particularly as regards mythology and religion, seemed quite incomprehensible.

At the head of the Baals of Canaan was the god

El. His wife was Asherah, a goddess who is also mentioned in the Bible. El married his three sisters, one of whom was Astarte. She is frequently referred to in the Old Testament as Ashtaroth. (Jud. 10:6ff.) El killed not only his brother but also his own son; he cut off his daughter's head, castrated his father, castrated himself, and compelled his confederates to do the same.

Little wonder that people in the Christian era were not prepared to believe stories of enormities of this sort. Among us it is accepted as a matter of course that every half-civilized community controls the morality of its citizens. But in Canaan in those days the cult of sensuality was regarded as the worship of the gods. Men and women prostitutes ranked as "sacred" to the followers of the religion, and the rewards for their "services" went into the temple treasuries as "offerings for the god."

The last thing the prophets and chroniclers did was to exaggerate. How well founded their harsh words were has only become fully understood since the great discoveries of Ras Shamra. On the north coast of Syria exactly opposite the east tip of Cyprus lies Mînet el-Beidâ, the "White Haven." The Mediterranean waves break here on dazzling, snow-white limestone rocks in a wonderful display of color, changing from light green to deep violet. Inland, great banks of clouds surround the lonely mountain top of Jebel Aqra. The natives say that long ago it was the dwelling place of the gods of their ancestors.

Near the sea in 1928 a peasant who was plowing discovered a long underground passage. Initial investigation showed that it led to a tomb. It was a sepulchral vault in the style of Mycenae. When the discovery was announced, France, which as mandatory power was in control of Syria, reacted with its customary alacrity. M. Dussaud, curator of Oriental antiquities in the Louvre, dispatched Professor Claude F. A. Schaeffer with some other experts to the "White Haven." Exciting discoveries awaited them.

Half a mile from the shore and the old Mycenae grave rose an artificial hill. Round its base flowed a pleasant rippling brook. It had always been called by

the natives Ras es Shamra, "Head of Fennel." Fennel
was actually growing on the old heap of ruins that
concealed the remains of the Phoenician royal city of
Ugarit. More than three thousand years ago it had
been wiped out for good by the onslaught of the Sea
Peoples.

Schaeffer had incredible luck with his excavations on
the "Head of Fennel." For here at last the long-sought
information about the religions of Canaan came to
light. Between two temples, one of them dedicated to
the god Baal and the other to the god Dagon, he
found among the houses of rich merchants the house
of the High Priest of Ugarit, who owned a handsome
library, as is clear from the large number of inscribed
tablets found there. Schaeffer's trained eye recognized
at once that the writer must have been using a hitherto
unknown Phoenician alphabet. It was surprisingly
quickly deciphered in 1930 by three scholars: Professor H. Bauer, of the University of Halle, Germany,
and C. Virolleaud and E. Dhorme, of France. The
bilingual documents—one of the languages is an ancient Canaanite dialect, which is something like pre-
Mosaic Hebrew—are exclusively concerned with the

Fig. 57. Phoenician merchantman.

gods and religions of old Canaan, with which Israel on
entering the Promised Land had its first fateful encounter.

The myths and practices described in this unique
collection of documents abounding in barbaric activities of gods and demigods indicate the particular

significance which was attached to the rites of the goddesses of fertility in Canaan.

The forms of worship which Canaan connected with fertility extended to everyday life. Under each of the houses that were excavated was found a burial vault in which the inhabitants of Ugarit buried their dead. Oddly shaped clay funnels were sunk into the ground through which water, wine, oil, and the flesh and blood of animal sacrifices were offered to the dead. The fertility cults did not hesitate to penetrate even the world beyond death. The feeding funnels leave us in no doubt about that. They are decorated with the appropriate symbols.

Mandrakes played a large part in the ritual of the living. Ancient Canaanites and Phoenicians ascribed aphrodisiac properties to these fleshy roots. They were supposed to be able to stimulate passion and cure barrenness.

Gruesome and ferocious are Astarte and Anath, goddesses of fertility and of war alike. The Baal epic of Ugarit depicts the goddess Anath: "With her might she mowed down the dwellers in the cities, she struck down the people of the seacoasts, she destroyed the men of the east." She drove the men into her temple and closed the doors so no one could escape. "She hurled chairs at the youths, tables at the warriors, footstools at the mighty men." She waded up to the knees, up to the neck, in blood. Human heads lay at her feet; human hands flew over her like locusts. "She tied the heads of her victims as ornaments upon her back, their hands she tied upon her belt." "Her liver was swollen with laughing, her heart was full of joy, the liver of Anath was full of exultation." "When she was satisfied she washed her hands in streams of human blood before turning again to other things."

Anath was the sister and wife of Baal, the god of storm and rain. His symbol was a bull's head.

Baal enriched the meadows with rain to make the cattle fat. He was also concerned with their propagation. When he died at the turn of the seasons, overpowered "like the bull under the knife of the sacrificer," his son took over his duties. "And the children of Israel did evil in the sight of the Lord and served Baalim." (Jud. 2:11) Quite recently an image of one of these gods was recovered on Israeli territory at Hazor. It was found in one of the heathen shrines which according to the Bible the Israelites erected in many places for the worship of strange gods. In the center of an area encircled with flat stones, with two altars for burnt offerings dating from the days before the monarchy, stood some weapons and a clay jar. It contained, together with other bronze votive figures, an image of a seated god—a "baal."

Professor Schaeffer also found in Ugarit small images and amulets of Astarte. They are made of clay and gold, and the goddess is naked. Snakes and pigeons, renowned in the ancient East for their fertility, are her symbols.

The goddesses of fertility were worshiped principally on hills and knolls. There their votaries erected for them Asherim and set out "sacred pillars," trees under which the rites were practiced, as the Bible repeatedly points out: "For they also built them high places, and pillars, and Asherim on every high hill and under every green tree." (I Kings 14:23—R.V.)

It is only since the results of scientific investigation into Canaanite gods and Phoenician religions have come to light that we can properly gauge the intensity of the moral struggle that the people of Israel had to face.

*Fig. 58. Gold plaquette of a naked goddess
of fertility.*

What temptation for a simple shepherd folk, what perilous enticement. More than once the Baal religions got a firm foothold and penetrated right into the temple of Yahweh, into the Holy of Holies.

Without its stern moral law, without its faith in one God, without the commanding figures of its prophets, Israel would never have been able to survive this struggle with the Baals, with the religions of the fertility goddesses, with the Asherim and the high places.

That was the reason for the "objectionable passages." In the interest of truth the matter could not be passed over in silence.

Ashurbanipal plunders Thebes—An empire stretching from the Nile to the Persian Gulf—The "great and noble Asnapper"—Big-game hunting with bow and arrow—Assyria's strength is exhausted—Crushed between two powers—Medes and Chaldeans arm—Scythian hordes in Palestine—Nineveh sinks in ruins—The Fertile Crescent breathes again—A Biblical slip of the pen—Gadd's discovery in London—Nebuchadnezzar, crown prince of Babylon

ART THOU BETTER THAN POPULOUS NO, THAT WAS SITUATE AMONG THE RIVERS, THAT HAD THE WATERS ROUND ABOUT IT . . . ? ETHIOPIA AND EGYPT WERE HER STRENGTH, AND IT WAS INFINITE. . . . YET WAS SHE CARRIED AWAY, SHE WENT INTO CAPTIVITY: HER YOUNG CHILDREN ALSO WERE DASHED IN PIECES AT THE TOP OF ALL THE STREETS. . . . (Nahum 3:8-10)

In 663 B.C. the Assyrians celebrated the greatest triumph in their whole history. King Ashurbanipal conquered the capital of Upper Egypt, No-Amon, which the Greeks called Thebes. According to Homer it had 100 gates and until then it had been regarded as impregnable. It was an event that caused an enormous stir in the world of the ancient Orient, in the Fertile Crescent itself, and as far as Greece. The Assyrians plundered the metropolis, whose temples contained boundless wealth. "I conquered the whole city. . . . silver, gold, precious stones, the whole contents of its palace, colored vestments, linen, magnificent houses, slaves, both men and women, two great obelisks of shining bronze weighing 2500 talents; I took the temple gates from their place and brought them to Assyria. Enormous spoils of priceless worth did I take with me from Thebes," exulted Ashurbanipal.

The Assyrian war machine had made a tabula rasa of the far-famed temple city on the Nile. Excavations fully confirm the description of the catastrophe given by the prophet Nahum and by the victor himself. The capital of Upper Egypt never recovered from his blow.

After this victorious expedition the world of those days lay at Assyria's feet. From the upper reaches of the Nile to the mountains of Armenia and the mouth of the Euphrates, the nations were under its yoke, their peoples reduced to vassals. But scarcely had Assyria reached the pinnacle of its might when the power of the empire began to wane. Ashurbanipal was not a conqueror or war lord of the caliber of his father Esarhaddon, to say nothing of his prodigious grandfather Sennacherib. Ashurbanipal, the "great and noble Asnapper" (Ezra 4:10) had already developed other interests.

Afer the long succession of bloodstained tyrants, this one Assyrian did the world an inestimable service. He ordered the transcription of the masterpieces of Akkadian literature, including the Babylonian Creation story. He commissioned the production of dictionaries and grammars of the various languages that were spoken in his colossal empire. The library that he built up in Nineveh was by far the largest and most important in the ancient East. Without this precious collection mankind would have been infinitely poorer in its knowledge of the thought and literature of the Fertile Crescent from earliest times.

Nevertheless, the wild streak in this last important scion of the race of Assyrian rulers was not completely tamed. As well as being a lover of art and literature, he loved hunting. Ashurbanipal was a big-game hunter in the proper sense of the word, and his successors in this pursuit can hardly compete with him. It was not with planes and armor-plated jeeps at sixty miles an hour, not with elephant howdahs equipped with telescopic sights, which enable the fatal shot to be fired from a safe distance where there is no threat of slashing paws or snapping teeth, that this big-game hunter of the ancient world set out to attack his prey. On these wonderfully vivid, large reliefs which were found in his palaces on the Tigris, he hunts in a light two-wheeled hunting car or on horseback with bow and arrow or javelin. According to the cuneiform texts, "30 elephants, 257 wild beasts, 370 lions" made up the splendid total of Ashurbanipal's bag.

"Woe to the bloody city! . . . There is a multitude of slain and a great number of carcases, and there is none end of their corpses; . . ." (Nahum 3:1, 3)

So the prophet Nahum announces the end of Nineveh, the end of its world empire and centuries of bloody tyranny. With the death of Ashurbanipal[1] the sudden and rapid collapse began. The new great

Fig. 59.

powers of Indo-Aryans and Semites gripped the gigantic structure between them like a vice, crushed it, and divided the colossal spoil between them.

To the northeast the kingdom of the Medes in the mountains of Iran had come into being. Then "Cyaxares came to power," wrote Herodotus, "and united all

---

[1] 626 B.C.

Asia beyond the Halys under him. Then he gathered together all his peoples and marched against Nineveh to take the city."

In the southeast of Mesopotamia a second adversary had sprung up whom the Assyrians had to take seriously. From the fringe of civilization south of the estuary of the Euphrates, where Ur of the Chaldees was also situated, Semitic tribes had pushed their way inland and had imported new vigor into the old kingdom of Babylon. They called themselves "Chaldeans." Merodach-Baladan who a century before had made a name for himself and had plagued Assyria for many years had been one of them.

Meantime his countrymen had succeeded in penetrating the whole country in a series of waves of invasion. In 625 B.C. a Chaldean assumed control over south Mesopotamia. Nabopolassar became king and founder of the Neo-Babylonian empire. The Chaldeans likewise had only one end in view, the destruction of Assyria.

At the same time as the two powers, north and south, were lying in wait to administer the death blow to Assyria, a wild horde burst out of the Caucasus into the Fertile Crescent, penetrated into Media and inundated the Assyrian empire. These were the Scythians. Looting and burning, they forced their way from Mesopotamia through Palestine to the very frontiers of Egypt. Through the maritime plain by the Mediterranean stormed this unruly mob of Scythian horsemen. Fearful and frightening rumors heralded their approach. The inhabitants of Judah must have seen them as they looked down from the mountains; the prophet Zephaniah foresaw with horror what would happen. "For Gaza shall be forsaken, and Ashkelon a desolation: they shall drive out Ashdod at the noonday and Ekron shall be rooted up. . . . In the houses of Ashkelon shall they lie down in the evening. . . ." (Zeph. 2:4, 7)

"They headed for Egypt," Herodotus related, "and while they were in Palestinian Syria, Psammitichus,[1]

_____
[1]Psam-tik I, 663-609 B.C.

King of Egypt went to meet them and persuaded them with gifts and pleas to go no further. And while the Scythians on their way back were in the Syrian city of Ashkelon, a few of them remained behind and plundered the temple of Aphrodite Urania. Those Scythians who had plundered the temple in Ashkelon together with their descendants for ever were smitten by the goddess with a woman's ailment."

Within ten years the Asiatic horsemen had disappeared again like an evil apparition.

In Palestine the name of a city kept the memory of the Scythians green. Beth-Shan was renamed Scythopolis.

Then the Medes and the Neo-Babylonians bore down upon the Assyrians on two fronts. They attacked from north and south at the same time. Ashur, the great city and fortress on the Tigris, was the first to fall in 614 B.C. "The king of Babylon and his army, which had set out to assist the Medes, did not arrive in time for the battle. The king of Babylon and Cyaxares[1] met each other among the ruins of the city," says a Neo-Babylonian chronicle, "and pledged themselves to friendship and a confederacy. . . . They took vast quantities of booty in the city and reduced it to a heap of rubble and ruins."

In 612 B.C. the alliance of Medes and Neo-Babylonians achieved its aim. After a "violent battle the city was taken." Nineveh was destroyed. "And he will stretch out his hand against the north and destroy Assyria: and will make Nineveh a desolation, and dry like a wilderness." Zephaniah had prophesied this (Zeph. 2:13), and now it had happened: the nerve center of Assyrian power destroyed and reduced to ashes. Nineveh for centuries with its armies of conquest and occupation, with torture, terror, and mass deportations had brought nothing but blood and tears to the ancient world.

The Fertile Crescent breathed again. Jubilation filled its afflicted peoples; new hope began to spring up, in which Judah shared.

---

[1] King of the Medes.

After the death of Ashurbanipal, when the hated
Assyrian colossus was shaken by the first signs of
ultimate collapse, King Josiah[1] had without hesitation
banned the practice of foreign religions in Jerusalem.
There was more to that than merely religious objec-
tions. It clearly signified the termination of the state
of vassalage of which the gods of Nineveh, imported
by compulsion, were symbolic. Together with these
compulsory deities, Josiah expelled all the Mesopotamian "workers with familiar spirits, and the wizards,
and the images and the idols." (II Kings 23:24) He
also cleared out all the Canaanite religious practices.
(II Kings 23:7)

Josiah's reforms paved the way for a renewed religious and national vitality which developed into a
regular frenzy when news of the fall of Nineveh confirmed their freedom.

Meantime something quite unexpected happened
which threatened to ruin everything. "Pharaoh-Nechoh
king of Egypt went up against the king of Assyria to
the river Euphrates: and king Josiah went against him,
and he slew him at Megiddo, when he had seen him."
(II Kings 23:29) This passage from the Bible is a
perfect example of how a single word can completely
change the meaning of a narrative. In this case the
wrong use of the little word "against" brands Josiah as
the accomplice of the hated tyrant. At some point or
other the word translated "against" had been wrongly
copied. In reality Pharaoh Necho went to the aid of
Assyria, that is, "toward." It was only through a chance
discovery that the Assyriologist C. I. Gadd found this
historical slip of the pen.

The place of discovery was quite outside the normal
archaeological pattern—it was a museum. In 1923 in
the British Museum Gadd was translating a badly
damaged fragment of cuneiform text that had been dug
up in Mesopotamia many years previously. It read as
follows: "In the month of Du'uz [June-July][2] the
king of Assyria procured a large Egyptian army and

[1] 639-609 B.C.
[2] 609 B.C.

marched against Harran to conquer it. . . . Till the month of Ulul [August–September] he fought against the city but accomplished nothing."

The "large Egyptian army" consisted of the forces of Pharaoh Necho.

After the fall of Nineveh, what remained of the Assyrian forces had retreated to northern Mesopotamia. Their king embarked upon the forlorn hope of re-conquering from there what he had lost. It was for this purpose that Pharaoh Necho had hastened to his aid. But when, after two months of fighting, not even the town of Harran had been recaptured, Necho re-tired.

It was the appearance of Egyptian troops in Palestine that decided Josiah to prevent the Egyptians at all costs from rendering military aid to the hated As-syrians. So it came about that the little army of Judah marched against the far superior Egyptian force, with the tragic ending at Megiddo. "Neko," wrote Herodotus, "also defeated the Syrians[1] in a land engagement at Magdolus."[2]

On the way back to Egypt, Pharaoh Necho assumed the role of overlord of Syria and Palestine. He made an example of Judah, so as to leave it in no doubt on whom the country now depended. Jehoahaz, Josiah's son and successor, was stripped of his royal dignities and taken as a prisoner to the Nile. (II Kings 23:31-34) In his stead Necho placed another son of Josiah upon the throne, Eliakim, whose name he changed to Jehoiakim. (II Kings 23:34)

Egyptologists have not been able so far to produce any hymns of triumph of Pharaoh Necho. Herodotus learned from Egyptian priests a century and a half later that Necho had presented to the temple of Apollo in Miletus "the garb in which he had accomplished these deeds" in thank offering for the participation of Greek mercenaries in his expedition. In the land he con-quered he left nothing but a stele. It bears his name in

---

[1]Judah.
[2]Megiddō.

hieroglyphic script. Its fragments were left lying in Sidon.

Four years later—605 B.C.—Necho's dream of suzerainty over Asia, as his predecessors had always called it, was at an end.

Even while he was collecting tribute in Palestine, decisions were being taken about his "conquest" elsewhere. After their joint victory the Medes and the Neo-Babylonians had divided the empire of Assyria between them. The Medes annexed the north and northeast; Babylon the south and southwest. Syria and Palestine thus fell to King Nabopolassar. But in the meantime he had grown old and was no longer fit for the fray. He therefore sent the crown prince of Chaldea, his son Nebuchadnezzar, to take possession of the new territories.

Necho made an attempt to repulse him but failed miserably. Near Carchemish, in the same region where four years previously he had endeavored to assist the last king of Assyria, he suffered total defeat at the famous passage across the Euphrates from Mesopotamia to north Syria. (Jer. 46:2)

Necho fled through Palestine followed by the jeers of the prophet Jeremiah: "Pharaoh king of Egypt is but a noise: he hath let the appointed time pass by. . . . The sound thereof shall go like the serpent, . . ." (Jer. 46:17, 22—R.V.)

After this shameful flight, Judah saw no more of Necho. "And the king of Egypt came not again any more out of his land: for the king of Babylon had taken, from the river of Egypt unto the river Euphrates, all that pertained to the king of Egypt." (II Kings 24:7) The crown prince of Chaldea was not able to exploit his victory at Carchemish. In the course of the battle news of the death of his father overtook him, and he had perforce to return to Babylon. After Nebuchadnezzar[1] had acceded to the throne, more important affairs of state kept him in his own country for the next few years. Judah was spared a fresh occupation for a time and was left to itself.

---

[1]605-562 B.C.

There are no contemporary records giving us the details of what happened in Judah around the turn of the sixth century. The Bible gives no clear picture of when, for example, the Chaldeans made their first appearance in the country, or of when they started to demand tribute. The Neo-Babylonian kings, unlike their predecessors the Assyrians, left no informative annals behind them. Inscriptions on buildings that have been preserved merely indicate historical events.

CHAPTER 6 / The Last Days of Judah

First deportation—King Jehoiachin in Babylonian court records—Discovery in the basement of the Berlin Museum —Nebuchadnezzar on the conquest of Jerusalem—Second punitive campaign—Dispatches on clay—Starkey's tragic death—Incendiary technique of Babylonian engineers—A clean slate for the archaeologists

IN HIS DAYS NEBUCHADNEZZAR KING OF BABYLON CAME UP, AND JEHOIAKIM BECAME HIS SERVANT THREE YEARS. (II Kings 24:7)

About the turn of the sixth century there took place the calamitous event which in a few years was to blot out Judah once and for all as a nation with a place in the history of the ancient Orient. Events now began to close in with frightening speed upon the tiny vassal state on the Jordan and its inhabitants, which were to result in Judah's most grievous hour of affliction. They ended with the road to exile and forcible removal to Babylon.

It began with refusal to pay tribute and rebellion against the new feudal lord. In 598 B.C. open revolt broke out in Judah. King Jehoiakim ". . . turned and rebelled against him." (II Kings 24:1)

At first Nebuchadnezzar did not intervene in person. Perhaps he did not think it sufficiently important; in a great empire, local rebellions are no rare occurrence. He was content to leave it, to begin with, to troops from Moab, Ammon, and Syria, strengthened by Chaldean regulars. They do not appear to have taken control of the situation, however, whereupon Nebuchadnezzar himself hurried to Judah.

He was already on his way to Palestine with a considerable force when Jehoiakim unexpectedly died. Jehoiakim's son followed him upon the throne: "Jehoiachin was eighteen years old when he began to reign, and he reigned in Jerusalem three months. . . . And Nebuchadnezzar king of Babylon came against

319

the city, and his servants did besiege it. . . . And he carried away all Jerusalem. . . . And he carried away Jehoiachin to Babylon. . . ." (II Kings 24:8-15)

In 597 B.C., as the Bible says, King Jehoiachin and his family were deported to Babylon as prisoners. But after twenty-five hundred years, who could hope to check up on the realiability of this factual statement? Nevertheless, shortly before the beginning of the twentieth century, an opportunity came the way of the archaeologists to find out something definite about the destination of the royal family of Judah.

In 1899 the German Oriental Society equipped a large expedition under the direction of Professor Robert Koldewey, the architect, to examine the famous ruined mound of Babil on the Euphrates. The excavations, as it turned out, took longer than anywhere else. In eighteen years the most famous metropolis of the ancient world, the royal seat of Nebuchadnezzar, was brought to light, and at the same time, one of the Seven Wonders of the World, the Hanging Gardens, loudly extolled by Greek travelers of a later day, and E-Temen-An-Ki, the legendary Tower of Babel. In the palace of Nebuchadnezzar and on the Ishtar Gate, which was situated beside it, countless inscriptions were discovered.

Nevertheless, the scholars were conscious of a certain disappointment. In contrast to the detailed records of Assyrian rulers, in which the names and fortunes of the kings of Israel and Judah were frequently given a historical setting, the Neo-Babylonian records hardly mentioned anything apart from the religious and architectural events of their day. They contained for example no corroboration of the fate of Judah.

Thirty years later, when the great finds at Babil had long since found their way into archives and museums, there emerged a number of unique documents from the immediate neighborhood of the Ishtar Gate—in Berlin!

On Museum Island, in the middle of the Spree in the heart of the German capital, the wonderful Ishtar Gate from Babylon had been reconstructed in the great Central Court of the Kaiser Friedrich Museum. Menacing and sinister, the bright yellow bodies of the long row of lions stood out against the deep blue of the glazed tiles on the Processional Way of Marduk.[1] As it had done by the Euphrates, so now it led astonished citizens of the twentieth century to the splendid gate, with its dragons and wild oxen, dedicated to the goddess Ishtar.

While deeply impressed visitors from all over the world stood in the Central Court upstairs in front of the lofty and brilliantly colored twin gate, and, as Nebuchadnezzar had done long ago, turned under its arch onto the Processional Way, 300 cuneiform tablets lying in the basement rooms of the museum were waiting to be deciphered.

Koldewey's team had rescued them from the outbuildings of Nebuchadnezzar's palace near the Ishtar Gate, had numbered them, and had packed them in boxes. Together with masses of brightly glazed tiles, bearing reliefs of lions, dragons, and wild oxen, they had made the long journey to Berlin, where, as luck would have it, the old tablets were lying in their packing cases by the Spree, almost exactly as they had been in Babylon, only a few yards under the Ishtar Gate.

After 1933 E. F. Weidner, the Assyriologist, took in hand the task of looking through the tablets and shards in the basement rooms of the Kaiser Friedrich Museum. He then translated them one by one. They contained nothing but court inventories, receipted accounts from the royal commissariat, book entries of ancient bureaucrats; nothing but ordinary everyday matters.

Despite that, Weidner stuck it out manfully day after day in the basement under the Ishtar Gate and worked at his translations tirelessly. Then, all of a sudden, his monotonous job came unexpectedly to life. Among this dull administrative rubbish Weidner suddenly found some priceless relics of red tape in the ancient world. On four different receipts for stores issued, among them best-quality sesame oil, he came upon a familiar Biblical name: Ja-U-Kinu—Jehoiachin!

There was no possibility of his being mistaken,

---

[1] Babylonian god.

because Jehoiachin was given his full title: King of the (land of) Judah. The Babylonian clay receipts, moreover, bear the date of the thirteenth year of the reign of King Nebuchadnezzar. That means 592 B.C., five years after the fall of Jerusalem and the deportation. In addition the Babylonian steward of the commissariat had mentioned in three cases five of the king's sons who were in charge of a servant with the Jewish name of "Kenaiah."

Other personnel on the rations from Nebuchadnezzar's stores are noted as "eight persons from the land of Judah," who possibly belonged to the retinue of King Jehoiachin, among them a gardener by the name of Salam-ja-a-ma.

Jehoiachin, the deposed King of Judah, lived with his family and his retinue in the palace of Nebuchadnezzar in Babylon. We may conclude from Weidner's discovery that the Biblical account in the Second Book of Kings may be thus supplemented. "And for his diet, there was a continual diet given him of the king of Babylon, every day a portion, until the day of his death, all the days of his life." (Jer. 52:34)

A sensational addition to the account of these events was made in 1955 through the examination of 2500-year-old cuneiform tablets which had long lain in peaceful oblivion in the British Museum. D. J. Wiseman was engaged in deciphering these tablets when to his great surprise he came across the following entry in the official records of the Babylonian royal house.

"In the seventh year, in the month Chislev, the king assembled his army and advanced on Hatti-land (Syria). He encamped over against the city of the Judaeans and conquered it on the second day of Adar (March 597). He took the king (Jehoiachin) prisoner, and appointed in his stead a king after his own heart (Zedekiah). He exacted heavy tribute and had it brought to Babylon."

Here we have the original account in Babylonian chronicles of the first conquest of Jerusalem by Nebuchadnezzar as it has been preserved for us in the Bible in the 24th chapter of the Second Book of Kings.

"And it came to pass in the ninth year of his reign,

in the tenth month, in the tenth day of the month, that Nebuchadnezzar, king of Babylon, came, he and all his host, against Jerusalem. . . . And the city was besieged unto the eleventh year of king Zedekiah." (II Kings 25:1, 2)

Eleven years had gone by since the capture of Jehoiachin and the first deportation to Babylon. The time had now come for Judah's fate to be sealed.

The last scene in the tragedy of this tiny nation provides a classic example of how Biblical narratives and archaeological discoveries illuminate the same event from different points of view, and how accurate are the statements of the prophet in the Second Book of Kings and in Chronicles alongside the official account. Jeremiah sketches with swift strokes of his brush scenes taken from the exciting and anxious events of the last days, which through discoveries in Palestine in our own day are confirmed as being startling in their accuracy and historically genuine.

After the first conquest in 597 B.C. Nebuchadnezzar allowed Judah to continue its existence as a vassal state. The successor to the throne, after Jehoiachin had been led off into captivity, was his uncle Mattaniah who was renamed Zedekiah by the Chaldean king. As we may conclude from Jeremiah 13:19, the territory of Judah was reduced: "The cities of the south shall be shut up and none shall open them."

The deportation of their kinsmen before their very eyes, the bitter experiences of a century and a half, the miserable fate of the northern kingdom, still only too fresh in their memories, nevertheless, did not extinguish the will to resist.

Fig. 60. Fortress of Lachish in Judah with double walls and triple gate (Reconstruction).

Soon indeed voices were being raised, denouncing Babylon and demanding the recovery of all that had been lost. (Jer. 28:1-4) The prophet Jeremiah raised his voice in warning, but it was the anti-Babylonian group which was more and more heeded. They egged the people on and eventually got the upper hand of the spineless and vacillating king. Alliances were struck with the bordering vassal states. There was a meeting of "messengers" from Edom, Moab, and Ammon as well as from the seaports of Tyre and Sidon in the presence of King Zedekiah in Jerusalem. (Jer. 27:3)

The fact that in 588 B.C. a new Pharaoh, Apries,[1] ascended the throne had clearly a decisive influence on the decision to revolt. (Jer. 44:30) The new ruler of Egypt must have given Judah assurances of armed help, for "Zedekiah rebelled against the king of Babylon." (II Kings 24:20)

In the "tenth month" (II Kings 25:1) of the same year, 588 B.C.—it was the "ninth year" of King Zedekiah—Nebuchadnezzar arrived with a strong army from Babylon. With the speed of lightning the punitive campaign against rebellious Judah was unfolded.

The Chaldean divisions of infantry, fast cavalry, and charioteers smashed all resistance and conquered city after city. Except for the capital, Jerusalem, and the frontier fortresses of Lachish and Azekah in the south, the whole land was finally subdued.

Jerusalem, Lachish, and Azekah were determined to fight to the end: "When the king of Babylon's army fought against Jerusalem and against all the cities of Judah that were left, against Lachish and against Azekah: for these defenced cities remained of the cities of Judah." (Jer. 34:7)

Impressive and enduring evidence of the last phase of this hopeless struggle lies before us. Twenty miles southwest of Jerusalem, the green valley of Elah pushes its way far into the mountains of Judah. This was the scene of the duel between young David and Goliath, the Philistine giant. (I Sam. 17:19ff.) The little brook out of which David gathered "five smooth stones" for

---

[1]588-568 B.C. Jeremiah calls him Hophra.

his sling still runs and burbles between its oak trees. (I Sam. 17:40)

From the river bed the hill slopes gently upward to a height of 1000 feet. From the top the cornfields and olive groves of the old plain of Philistia can be seen stretching away to the far horizon where they meet the silver sparkle of the Mediterranean. On this spot Dr. Frederick J. Bliss, a British archaeologist, identified a fort with eight stout towers as ancient Azekah, one of the frontier fortresses which, as we have seen, remained unconquered. Just about twelve miles to the south the ruins of Lachish were found to contain valuable evidence. The archaeologist J. L. Starkey disinterred them in the thirties when the Wellcome-Marston expedition from the United Kingdom investigated the ruins of the great city gate, where the battle was fiercest. Eighteen ostraca (inscribed clay shards) contained information about forward posts, observation posts, and strong points held by Judahite troops which had not yet been overwhelmed. These dispatches on clay had been sent to "Jaosh," the "commandant of the fort of Lachish," during that fateful "tenth month" of the year 588 B.C. The messages, scratched out in haste, indicate with every line the frightful tension that existed just before the collapse. One of the last of these eyewitness reports reads: "May Yahweh grant that my lord should hear good tidings. . . . we are watching for the signal stations of Lachish, according to the signals which my lord has given. . . . we are no longer receiving signals from Azekah." This message told Jaosh, the commanding officer at Lachish, that Azekah had fallen. Nebuchadnezzar could now withdraw his engineers for the attack on the last fortress but one.

British archaeologists with the Wellcome-Marston expedition obtained information in 1938 about the terrible end of Lachish, after six strenuous seasons of excavating.

It was the last success that was to crown the career of James Lesley Starkey, the famous excavator of Lachish. During the Palestinian troubles which had broken out, he was shot, at the age of forty-three, by Arabs in the neighborhood of Hebron on the road from

Lachish to Jerusalem. His death was a tragic case of mistaken identity; in the course of the protracted excavations he had grown a beard and the Arabs took him for a Jew.

In 701 B.C. the storm troops of Sennacherib, King of Assyria, had rushed the walls of Lachish with "tanks" fitted with battering rams. Nebuchadnezzar's special detachments adopted an entirely different technique to force the city to surrender.

Investigation of the stratum that marked the Babylonian work of destruction produced, to Starkey's astonishment, ashes. Ashes in incredible quantities. Many of the layers are several yards thick and are still —after twenty-five hundred years—higher than the remains of the solid walls of the fortress. Nebuchadnezzar's engineers were specialists in the art of incendiarism, past masters at starting conflagrations.

Whatever wood they could lay hands on they dragged to the spot, stripped the whole area around Lachish of its forests and thickets, cleared the hills of timber for miles around, piled the firewood as high as a house outside the walls and set it alight. Countless olive groves were hacked down for this purpose: the layer of ashes contains masses of charred olive stones.

Day and night sheets of flame leapt sky high; a ring of fire licked the walls from top to bottom. The besieging force piled on more and more wood until the white-hot stones burst and the walls caved in.

So Lachish likewise fell and only Jerusalem still offered resistance. The whole weight of the Babylonian war machine could now be directed against it. It was impossible to use the new incendiary technique in this case, for the forests around Jerusalem had, since the time of the patriarchs and of Joshua's conquest, been reduced to miserable little plantings and undergrowth. (Josh. 17:15, 18) They therefore preferred to storm Jerusalem with the approved technique of battering rams and siege engines. For eighteen months Jerusalem was besieged and heroically defended: "And the city was besieged unto the eleventh year of king Zedekiah." (II Kings 25:2)

What made the defenders hold out, despite the fact that famine had long been raging in the city and was taking a heavy toll, was a desperate hope that Egypt might come to their assistance. It seemed that this hope was to be fulfilled, for the Babylonians suddenly withdrew. "The Pharaoh's army was come forth out of Egypt: and when the Chaldeans that besieged Jerusalem heard tidings of them, they departed from Jerusalem." (Jer. 37:5) An army did in fact at that time come up from the Nile under Pharaoh Apries, as Herodotus also mentions. Its destination was, however, not Jerusalem. Apries was making an attack by land and sea against the Phoenician ports.

Archaeologists have found evidence on fragments of Egyptian monuments of Pharaoh's presence in Tyre and Sidon at that time. So it came about as Jeremiah had prophesied: "Behold, Pharaoh's army, which is come forth to help you, shall return to Egypt unto their own land." (Jer. 37:7) After a few days the enemy was back in front of Jerusalem, the siege continued with the utmost fury, and the end could no longer be delayed.

"And the city was broken up, and all the men of war fled by night, by the way of the gate between two walls which is by the king's garden." (II Kings 25:4) Thanks to the result of excavations, the route taken by the defenders in their flight can now be reconstructed without difficulty. King Hezekiah had strengthened the old fortifications of the city of David by a second wall on the south side. (II Chron. 32:5) Remains of this have been discovered.

The moment the enemy entered the city through a breach in the walls, the defenders retreated in the first instance behind the double-walled southern part of the fortifications and only with the onset of darkness did they escape through an outer gate into freedom and then over the hills to Jericho. In the process King Zedekiah was taken. His children were "slaughtered" before his eyes; he himself had his eyes put out (II Kings 25:7)—the harsh Babylonian martial law for traitors. This cruel punishment by blinding is frequently attested on pictorial reliefs.

Jerusalem was given over to plundering: the royal palace and the Temple were set on fire, and the city walls and fortifications were razed to the ground. The order to destroy was given to "Nebuzar-Adan, captain of the guard" (II Kings 25:8), a grand vizier who appears in the Babylonian list of court officials as "Nabu-Seri-Idinnam." Once more, in 587 B.C., part of the population was deported. (II Kings 25:11) Nebuchadnezzar erased the royal house of David, which

Fig. 61.

had reigned without interruption for 400 years. The land of Judah became a Babylonian province. Those who were left waged a *maquis* type of war from their hideouts in the mountains and claimed as their victim Gedaliah who had been appointed governor by the Babylonians. The third deportation was a reprisal for this, and it was also the last. (Jer. 52:30) Little groups of Judahites were able to escape it by fleeing to Egypt. (II Kings 25:26; Jer. 43:7) The curtain of history was lowered on an empty land. The tribes of Israel were scattered to the four winds.

Scholars like S. A. Cook and C. C. Torrey have denied the truth of the Biblical tradition of this carrying off into exile. In their view there was never a mass deportation from Judah; at the most some of the nobility were imprisoned in Babylon.

Excavations indicate the exact opposite. Since 1926 a considerable number of towns and fortresses in Judah have been either wholly or partly excavated and carefully examined with a view to establishing the date of their destruction or depopulation. "The results," says Professor Albright, "are uniform and convincing: many towns were destroyed at the beginning of the 6th century and were never again resettled. There is not a single known case of a town in Judah being continuously inhabited during the exile." The Babylonians permanently destroyed and depopulated Judah: in brief, as far as archaeology is concerned they made a clean sweep.

Six hundred and fifty years after the children of Israel had, under Joshua, set foot on the Promised Land there was not one of their descendants still in it. The prophetic threats and warnings had been fulfilled; the judgment of God which had been proclaimed had come upon them: "Behold . . . saith the Lord . . . I will make the cities of Judah a desolation without an inhabitant." (Jer. 34:22)

The story of the children of Israel is at an end—the story of the Jews begins.

VII / From the Exile to the Maccabean Kingdom: From Ezekiel to John Hyrcanus

*Good advice from the prophet Jeremiah—The firm of
Murashu and Sons, Nippur—Interest 20 per cent—Farmers
and shepherds turned traders—Koldewey excavates Baby-
lon—The greatest city in the ancient world—Tower of
Babel 300 feet high—Chamber of Commerce on the
Euphrates*

BUILD YE HOUSES, AND DWELL IN THEM: AND PLANT
GARDENS, AND EAT THE FRUIT OF THEM . . . THAT
YE MAY BE INCREASED THERE AND NOT DIMINISHED.
AND SEEK THE PEACE OF THE CITY WHITHER I HAVE
CAUSED YOU TO BE CARRIED AWAY CAPTIVES. (Jer.
29:5-7)

So wrote the prophet Jeremiah from Jerusalem to the
elders, priests, prophets and to the whole nation that
at Nebuchadnezzar's bidding had been carried off to
Babylon. Following his well-considered advice, they
sought and found "the peace of the city" and did not
fare at all badly. The Exile in Babylon was not to be
compared with the harsh existence of the children of
Israel on the Nile, in Pithom, and Raamses in the days
of Moses. Apart from a few exceptions (Isa. 47:6)
there was no heavy forced labor. Nowhere is there any
mention of their having to make bricks by the Euphrates. Yet Babylon ran what was probably the greatest brickmaking industry in the world at that time. For
never was there so much building going on in Mesopotamia as under Nebuchadnezzar.

Anyone who took Jeremiah's advice as his guide got
on well; some, indeed, very well. One family that had
made the grade has left to posterity its dust-covered
business documents on clay: Murashu and Sons—
International Bank—Insurance, Conveyancing, Loans
—Personal and Real Estate—Head Office: Nippur;
Branches Everywhere—a firm with a reputation
throughout the world, the "Lloyd's" of Mesopotamia.

The Murashus—displaced persons from Jerusalem —had done well for themselves in Nippur since 587 B.C. They were an old established office. Their firm still stood for something in Mesopotamia, even in the Persian era. The "books" of Murashu and Sons are full of detailed information about the life of the exiles, such as their names, their occupations, their property.

Scholars from the University of Pennsylvania discovered some of the Jewish firm's deeds stored in its former business premises in Nippur. They were in great clay jars, which, in accordance with security precautions in those days, had been carefully sealed with asphalt. It was not only Assyriologists who read the translations of these documents with delight.

The offices of Murashu and Sons were a hive of activity. For a hundred and fifty years they enjoyed the confidence of their clients, whether it was a matter of conveyance of large estates and sections of the canals or of slaves. Anyone who could not write, when he came eventually to add his signature, put, instead of his name, the print of his finger nail on the documents. It corresponded to putting a cross, in the presence of witnesses, as illiterates do today.

One day three jewelers called on Murashu and Sons. "Elil-Aha-Idinna and Belsunu and Hatin said to Elil-Nadin-Sum, son of Murashu: In the case of this emerald ring, we give a twenty years' guarantee that the stone will not fall out of the gold. If the emerald falls out of the ring before the expiry of twenty years, Elil-Aha-Idinna, Belsunu and Hatin undertake to pay damages to Elil-Nadin-Sum amounting to 10 Minas of silver." The document is signed by seven people. Before the lawyer's name the clay bears the imprint of three finger nails. These are the signatures of the three jewelers, who were unable to write.

An exiled Jew, Mannudannijama, came to Murashu and Sons, because he wanted to arrange a deed of conveyance with a Babylonian concerning an important herd of cattle: "13 old rams, 27 two year old rams, 152 lambing ewes, 40 year old rams, 40 year old ewe-lambs, an old he-goat, a two year old he-goat . . . a total of 276 white and black, large and small sheep and goats . . . cash on delivery . . . Mannudannijama to be responsible for pasture, feeding, and safe custody . . . Nippur, the 25th of Ulul . . . Signed: Fingernail of Mannudannijama."

Securities for those imprisoned for debt were deposited with the bank. There were special departments for all eventualities of life. The rate of interest was 20 per cent, not introduced by Murashu, let it be said. That was the normal rate in those days.

Murashu and Sons may serve as an example of the profession, which, since the days of the Exile, has been associated with the children of Israel. It became for them the profession par excellence and has remained so until now—that of merchant and trader. In their homeland they had been only peasants, settlers, cattle breeders, and tradesmen. The law of Israel had made no provision for commerce; it was an alien occupation. The word "Canaanite" was for them synonymous with "shopkeeper," "merchant," people whom the prophets had vigorously castigated for their sins. "He is a merchant, the balances of deceit are in his hand: he loveth to oppress." (Hos. 12:7; Amos 8:5, 6)

The switch over to this hitherto forbidden profession was extremely clever, a fact that is seldom properly understood; for it proved to be, in the last resort, when added to a tenacious attachment to their old faith, the best guarantee of the continuance of Israel as a people. As farmers and settlers scattered throughout a foreign land, they would have intermarried and interbred with people of other races and in a few generations would have been absorbed and would have disappeared. This new profession demanded that their houses should be in more or less large societies, within which they could build themselves into a community and devote themselves to their religious practices. It gave them cohesion and continuity.

The Israelites could have chosen no better training college. Babylon, as an international center of trade, industry, and commerce, was the great school for the cities and capitals of the whole world that from then on were to become the home of the homeless. The metropolis, whose ruins after 2500 years still betray its ancient power and glory, had no equal in the ancient world.

Sixty miles south of busy Baghdad the desert is churned up, scarred and furrowed. As far as the eye can see, there stretches a maze of trenches, rubble heaps, and pits which bear witness to the efforts of German archaeologists, over a period of eighteen years. As a result of this prolonged campaign,[1] Professor Robert Koldewey has been able to bring to light the fabulous Babylon of the Bible.

Less than fifty years after the excavations, the site presents a dismal and chaotic appearance. Wind and desert sand are slowly but relentlessly covering up again the gigantic skeleton of the old metropolis. Only on one side a few block-like towers stand out with sharply defined silhouette against the sky. Their brick walls, once brightly tiled, are bleak and bare. Here at the Ishtar Gate began the long Processional Way. Where it ends, a massive hump on the other side of the city proclaims the presence of one of the greatest edifices of the ancient world, the Tower of Babel.

The pomp and glory, the power and might of the city that "sinned against the Lord" (Jer. 50:14) were all destroyed and disappeared. It was never again inhabited. Could the oracle of the prophet Isaiah have been more completely fulfilled?

"And Babylon, the glory of kingdoms, the beauty of the Chaldeans' pride shall be as when God overthrew Sodom and Gomorrah. It shall never be inhabited, neither shall it be dwelt in from generation to generation. . . . But wild beasts of the desert shall lie there: and their houses shall be full of doleful creatures: and ostriches shall dwell there. . . . And wolves shall cry in their castles and jackals in the pleasant palaces." (Isa. 13:19-23—R.V.)

It is a long time now since the site was deserted by jackals and owls and more so by ostriches. Even the mighty Euphrates has turned its back on it and has chosen a new bed. Once upon a time the arrogant walls

[1] 1899-1917.

of the city and the lofty Tower were reflected in its waters. Now a silhouette of palm trees in the distance indicates its new course. The little Arab settlement of Babil preserves in its name the memory of the proud city, but it lies some miles north of the ruins.

"Babylon Halt" is written in Arabic and English on the signboard of the station on the Baghdad railway, which lies a few hundred yards from the mounds and allows the visitor, a rare occasion these days, to make a tour of the desolate yellowish-brown ruins. Here he is surrounded by the silence of utter solitude.

The ruins preserved as their most precious treasure documents of imcomparable value. It is thanks to them that we are able today to reconstruct an accurate picture of the time of the Jewish Exile which was also the period of Babylon's greatest prosperity.

"Is not this great Babylon, that I have built for the house of the kingdom, by the might of my power, and for the honour of my majesty?" (Dan. 4:30) These words, which Daniel puts into the mouth of King Nebuchadnezzar, do not exaggerate. Hardly any other monarch in the past was such an assiduous builder. There is scarcely any mention of warlike activities, conquests and campaigns. In the forefront there is the constant building activity of Nebuchadnezzar. Hundreds of thousands of bricks bear his name, and the plans of many of the buildings have been preserved. Babylon, in fact, surpassed all the cities of the ancient Orient; it was greater than Thebes, Memphis and Ur, greater even than Nineveh.

"The center of the city, which is full of three- and four-storied buildings, is traversed by dead straight streets not only those that run parallel to the river but also the cross streets which lead down to the water side." So Herodotus describes what he himself had seen. The town plan of Babylon is not so different from the blueprints for an American city.

Coming from Palestine, even from proud Jerusalem, the exiles had known only narrow twisting streets, little better than alleys. In Babylon, however, they made the acquaintance of streets as broad as avenues and as straight as though they had been drawn with a ruler.

Every one of them bore the name of one of the gods in the Babylonian pantheon. There was a Marduk Street and a Zababa Street on the left bank of the river. In the right-hand corner of the city they crossed the streets of the moon god Sin and of Enlil, the "Lord of the World." On the right bank Adad Street ran from east to west and intersected the street of the sun god Shamash.

Babylon was not only a commercial metropolis but a religious one, as can be seen from an inscription: "Altogether there are in Babylon 53 temples of the chief gods, 55 chapels of Marduk, 300 chapels for the earthly deities, 600 for the heavenly deities, 180 altars for the goddess Ishtar, 180 for the gods Nergal and Adad and 12 other altars for different gods."

Polytheism of this kind, with worship and ritual that extended to public prostitution, must have given the city, in terms of the present day, the appearance of an annual fair.

"But the most vicious practice of the Babylonians is the following," wrote Herodotus in shocked astonishment (I:199). "Every woman in the country must take her seat in the shrine of Aphrodite, and once in her life consort with a stranger. . . . And only when she has been with him, and done her service to the goddess, is she allowed to go home: and from then on no gift is great enough to tempt her. All the women who are tall and beautiful are quickly released: but the unattractive ones have to wait for a long time before they can fulfil the law: some of them have to wait three or four years."

The abominable temptations and enticements which were part of everyday life in Babylon remained indelibly fixed in the minds of the exiled Jews. Through the centuries until the time of Christ the brilliant metropolis was for them "Babylon the Great, the mother of harlots and abominations of the earth." (Rev. 17:5) The idea of Babylon as a cesspool of vice is rooted in the vocabulary of every modern language.

The German archaeologists had to clear away over a million cubic feet of rubble before they exposed part of the temple of Marduk on the Euphrates, which had been rebuilt under Nebuchadnezzar. The structure, including its outbuildings, measured approximately 1500 by 1800 feet. Opposite the temple rose the ziggurat, the tower of Marduk's sanctuary.

"Go to, let us make brick, and burn them thoroughly. And they had brick for stone, and slime had they for mortar. And they said, Go to, let us build us a city, and a tower whose top may reach unto heaven: and let us make us a name. . . ." (Gen. 11:3, 4)

The bricklaying technique described in the Bible at the building of the Tower of Babel corresponds with the findings of the archaeologists. As the investigations confirmed, actually only asphalted bricks were used in the construction, especially in the foundations. That was clearly necessary for the security of the structure in accordance with building regulations. In the neighborhood of the river the regular rise in the level of the water and the constant dampness of the ground had to be borne in mind. Foundations and stonework were therefore made waterproof and dampproof with "slime," that is, asphalt.

The beginning of the building of the Tower of Babel is described in the Book of Genesis and comes before the days of the patriarchs. Abraham lived, as we can gather from what has been discovered at Mari, in the nineteenth century B.C. Is this a contradiction? The history of the tower "whose top may reach unto heaven" points back into the dim past. More than once it had been destroyed and rebuilt. After the death of Hammurabi the Hittites tried to raze the mighty structure to the ground. Nebuchadnezzar merely had it restored.

Seven stages, "seven squares," rose one above the other. A little tablet belonging to an architect which was found in the temple expressly mentions that length, breadth, and height were equal and that only the terraces had different measurements. The length of the sides at the base is given as being rather more than 290 feet. The archaeologists measured it as 295 feet. According to that the tower must have been almost 300 feet high.

The Tower of Babel was also involved in dubious

religious rites. Herodotus described them: "On the topmost tower there is a spacious temple, and inside the temple stands a couch of unusual size richly adorned, with a golden table by its side. There is no statue of any kind set up in the place, nor is the chamber occupied at nights by anyone but a single native woman, who, as the Chaldeans, the priests of this god, affirm, is chosen for himself by the deity out of all the women of the land. They also declare— but I for my part do not believe it—that the god himself comes down into the temple and sleeps upon the couch. This is like the story told by the Egyptians of what takes place in Thebes, where a woman always sleeps in the temple of the Theban Zeus. . . ."

On the streets and squares among the temples, the chapels, and the altars, trade and commerce flourished. Solemn processions, heavily laden caravans, traders' barrows, priests, pilgrims, merchants surged to and fro, colorful and noisy. Religious life and business life were so closely associated in Babylon's everyday affairs that they often dovetailed into each other as they did in the temples. What else could the priests do with all the sacrificial animals, all the "tithes" that were presented daily on the altars, many of them quickly perishable, apart from turning them into money as soon as possible. Just as in Ur, the temple authorities in Babylon ran their own department stores and warehouses. They also ran their own banks to invest their revenues to the best advantage.

Outside the double walls of the city, which were broad enough "to allow a four-horse chariot to turn on them,"[1] lay the "Chambers of Commerce." It was on the riverbank that prices were fixed and exchange rates established for the commodities that arrived by boat. "Karum," or "quay," was the name the Babylonians gave to what we now call the Exchange. As well as taking over the Quay, or Exchange, from the Babylonians, the Old World has also taken over its system of weights and measurements.

However much the Jews may have sought "the

---

[1] Herodotus.

peace of the city" and found it, however much they
may have learned in the cities of Babylonia that would
profit future generations, broaden their own outlook,
and raise their standard of living, all of which would
benefit future generations in many ways, nevertheless,
their heart yearnings for their distant little homeland
on the Jordan left them no inward peace. They could
not forget the city of David, their beloved Jerusalem.
"By the rivers of Babylon, there we sat down; yea, we
wept, when we remembered Zion." (Ps. 137) These
were no empty words, for thousands of them set out
on the difficult journey home. They rebuilt their shattered city and the temple of Yahweh. Without a pas-
sionate longing for the homeland they had lost that
would never have happened.

The old world about 500 B.C.—Last spasms before the end—Escape into the past—Nabonidus restores ancient buildings—First museum in the world at Ur—Semitic empires make their exit—The birth of the west

BEHOLD EVIL SHALL GO FORTH FROM NATION TO NATION AND A GREAT WHIRLWIND SHALL BE RAISED UP FROM THE COASTS OF THE EARTH. (Jer. 25:32)

The hands of the cosmic clock are approaching 500 B.C. The ancient Orient has over 3000 years on its back. The nations in the Fertile Crescent and on the Nile have grown old. Their creative impulse is exhausted; they have fulfilled their task, and the time is drawing near for them to step off the stage of history.

The sun of the ancient Orient is setting and its peoples are vaguely conscious of the approaching night. Yet, there is to be a last flicker of life among these weary nations; they summon up enough strength for one last effort. From Egypt to the lands on the Euphrates and the Tigris it is as though there is to be one final attempt to rise before sinking into insignificance. Were they looking back and thinking of the leading role they had played on the world's stage? It would almost seem that they did. Their monarchs look back to the great symbols of their glorious past. They believe that with a new display of strength they can delay the inevitable.

Pharaoh Necho and Pharaoh Apries made great efforts to reconquer Syria and Palestine. The Old Kingdom with its "campaigns against Asia" became the ideal of the XXVIth dynasty.[1] Large navies were built, and an attempt was made to restore the old canal between the Nile and the Red Sea.

Even though the new manifestations of strength

---

[1] 663-525 B.C.

bore no fruit, and success eluded their military exploits, nevertheless the example of the great days of the builders of the Pyramids lent vitality in other directions. Painters and sculptors copied the works of their great predecessors. Names of Pharaohs of the third millennium were engraved on new scarabs. Ancient official titles and court titles were revived, the Civil Service was, as it were, antiquarianized.

The same thing happened in Phoenicia on the Mediterranean coast. In 814 B.C. Carthage was founded as a North African colony of the city of Tyre. By this time the power of these Phoenician merchant sailors had reached its limit. From the Black Sea to the Straits of Gibraltar they had trading posts and bases along the shores of the Mediterranean. A century later the Greeks had inherited their world trade. Sanchuniathon, the priest, wrote the history of Phoenicia. He was commissioned by a king to copy old inscriptions and texts, which Philo of Byblos was to use much later as the source for his history.

With Ashurbanipal[1] the Assyrian Empire reached the zenith of its power. It stretched from the Persian Gulf to Upper Egypt. The tiger of the ancient Orient had eaten his fill, and the ruler of the most powerful of all conquering nations allowed himself to be painted in an arbor of grapevines, reclining on soft cushions and being handed a goblet of wine. Collecting old books was his hobby, and he had the biggest library in the ancient world. On his instructions the repositories of old temples were ransacked in a search for lost documents. His scribes made copies of thousands of tablets from the reign of the great Sargon I (2350 B.C.). The hobby of his brother Shamash-Shumukin of Babylonia went even further. He had the events of his day written up in the ancient language of Sumeria.

Nebuchadnezzar, too,[2] the last great ruler on the throne of Babylon, was afflicted with this longing for old, forgotten, far-off things. His court chroniclers had to compose inscriptions in Old Babylonian, which

----

[1] 669-626 B.C.
[2] 605-562 B.C.

nobody could either speak or read. Architecture and literature flourished once again among the Chaldeans.

Observing the sky in the interests of astrology led to undreamed-of advances. They were able to predict eclipses of the sun and moon. In the Babylonian School of Astronomy about 750 B.C. observations of heavenly bodies were recorded and continued without interruption for over 350 years, the longest series of astronomical observations ever made. The accuracy of their reckoning exceeded that of European astronomers until well into the eighteenth century.

Nabonidus[1] may well have been the first archaeologist in the world. This monarch, the last of the Babylonian rulers, caused ruined shrines and temples to be excavated, old inscriptions to be deciphered and translated. At Ur he restored the staged tower which had been weakened by age, as was shown by the finds at Tell al Muqayyar.

Princess Bel-Shalti-Nannar, sister of the Belshazzar in the Bible, had the same interests as her father Nabonidus. Woolley discovered in an annex to the temple in Ur, where she had been priestess, a regular museum with objects which had been found in the southern states of Mesopotamia—probably the earliest museum in the world. She had actually carefully catalogued her collection piece by piece on a clay cylinder. This is, in Woolley's words, the "oldest museum guide known."

One people alone, broken up into many parts and at that time scattered far and wide throughout the Fertile Crescent, did not succumb to surfeit or slackness: the children of Israel, descendants of the patriarchs, were filled with eager hope and had a definite end in view. They did not disappear; they found the strength to preserve themselves for new millennia up to the present day.

For fifteen hundred years mankind's brightest light had come from the Fertile Crescent, the oldest center of civilization since the Stone Age. About 500 B.C. darkness fell, imperceptibly but irresistibly, over the

[1]555-538 B.C.

lands and peoples who had within them the seed of all that would come after them—but in other lands.

A new light was already shining from the mountains of Iran: the Persians were coming. The great Semitic states and Egypt had fulfilled their assignment in history: the most significant and decisive part of man's early existence had helped to prepare the ground for the Indo-Germanic kingdoms which gave birth to Europe.

From the extreme southeastern tip of the continent the light traveled farther and farther west: from Greece to Rome, across the barrier of the Alps, across Western Europe and up to Scandinavia and the British Isles. Light from the East!

On its way, within a few centuries, new civilizations would appear, art would reach unimagined heights of beauty and harmony, the human mind in the philosophy and science of the Greeks would soar to pinnacles denied to the ancient Orient.

On its way, the light would also bring the varied, colorful legacy of the ancient Orient, from a practical system of weights and measures to astronomy, it would bring writing, the alphabet, and—the Bible.

CHAPTER 3 / **Cyrus, King of Persia**

Two famous dreams—Cyrus unites Media and Persia—The writing on the wall—Belshazzar was merely crown prince—Peaceful entry into Babylon—Persian toleration

THUS SAITH THE LORD TO HIS ANOINTED, TO CYRUS, WHOSE RIGHT HAND I HAVE HOLDEN, TO SUBDUE NATIONS BEFORE HIM; AND I WILL LOOSE THE LOINS OF KINGS, TO OPEN BEFORE HIM THE TWO LEAVED GATES; AND THE GATES SHALL NOT BE SHUT. (Isa. 45:1)

Seven years after Nebuchadnezzar's death, Nabonidus, the "first archaeologist," ascended the throne of Babylon in 555 B.C. He was to be the last ruler from Mesopotamia, for events in the highlands of Iran suggested that world history was quickly heading for a great revolution.

Five years after the accession of Nabonidus, the new era began with the Persians' rise to power. The Medes, who since the fall of Nineveh in 612 B.C. had shared the stricken Assyrian empire with the Babylonians, were unexpectedly overcome by their neighbors and vassals, the Persians. Astyages, king of the Medes, was beaten by his own grandson, Cyrus.

In the ancient world great men were wont to herald their arrival in extraordinary ways; often the remarkable circumstances of their birth took them outside the normal framework of the lives of their contemporaries. Two unusual dreams are said to have decided the destiny of Cyrus. They were gossiped around the whole of the ancient Orient and in this way came to the ears of Herodotus, who recorded them:

"Astyages . . . had a daughter who was named Mandane. He dreamt that from her such a stream of water flowed forth as not only to fill his capital but to flood the whole of Asia. This vision he laid before such of the Magi as had the gift of interpreting dreams, who expounded its meaning to him in full, whereat he was greatly terrified. On this account, when his daughter was of marriageable age, he would not give her to any of the Medes lest the dream should be accomplished, but married her to a Persian by name Cambyses. . . ."

When Mandane was living with Cambyses, Astyages in the very first year saw another vision. He fancied that a vine grew from the womb of his daughter and overshadowed the whole of Asia. After this dream, which he submitted also to the interpreters, he sent to Persia and fetched away Mandane, who was now with child, and was not far from her time. On her arrival he set a watch over her, intending to destroy the child to which she should give birth; for the Magian interpreters had expounded the vision to foreshow that the offspring of his daughter would reign over Asia in his stead. To guard against this, Astyages, as soon as Cyrus was born, sent for Harpagus, a man of his own house and the most faithful of the Medes . . . and addressed him thus: "Take the child born of Mandane: carry him with thee to thy home and slay him there. . . ."

Harpagus found that he had no heart to carry out this murderous command of the child's grandfather. No more had a shepherd to whom he deputed the task. So Cyrus remained alive.

It was not only the birth and boyhood of Cyrus that were wrapped in legend. This Persian king's son, descended from the royal race of Achaemenes, has, more than any other prince of the ancient world, caught the imagination and evoked the admiration of all nations. Xenophon, the Greek, celebrated the foundation of his empire in a complete romance, the *Cyropaedia*.

The Bible remembers him as an enlightened monarch. His unparalleled, swift, and brilliant rise to power was marred by no deed of violence. His able and humane policy made him one of the most attractive figures in the ancient Orient. The most repugnant feature of oriental monarchs before him, despotic cruelty, was foreign to this Persian.

The figure of Cyrus became a hard fact of history

in 550 B.C. In that year he captured Ecbatana, capital of the kingdom of Media. His royal grandfather Astyages was banished. Cyrus amalgamated Media with the Persian kingdom. Babylonia, Lydia in Asia Minor, and Sparta formed an alliance against the conqueror. Croesus, King of Lydia—his name is still proverbial for great riches—attacked the Persians. Cyrus took Sardis,[1] his capital, and defeated him.

The way to Babylonia was open and Babylon lay invitingly before him. Against the background of such a situation, a strange and mysterious story got about, which, since it has been recorded in the Bible, has gripped the imagination of the western world:

"Belshazzar the king made a great feast to a thousand of his lords, and drank wine before the thousand. . . . They drank wine, and praised the gods of gold, and of silver, of brass, of iron, of wood and of stone. In the same hour came forth fingers of a man's hand, and wrote over against the candlestick upon the plaister of the wall of the king's palace. . . . Then the king's countenance was changed, and his thoughts troubled him, so that the joints of his loins were loosed, and his knees smote one against another. . . . And the king spake and said to the wise men of Babylon, Whosoever shall read this writing, and shew me the interpretation thereof, shall be clothed with scarlet, and have a chain of gold about his neck, and shall be the third ruler in the kingdom." (Dan. 5:1, 4-7) "Mene, Mene, Tekel, Upharsin" were the words on the wall which have become famous. They mean: "God hath numbered thy kingdom." "Thou art weighed in the balances and art found wanting." "Thy kingdom is divided and given to the Medes and Persians." (Dan. 5:25-28)

When Joseph in Egypt was able to interpret Pharaoh's dreams of the seven fat kine and the seven lean kine and of the ears of corn, he was made second man in the kingdom, grand vizier.

What was the meaning of the promised reward for explaining the meaning of the mysterious writing: to

---

[1] 50 miles east of Smyrna.

be "the third ruler in the kingdom"? This Biblical statement was unintelligible and was explained only with the help of archaeology.

Who Belshazzar was has now been established by cuneiform texts from his own father. He was not, in fact, as the Book of Daniel says (5:2) the son of Nebuchadnezzar, but of Nabonidus, who says in an inscription: "And put into the heart of Belshazzar, my first-born son, the fruit of my loins, fear of thy sublime divinity, that he commit no sin, and that he may have fulness of life." Thus it is clear that Belshazzar was crown prince; therefore, the second man in Babylonia. He could only therefore hold out a promise of third highest place in the kingdom.

The story of Belshazzar's feast and the writing on the wall reflects through the eyes of the prophets a contemporary political situation. In 539 B.C. Cyrus turned his attack against Nabonidus, and the Babylonian army was defeated. With that the hours of the last great Mesopotamian empire were numbered.

"Come down, and sit in the dust, O virgin daughter of Babylon: there is no throne, O daughter of the Chaldeans." (Isa. 47:1)

A year after the battle Cyrus, king of Persia, made his triumphal entry into conquered Babylon.

Hittites, Kassites, Assyrians had at various times threatened the great city with the same fate. This conquest, however, did not follow the normal pattern. It was without a parallel in the military practice of the ancient Orient; for this time there were no columns of smoke rising from behind shattered walls, no temples or palaces razed to the ground, no house plundered, no man was butchered or impaled. The clay cylinder of Cyrus narrates in Babylonian script what took place:

"As I entered Babylon in peace, and established my royal residence in the palace of the princes amid jubilation and rejoicing, Marduk, the great lord, warmed the hearts of the Babylonians towards me, while I for my part devoted myself daily to do him reverence. My troops wandered peacefully widespread throughout Babylon. In all Sumer and Akkad I let no man be afraid. I concerned myself with the internal affairs of Babylon and all its cities. The dwellers in Babylon . . . I freed from the yoke that ill became them. I repaired their houses, I healed their afflictions. . . . I am Cyrus, king of all, the great king, the mighty king, king of Babylon, king of Sumer and Akkad, king of the four corners of the earth. . . ."

The last sentences almost suggest that the Biblical Chronicler had known the text of the clay cylinder. "Thus saith Cyrus, king of Persia. All the kingdoms of the earth hath the Lord God of heaven given me. . . ." (II Chron. 36:23) That rulers should make tolerance, including religious tolerance, their motto was uncommon and distinguished the Persian king from the first.

After his entry into Babylon Cyrus at once had the images and shrines of the local gods set up again. He was concerned with "the daily worship of the chief god of the city—Marduk." In the city of Ur he did the same. On a broken cylinder which was preserved among the ruins Cyrus himself says: "Sin, the light of heaven and earth, with his favourable omens gave into my hands the four corners of the earth. I brought the gods back into their sanctuaries."

His tolerance was also to the advantage of the Jews. After these many years of exile their dearest wish was now to find fulfillment.

CHAPTER 4 / Return to Jerusalem

The edict of Cyrus—The trek of the 42,000—A caravan of fateful significance—Starting work on the ruins—A lonely grave in Pasargadae—Rebuilding the Temple—The Persian Empire: from the Nile to India—Duncan finds Nehemiah's work—The secret of the "thick water"—A theocratic state —Judah coins stamped with the Athenian owl—A Persian province for two centuries

IN THE FIRST YEAR OF CYRUS THE KING, THE SAME CYRUS THE KING MADE A DECREE CONCERNING THE HOUSE OF GOD AT JERUSALEM, LET THE HOUSE BE BUILDED, THE PLACE WHERE THEY OFFERED SACRIFICES, AND LET THE FOUNDATIONS THEREOF BE STRONGLY LAID: THE HEIGHT THEREOF THREESCORE CUBITS, AND THE BREADTH THEREOF THREESCORE CUBITS. (Ezra 6:3)

This meant permission for them to return to Jerusalem. The text of the royal decree is in imperial Aramaic, the new official language of the Persian government. Archaeology has been able to establish the authenticity of this permit, which was incorporated in Chapter 6 of the Book of Ezra.

It was a matter of reparation. It is clear from the terms of the enactment that the Persians regarded themselves as successors of the Babylonians: ". . . let the expenses be given out of the king's house. And also let the golden and silver vessels of the house of God, which Nebuchadnezzar took forth out of the temple which is at Jerusalem, and brought unto Babylon, be restored and brought again unto the temple, which is at Jerusalem, every one to his place, and place them in the house of God." (Ezra 4:5, 6)

The carrying out of the order was entrusted by Cyrus to Sheshbazzar,[1] the governor (Ezra 5:14), a

---

[1] It is thought that Sheshbazzar is the same as Shenazar, the fourth son of King Jehoiachin. (I Chron. 3:18)

prince of Judah, and probably a member of the house of David.

It is understandable that fifty years after the deportation not everyone would take advantage of this permission to return to the land of their fathers. In any case it was a risky business to leave this wealthy country of Babylon, where they had established themselves and where most of them had grown up, and to set out on the difficult road back to the ruins of a ravaged land. Despite this, in the spring of 537 B.C., after long preparations a lengthy caravan set out on the trail toward the old homeland. "The whole congregation together was forty and two thousand three hundred and threescore. Beside their servants and their maids, of whom there were seven thousand three hundred thirty and seven, and there were among them two hundred singing men and singing women. Their horses were seven hundred thirty and six: their mules two hundred forty and five, their camels four hundred thirty and five, their asses six thousand seven hundred and twenty." (Ezra 2:64-67)

The Old Testament gives us no information about the trek of this vast throng, nor have we so far any other contemporary evidence. But it requires no great imagination to picture the long procession, with its priests and singers, its porters, its women and children, slowly making its way upriver by the banks of the mighty Euphrates.

Almost 800 miles have to be covered between Babylon and distant Jerusalem, with the clouds of dust churned up by the caravan as a faithful companion throughout the whole journey. One day they would pass the site of old Mari. They would reach the spot where, on the opposite side of the river, the Balikh, on whose lower reaches Haran was situated, enters the Euphrates.

From then on the returning exiles were following the same track which had been taken by Abraham 1400 years earlier, when he left the land of his fathers to go to Canaan, via Damascus and along the foot of Hermon to the Lake of Galilee. Then came the day when from among the brown peaks of the mountains of

Judah the desolate ruins of the city of Zion rose before their eyes—it was Jerusalem.

What fateful significance this journey had for the generations that were still to come!

"The future of the world lay in this procession to Jerusalem," says the American writer and educator Mary Ellen Chase, who has been lecturing in colleges and universities on "The Bible as Literature" since 1926. "It rested with it whether we should have a Bible at all as we know it—the Bible, the Jewish faith, Christianity and many centuries of western culture. If there had been no return to Jerusalem, Judah would assuredly have shared by and large the fate of Israel, become intermingled with the East and eventually been lost as a united people."

Soon after their arrival in Jerusalem, the foundations of the new Temple were laid amid great enthusiasm. But then the work slackened off. (Ezra 5:16) The great enthusiasm of the returned settlers

Fig. 62. Mausoleum of Cyrus.

quickly waned; life was too hard and barren in this depopulated land, where dilapidated houses provided the scantiest of shelter. Added to this was the problem of making a living; as Haggai said, "ye run every man unto his own house." (Hag. 1:9) Everyone was too concerned with his own problems.

The rebuilding advanced but slowly. The first settlers were poor and, as the remains of their household belongings indicate, few in number. The objects that have been discovered clearly reflect the harshness of that first early stage.

Cyrus, the liberator, died on an expedition to the East in 530 B.C. and was buried in the royal palace of Pasargadae near Persepolis.[1] His palace was built in the form of individual pavilions; each one lay in the center of a magnificent garden, the whole area enclosed by a high wall.

On the southern slopes of a long range of hills there still stands among the rough grass of the highlands a small unpretentious stone building dating from the time of Cyrus. Six square blocks form the steps that lead up to a small chamber, above the entrance to which there could at one time be read the following

Fig. 63.

plea: "O man, whoever you are and whenever you come—for I know that you will come—I am Cyrus, who gave the Persians their empire. Do not grudge me this patch of earth that covers my body." Alas, the small stone chamber in which a golden sarcophagus enclosed the mortal remains of the great Persian is now as empty as the place above the entrance which

[1]Thirty miles northeast of Shiraz in southern Iran, famous in modern times as a center of carpet weaving.

bore the inscription. Occasionally shepherds with their flocks pass unconcernedly by this forgotten spot, as they did in olden times, across the wide plateau where the lion is still lord of the chase.

Cyrus was followed by his son Cambyses II.[1] With the conquest of Egypt, Persia became under him the greatest empire that the world had ever seen; it stretched from India to the Nile.

It was not until the reign of his successor, Darius I,[2] that the rebuilding of the Temple in Jerusalem was finally taken in hand. Almost twenty years had passed since the foundations had been laid. At the request of the official responsible for the administration of Judah, the Satrap of Transeuphrates, Darius I expressly confirmed the permit issued by Cyrus. The official exchange of letters with the Persian court on this matter can be found in the Book of Ezra (5:6-6:12).

There is no longer any doubt as to the historicity of these documents. Numerous contemporary texts of a different type indicate how zealously Darius I promoted religion in every way, just as his predecessor had done, not only in Palestine but also in Asia Minor and in Egypt. For example, the inscription of Usahor, an Egyptian doctor, runs as follows: "King Darius— may he live for ever—commanded me to go to Egypt . . . and make up once more the number of the holy scribes of the temple and bring new life into what had fallen into decay. . . ."

Darius wrote to Gadata the steward of his demesnes in no uncertain manner. He took him sharply to task for his attitude to the priesthood of the temple of Apollo in Magnesia: "I hear that you are not carrying out my instructions properly. Admittedly you are taking trouble over my estates, in that you are transferring trees and plants from beyond the Euphrates to Asia Minor. I commend this project and the court will show its gratitude. But in disregarding my attitude to the gods you have provoked my displeasure and unless you change your tactics you will feel its weight.

---

[1] 530-522 B.C.
[2] 522-486 B.C.

For you have taken away the gardeners who are sacred to Apollo and used them for other gardening jobs of a secular character, thereby showing a lack of appreciation of the sentiments of my ancestors toward the god who has spoken to the Persians. . . ."

The efforts of the returned exiles were for many years confined exclusively to rebuilding the Temple at Jerusalem. Building operations started in October-November, 520 B.C., and by March 12, 515 B.C., they were completed.[1]

They had to wait for the city wall until the next century. It was not until the time of Nehemiah, who was installed as independent governor of Judah by King Artaxerxes I[2] of Persia in 444 B.C., that they began work on the wall, which was finished in record time. "So the wall was finished . . . in fifty and two days." (Neh. 6:15) A new wall in fifty-two days? Impossible! Nehemiah himself tells us of "the walls of Jerusalem which were broken down, and the gates thereof were consumed with fire." (Neh. 2:13) The walls were thus merely repaired. And that must have happened in a hurry. For the neighboring tribes— above all, the Samaritans—wanted to stop the refortification of Jerusalem by every means in their power. The Jews had to be constantly on the lookout, "everyone with one of his hands wrought in the work, and with the other hand held a weapon." (Neh. 4:17)

It is no different today in the case of the building operations of farmers, workers, and shepherds in the modern state of Israel.

The speedy filling up of holes and patching up of gaps in the walls reflect the pressure of the time factor and the feverish anxiety with which the work went forward. The British archaeologist J. Garrow Duncan dug up parts of the wall on the little hill to the southeast above the Gihon spring. In his report he says:

---

[1] Zech. 1:1; the eighth month of the second year of Darius= October-November, 520 B.C. (start of building operations) (Ezra 6:15); the third day of the month of Adar (Babylonian: Addaru) in the sixth year of Darius=March 12, 515 B.C. (completion of Temple).
[2] 465-424 B.C.

Fig. 64. Stamp on Judahite pitcher bearing the inscription "Jerusalem."

"The stones are small, rough, irregular and unequal. Some of them are unusually small and seem to be merely chips broken off from bigger stones, just as if they were using any kind of material that came to hand. The large holes and hollow spaces are filled up with a haphazard mixture of clay plaster mixed with tiny chips of stone. . . ."

During the time that Nehemiah was governor of Jerusalem we are told how the holy fire of the Temple was rediscovered. The first two chapters of II Maccabees tell how Nehemiah "sent in quest of the fire the descendants of the priests that hid it." They "had found no fire but thick water." When at Nehemiah's command they poured this thick water over "the wood and the things laid thereupon" "there was kindled a great blaze so that all men marvelled." (II Macc. 1:21-22) Nobody paid much attention to the observation that followed: "And Nehemiah and they that were with him called this thing Nephthar." (II Macc. 1:36) Yet this passage in the Bible contains a very clear hint regarding a quite specific mineral product which must have been well known to the Israelites, and it is only very recently that this was recognized. In the new state of Israel petroleum, or naphtha—the word is of Babylonian derivation—has in fact been found. Since 1953, drilling near the Dead Sea, in the Negeb and in the neighborhood of Askelon has led to the successful opening of Israeli oil wells.

Was it surprising that the suggestion was made after this discovery that petroleum may have been involved in the divine judgment on Mount Carmel? (I Kings 18:34-38) Was Elijah perhaps guilty of pious deception when he covered his altar with petroleum and not with water, before setting it alight to the astonishment of the priests of Baal?

The rebuilding of the Temple and of the old city of David makes it abundantly clear that Israel knew full well that the days of the monarchy had gone forever and that only the inward solidarity of a religious community could guarantee the further existence of the tiny state in face of what political developments might be in store for them. With this end in view they made the holy city the center of Jewry, both for those Jews who lived in the homeland of Judah and for those who were scattered throughout the world. The High Priest of the new Temple at Jerusalem became head over all Israel. The little theocracy in Palestine took no noteworthy part in the affairs of the world during the subsequent centuries. Israel turned its back on politics.

With Persian approval the Law of God became the law of Israel, indeed, of Jews everywhere, as the Book of Ezra clearly indicates. (Ezra 7:23-26) This Biblical

Fig. 65. Coins from Judah with Zeus and the owl of Athens (Persian era).

passage is convincingly borne out by another document from the same period. In 1905 three papyrus documents were discovered on the palm-covered Island of Elephantine, which lies beside the first cataract of the Nile near the Aswan dam. They are written in imperial Aramaic and date from the year 419 B.C. One of them is a message from King Darius II of Persia containing instructions as to how the Feast of the Passover is to be celebrated. The recipients of the letter were the Jewish military colony in Elephantine. The sender signs himself Hananiah, "agent for Jewish affairs at the court of the Persian governor of Egypt."

For two centuries the Persians were liege lords of Jerusalem. The history of Israel during this period seems to have been subjected to no violent variations. The Bible makes no mention of it, nor have the layers of rubble anything significant to tell us of this long space of time. At all events there is a complete absence of large buildings, or objects of art and craft among the archaeological trophies recovered from the appropriate layer. Fragments of simple household utensils prove how miserably poor life in Judah must have been at that time.

Nevertheless, in the course of the fourth century B.C. coins appear. They bear the proud inscription "Yehud"—Judah. Clearly the Persians had allowed the High Priest to mint silver coins. They are adorned with the image of Zeus and the owl of Athens in the manner of Attic drachmas, proving how strongly—long before Alexander the Great—Greek trade and influence had been able to penetrate the whole of the East.

CHAPTER 5 / Under Greek Influence

*Alexander the Great in Palestine—Causeway forces capit-
ulation of Tyre—Siege towers 160 feet high—Alexandria,
the new metropolis—Ptolemies occupy Judah—Seventy-two
scholars translate the Bible—Pentateuch in Greek—The
Septuagint came from Pharos—A stadium below the Temple—High Priest in "gaming house"—Jewish athletes give
offense*

AND IT CAME TO PASS, AFTER THAT ALEXANDER THE
MACEDONIAN, THE SON OF PHILIP, WHO CAME OUT
OF THE LAND OF CHITTIM,[1] AND SMOTE DARIUS KING
OF THE PERSIANS AND MEDES, IT CAME TO PASS, AFTER
HE HAD SMITTEN HIM, THAT HE REIGNED IN HIS
STEAD, IN FORMER TIME, OVER GREECE. AND HE
FOUGHT MANY BATTLES, AND WON MANY STRONG-
HOLDS. . . . (I Maccabees 1:1—R.V.)

In the fourth century B.C. the center of political power
gradually shifted from the Fertile Crescent to the West.
The prelude to this development, which was of decisive
importance for the whole world, had been two famous
battles in the previous century, in both of which the
Greeks put a halt to any further Persian advance. At
Marathon in 491 B.C. they defeated the Persian armies
of Darius I. At Salamis, off Athens, they smashed the
Persian fleet eleven years later, in 480 B.C.

With the victory of Alexander the Great[2] over
Darius III,[3] King of Persia, in 333 B.C. at Issus, near
the present-day seaport of Alexandretta in north Syria,
the Macedonians arrogated to themselves the leading
role among the nations of the world.

Alexander's first target was Egypt. At the age of
twenty-four, he marched south with a picked force of
32,000 infantry and 5000 cavalry, accompanied off-

---

[1]Greece.
[2]336-323 B.C.
[3]336-331 B.C.

shore by a fleet of 160 ships. Twice he was held up on the coast of Syria and Palestine.

The first occasion was at Tyre. This Phoenician city, heavily fortified and protected by stout high walls, was built on a small island which guarded the coastline. Alexander performed here a miracle of military ingenuity by building a 2000-foot mole in the sea out to the island city. To safeguard the operations, mobile protective shields, so-called "tortoises," had to be employed. Despite this the construction of the causeway was greatly hindered by an incessant hail of missiles. Meantime his engineers were on shore building veri-

Fig. 66. Alexander the Great built a 650-yard causeway across to Tyre.

table monsters—"Hele-poleis." These were mobile protective towers many stories high, which held detachments of bowmen and light artillery. A drawbridge on the front of the towers enabled a surprise attack to be made on the enemy's walls. They were the highest siege towers ever used in the history of war. Each of them had twenty stories and the topmost platform towered, at a height of over 160 feet, far above the highest city walls.

When, after seven months' preparation, these monsters, bristling with weapons, slowly and clumsily rolled toward Tyre, the fate of the maritime stronghold, which was considered to be impregnable, was sealed.

The second check came from Gaza, the old Philistine city. But this siege lasted only two months, and then the road to the Nile lay open.

The siege of Gaza in southwest Palestine especially must have made some impact on the Jews. The noise of troops marching down the coast below them and camping there must have been heard on their hills above. Yet the Bible has as little to say about these events as indeed about the whole period of Greek supremacy for almost 150 years. Its historians do not take us beyond the end of the kingdoms of Israel and Judah and the creation of the theocracy under Persian sovereignty. It is only with the beginning of the Maccabean wars that it embarks once more upon detailed history.

Fig. 67. Alexander's mobile siege-towers were 160 feet high.

But Flavius Josephus, the Jewish historian, gives an account that is not found in the Bible of the campaign of the victorious Greeks through Syria and Palestine at this time. After the capture of the fortress of Gaza, he says, Alexander the Great came to Jerusalem. The people and Jaddua the High Priest received him with great ceremony. Alexander offered sacrifices in the Temple and granted the people favors.

Alexander can hardly have found time for a trip to Jerusalem, since he had already been held up for nine months by the resistance of Tyre and Gaza. After the fall of Gaza, he hurried on by the quickest road to Egypt, leaving the conquest of the territory inland to his general, Parmenio, who had no difficulty in subduing the country. Only Samaria, the seat of the governor of the province, had to be forcibly brought to heel. As a punishment it had a colony of Macedonians settled in it.

Jerusalem and the province of Judah seem to have submitted to their new masters without more ado. At all events no contemporary source has so far suggested that there was any resistance from the theocracy.

The visit of Alexander to Jerusalem is probably only a legend which nevertheless contains a grain of truth. It bears eloquent witness to the fact that the Greek conqueror too tolerated the way of life of the theocracy of Judah. It was left unmolested as a religious community. This is quite in accord with what archaeology has been able to establish. There are no traces of either a Greek conquest or a Greek occupation of Judah at that time. Only in the neighboring city of Samaria a strong Greek fortress came into existence about 322 B.C. Excavations disclosed a whole series of round towers. They lean against the old casemated wall which was built in the days when Samaria was still the capital of the kingdom of Israel.

Alexander remained in Egypt, which welcomed him as a liberator, during the winter of 332-331 B.C. On the outermost tip of the Nile Delta, he founded the city of Alexandria, which was destined for the role of the metropolis of the new age. It quickly blossomed into the center of a new intellectual life which attracted the best minds of the Greek and oriental world within its orbit.

At its foundation Alexander issued instructions

which were to be of the highest significance in future days. He guaranteed to the Jews—descendants of the refugees in the Babylonian era—the same rights as were accorded to his own countrymen. This provision, carried on by the successors of the great Macedonian, led to Alexandria's becoming subsequently one of the great reservoirs of Jewish life and culture.

The name of the city founded by Alexander does not appear in the Bible earlier than the Book of Acts: "And a certain Jew named Apollos, born at Alexandria, an eloquent man and mighty in the scriptures, came to Ephesus." (Acts 18:24)

On the way to one of the greatest and most successful military expeditions known to history, Alexander marched once more through Palestine. Every country in the ancient East fell before him. He pressed on to the Indus, almost to the foot of the Himalayas. On the way back he was attacked by a fever. Alexander died in Babylon at the age of thirty-three on June 13, 323 B.C.

"Behold ye among the nations, and regard, and wonder marvellously . . . . For, lo, I raise up the Chittites,[1] that bitter and hasty nation, which march through the breadth of the earth. . . ." (Hab. 1:5, 6—R.V.) So writes the prophet Habakkuk in Jerusalem and asks his God in wonderment: "Wherefore lookest thou upon them that deal treacherously, and holdest thy peace when the wicked swalloweth up the man that is more righteous than he?" (Hab. 1:13— R.V.)

In view of the fact that, long before Alexander, the Greeks had been stretching out their feelers in a thousand ways in the direction of Mesopotamia and Egypt, we can only shake our heads in amazement at the ignorance of the ways of the world which this question reflects. Time seems to have been standing still in the little theocracy, and the life of its tiny religious com-

---

[1]"Chittites," i.e., Greeks, should be read here instead of Chaldeans. The author adopts Duhm's view that Kasdim (Chaldeans) should read Kittim (Greeks).—Translator's note.

munity appears to have been influenced only by the
Torah, the Law of God.

A long way back there had been Greek mercenaries
in the armies of Pharaoh Psamtik II and Nebuchadnezzar, King of the Chaldeans. It was also a long time
since the first Greek forts and trading stations had
started to spread along the coast of Syria and Palestine. In the fifth century B.C. there were already
highly educated Greeks traveling and studying in all
countries of the ancient Orient: Herodotus and
Xenophon, Hecataeus and Ctesias.

Were these men in their theocratic community no
longer able to recognize or understand the signs of the
times? Or did they intentionally shut their eyes and
blindly hope to keep the future at bay?

If so they must have had all the ruder awakening
when they came face to face with Greece but a few
steps from the sanctuary of the Temple and could disguise from themselves no longer that Jewish youth had
fallen completely for the sport of throwing the discus,
which had been imported from Greece. Athletic contests on the Greek pattern quickly found an enthusiastic response among the young people.

Greece was not a danger to the Jews by reason of its
growing ascendancy, or militarism, or seductive temptations. The danger lay far more in the freer atmosphere of a fabulous modern world. Hellas with its
Pericles, Aeschylus, Sophocles, Euripides, with its
Phidias and Polygnotus, its Plato and its Aristotle, had
climbed up to a new stage in human development.

Undisturbed by the new era of mankind the tiny
theocracy went on obstinately in its own way, held
tenaciously and inflexibly to its traditions and to the
past. Despite all this it was forced to join issue with
the new ideas. But there was still time enough before
the second century B.C.

"So Alexander . . . died. And his servants bore rule
every one in his place. And after his death they all
put crowns upon themselves: so did their sons after
them many years: and evils were multiplied in the
earth." (I Macc. 1:7-9)

The idea behind the struggle for power of Alexander's captains, the Diadochi, is not unknown even in twentieth-century politics. In its original form it was no more than an advertisement for the profession of army commanders. Alexander's generals had no scruples about getting rid of his whole family by murdering them: Philip Arrhidaeus his half-brother, his

Fig. 68.

mother Olympia, his widow Roxana and his posthumous son. The conflict came to a head in the division of the empire into three kingdoms.

The kingdom of Macedonia in northern Greece was the first. The kingdom of the Seleucids, which extended from Thrace through Asia Minor and Syria to the borders of India, was another. Antioch in the north of Syria, situated on the lower reaches of the Orontes, was founded as capital of this second and by far the largest of the successor states. Thereafter almost all the Seleucid monarchs added to their own names the name of this city: Antiochus.

The third was the Ptolemaic kingdom on the Nile, with Alexandria as its capital. It was ruled by a dynasty whose last representative, Cleopatra, has ever since enjoyed a certain amount of fame for having so successfully turned the heads of her distinguished contemporaries Julius Caesar and Mark Anthony.

Ptolemy I was the first ruler of this dynasty. While he was still a general Ptolemy had entered Jerusalem in 320 B.C. The incorporation of the theocracy of Judah into the kingdom of the Hellenistic Ptolemies meant more than merely another change of government. It was much more the first step on the way to the realization of what the Bible significantly paraphrases in the Book of Genesis: "God shall enlarge Japheth and he shall dwell in the tents of Shem. . . ." (Gen. 9:27)

According to Genesis, Noah had three sons, Shem, Ham, and Japheth, who became the ancestors of three racial groups. From Shem came the Semites, from Ham the Hamites, living in Africa. The descendants of Japheth are, however, Aryans according to their location, which the Bible gives with great accuracy. Among them the Kittim, the Greeks, are specifically mentioned.

Two unusually farsighted rulers, Ptolemy I and his son Ptolemy II Philadelphus, developed their capital city of Alexandria into a nursery of Hellenistic culture and learning, whose fame extended far beyond the borders of its own kingdoms and made it a radiant center of attraction for emigrants from Judah among others. In this crucible they steeped themselves in the beauty of the Greek language, the only means of tasting the delights of the prodigious advances of the human mind and the human spirit. It was the international language of learning and of commerce, the language of tens of thousands of Israelites who knew no other home.

The rising generation no longer knew Hebrew as their mother tongue. They could no longer follow the sacred text in the services of the synagogue. Thus it came about that the Jews in Egypt decided to translate the Hebrew scriptures. About 250 B.C. the Torah was translated into Greek, a fact of immeasurable import for Western civilization.

The translation of the Bible into the Greek tongue was for the Jews in Egypt such an incredible step forward that legend took hold of it. The story is told in an apocryphal letter of Aristeas of Alexandria.

Philadelphus,[1] the second of the Ptolemaic dynasty, took great pride in the fact that he possessed a collection of the finest books in the world. One day the librarian said to the monarch that he had brought together in his 995 books the best literature of all nations. But, he added, the greatest books of all, the five books of Moses, were not included among them. Therefore, Ptolemy II Philadelphus sent envoys to the High Priest to ask for a copy of these books. At the same time he asked for men to be sent who could translate them into Greek. The High Priest granted his request and sent together with the copy of the Torah seventy-two learned and wise scribes. Great celebrations were organized in honor of the visitors from Jerusalem, at whose wisdom and knowledge the king and his courtiers were greatly astonished. After the festivities they betook themselves to the extremely difficult task which had been assigned to them, and for which there was neither prototype nor dictionary. They set to work out at sea, on the Island of Pharos off Alexandria, at the foot of one of the Seven Wonders of the World—the 300-foot-high lighthouse which Ptolemy II had erected as a warning for shipping far and near. Each of them worked in a cell by himself. When the scholars had completed their work and the translations were compared with one another all seventy-two are said to have corresponded exactly, word for word. Accordingly, the Greek translation of the Bible was called the "Septuagint," meaning "the Seventy."

What had previously been made known only in the sanctuary, only in the old tongue, and only to the one nation was now all at once available and intelligible for people of other tongues and other races. The hitherto carefully guarded door into the "tents of Shem" was thrown wide open.

Judah's attachment to the kingdom of the Ptolemies lasted for more than a hundred years. Then the Seleucids of Antioch forced their way southward, an

---

[1] 285-246 B.C.

expansion for which they had long been striving. After a victorious battle against Ptolemy V at the sources of the Jordan, Antiochus III, called "the Great," took over Palestine, in 195 B.C., and Judah thereby once more came under a new sovereignty.

Gradually the foreign seed began to sprout even in the theocracy. The manifold and enduring influence of the Greek attitude of mind, which had been infiltrating since Alexander's victorious campaigns, became more and more apparent.

When "Antiochus surnamed Epiphanes . . . reigned in the hundred and thirty and seventh year of the kingdom of the Greeks" (I Macc. 1:10) and "Jason . . . labored underhand to be high priest . . . he forthwith brought his own nation to the Greekish fashion. . . . For he built gladly a place of exercise under the tower itself, and brought the chief young men under his subjection. . . . Now such was the height of Greek fashions, and increase of heathenish manners through the exceeding profaneness of Jason, that ungodly wretch and no high priest; that the priests had no courage to serve any more at the altar, but despising the temple, and neglecting the sacrifices, hastened to be partakers of the unlawful allowance in the place of exercise, after the game of Discus called them forth." (II Macc. 4:7-14)

This "place of exercise"—Luther even translated it as a "gaming-house"—was nothing more or less than a stadium. Why then so much excitement over a sports ground? Gymnastics in Jerusalem—discus throwers and sprinters in the Holy City—it sounds perhaps unusually progressive but why should Yahweh be displeased at it? How could a High Priest be denounced as ungodly on that account?

Between the method of playing games today and playing games in those days there is a slight but very essential difference. It has nothing to do with the exercises themselves, which have remained practically the same for more than 2000 years. The difference lies in dress. True to the Olympic pattern, games were played completely naked. The body could be "covered" only with a thin coat of oil.

Nakedness itself must have been regarded by all orthodox believers in Judah as a challenge. They firmly believed in the corruption of human nature from youth onward and in the sinfulness of the body. It is impossible that athletics in full view of the Temple, only a few steps from the Holy of Holies, should not have been regarded as an outrageous insult or that it should not have given rise to vigorous opposition. According to contemporary sources the High Priest, Jason, had located the stadium in the heart of Jerusalem, in the valley[1] which bordered the Temple hill.

But that was not the end of the scandal. It was not long before Jewish athletes were guilty of a serious crime against the Law—they "made themselves uncircumcised" (I Macc. 1:15) The Greek conception of beauty and the circumcision of Jewish athletes displayed in full view of the public eye were two irreconcilable things. Jewish teams—not in Jerusalem among their own people naturally—met with scorn and ridicule, and even aversion, as soon as they appeared in contests away from home. The Bible speaks of "the game that . . . every fifth year was kept at Tyrus." (II Macc. 4:18) Many of them must have suffered so much from the disgust that they encountered that they sought a remedy. Other translations refer to a surgical operation which restored the natural state. (See Kautzsch on I Macc. 1:15)

Nakedness had come for a second time to be Judah's great temptation. Nakedness had been the outstanding characteristic of the fertility goddesses of Canaan; nakedness was now paraded by the athletes in the sports grounds that had sprung up all over the country. In those days a much deeper significance was attached to athletics than to sport in the modern sense. They were religious exercises, dedicated to the foreign Greek gods Zeus and Apollo. The reaction of orthodox Judaism to this revival of a real threat to their religion could only be uncompromising.

Their new overlords, the Seleucids, gave them all too soon every reason to be so.

---

[1]Josephus calls it the "Tyropoeon," i.e., (Valley) of the cheese-makers.

chapter 6 / The Battle for Religious Liberty

Tax official plunders Jerusalem—Worship of Zeus in the Temple—The revolt of the Maccabees—The Battle of the Elephants at Bethlehem—Americans find Beth-Zur—Coins from Antioch among the rubble—Canteen supplies from Rhodes—Pompey storms Jerusalem—Judah becomes a Roman province

AND TAKING THE HOLY VESSELS WITH POLLUTED HANDS, AND WITH PROFANE HANDS PUTTING DOWN THE THINGS THAT WERE DEDICATED BY OTHER KINGS TO THE AUGMENTATION AND GLORY AND HONOR OF THE PLACE HE GAVE THEM AWAY. (II Macc. 5:16)

King Antiochus IV,[1] called Epiphanes, plundered and desecrated the Temple in Jerusalem in 168 B.C. Plundering temples was his specialty, so his contemporaries tell us. Polybius, the Greek historian, observed in his forty-volume *History of the World* that Antiochus IV had "despoiled most sanctuaries."

However, the treasures of the Temple were not enough for the Seleucid king. He sent in addition his chief tax collector Apollonius with an armed force to Jerusalem. This man, "when he had taken the spoils of the city, (he) set it on fire, and pulled down the houses and walls thereof on every side. But the women and children took they captive, and possessed the cattle." (I Macc. 1:29-32; II Macc. 5:24ff.)

Throughout the turbulent changes of its past history, Israel had been spared none of the horror and ignominy which could befall a nation. But never before, neither under the Assyrians nor under the Babylonians, had it received such a blow as the edict issued by Antiochus Epiphanes by which he hoped to crush and destroy the faith of Israel. "And the king sent letters by the hand of messengers unto Jerusalem and

[1]175-163 B.C.

the cities of Judah, that they should follow laws strange to the land." (I Macc. 1:44)

The worship of Olympian Zeus was set up in the Temple of Yahweh. For taking part in any Jewish religious ceremonies—the traditional sacrifices, the sabbath, or circumcision—the penalty was death. The holy scriptures were destroyed. This was the first thoroughgoing religious persecution in history.

But Israel gave the world an example of how a nation that refuses to be untrue to itself can and must react to a violation of its conscience of this kind. There were of course even in those days weak characters who chose the way of least resistance. Nevertheless many ". . . chose rather to die, that they might not be defiled. . . ." (I Macc. 1:63) But it was the resolute and fervent faith of an old man that first kindled the torch of revolt in the land.

Modin was the name of a small village twenty miles from Jerusalem on the western fringe of the highlands of Judah. Today it is the market town of El-Medieh. Here lived the priest Mattathias with his five sons. When Antiochus' officers came to Modin to force the inhabitants to "forsake the law," to offer sacrifices and to burn incense, Mattathias steadfastly refused to obey the order, and when he saw one of his countrymen offering a sacrifice, he could not "forbear to show his anger according to judgment: wherefore he ran and slew him upon the altar. Also the king's commissioner, who compelled men to sacrifice, he killed at that time, and the altar he pulled down." (I Macc. 2:1-25) This act was the signal for open resistance, for a life-and-death struggle for religious freedom—the Wars of the Maccabees.

Mattathias and his sons escaped. In their secret haunts in the mountains and in caves they gathered round them a band of those who shared their beliefs and with their assistance waged bitter guerrilla warfare against the occupying power. After the death of the old priest, his son Judas, whose surname was Maccabaeus,[1] became the leader.

---

[1] I.e., "Hammer."

It was in the highlands of Judah that the rebels achieved their first successes. Their achievements were indeed remarkable. This small untrained and badly equipped band mastered the well-drilled and numerically superior occupation troops. Beth-Horon, Emmaus, and Beth-Zur were captured. The Seleucids had to retreat until reinforcements arrived from Antioch. Judas Maccabaeus liberated Jerusalem in 164 B.C. and restored the old order in the Temple. The altar was rebuilt and sacrifices to Yahweh were offered as in former times. (I Macc. 4:36ff.)

In the course of military expeditions which took him more and more across the frontiers of the province of Judah, Judas Maccabaeus entered Galilee and Transjordan and wherever there were Israelites who remained true to the old faith. On the way to Idumaea, the old town of Hebron, in southern Judah, was besieged and destroyed. This continuing good fortune of Judas Maccabaeus in battle compelled King Antiochus V Eupator,[1] son of Epiphanes, to intervene with a large armed force. In the decisive battle, which took place a few miles southwest of Bethlehem, near Beth-Zechariah,[2] the Seleucids employed elephants, flanked by detachments of cavalry. The Maccabees were unable to cope with this colossal superiority and were defeated. Dissension among themselves drove the victors to make peace with surprisingly favorable terms for the vanquished. The decrees of Antiochus IV Epiphanes of 167 B.C. were rescinded, liberty of worship was guaranteed, and the religious community at Jerusalem was once more recognized. (I Macc. 6:30ff., 58ff.)

The aims of the Jewish rebellion had been achieved. Not content with that, the Maccabees wanted political independence as well as freedom of religion. The successors of Judas Maccabaeus, his brothers Jonathan and Simon, began the struggle anew. It ended in 142 B.C. under Simon, with Syria granting them also political freedom. (I Macc. 15:1ff.)

A fortress that was in the midst of the struggle and

---

[1]163-162 B.C.
[2]Now Bet-Iskarje.

changed hands several times was Beth-Zur.[1] The results of excavation correspond to the historical circumstances described in the First Book of the Maccabees.

"Khirbet et-Tubeka" is the modern name of this once hotly contested spot. It controls the old road from Jerusalem to Hebron on the frontier between Judah and Idumaea which lies to the south of it. In 1931 the American archaeologists W. F. Albright and O. P. Sellers found here a large collection of coins. Out of a total of over 300, there were 126 stamped with the names of Antiochus Epiphanes and Antiochus Eupator.

The hill still bears the foundations of a powerful fortress in which three stages of construction can be clearly distinguished. Only fragments remain of the lowest and oldest. They date from Persian times. The next stage above it is of oriental character. This is the work of Judas Maccabaeus, dating from the first period of his successful revolt. "And they set there a garrison to keep it, and fortified Bethsura to preserve it: that the people might have a defence against Idumaea." (I Macc. 4:61)

After the Battle of the Elephants near Beth-Zechariah, Antiochus V Eupator occupied this border fortress: "So the king took Bethsura, and set a garrison there to keep it." (I Macc. 6:50)

The troops of the Seleucids likewise have left unmistakable traces of their stay. As the archaeologists were able to establish, these consisted of relics of their catering arrangements which were found among the ruins of the walls erected by Judas Maccabaeus. Part of the rations of these soldiers was wine of excellent quality from the hills of Greece. From the handles of the jars, which lay about among the mass of broken earthenware, Albright and Sellers were even able to tell where the wine came from. A wine merchant in Rhodes must have been the army's principal supplier.

That was in 162 B.C. A year later the Seleucids fortified Beth-Zur anew. A new citadel, with characteristic Hellenistic masonry, arose upon the ruined Maccabean walls. Their general, Bacchides, "repaired the

---

[1] Or Beth-Sur.

strong cities in Judah. . . . He fortified also the city Bethsura . . . and put forces in them and provision of victuals." (I Macc. 9:50-52)

The Biblical record ends with the murder of Simon, brother of Judas Maccabaeus. The spiritual and political leadership of Judas was transferred, with the office of High Priest, to Simon's son John. He was called John Hyrcanus. "John, the High Priest, and the Jewish people" and "John the High Priest, Head of the Jewish people" are the inscriptions on the coins which he had minted and which have since been found. We are indebted to Flavius Josephus's careful account of the his-

Fig. 69.

tory of the period for accurate information about this Maccabee and his successors.[1]

By dint of incessant and purposeful fighting the frontiers of Judah were extended farther and farther. Under Alexander Jannaeus[2] they enlarged their territories until they almost covered the area previously occupied by the kingdoms of Israel and Judah.

As time went on the Seleucids became less and less serious adversaries. They lacked the strength to cope with the Maccabees when Rome—now, having overthrown Hannibal of Carthage,[3] undisputed mistress of the western Mediterranean—had expanded its sovereignty beyond Greece into Asia Minor.

Pompey, the Roman general, marched through the kingdom of the Seleucids into Palestine. After a three months' siege Roman legions entered Jerusalem in 63 B.C. Judah became a Roman province.

With this event the political independence of Israel came to an abrupt end.

---

[1] Josephus calls them "Hasmoneans," from the name of their ancestor the father of Mattathias. (*Wars of the Jews*, I:1.3)

[2] 103-76 B.C.

[3] At the battle of Zama in 202 B.C.

DIGGING UP
THE NEW TESTAMENT

I / Jesus of Nazareth

CHAPTER 1 / Palestine on Mare Nostrum

A province of the Roman Empire—Greek cities on the Jordan—The New Testament—The governor appears in history—A census every fourteen years

BUT WHEN THE FULNESS OF THE TIME WAS COME, GOD SENT FORTH HIS SON. . . . (Gal. 4:4)

In the wide circle of countries which surround Mare Nostrum[1] from North Africa and Spain to the shores of Asia Minor, the will of Rome, now mistress of the world, reigned supreme. After the disappearance of the great Semitic empires of the Fertile Crescent, Palestine was drawn into the new world and shared its destinies. Roman occupation troops enforced the will of Rome in a land that was ruled and exploited by men who were likewise nominees of Rome.

Life in the Roman Empire took on more and more the stamp of Greece; Roman civilization was to a large extent Greek civilization. Greek was the world language which united all the subject peoples of the East.

Anyone wandering through Palestine at the turn of the eras might have imagined he was in Greece. Across the Jordan lay out-and-out Greek cities. The "Ten Cities"[2] of the gospels (Matt. 4:25; Mark 5:20) took Athens as their model: they had temples that were sacred to Zeus and Artemis; they had their theater, their pillared forum, their stadium, their gymnasium, and their baths. Greek in architecture as well as in the habits of their citizens were likewise Caesarea, the seat of Pilate's government, which lay on the Mediterranean south of Carmel, Sepphoris, and Tiberias which lay a few miles north of Nazareth on the Lake of Galilee, Caesarea Philippi built at the foot of Hermon, and likewise Jericho. Only the many small towns and villages in

---

[1]The Roman name for the Mediterranean.
[2]Greek=Dekapolis.

Galilee as in Judah had retained their Jewish style of architecture. It was in these genuine Jewish communities that Jesus lived and worked, and nowhere do the gospel writers speak of his ever having lived *in* one of the Greek cities but only in their neighborhood. (Mark 7:31)

Nevertheless, Greek dress and much of the Greek way of life had long before Jesus' day penetrated into the purely Jewish communities. Natives of Galilee and Judah wore the same sort of clothes as were worn in Alexandria, Rome, and Athens. These consisted of tunic and cloak, shoes or sandals, with a hat or a cap as head covering. Furniture included a bed, and the Greek habit of reclining at meals was generally adopted.

The Old Testament covers a period of nearly 1200 years if we reckon from the Exodus from Egypt under Moses, or nearly 2000 years if we reckon from the time of the patriarchs. The New Testament, on the other hand, covers a period of less than 100 years. From the beginning of the ministry of Jesus to the end of the Acts of the Apostles is only a little more than thirty years. The Old Testament largely reflects the varied history of the people of Israel: the New Testament is concerned with the life and sayings of a few individuals: it revolves exclusively round the teaching of Jesus, round his disciples and the apostles.

Archaeology cannot produce extensive evidence from the world of the New Testament. For the life of Christ offers nothing that would leave any material traces of this earth: neither royal palaces, nor temples, neither victorious campaigns nor burned cities and countrysides. Jesus was essentially a man of peace; he taught the Word of God. Archaeologists have recognized their task to be that of reconstructing his environment and rediscovering the villages and cities where he lived, worked, and died. Yet, for this purpose they have been given a unique guide. No event out of the whole of Greco-Roman history, no manuscript of any classical author has come down to posterity in anything like so many ancient copies as the scriptures of the New Testament. They can be numbered in thousands and the oldest and most venerable among them are only a few decades removed from the time of Christ.

A manuscript containing part of St. John's Gospel, for example, the famous Papyrus Bodmer II, comes from the time of Trajan, the Roman emperor who reigned from A.D. 98-117. This precious document in Greek script, so far the oldest New Testament writing, was discovered by a lucky chance in Egypt in 1935.

"And it came to pass in those days that there went out a decree from Caesar Augustus, that all the world should be taxed. (And this taxing was first made when Cyrenius was governor of Syria.) And all went to be taxed, every one into his own city. And Joseph also went up from Galilee, out of the city of Nazareth, into Judaea, unto the city of David, which is called Bethlehem (because he was of the house and lineage of David), to be taxed with Mary his espoused wife. . . ." (Luke 2:1-5)

The census is by no means the invention of modern statisticians. Practiced in ancient times, it fulfilled then as now two extremely reasonable purposes. It provided the relevant information, first, for calling up men for military service and, second, for taxation purposes. In subject countries it was the second of these that chiefly concerned the Romans.

Without exacting tribute from its foreign possessions, Rome would never have been able on the strength of its own resources to afford the luxury of its much admired magnificent buildings and sporting grounds, its extravagant way of living, or its expensive system of administering its empire. Roman emperors were able to guarantee their people *panem et circenses*—"bread and circuses"—on a grand scale at no cost to themselves. Egypt had to provide the corn for the free bread; and the great arenas for the games were built by slaves with money derived from tribute.

The census, as the Romans themselves called it, took place in the Empire every fourteenth year. It affected not only the *cives Romani,* the Roman citizens, but also those of Spain and Gaul. It covered Egypt as well as Syria and Palestine.

Cyrenius the governor was the Senator P. Sulpicius Quirinius, who is otherwise known to us from Roman documents. The Emperor Augustus rated highly the outstanding ability of this social climber both as soldier and as administrator. He was born in modest circumstances near Tusculum in the Alban hills, a place which was reckoned among the favorite resorts of the noble Roman families.

In A.D. 6 Quirinius went as legate to Syria. Coponius was sent with him from Rome to be the first procurator of Judaea. Between A.D. 6 and 7 they carried out a census, but this cannot be the one referred to by St. Luke, since by that time Jesus was over ten years old. According to the Biblical narrative the census decreed by Caesar Augustus took place about the year Christ was born.

For a long time it seemed as though St. Luke had made a mistake. It was only when a fragment of a Roman inscription was discovered at Antioch that the surprising fact emerged that Quirinius had been in Syria once before on a mission from the Emperor Augustus in the days of Saturninus the Proconsul. At that time his assignment had been purely military. He led a campaign against the Homanadenses, a tribe in the Taurus Mountains in Asia Minor. Quirinius established his seat of government as well as his headquarters in Syria between 10 and 7 B.C.

A suggestion by Origen—Halley's comet over China—Kepler's observations in Prague—Astronomical tablets found at Sippar—Babylonian astronomers' records—Modern astronomical calculations—December frost in Bethlehem

NOW WHEN JESUS WAS BORN IN BETHLEHEM OF JUDAEA, IN THE DAYS OF HEROD THE KING, BEHOLD, THERE CAME WISE MEN FROM THE EAST TO JERUSALEM, SAYING, WHERE IS HE THAT IS BORN KING OF THE JEWS? FOR WE HAVE SEEN HIS STAR IN THE EAST, AND ARE COME TO WORSHIP HIM. (Matt 2:1-2)

International expeditions of astronomers have been regarded as a matter of course for a long time now. Scientists from all countries, laden with special instruments and measuring apparatus, stream into every corner of the globe when there is a total eclipse or some other important astronomical phenomenon to be observed.

For centuries St. Matthew's story of the Messianic star has exercised men's imaginations. Laymen and experts alike have expressed their views on the subject and these have found expression in a considerable volume of literature. Anything that has ever moved across the canopy of heaven, as well as much that has only existed in men's imaginations, has been dubbed the "Star of Bethlehem."

That this is a case of a phenomenon in the sky of quite an unusual type is indicated by the Bible in unmistakable terms. Astronomers are the experts in these matters of heavenly phenomena, and we should therefore expect from them an explanation that would fit in with modern scientific knowledge.

If we think of a sudden bright light in the sky, we can reckon with only two types, apart from shooting stars: either a comet or a new star, technically known as a "nova."

Conjectures of this kind were expressed in early times. Origen, one of the Christian Fathers, who lived in Alexandria about A.D. 200 wrote as follows: "I am of the opinion that the star which appeared to the Wise Men in the East was a new star which had nothing in common with those stars which appear either in the firmament or in the lower levels of the atmosphere. Presumably it belonged to the category of these heavenly fires which appear from time to time and have been given names by the Greeks depending on their shape, either comets, or fiery beams, or starry hosts, or starry tails, or vessels or some such name."

Bright comets, often with tails stretching half across the sky, have always made a deep impression on men's minds. They were held to portend special events. Is it surprising that this most magnificent of all stellar spectacles should be associated with the idea of the star of the Wise Men of the East? Artists seized upon this attractive motif: in many popular representations of the crib in pictures of the birth of Christ a radiant comet shines over the manger bed of Bethlehem.

Excavations and ancient writings that have come to light have produced astonishingly detailed information about astronomical occurrences stretching back over thousands of years. We now possess notes and observations from Greek, Roman, Babylonian, Egyptian, and Chinese sources.

After the assassination of Caesar, shortly after the Ides of March in 44 B.C., a brilliant comet was seen. Seventeen years before the turn of the era another extremely bright comet appeared suddenly and was observed for a whole night in Mediterranean countries. The next dazzling comet to be reported was in the year A.D. 66 shortly before Nero committed suicide.

Between these two there is another account with most precise details, this time from Chinese astronomers. Their observations are recorded in the Wen-Hien-Thung-Khao *Encyclopedia* of the Chinese scholar Ma Tuan-Lin: "In the first year of [the Emperor] Yuen-yen, in the 7th month, on the day Sin-Ouei [25 August] a comet was seen in the region of the sky known

THE STAR OF BETHLEHEM 387

as Toung-Tsing [beside the Mu of the Gemini]. It passed over the Ou-Tschoui-Heou [Gemini], proceeded from the Ho-Su [Castor and Pollux] in a northerly direction and then into the group of Hien-Youen [the head of Leo] and into the house of Thaiouei [tail of Leo]. . . . On the 56th day it disappeared with the Blue Dragon [Scorpio]. Altogether the comet was observed for 63 days."

This very full account from ancient Chinese sources contains the first description of the famous Halley's comet, that great trailing star which always reappears close to the sun after an interval of seventy-six years. The last time it was seen was between 1909 and 1911. The strange display will be seen again in 1986, for the comet keeps to a strict time schedule on its tremendous elliptical course through space. But it is not always visible and not equally visible everywhere. Thus, in the year 12 B.C. in China it was an astral phenomenon that could be accurately observed in all its phases; whereas in the Mediterranean countries, in Mesopotamia and Egypt, there is no mention whatever at that time of a heavenly body of such striking and impressive brilliance.

The same is true of "new stars." These "novae" are constellations in space which suddenly burst asunder in an atomic explosion of colossal magnitude. Their radiance, which outshines the light of all other stars, is so noticeable and so unusual that it is always remarked upon. About the turn of the era, the blazing light of a new star is only twice mentioned, in 134 B.C. and A.D. 173. None of the old sources and traditions says anything about a bright comet or a new star in the Mediterranean world about the year zero.

Shortly before Christmas 1603, on December 17, the Imperial Mathematician and Astronomer Royal Johannes Kepler was sitting through the night high above the Moldau in the Hradçyn in Prague, observing with his modest telescope the approach of two planets. "Conjunction" is the technical name for the position of two celestial bodies on the same degree of longitude. Sometimes two planets move so close to each other that they have the appearance of a single larger and more brilliant star. That night Saturn and Jupiter had a rendezvous in space within the constellation of Pisces.

Looking through his notes later Kepler suddenly remembered something he had read in the rabbinic writer Abarbanel, referring to an unusual influence which Jewish astrologers were said to have ascribed to this same constellation. Messiah would appear when there was a conjunction of Saturn and Jupiter in the constellation of Pisces.

Could it have been the same conjunction at the time of the birth of Christ as Kepler had observed at Christmastide in 1603? Kepler checked his calculations again and again. He was a mixture of scholar and quack, astronomer and astrologer, a disciple of those doctrines which had been put in the same class as mixing poisons as far back as the Code of Justinian. The result was a threefold conjunction within the space of a year. Astronomical calculations gave the year as 7 B.C. According to astrological tables it must have been 6 B.C. Kepler decided in favor of 6 B.C. and consequently dated the conception of Mary 7 B.C.

His fascinating discovery was published in a number of books, but this enlightened genius who established the planetary laws named after him eventually steeped himself overmuch in the realm of mysticism. Consequently, Kepler's hypotheses were for a long time

Fig. 70. Conjunction of Mercury, Jupiter and Saturn in December 1603 according to Kepler.

rejected and finally disregarded. It was not until the nineteenth century that astronomers remembered them again. But even then it was impossible to produce clear scientific proof.

Science has provided it in our own day. In 1925 the German scholar P. Schnabel deciphered the "Papers" in Neo-Babylonian cuneiform of a famous professional institute in the ancient world, the School of Astrology at Sippar in Babylonia. Among endless series of prosaic dates of observations he came across a note about the position of the planets in the constellation of Pisces. Jupiter and Saturn are carefully marked in over a period of five months. Reckoned in our calendar the year was 7 B.C.!

Archaeologists and historians have to reconstruct their picture of a bygone age with enormous effort from monuments and documents, from individual discoveries and broken fragments. It is simpler for the modern astronomer. He can turn back the cosmic clock at will. In his planetarium he can arrange the starry sky exactly as it was thousands of years ago for any given year, any month, even any day. The position of the stars can be calculated backwards with equal precision.

In the year 7 B.C. Jupiter and Saturn did in fact meet in Pisces and, as Kepler had already discovered, they met three times. Mathematicial calculations established further that this threefold conjunction of the planets was particularly clearly visible in the Mediterranean area.

The timetable of this planetary encounter when it is presented in the prosaic dating system of modern astronomical calculations goes something like this: About the end of February in 7 B.C. the clustering began. Jupiter moved out of the constellation Aquarius toward Saturn in the constellation of Pisces. Since the sun at that time was also in the sign of Pisces, its light covered the constellation. It was not until April 12 that both planets rose in Pisces heliacally with a difference of 8 degrees of longitude. "Heliacal" is the word used by astronomers to indicate the first visible rising of a star at daybreak.

On May 29, visible for fully two hours in the morn-

Fig. 71. Third conjunction of Jupiter and Saturn on December 4th in 7 B.C. in the constellation of Pisces.

ing sky, the first close encounter took place in the twenty-first degree of Pisces with a difference of 0 degrees of longtitude and of 0.98 degrees of latitude.

The second conjunction took place on October 3 in the eighteenth degree of the constellation of Pisces.

On December 4, for the third and last time, a close encounter of the planets Jupiter and Saturn took place. This time it was in the sixteenth degree of Pisces. At the end of January in the year 6 B.C. the planet Jupiter moved out of Pisces into Aries.

"We have seen his star in the east" (Matt. 2:2), said the Wise Men, according to the Authorized Version. The translation is, however, incorrect, for the words "in the east" are in the original "En té anatolé," the Greek singular, but elsewhere "the east" is represented by "anatolai," the Greek plural. The singular form "anatolé" has, it is maintained, quite a special astronomical significance in that it implies the observation of the early rising of the star, the so-called heliacal rising. The translators of the Authorized Version could not have known this.

When "en té anatolé" is translated properly Matt.

2:2 reads as follows: "We have seen his star appear in the first rays of dawn." That would have corresponded exactly with the astronomical facts.

But why this ancient learned expedition of the three Wise Men to Palestine when, as we know, they could see the occurrence just as well in Babylon? The sky-gazers of the East in their capacity as astrologers attached a special significance to each star. According to the Chaldeans, Pisces was the sign of the West, of the Mediterranean countries; in Jewish tradition it was the sign of Israel, the sign of the Messiah. The constellation of Pisces stood at the end of the sun's old course and at the beginning of its new one. What is more likely than that they saw in it the sign of the end of an old age and the start of a new one?

Jupiter was always thought of by all nations as a lucky star and a royal star. According to old Jewish tradition Saturn was supposed to protect Israel; Tacitus equates him with the god of the Jews. Babylonian astrology reckoned the ringed planet to be the special star of the neighboring lands of Syria and Palestine.

Since Nebuchadnezzar's time, many thousands of Jews had lived in Babylon. Many of them may have studied at the School of Astrology in Sippar. This wonderful encounter of Jupiter with Saturn, guardian of Israel, in the constellation of the "West country" of the Messiah, must have deeply moved the Jewish astrologers, for, according to astrological ways of thinking, it pointed to the appearance of a mighty king in the west country, the land of their fathers. To experience that in person, to see it with their own eyes, that was the reason for the journey of the wise astronomers from the East.

This is what may have happened: on May 29 in the year 7 B.C. the first encounter of the two planets was observed from the roof of the School of Astrology at Sippar. At that time of year the heat was already unbearable in Mesopotamia. Summer is no time for long and difficult journeys. Besides that they knew about the second conjunction on October 3. They could predict this encounter in advance as accurately as future eclipses of the sun and moon. The fact that October 3 was the Jewish Day of Atonement may have been taken as an admonition, and at that point they may have started out on their journey.

Travel on the caravan routes even on camels, the swiftest means of transport, was a leisurely affair. If we think in terms of a journey lasting about six weeks, the Wise Men would arrive in Jerusalem toward the end of November.

". . . where is he that is born King of the Jews? for we have seen his star in the east, and are come to worship him. When Herod the king had heard these things, he was troubled, and all Jerusalem with him." (Matt. 2:2-3) For these eastern astronomers that must have been the first and obvious question, which would, however, arouse nothing but startled concern in Jerusalem. In the Holy City they knew nothing about schools of astrology.

Herod, the hated tyrant, was alarmed. The announcement of a new-born king brought his sovereignty into question. The people, on the other hand, were pleasurably startled, as appears from other historical sources. About a year after this conjunction of planets, which has just been described, a strong Messianic movement came into being. Flavius Josephus, the Jewish historian, records that about this time a rumor went around that God had decided to bring the rule of the Roman foreigners to an end and that a sign from heaven had announced the coming of a Jewish king. Herod, who had been appointed by the Romans, was, in fact, not a Jew but an Idumaean.

Herod did not hesitate. He "gathered all the chief priests and scribes of the people together" and "demanded of them where Christ should be born." They searched through the ancient sacred scriptures of the nation and found the allusion which is contained in the book of the prophet Micah, who had lived 700 years before in the kingdom of Judah: "But thou, Bethlehem Ephratah, though thou be little among the thousands of Judah, yet out of thee shall he come forth unto me that is to be ruler in Israel. . . ." (Micah 5:2)

Herod therefore summoned the Wise Men and "sent them to Bethlehem." (Matt 2:4-8) Since Jupiter and

Saturn came together for the third time in the constellation of Pisces on December 4, "they rejoiced with exceeding great joy" and set out for Bethlehem, "and lo, the star, which they saw in the east, went before them" (Matt. 2:10, 9)

On the road to Hebron, five miles from Jerusalem, lies the village of "Bet Lahm," which was the old Bethlehem of Judah. The ancient highway, which Abraham had once passed along, lay almost due north and south. At their third conjunction the planets Jupiter and Saturn appeared to have dissolved into one great brilliant star. In the twilight of the evening they were visible in a southerly direction, so that the Wise Men of the East on their way from Jerusalem to Bethlehem had the bright star in front of their eyes all the time. As the gospel says, the star actually "went before them."

Every year millions of people all over the world hear the story of the Wise Men of the East. The Star of Bethlehem, a symbol always associated with Christmas, impinges on life in other ways. In biographical dictionaries and on tombstones it has its place beside the date of birth.

Christendom celebrates Christmas from December 24 to 25. Astronomers and historians, secular and ecclesiastical, are, however, unanimously agreed that December 25 of the year A.D. 1 was not the authentic date of the birth of Christ, as regards either the year or the day. The responsibility for this lies at the door of the Scythian monk Dionysius Exiguus, who made several mistakes and miscalculations. He lived in Rome, and in the year 533 he was instructed to fix the beginning of the new era by working back. But he forgot the year zero which should have been inserted between 1 B.C. and A.D. 1. He also overlooked the four years when the Roman Emperor Augustus had reigned under his own name Octavian.

The Biblical tradition gives us this clear indication: "Now when Jesus was born in Bethlehem of Judaea, in the days of Herod the king. . . ." (Matt. 2:1) We know from numerous contemporary sources who Herod was and when he lived and reigned. In 40 B.C. Herod was designated King of Judaea by the Romans. His reign ended with his death in 4 B.C. Jesus must therefore have been born before 4 B.C.

December 25 is referred to in documents as Christmas Day in A.D. 354 for the first time. Under the Roman Emperor Justinian,[1] it was recognized as an official holiday. An old Roman festival played a major part in the choice of this particular day. December 25 in ancient Rome was the "Dies Natalis Invicti," the "birthday of the unconquered," the day of the winter solstice and at the same time, in Rome, the last day of the Saturnalia, which had long since degenerated into a week of unbridled carnival and therefore a time when the Christians could feel most safe from persecution.

Meteorologists as well as historians and astronomers have something of importance to contribute to this question of fixing the date of the birth of Jesus. According to St. Luke: "And there were in the same country shepherds abiding in the field, keeping watch over their flock by night." (Luke 2:8)

Meteorologists have made exact recordings of the temperature at Hebron. This spot in the southern part of the highlands of Judah exhibits the same climatic conditions as Bethlehem, which is not far distant. The temperature readings show over a period of three months that the incidence of frost is as follows: December, 2.8°; January, 1.6°; February, 0.1°. The first two months have also the greatest rainfall in the year, approximately 6 inches in December and nearly 8 inches in January. According to all existing information the climate of Palestine has not changed appreciably in the last 2000 years; consequently, modern accurate meteorological observations can be taken as a basis.

At Christmastime Bethlehem is in the grip of frost, and in the Promised Land no cattle would have been in the fields in that temperature. This fact is borne out by a remark in the Talmud to the effect that in that neighborhood the flocks were put out to grass in March and brought in again at the beginning of November. They remained out in the open for almost eight months.

[1] A.D. 527-565.

Around Christmastime nowadays both animals and shepherds are under cover in Palestine.

What St. Luke tells us points therefore to the birth of Jesus as having taken place before the onset of winter, and the description of the brilliant star in St. Matthew's gospel points to the year 7 B.C.

Mataria near Cairo—A famous herbal garden—Place of pilgrimage near the On of the Bible—Queen Cleopatra's balsam garden

AND WHEN THEY WERE DEPARTED, BEHOLD, THE ANGEL OF THE LORD APPEARETH TO JOSEPH IN A DREAM, SAYING, ARISE, AND TAKE THE YOUNG CHILD AND HIS MOTHER, AND FLEE INTO EGYPT, AND BE THOU THERE UNTIL I BRING THEE WORD: FOR HEROD WILL SEEK THE YOUNG CHILD, TO DESTROY HIM. WHEN HE AROSE, HE TOOK THE YOUNG CHILD AND HIS MOTHER THERE UNTIL THE DEATH OF HEROD. . . . (Matt. 2:13-15)

Anyone fleeing the country for safety goes, if he can, to some place where he will be among his own kith and kin. Anyone taking an infant as well will tend to prefer a place as near the frontier as possible.

On the road from Palestine to Egypt, about six miles north of Cairo, lies the quiet little village of Mataria. It is on the right bank of the Nile. There is therefore no need to cross the wide river. From among the great fields of sugar cane peeps the dome of Sanctae Familiae in Aegypto Exuli, the Church of the Holy Family. The ancient tales that have woven themselves round the nearby tiny garden seemed a good enough reason for French Jesuits to build the little church.

Today, as of old, pilgrims from all over the world pass through the creaking gate into the garden and stand in front of the great decayed bole of a sycamore[1] called the "Tree of the Holy Virgin." In its hollow trunk, says a pious legend, Mary and the infant Jesus hid from their pursuers during their flight. A spider is said to have spun such a close web over the fugitives that they were not discovered.

There has been much dispute over the real age of the

---

[1]Fig tree.

venerable tree. Its existence is not attested by eyewitnesses beyond a few centuries back. But there is another tale about this village which is nearly 2000 years old. In the Middle Ages the garden at Mataria was famous as a herbal garden because it produced plants which were not found anywhere else in Egypt. "Slender little trees which are no higher than the belt of your riding breeches and resemble the wood of the wild vine," wrote Sir John Mandeville, who saw them during his travels in 1322. What he was describing were balsam bushes.

How these precious shrubs came to Egypt is recounted by the trusty historian Flavius Josephus. After the murder of Caesar, Mark Anthony came to Alexandria. Cleopatra, the ambitious Queen of Egypt, had a liaison with him.

Secretly she was planning the restoration of the old sphere of power of her ancestors, which involved getting back Palestine. Several times she visited the land of Judaea and Jerusalem and even tried to ensnare King Herod and win over to her side this nominee of Rome. Although Herod was anything but a misogynist, he was much too able and much too realistic not to know very well that an adventure of this sort would bring about his ears the wrath of the powerful Anthony. Nevertheless, his rejection of Cleopatra almost cost him his head. Her feminine vanity deeply wounded, she intrigued with Mark Anthony against Herod. She brought it about that the king of the Jews was summoned to Alexandria to answer grave charges.

Cleopatra had played her cards skillfully, but Herod was the bigger fox. Laden with gold treasure, he went to visit Mark Anthony and was able to soothe his feelings by bribing him. Another deep humiliation for the queen! But she did not come away empty-handed. Herod had to vacate in her favor the whole of the valuable seacoast of Palestine with all its cities. Mark Anthony presented them to his mistress as her personal property. In addition, the city of Jericho on the Jordan with its surrounding plantations, which contained in large fragrant gardens most valuable plants, reared from seeds which the Queen of Sheba was said to have brought once upon a time as a present to the great Solomon—balsam bushes.

The new owner, as Josephus expressly mentions, took cuttings of it home with her. They were planted on her instructons in the temple gardens at Heliopolis, the "On" of the Bible. (Gen. 41:50) Under the care of skilled Jewish gardeners from the Jordan Valley, these rare and precious shrubs throve on the Nile—the herbal garden of Mataria.

Thirty years later—Cleopatra and Mark Anthony had long since committed suicide after their defeat in the naval battle of Actium—Joseph, Mary, and Jesus are said to have found safe refuge among the Jewish gardeners in the fragrant balsam gardens of Mataria. Many trails keep on leading again and again to this same spot. Perhaps one day one of them will turn out to be historically true.

CHAPTER 4 / Nazareth in Galilee

Death of King Herod, "the most cruel tyrant"—Unrest in the land—Checking Jerusalem's finances—Sabinus steals the Temple treasures—Varus crucifies 2000 Jews—A town of carpenters—Where Jesus grew to manhood

BUT WHEN HEROD WAS DEAD, BEHOLD, AN ANGEL OF THE LORD APPEARETH IN A DREAM TO JOSEPH IN EGYPT, SAYING, ARISE, AND TAKE THE YOUNG CHILD AND HIS MOTHER, AND GO INTO THE LAND OF ISRAEL: FOR THEY ARE DEAD WHICH SOUGHT THE YOUNG CHILD'S LIFE. . . . BUT WHEN HE HEARD THAT ARCHELAUS DID REIGN IN JUDAEA IN THE ROOM OF HIS FATHER HEROD, HE WAS AFRAID TO GO THITHER. (Matt. 20:19, 20, 22)

Herod died at the age of seventy in 4 B.C., thirty-six years after Rome had made him king. It is said that immediately after his death there occurred an eclipse of the moon which modern astronomers reckon to have happened on March 13.

Flavius Josephus passes harsh judgment on him when he comes to write about Herod a few decades later. "He was no king but the most cruel tyrant who ever ascended the throne. He murdered a vast number of people, and the lot of those he left alive was so miserable that the dead might count themselves fortunate. He not only tortured his subjects singly but ill-treated whole communities. In order to beautify foreign cities, he robbed his own and made gifts to foreign nations that were paid for with Jewish blood. The result was that, instead of their former prosperity and time-honored customs, the people fell victim to utter poverty and demoralization. Within a few years the Jews suffered more misery through Herod than their forefathers had done in the long period since they left Babylon and returned under Xerxes."

In thirty-six years hardly a day passed without someone being sentenced to death. Herod spared no one,

399

neither his own family nor his closest friends, neither the priests nor least of all the people. On his list of victims stand the names of the two husbands of his sister Salome, his wife Mariamne, and his sons Alexander and Aristobulus. He had his brother-in-law drowned in the Jordan and his mother-in-law, Alexandra, put out of the way. Two scholars who had torn down the golden Roman eagle from the gateway of the Temple were burned alive. Hyrcanus, the last of the Hasmoneans, was killed. Noble families were exterminated root and branch. Many of the Pharisees were done away with. Five days before his death the old man had his son Antipater assassinated. And that is only a fraction of the crimes of this man who "ruled like a wild beast." The Massacre of the Innocents at Bethlehem, which the Bible lays at his door (Matt. 2:16), fits in perfectly with this revolting picture of his character.

After the murder of Antipater, Herod on his deathbed made a will in which he nominated three of his younger sons as his successors. Archelaus was to succeed to the kingdom, Herod Antipas and Philip were to be tetrarchs, rulers of Galilee and Peraea, part of Transjordan, and the territory northeast of the Lake of Galilee. Archelaus was acknowledged as king by his family and was acclaimed by Herod's mercenaries—Germans, Gauls, and Thracians. But throughout the country the news of the despot's death brought uprisings of a violence that had seldom been seen among Jewry. Their burning hatred of the house of Herod was mingled with their loathing of the Romans.

Instead of lamenting the death of Herod, they proclaimed their grief over the deaths of his innocent victims. The people demanded that the learned Jehuda ben Saripha and Mattathias ben Margoloth, who had been burned like torches, should be atoned for. Archelaus replied by sending his troops to Jerusalem. There 3000 people were butchered on one day alone. The courts of the Temple were strewn with corpses. This first act of Archelaus revealed at one stroke the true character of the man—Herod's son yielded nothing to his father in cruelty and injustice.

However, the will had to be approved by the Emperor Augustus. Archelaus and Herod Antipas accordingly set out for Rome one after the other. At the same time fifty of the elders representing the people of Israel hastened to Augustus to beseech him to rid them of this "monarchy." In the absence of the Herodians, the unrest assumed more serious proportions. As a security measure a Roman legion was dispatched to Jerusalem. Right in the midst of this turmoil, as luck would have it, there arrived one of the hated Romans in the person of Sabinus, agent of the Imperial Treasury. Disregarding all warnings, he took up his abode in Herod's palace and proceeded to audit the taxes and tribute of Judaea.

Masses of pilgrims were streaming into the Holy City for the Feast of Weeks. Bloody clashes ensued. Bitter fighting broke out in the Temple area. Stones were thrown at the Roman troops. They set fire to the arcades, then rushed into the Temple and pillaged all they could lay hands on. Sabinus himself relieved the Temple treasury of 400 talents, at which point he had to retreat precipitately to the palace and barricade himself in.

Revolt spread from Jerusalem through the country like wildfire. The royal palaces of Judaea were plundered and set ablaze. The governor of Syria hastened to the scene with a powerful Roman army strengthened with troops from Beirut and Arabia. As soon as the marching columns appeared in sight of Jerusalem, the rebels fled. They were pursued and captured in droves. Two thousand men were crucified.

The Roman governor of Syria who issued this order wrote his name in the history books through a decisive defeat which he suffered in A.D. 9. He was Quintilius Varus, who was posted from Syria to Germany and lost the battle of the Teutoburgian Forest.

This was the terrifying situation when Joseph, on his way back from Egypt, "heard that Archelaus did reign in Judaea in the room of his father Herod." It was for this reason that "he was afraid to go thither."

"And he came and dwelt in a city called Nazareth." (Matt. 2:23) Many a scholar and writer has extolled the beauty of the place where Jesus spent his childhood and youth. St. Jerome called Nazareth "the Flower of

Galilee." Present-day Nazareth is a little town of 8000 souls. In the arcades of its lanes and alleyways a surprising number of carpenters run their open-air workshops and sell their wares. Wooden yokes for oxen, plows, and a variety of other implements used by smallholders in the past as well as today are manufactured there.

As in the time of Jesus women draw water in jars, which they skillfully balance on their heads, from a well at the foot of the hill where a little spring supplies it. Ain Maryam, "Mary's Well," has been the name of this fountain from time immemorial. It provides the only water supply for far and near.

Old Nazareth has left many traces behind. It lay farther up the hill than the modern village, and there, 1200 feet above sea level, its little houses with their clay walls clustered together, was one of them belonging to Joseph the carpenter.

Nazareth, like Jerusalem, is surrounded by hills. But how different is the character of the two scenes, how unlike are they in appearance and atmosphere. There is an air of menace and gloom about the Judaean mountains. They provide a noble and austere background for a world which gave birth to the prophets, those uncompromising fighters who pitted their wills against the whole world, who stormed against wrongs of every sort, against immorality, against perversions of justice, who pronounced judgment upon the peoples and rebuked the nations.

Peaceful and charming by contrast are the gentle contours of the environs of Nazareth. Gardens and fields surround the little village with its farmers and its craftsmen. Groves of date palms, fig trees, and pomegranates clothe the encircling hills in friendly green. The fields are full of wheat and barley, vineyards yield their delicious fruit, and everywhere on the highways and byways grows an abundance of richly colored flowers.

This is the countryside which supplied Jesus with so many of those lovely parables, the parables of sowing and harvesting, of the wheat and the tares, of the mustard seed, the vineyard, and the lilies of the field.

Yet old-time Nazareth was not wholly out of touch

with the busy world. The Roman military road from the north, which came down through the hills of Galilee, passed Nazareth on its way, and not far south an ancient caravan route, the busy road for all trade between Damascus and Egypt, crossed the plain of Jezreel.

The witness of Josephus—A forbidden marriage—Herod Antipas orders an arrest—The castle of Machaerus in Moab—The dungeon of death—Princess Salome—Capernaum on the sea—Ruins in a eucalyptus grove—The place where Jesus taught

THEN COMETH JESUS FROM GALILEE TO JORDAN, UNTO JOHN, TO BE BAPTISED OF HIM. (Matt. 3:13)

This was the event which took Jesus for the first time from his Nazareth home. After the years of childhood and youth, about which we are told almost nothing, he stepped onto the stage for his public ministry. "And Jesus himself, when he began to teach, was about thirty years of age." (Luke 3:23—R.V.)

John preached and baptized in the Jordan Valley south of Jericho, where the river is crossed by the well-known ford. He was, therefore, in the territory of Herod Antipas, the tetrarch appointed by Rome. Apart from his baptism of Jesus it is principally through his tragic end that John has become known throughout the world. He was beheaded.

Did the godly Baptist who appears at the decisive turning point in Jesus' life exist at all? His contemporary, Josephus, tells us that John was a high-minded man "who urged the Jews to strive toward perfection and exhorted them to deal justly with one another and walk humbly with God and to present themselves for baptism. As they flocked to him from all directions, Herod began to be alarmed lest the influence of such a man might lead to disturbances. In consequence of Herod's suspicions John was put in chains, sent to the castle of Machaerus and there beheaded."

"For Herod had laid hold on John, and bound him and put him in prison for Herodias' sake. . . ." (Matt. 14:3; Mark 6:17; Luke 3:19) According to the gospels this alarm was the reason for John's arrest. Josephus has some more background detail to offer. In the course of a trip to Rome, Herod got to know Herodias, his brother's wife, and was so much attracted by her that he ventured a proposal of marriage. Herodias agreed and brought with her into the marriage her daughter Salome. According to Mosaic law, marriage with a sister-in-law was forbidden, and, according to the gospels, John the Baptist denounced it, an offense which in the eyes of the enraged Herodias could only be expiated by his death.

Josephus puts the event in a concrete historical setting, the castle of Machaerus, one of the numerous strongholds which Herod the Great had built in Palestine.

Machaerus, the place where John forfeited his life, lies in dark and rugged country on the east side of the Dead Sea. No road links this isolated spot with the outside world. Narrow paths lead up from the Valley of the Jordan into the bare and desolate mountains of what was once Moab. In the deep wadis a few Bedouin families wander with their flocks over the scanty rough grass.

Not far from the river Arnon one lofty peak rises above the round humps of the other mountains. Its summit, which is swept by chill winds, is still crowned with ruins. "El-Mashnaka," "The Hanging Palace," is what the Bedouins call this deserted place. This was the fortress of Machaerus. Far to the north can be seen with the naked eye the part of the Jordan Valley where John baptized the people and where he was arrested.

So far no excavations have been carried out among the ruins of "El-Mashnaka," and few have visited the lonely spot at all. Below the summit the rock face is at one point hollowed out to a considerable depth. Narrow passages lead into a large vaulted chamber which from time to time provides shelter for nomads and their flocks when sudden storms take them by surprise among the mountains of Moab. From the carefully shaped walls it is obvious that this was once the castle dungeon. This gloomy vault sheltered John the Baptist after his arrest, and it was here that he was beheaded.

Anyone who has heard of the beheading of John associates automatically with it the name of Salome, and thinks at once of the daughter of Herodias, who at her mother's behest is said to have asked for the head of John as a reward for her dancing. This Salome has taken her place in the literature of the world. Oscar Wilde wrote a play *Salome;* Richard Strauss made the story of this Jewish princess the theme of his famous opera *Salome;* and even Hollywood has used the story of Salome as the subject of one of its spectacular films.

But in the New Testament we may search in vain for the name of this princess. The Bible makes no mention of Salome. In the story of John the Baptist she is simply called the "daughter of Herodias." (Mark 6:22)

It is Josephus who has told us the name of this "daughter of Herodias." A small coin has preserved her appearance for posterity. She is depicted on it with her husband Aristobulus. The coin bears the inscription "King Aristobulus—Queen Salome." Salome must have been about nineteen years old when John the Baptist was beheaded.

"Now when Jesus had heard that John was cast into prison he departed into Galilee: and leaving Nazareth, he came and dwelt in Capernaum, which is upon the sea coast, in the borders of Zabulon and Nephthalim." (Matt. 4:12, 13)

During the short course of Jesus' ministry, which according to the evangelists Matthew, Mark, and Luke, cannot have lasted more than a year and a half, one place always takes priority. Matthew, indeed, on one occasion calls it "his own city" (Matt. 9:1): Capernaum on the Lake of Galilee. At the north end, not far from the spot where the fast-running waters of the Jordan pour into the lake, the shore curves into a small bay. Out of the dark greenness of eucalyptus bushes comes a glint of white stone flags with four pillars rising out of them. Tufts of grass sprout from between the paving stones of the courtyard; shattered columns and blocks of basalt with carved ornamentation lie strewn around. All that remains of what was once the entrance are the broad steps of a staircase, the last remnants of a one-time splendid synagogue.

That is all that is left to bear witness to ancient Capernaum.

In 1916 the German archaeologists H. Kohl and C. Watzinger discovered hidden under rubble and overgrown with grass the fragmentary remains of this edifice. Franciscans rebuilt part of the old façade out of the ruins. The walls of the original building consisted of white limestone; on three sides it was surrounded by rows of tall pillars. The interior, measuring 80 by 50 feet, was decorated with sculptures of palms, vine branches, lions, and centaurs. From there the view through a large window ranged southward over the broad surface of the lake to where Jerusalem lay behind the pale blue outlines of distant hills.

Both archaeologists were convinced that they had found the synagogue of Capernaum, dating from the time of Christ. But in the whole of Palestine there is not one synagogue left from those days. When the Romans in two bloody wars razed Jerusalem to the ground and the inhabitants of the ancient country were scattered to the four winds, their sanctuaries also fell a prey to destruction.

This building came into being for the first time about A.D. 200 on top of the ruins and foundations of the synagogue in which Jesus often stood and taught on the Sabbath day: "And they went into Capernaum; and straightway on the sabbath day he entered into the synagogue and taught." (Mark 1:21)

Most of the inhabitants of the little town of Capernaum lived on the natural riches of the lake. Huts and houses in large numbers nestled quietly on the gentle slopes or surrounded the synagogue. On the day when Jesus came from Nazareth to Capernaum, he took the first decisive step toward proclaiming his message: "Now as he walked by the sea of Galilee, he saw Simon and Andrew his brother, casting a net into the sea; for they were fishers. And Jesus said unto them: Come ye after me, and I will make you fishers of men." (Mark 1:16-17) He met another pair of brothers, James and John, as they were mending their nets. The first people to listen to his words, to accept his teaching and to become his disciples, were simple men, fishermen of Galilee.

Jesus often wandered up from the lake into the Galilean hills and preached in many of the towns and villages, but always returned to the little fishing town; it remained the main center of his mission. And when, one day, he left Capernaum and set out with twelve disciples for Jerusalem, it was his last journey.

CHAPTER 6 / The Last Journey, Trial and Crucifixion

Detour through Transjordan—The tax collector of Jericho —View from the Mount of Olives—Arrest on the Mount of Olives—The "clubs" of the high priests—The Procurator Pontius Pilate—Vincent discovers the "Pavement"—Scourging in the courtyard of the Antonia—"The most cruel form of execution"—A crown of Syrian Christ's-thorn—A drink to stupefy—Heart failure as the cause of death—Crurifragium hastens the end—A solitary tomb under the Church of the Holy Sepulchre—Tacitus mentions "Christus"—The evidence of Suetonius

THEN HE TOOK UNTO HIM THE TWELVE AND SAID UNTO THEM, BEHOLD WE GO UP TO JERUSALEM, AND ALL THINGS THAT ARE WRITTEN BY THE PROPHETS CONCERNING THE SON OF MAN SHALL BE ACCOMPLISHED. (Luke 18:31)

Out of all the journeys that Jesus undertook in his lifetime, one can be traced without difficulty—his last journey through Palestine, the journey from Capernaum to Jerusalem.

He went a long way round to get there. The shortest route from Galilee to the Holy City lies directly south through the hills of Samaria. The path keeps to the hills, over the tops of Gerizim and Ebal, the site of ancient Shechem, and then on through Bethel into the heart of Judah, along the old high road which Abraham followed with his family and his flocks.

It took three days to make this journey on foot from Galilee to Jerusalem.

Jesus, too, would have chosen this road through Samaria (Luke 9:51-56), but since the anti-Jewish feeling among the Samaritans was well known, it seemed doubtful to him whether they would permit his little company to pass through their territory. To make sure, he sent his disciples James and John in advance. And, indeed, the Samaritans refused permission.

Jesus and his disciples therefore went by way of "the borders of Judaea and beyond Jordan." (Mark 10:1—R.V.) The road goes downstream through the middle of the wide and torrid valley, where the banks alone are fringed with tropical growth, with little clumps of tamarisks and poplars, with castor oil and liquorice trees. There is solitude and stillness in the "pride of Jordan." (Zech. 11:3; Jer. 12:5) For the valley, which for nine months of the year is as sultry as the tropics, is but thinly populated.

At the ancient ford, where once the children of Israel under Joshua's leadership had passed over in safety, Jesus crossed the Jordan and arrived in Jericho. (Luke 19:1) It was no longer the fortified city of old Canaan, entrenched behind its walls. On the south side of the hill lay a new, up-to-date city, built by Herod the Great, a gem of Greco-Roman architecture. At the foot of the citadel called Cyprus, a magnificent palace had arisen. A theater, an amphitheater, cut into the hillside, and a circus, all adorned with dazzling white pillars, sparkled in the sunlight. Magnificent fountains played in the luxuriant gardens with their massed banks of flowers. Outside the town stretched the balsam plantations, the most precious plants in the whole of the Mediterranean land, while deep palm groves offered coolness and shade.

Jesus spent the night in Jericho in the house of the Jewish tax collector Zacchaeus (Luke 19:2ff.), far away from all this magnificence. He could not have avoided Jericho, which was a center of Greek paganism, for the road to Jerusalem led through the city.

It is twenty-three miles from Jericho to Jerusalem, twenty-three miles of dusty road winding and twisting between steep and almost barren cliffs nearly 4000 feet high. Hardly anywhere else in the world can there be a stronger contrast than this short stretch of road affords. Straight from the wonderfully luxuriant growth and the sheer unbearable heat of a tropical sun by the Jordan's banks, one is whisked into the chill air of forbidding and barren mountain peaks.

This was the road, like a prelude to the end, which Jesus followed with his disciples a week before the

Passover. This was the time when Jews from far and near flocked to celebrate the feast in the Holy City.

At the highest point on the road, which is almost at the end of the journey, the Holy City emerges from behind the top of the Mount of Olives, as if some wizard had conjured it out of the hills. The view that Jerusalem presented to Jesus and the disciples can be imagined from a contemporary description: "Anyone who has not seen Jerusalem in all its beauty has never beheld a great and lovely city in all his life; and anyone who has not seen the structure of the second Temple has never seen an impressive building in his life." This was the proud verdict of the Jewish rabbis of the time.

Research into the appearance of old Jerusalem has been summed up by Garstang in the following words: "At no point in their history can the Temple and the city have presented a more wonderful picture. The rhythm and harmony of Greco-Roman art, which stood out so marvelously against the eastern sky, repressed the extravagant architectural tendencies of Herod, and brought order and good taste into the traditional chaos of the city."

The great walls towered 250 feet high above the valley. Behind their battlements rose the contours of mighty edifices from a constricted checkerboard of houses, streets, and alleys.

Immediately opposite the Mount of Olives lay the Temple, right in the foreground and outshining all other buildings in its magnificence. Its façade, 150 feet high and of equal breadth, faced eastward and consisted entirely of light marble. Its decorations were of pure gold. Pillared colonnades hemmed in the spacious courts and vestibules. The crowning glory was, however, the Tabernacle in the center, sparkling "like a snow capped mountain," to quote Josephus' words.

Directly on the northwest side of the Temple wall rose the Tower of Antonia, perched on a rocky eminence. Each of its four great corner turrets measured nearly 120 feet high. A viaduct led from the south side of the Temple area to the palace of the Hasmoneans in the upper city. At the highest point in the city stood Herod's palace by the west wall, likewise surmounted by three towers 130, 100, and 80 feet high. Herod had named them Hippicus, Phasael, and Mariamne. From this point a thick wall ran through the sea of houses to the Temple area, thus dividing the heart of the city once more into two sections.

There is an indomitable air about this city, with its multiplicity of fortifications, walls, and towers surrounding its Temple. As the sightseer looks over Jerusalem, he almost feels that he is breathing in its obstinacy, rigidity, and inflexibility. It was these very attributes of obstinacy, rigidity, and inflexibility that helped Israel for more than a thousand years to stand out against every world power. These same qualities were also responsible for the eventual destruction of Jerusalem and the ejection of Israel from the land of their fathers.

Jesus predicted the future fate of Jerusalem. "And when he was come near, he beheld the city, and wept over it." (Luke 19:41)

"And straightway in the morning the chief priests held a consultation with the elders and scribes and the whole council, and bound Jesus, and carried him away, and delivered him to Pilate. . . . And so Pilate willing to content the people . . . delivered Jesus, when he had scourged him, to be crucified." (Mark 15:1, 15)

The descriptions of the trial, sentence, and crucifixion in the four gospels have been checked with scientific thoroughness by many scholars and have been found to be historically reliable accounts even to the last detail. The chief witnesses for the prosecution against Jesus have been indirectly attested, and the place where sentence was pronunced has been accurately ascertained by excavations. The various incidents in the course of the trial can be verified from contemporary sources and modern research.

With the arrest the incomparable tragedy began to unfold. Jesus had gathered his disciples round him in the Garden of Gethsemane on the Mount of Olives, "and immediately, while he yet spake, cometh Judas, one of the twelve, and with him a great multitude with swords and staves, from the chief priests and the scribes and the elders." (Mark 14:43)

A taunt song in the Talmud reminds us of the

"clubs" and "staves" of the Boethusian high priests who had been in control since Herod's day:

"A plague on the house of Boethus: a plague on their clubs!
A plague on the house of Annas: a plague on their spying!"

It ends: "For they are high priests and their sons are in the Treasury, and their sons-in-law in the Government and their servants beat the people with staves."

Among the high priests who are expressly named is one well known to us: the "Annas" in the gospels. "Then the band and the captain and officers of the Jews took Jesus, and bound him, and led him away to Annas first: for he was father-in-law to Caiaphas, which was the high priest that same year. Now Caiaphas was he, which gave counsel to the Jews, that it was expedient that one man should die for the people." (John 18:12-14)

Joseph ben Caiaphas had been appointed high priest by the Roman procurator Valerius Gratus. He remained in office[1] under Valerius' successor, Pontius Pilate, also.

After his arrest, Jesus was brought before the High Council—the Sanhedrin—which at that time was the highest Jewish authority and combined within itself all spiritual and temporal power. At the same time it functioned as the highest judicial court of the Jews. It met below the Temple near the bridge that gave access to the upper city.

What were the grounds on which the council condemned Jesus to death?

"The expectation of the old Jewish prophets which centered on a future Messianic king," writes Professor Martin Noth, "had developed during the long period of foreign domination into hope of a political liberator; and the greater the resentment of the Roman government of the country the more this picture of a Messianic conqueror who would destroy the hateful foreign power filled their minds. Measured by these standards Jesus of Nazareth could not be the Messiah they were waiting

[1]From A.D. 18 to 36.

for. . . . But if Jesus of Nazareth was not the Messiah, 'the Christ,' then he must be a fraud and an impostor. And if he was a fraud and an impostor, then for the safety and peace of the religious life of Jerusalem he must be got rid of. . . . The fact that Jesus during his trial claimed to be the Messiah and therefore, on the basis of Old Testament teaching, the Son of God, was sufficient ground for condemning him to death on a charge of outrageous blasphemy."

According to the existing law, the sentence had to be confirmed by the Roman procurator, to whom belonged the so-called *ius gladii*. Only he could authorize the death penalty. The procurator of Judaea was Pontius Pilate.[1]

Contemporaries, such as Josephus and Philo of Alexandria, describe him as an extortioner, a tyrant, a blood sucker, and a corruptible character. "He was cruel and his hard heart knew no compassion. His day in Judaea was a reign of bribery and violence, robbery, oppression, misery, executions without fair trial and infinite cruelty."[2] That Pilate hated and despised the Jews was made unmistakably plain to them again and again.

Pilate must have recognized at once that the ac-

Fig. 72. Coins of the Roman Procurator, Pontius Pilate.

cused man, Jesus, was the object of a hatred that had been stirred up by the Pharisees. That alone must have been sufficient reason for him to reject their demand and to acquit him. Indeed, first of all and without hesitation, he actually declared him to be innocent:

---

[1] A.D. 26-26.
[2] Philo of Alexandria, A.D. 25-50.

"Then said Pilate to the chief priests and to the people, I find no fault in this man." (Luke 23:4)

But the mob, incited and goaded by the councilors, tumultuously repeated their demand for the death penalty. Pontius Pilate gave in.

How was it that this tyrannical enemy of the Jews yielded to their request?

St. John's Gospel contains a cogent explanation: "But the Jews cried out, saying, if thou let this man go, thou art not Caesar's friend: whosoever maketh himself a king, speaketh against Caesar." (John 19:12)

This was a dangerous political threat that clearly implied reporting Pilate to Rome for neglect of duty in acquitting a rebel. "Making himself a king" meant treason against the Roman Emperor. According to the Lex Juliana the penalty for that was death. Pilate was afraid of this unambiguous threat. He had not forgotten that the Jews had carried it out once before.

As Philo tells us, Pontius Pilate had brought to Jerusalem the golden shields bearing the emperor's name and hung them up in Herod's palace in the middle of the city. That was a serious offense against the rights of the Jewish religious community, which had been guaranteed by Rome. It was a challenge. He scornfully rejected their request to have the golden shields removed from the Holy City. Thereupon, the Jews appealed to Rome and secured their rights. The Emperor Tiberius himself ordered the removal of the golden shields. Because of this and sundry other arbitrary actions, which ran counter to Roman colonial policy, Pontius Pilate's reputation in Rome was at a low ebb at the time of the trial.

"When Pilate therefore heard that saying, he brought Jesus forth, and sat down in the judgement seat, in a place that is called the Pavement, but in the Hebrew, Gabbatha. . . . Then delivered he him therefore unto them to be crucified." (John 19:13, 16)

The Pavement in Pilate's court, where this scene took place, survived even the destruction of Jerusalem in A.D. 70. Its rediscovery was the result of years of work on the part of the archaeologist Father L. H. Vincent. His success was due to the exact description given in

St. John's Gospel. The Authorized Version has translated the word "Lithostroton" by "Pavement." It means a stone pavement. The Aramaic word "Gabbatha" means "raised ground."

Just beside the northwest perimeter wall of the Temple there lay in the time of Jesus the powerful Tower of Antonia. It stood upon a rocky eminence, therefore on "raised ground." Herod I had built it and called it after a friend. The Roman occupation troops had taken it over as a garrison. In A.D. 70, at the conquest of Jerusalem, Titus had the castle of Antonia demolished. Later buildings arose upon the ruins.

On the spot where the courtyard of the Antonia had been, Vincent was able to establish the existence of a large flat pavement nearly 3000 yards square built in the Roman style and typical of the time of Jesus.

This was where Jesus stood before Pilate while the mob howled outside. It was on this Pavement, too, that the scourging took place. (John 19:1) This always preceded crucifixion, as Josephus expressly mentions twice. For this horrible punishment the body was stripped naked and flogged until the flesh hung down in bloody shreds.

Then Jesus was seized by Roman soldiers to complete the sentence of crucifixion. Cicero calls it "the most cruel and most frightful means of execution." Josephus recoils from it as "the most pitiable of all forms of death." This typically Roman death penalty was unknown in the Jewish penal code.

Still inside the court buildings the soldiery vented their wanton mischief on Jesus and "clothed him with purple and platted a crown of thorns and put it about his head." (Mark 15:17) Thus far, botanists have not been able to agree on what sort of plant this was. The only thing that is certain is that the "Christ's Crown of Thorns"[1] familiar in Europe and the United States in the present day has nothing to do with the Biblical crown of thorns. "It is a native of Madagascar and was completely unknown in Jesus' day," says the American botanist Dr. Harold Moldenke. Many other ex-

---

[1] Euphorbia milii Desmoul.

perts assume that the crown of thorns was woven from the Syrian Christ's-thorn,[1] hence, its name. The Syrian Christ's-thorn is a bush or small tree, ten to fifteen feet high, with pliant white twigs. Its stipulae have each two strong thorns which curve backward. According to Dr. G. E. Post, who is an expert on these matters, this plant grows in the neighborhood of old Jerusalem, especially in the area where Golgotha is said to have been.

The way from the courthouse to Golgotha was mercifully short, "for the place . . . was nigh to the city" (John 19:20), beside the main road which entered Jerusalem from the northwest. A pilgrim from Bordeaux who visited Jerusalem in the year 333 specifically mentioned "the hill of Golgotha[2] where the Lord was crucified."

"And they gave him to drink wine mingled with myrrh: but he received it not." (Mark 15:23) Similar acts of mercy are frequently recorded on other occasions. We read in an old Jewish Baraita: "Anyone who is led out to execution is given a small piece of incense in a beaker of wine to numb his senses. . . . The good women of Jerusalem have a custom of dispensing this generously and bringing it to the victims." Moldenke, who has done much research into Biblical flora, has this to say: "Wine mixed with myrrh was given to Jesus just before the Crucifixion to lessen the pain, just as in the days before anesthetics, intoxicating drinks were poured into the unfortunate patients on the eve of big operations." Jesus, however, declined the drink and endured with all his senses the torture of being nailed to the cross.

"And it was the third hour and they crucified him." (Mark 15:25) According to our division of time the "third hour" in the ancient East is 9 A.M. "And at the ninth hour," in our reckoning 3 o'clock in the afternoon, the tragedy came to an end. "And Jesus cried with a loud voice, and gave up the ghost." (Mark 15:34, 37)

---

[1] Paliurus spina-christi or Zizyphus jujuba.
[2] Monticulus Golgotha.

What was the cause of Jesus' death? Some years ago Dr. Hermann Mödder of Cologne carried out scientific tests in an attempt to answer the question from a medical point of view. In the case of a person suspended by his two hands the blood sinks very quickly into the lower half of the body. After six to twelve minutes blood pressure has dropped by 50 per cent, and the pulse rate has doubled. Too little blood reaches the heart and fainting ensues. This leads to a speedy orthostatic collapse through insufficient blood circulating to the brain and the heart. Death by crucifixion is therefore due to heart failure.[1]

It is a well-authenticated fact that victims of crucifixion did not usually die for two days or even longer.

Fig. 73. It was in a Palestinian tomb of this sort, with a millstone rolled across the entrance, that Christ was buried.

On the vertical beam there was often a small support attached called a "sedile" (seat) or a "cornu" (horn). If the victim hanging these eased his misery from time to time by supporting himself on this, the blood returned to the upper half of his body and the faintness passed. When the torture of the crucified man was finally to be brought to an end, the "crurifragium" followed: his legs were broken below the knee with

---

[1] Coronary insufficiency.

blows from a club. That meant that he could no longer ease his weight on the footrests and heart failure quickly followed.

Jesus was spared the "crurifragium." "Then came the soldiers, and brake the legs of the first, and of the other which was crucified with him. But when they came to Jesus, and saw that he was dead already, they brake not his legs." (John 19:32-33)

The Jews had asked Pilate for the "crurifragium," for it was "the day before the sabbath" (Mark 15:42; Luke 23:54) and also the day of preparation for the Passover. According to Jewish law the bodies of victims after crucifixion were not allowed to remain hanging overnight. (Deut. 21:23) And at 6 P.M. the Sabbath of Passover week began, when all kinds of normal activity were forbidden. The imminence of this important festival explains the precipitate haste of the events that preceded it: the arrest by night, the condemnation, the execution and burial of Jesus all within a few hours.

It is barely a thousand paces from the Ecce Homo arch, the site of Pilate's judgment seat, along the narrow Via Dolorosa, to the Church of the Holy Sepulchre.

In 326 the Emperor Constantine erected a magnificent sepulchral tower over the tomb of Jesus which had just then been rediscovered. Richly decorated pillars supported a roof of gilded beams, as can be seen from old books on pilgrimages and early Christian art. Today the Church of the Holy Sepulchre is a chaotic jumble of dim chapels. Every branch of the Christian Church has established for itself a little place of worship in this holiest of all the sites of Christendom.

In the Chapel of the Holy Sepulchre a well-worn flight of steps leads down to a grotto where a six-foot-long tomb is hewn out of the rock. Is this the burial place of Jesus?

Over a thousand graves have been found in Palestine dating from this period, but all of them were in cemeteries or family vaults. This tomb, however, is by itself. According to the gospel tradition, Jesus was the first to be laid in a great sepulchre: "And when Joseph had taken the body, he wrapped it in a clean linen cloth,

and laid it in his own new tomb, which he had hewn
out in the rock: and he rolled a great stone to the door
of the sepulchre, and departed." (Matt. 27:59-60)

One question has always been pressing for an answer
since early times: How is it possible that apart from
the books of the New Testament no contemporary records exist which deal with the events in those days?
"World history at the time took no notice of him
[Jesus of Nazareth]," writes Professor Martin Noth in
his important *History of Israel.* "For one short moment his appearance stirred men's minds in Jerusalem;
then it became an episode in past history and people
had to concern themselves with what seemed more important things. And yet this was a final and decisive
crisis in the history of Israel. It was only when the numbers of his followers made them a force to be reckoned
with in terms of world history that his name began to
be mentioned at all."

Josephus, in his *Antiquities of the Jews,* which he
wrote in the last part of the first century of the Christian Era, in referring to the early Christian community
in Jerusalem, speaks of "Jesus who was called Messiah."[1] Tacitus the Roman historian mentions Jesus specifically in his *Annals*[2] while explaining the meaning of
the word "Christians": "Christ, from whom they derive
their name, was condemned to death by the procurator
Pontius Pilate in the reign of the Emperor Tiberius."

The most important comment comes, however, from
the Roman Suetonius.[3] He is describing a Messianic
movement during the reign of Claudius, who was Roman emperor from A.D. 41 to 54. Suetonius says of him
in his book *The Twelve Caesars:* "He drove the Jews
out of Rome who were rioting because of Chrestus."
The writer Orosius mentions that this expulsion took
place in the ninth year of Claudius's reign, that is,
A.D. 49. That means that a Christian community is attested in Rome not more than fifteen to twenty years
after the Crucifixion.

---

[1]*Antiquities,* XX:9, para. 200.
[2]*Annals,* XV:44; written A.D. 115-117.
[3]A.D. 65-135.

Fig. 74.

There is, in the Acts of the Apostles, an amazing corroboration of this Roman evidence. When Paul came from Athens to Corinth, he found there "a certain Jew named Aquila, born in Pontus, lately came from Italy, with his wife Priscilla: because that Claudius had commanded all Jews to depart from Rome." (Acts 18:2)

II / In the Days of the Apostles

CHAPTER 1 / In the Steps of St. Paul

*The tentmaker from Tarsus—A triumphal arch in Antioch
—Galatia, a Roman province—J. T. Wood digs in Ephesus
—The temple of Artemis—The ruins of the gateway of
Philippi—In ancient Corinth—A meat market with a cool-
ing system—"The Hebrew Synagogue"—A prisoner on the
way to Rome*

AND YE SHALL BE WITNESSES UNTO ME, BOTH IN
JERUSALEM, AND IN ALL JUDAEA, AND IN SAMARIA,
AND UNTO THE UTTERMOST PART OF THE EARTH.
(Acts 1:8)

"I am a man which am a Jew of Tarsus, a city in
Cilicia, a citizen of no mean city." Thus Paul, who was
by trade a tentmaker (Acts 18:3), describes himself
in Acts 21:39. Tersoos, a little town of 20,000 inhabitants lying at the foot of the Taurus mountains in
the south of Turkey, has preserved none of its former
glory. Paul had every reason to laud his native city to
the skies. An inscription calls Tarsus "the great and
wondrous metropolis of Cilicia," and the Greek geogra-
pher Strabo[1] mentions that Tarsus had a university to
match those of Athens and Alexandria. The famous
teacher of the Emperor Augustus, Athenodorus the
philosopher, was one of its sons. All that remains from
the past is its tentmaking. As in Paul's day, the material
comes from flocks of goats who grow magnificent thick
coats among the Taurus mountains where the snow lies
right up to the month of May.

Long journeys by sea and land, such as Paul undertook, were in those days nothing out of the ordinary.
Roman roads were in their way the finest that even
western Europe knew until the railways began to be
built in the nineteenth century. An inscription on the
tombstone of a Phrygian merchant in the heart of modern Turkey proudly proclaims that in his lifetime he

---

[1] 63 B.C.-A.D. 20.

made seventy-two journeys to Rome alone. The busy, well-maintained imperial roads were equipped with halts for changing chariots and horses. Inns and hostelries offered rest and refreshment to travelers. A special police force was responsible for the protection of the roads against the attacks of brigands.

The marvelous network of roads throughout the vast empire—a masterpiece of Roman skill and organization—together with the Greek language, which Paul could make use of on all his journeys contributed as much to the speedy spread of Christianity as the wide dispersal of Jewish communities. "Jerusalem is not only the capital of Judaea," wrote King Herod Agrippa I[1] to the Emperor Caligula, "but also of most countries in the world through the colonies which it established in neighboring lands when it had the opportunity."

Even last century scholars had begun to search for the cities in Asia Minor whose names have become so familiar to the Christian world through the Acts of the Apostles and the Epistles of St. Paul. Where were the places whose inhabitants received the famous Epistle to the Galatians?

In 1833, Francis V. J. Arundell, a British chaplain in Smyrna, discovered the ancient "Antioch in Pisidia" (Acts 13:14) near the Turkish town of Yalovach. North of the Taurus a great arched aqueduct sweeps down from the majestic scenery of the Sultan-dagh Mountains into the valley. In the early twenties of this century scholars of the University of Michigan stood entranced before the remains of monuments of unique beauty. In the center of the old city the archaeologists uncovered a broad flight of steps at the top of which stood three triumphal arches. Marvelous reliefs depicted the victories of the Emperor Augustus on land, while a frieze with Poseidon, Tritons, and dolphins commemorated the naval victory of Augustus at Actium. In the Roman quarters they found the gaming tables where the soldiery whiled away their leisure hours. The archaeologists were looking at the Antioch, so often

---

[1] King Agrippa (A.D. 37-44); see Acts 12.

mentioned, where Paul founded a church on his first missionary journey. (Acts 14:21)

And they "came unto Iconium . . . unto Lystra and Derbe, . . . and unto the region that lieth round about: and there they preached the gospel." (Acts 13:51; 14:6, 7)

Konia, sixty miles southeast of Antioch and main station on the Anatolian Railway, was the Iconium of Paul's missionary activity. In 1885 Professor J. R. Sitlington Sterrett discovered the remains of an altar in the mountains twenty-five miles farther south. A thick stone slab bore a Latin inscription to the effect that a Roman colony had existed on this site. He was able to decipher the name Lustra.[1] A day's journey further on, Sterrett also discovered the ancient Derbe. These four cities, Antioch, Iconium, Lystra, and Derbe, belonged in Paul's day to the Roman province of Galatia, the home of the "Galatians."

On the Island of Cyprus near the ancient town of Paphos a Roman inscription came to light. It made mention of Paulus, the proconsul who is described as "a prudent man" in the book of Acts (13:7). Likewise, the riot at Ephesus, as the New Testament depicts it, has become a living reality thanks to the tireless efforts of the archaeologists.

"For a certain man named Demetrius, a silversmith, which made silver shrines for Diana, brought no small gain unto the craftsmen: whom he called together with the workmen of like occupation, and said: Sirs, ye know that by this craft we have our wealth." He then went on to incite them: "not alone at Ephesus, but almost throughout all Asia, this Paul hath persuaded and turned away much people" and graphically described how they would all be reduced to starvation as a result. "Great is Diana of the Ephesians!" was the answering cry. "And the whole city was filled with confusion: and having caught . . . Paul's companions in travel, they rushed with one accord into the theatre." (Acts 19:24-29)

---

[1] I.e., Lystra.

This story fired an English architect, J. T. Wood, with a desire to investigate the Temple of Artemis,[1] which was widely renowned in the ancient world. The British Museum put funds at his disposal for this enterprise, and in the beginning of May, 1863, Wood landed on the coast opposite the Island of Samos. If he had not been so incredibly persistent and obsessed with his purpose, he well might never have achieved it. For six long years he dug down doggedly through layer after layer of what was left of the masonry of the old city and found nothing. Eventually, while digging in the old amphitheater, the site of the riot, he found a signpost which put him on the right road.

An inscription listed several gold and silver images of Artemis, from two to six pounds in weight, which were to be offered as a gift to the goddess and placed in the temple. The vanity of that Roman donor showed Wood the way to the fulfillment of his dream without further ado, for in order to ensure that the greatest possible number of people would admire his gifts, he had described in detail the exact route along which they were to be borne in solemn procession, on the goddess' birthday, from the temple to the ceremony in the amphitheater and back again.

They were to be carried in through the Magnesian Gate. . . . Wood searched for the gate and found it, followed the prescribed route, and found himself a mile northeast of the city at the finishing point of the procession, which was also the end of his own indefatigable quest.

Under nearly twenty-five feet of soil and rubble he came upon a magnificent pavement, the bases of massive pillars, and great stone cylinders adorned with sculptures—the Temple of Artemis. Dinocrates, the famous Alexandrian architect, had designed the shrine; Alexander the Great had been responsible for completing it in such splendor that in ancient times the temple was admired as one of the Seven Wonders of the World.

The foundations measured 390 feet long by 260 feet

---

[1] Artemis, the Greek goddess of hunting, was called Diana by the Romans.

broad, sheets of white marble covered the roof, and a hundred columns 65 feet high led the way into the interior of the temple, which was extravagantly decorated with sculptures, paintings, and gold ornamentation.

Thirty-five years later one of Wood's countrymen, David G. Hogarth, found under the shattered altar a large collection of statues of the goddess made of bronze, gold, ivory, and silver. They had been made by those craftsmen and workers who scented in Paul's preaching of the gospel at Ephesus a threat to their livelihood and therefore responded to Demetrius with cries of "Great is Diana of the Ephesians!"

"Immediately we endeavoured to go into Macedonia, assuredly gathering that the Lord had called us for to preach the gospel unto them. Therefore loosing from Troas. . . ." (Acts 16:10, 11)

Where once the proud stronghold of Priam's Troy held sway, St. Paul boarded a sailing ship for his first journey to Europe. Near the fishing village of Kavalla[1] he set foot on European soil and set out on the ancient Via Egnatia which climbed up into the wild mountains of Macedonia to Philippi.

Can anyone hear the name of this city without thinking of the ominous words: "Thou shalt see me at Philippi"? For it was here in 42 B.C. that the legions of Anthony and young Octavian won a brilliant victory over Brutus and Cassius who had assassinated Caesar in an attempt to save the republic of Rome from dictatorship. But who reflects that it was outside the walls of Philippi that St. Paul won for Christianity its first congregation on European soil?

French archaeologists on the strength of the concrete evidence in the book of Acts excavated the Roman colony. They found the old forum, the temples and public buildings, the pillared arcades, the paved streets and squares with their rain gutters still intact. At the western exit of the city a great colonial archway spanned the Via Egnatia which soon afterward crossed the swift, narrow River Gangites. "And on the sabbath day we

---

[1] Then Neapolis.

went forth without the gate by a river side where we supposed there was a place of prayer." (Acts 16:13—R.V.) On the banks of the Gangites, Paul's first convert was Lydia, the seller of purple.

By way of Thessalonica[1] and Athens, where he preached only for a short time, St. Paul turned his steps toward Corinth.

In 1893 dredgers cut a narrow channel through the isthmus which joined the Peloponnese with the mainland and thus realized a plan which was already in the minds of notable figures in the ancient world, Alexander the Great and Julius Caesar. In A.D. 63 Nero had indeed begun to put the plan into effect. After a song in praise of Neptune, in which he accompanied himself on the harp, he dug the first sod with a golden spade. From Palestine 6000 Jews had been commandeered to cut the canal, which was, however, very quickly filled in again when the suspicion was voiced that a breach in the land might wash away the Peloponnese.

Three years after the first ship passed through the new canal, the American School of Classical Studies began to search for the renowned and important trading and packing center of Corinth, where the wares of the ancient Orient met those of Europe. Here, too, the archaeologists followed the footsteps of St. Paul to the places which, if they could only speak, could tell so much about his activities.

The road from Lechaeum, the west harbor, led into the heart of the old city of Corinth. Through the great marble arch of the Propylaeum it debouched into the market place, the agora. In those days the business quarter lay to the west of Lechaeum Street, and colonnades led past its shops and up to the steps of the Temple of Apollo. What aroused genuine admiration among the hygienically minded Americans was the ingenious system of water mains that they found immediately under the houses which fronted the broad and handsomely paved market place. It obviously provided the shops with a constant supply of fresh mountain wa-

---

[1] Now Salonika.

ter to keep fresh such foodstuffs as were liable to perish quickly. An inscription at this place dating from the last years of the reign of Augustus actually mentioned a "meat market." The Christians in Corinth were allowed to make their purchases in these shops without scruple. "Whatsoever is sold in the shambles, that eat" is Paul's advice to the church in I Corinthians 10:25.

At the marble steps of the Propylaeum the excavators found a heavy stone lintel on which they were able to decipher the words "Hebrew Synagogue" clearly cut out in Greek letters. The house in which Paul proclaimed the new doctrine must have stood beyond the colonnade in the region of Lechaeum Street. For "he reasoned in the synagogue every sabbath, and persuaded the Jews and the Greeks." (Acts 18:4) Among the ruins of the numerous dwelling houses in the same quarter of the city must certainly be those of the house of the Justus whom Paul lodged with, "whose house joined hard to the synagogue." (Acts 18:7)

Finally the archaeologists found in the market place a raised platform, on which a Latin inscription indicated that it had been the rostra, the judgment seat. "And when Gallio was the deputy of Achaia, the Jews made insurrection with one accord against Paul, and brought him to the judgment seat, saying, This fellow persuadeth men to worship God contrary to the law." Gallio, however, declined to intervene "and drave them from the judgment seat." (Acts 18:12-16)

The detailed reproduction of the trial scene made it possible to establish the exact time that Paul spent in Corinth. Lucius Junius Annaeus Novatus Gallio—which was the governor's full name—was the worthy offspring of a highly respected family. His brother Lucius Annaeus Seneca, the great Roman philosopher and tutor of Nero, dedicated two books to him.[1] And the poet Statius called him the "beloved Gallio."

In old Delphi a letter of the Emperor Claudius came to light, from which it appeared that Gallio must have been in Corinth from A.D. 51 to 52. The letter contains

---

[1] *De Ira* and *De Vita Beata.*

the words, "As Lucius Junius Gallio, my frind the proconsul of Achaia,[1] wrote . . ." and is dated at the beginning of the year A.D. 52. According to a decree of Claudius, newly appointed officials had to leave Rome for their provinces on June 1. Gallio must therefore have arrived in Achaia about July 1, A.D. 51. Paul "continued there a year and six months, teaching the word of God among them" (Acts 18:11) until the Jews became incensed and dragged him before the governor. Thus, it is highly probable that the apostle went to Corinth at the beginning of A.D. 50.

Two years after the Crucifixion of Christ the fanatical persecutor of the Christians, Saul of Tarsus,[2] was converted to Christianity. (Acts 9:3ff.) Almost exactly thirty years later the great missionary and evangelist embarked upon his last journey, this time as a prisoner. In Judaea, Festus had been procurator since A.D. 61. He sent Paul to Rome in the custody of the centurion Julius to face a serious charge. (Acts 27:1) There Paul was allowed "to dwell by himself with a soldier that kept him." (Acts 28:16)

"And Paul dwelt two whole years in his own hired house, and received all that came in unto him, preaching the kingdom of God, and teaching those things which concern the Lord Jesus Christ with all confidence, no man forbidding him." With these words St. Luke concludes his narrative in the book of Acts.

In the persecution of the Christians which took place under Nero, Paul died a martyr's death. As a Roman citizen, he did not die on a cross as Peter did but was beheaded.

---

[1] The Peloponnese was in Roman times the provice of Achaia.
[2] Later called St. Paul.

CHAPTER 2 / The Grave of St. Peter

*Caligula's racecourse—As Rome burned—Vatican hill—
The cemetery on the Via Cornelia—The Emperor Constantine builds a church—The new cathedral—Bernini's
find in 1626—Commissioned by Pius XII—Investigations
by Dr. Kaas—Digging under St. Peter's—The most important discovery in Christian archaeology*

AND I SAY ALSO UNTO THEE, THAT THOU ART PETER;
AND UPON THIS ROCK I WILL BUILD MY CHURCH:
AND THE GATES OF HELL SHALL NOT PREVAIL
AGAINST IT. (Matt. 16:18)

After its conquest by Islam in 637, the Holy Land was,
except in the time of the Crusaders, a closed book to
Christians throughout the rest of the world for many
centuries. The only place on earth, apart from the Orient, where Christian tradition had been maintained
without interruption for almost 2000 years, where a
living chain has maintained the connection from generation to generation between the time of Jesus and his
disciples and our own day, is Rome with its Church of
St. Peter.

Who was Peter? What do we know of him from the
New Testament? Simon was a fisherman in Capernaum
on the shores of the Lake of Galilee. His brother Andrew "brought him to Jesus. And when Jesus beheld
him, he said, Thou art Simon the son of Jona: thou
shalt be called Cephas." (John 1:42) Cephas is Petros
in Greek and means "a rock." Thus, he became Peter,
one of the first of Jesus' disciples.

After the death of Jesus, Peter was the first apostle
to convert pagans. (Acts 10) He was the leader of the
first Christian community in Jerusalem and Judaea and
later extended his activity beyond Palestine. Two of his
letters to the Christians of Asia Minor remind us of
this. In St. John's Gospel there is a dialogue between
Jesus and Peter that refers to the kind of death he
would die at an advanced age.

"When thou wast young, thou girdedst thyself, and walkedst whither thou wouldest: but when thou shalt be old, thou shalt stretch forth thy hands, and another shall gird thee, and carry thee whither thou wouldest not. This spake he, signifying by what death he should glorify God." (John 21:18-19) Legend and church tradition, in story and writing, connect up with this meager New Testament utterance concerning Peter. They tell of his martyr's death in Rome; they specify the place where his bones were laid to rest—under the high altar in the Basilica of St. Peter.

On what is now the broad piazza in front of St. Peter's Church there could be heard in the days of the first Christians the cracking of whips, the thunder of horses' hooves on the trembling ground, and the roar of thousands of throats filling the air. The Emperor Caligula[1] had built a chariot racecourse here, of which the only evidence now is the tall slender obelisk on the piazza which Caligula himself had brought by sea from Egypt.

In July, 64, thick, acrid smoke billowed across the city; flames leapt out of palaces and raged through the streets and squares. Rome was ablaze. Rumor whispered that Nero was responsible. But at the time the Emperor was away from Rome at Antium. He hurried back to the city and made every effort to have the fires put out. It was a slow business, however, and he looked around to see at whose door the blame could be laid for this base act of incendiarism. The Christians, "men with a new and dangerous superstition," in Suetonius' words, the "sect," which through the people's ignorance and hatred of what they did not understand was accused of all possible crimes, became the victims.

From then on the racecourse beheld a scene of horror. On the sand of the arena adherents of Christianity were tortured. Hosts of devout believers had tar poured over them and were set alight like torches or were nailed to a cross. Among them, according to legend, was Peter.

---

[1] A.D. 37-41.

According to Roman law the body of a victim of execution had to be delivered to his next of kin. On the night of his death on the cross, it is said, Peter's followers buried his body. As in the case of Jesus on the hill of Calvary, it was wrapped in linen and secretly taken to a pagan burial ground on the Via Cornelia, behind the stone structure of the arena. This pagan cemetery lay on a knoll called Vaticanus. The Latin word vatis means a "prophet" or "soothsayer." In days gone by there had been an Etruscan oracle on this spot.

Peter found a resting place here among many other graves. St. Anacletus erected the first shrine over the grave of the apostle. He had been ordained priest by St. Peter and became the third Bishop of Rome. Everyone who passed could see the memorial on the hill. "Go therefore to the Vatican and to the Ostian way and you will see the memorials of the founders of the Church of Rome," wrote Gaius the priest in the third century.

Although it was not safe to be found there, the Christians chose the grave of the apostle as their meeting place from the start. The Acts of St. Sebastian record that St. Zoe was arrested there and led away to be tortured. Later, pilgrims from other countries came secretly to Rome: St. Marcius with his wife and sons from distant Persia in 269, and St. Maurus from Africa in 284, and others.

Tribulation and persecution did not end until Constantine[1] became the first Christian Roman Emperor. Constantine gave permission to Pope Sylvester I to build a large church on the Via Cornelia over the old burial place of Peter and the early Christian popes. Peter's grave was not interfered with, and the superstructure of the grave became the high altar. The stones for the building came from the old circus of Caligula. The north wall of the arena was included in the foundations of the church, and the south end of the church extended into the racecourse.

The church took a quarter of a century to build, from 326 to 349. Thirty-five steps led up to a broad open courtyard paved with marble which was sur-

---

[1] A.D. 306-337.

rounded by cloisters. In the middle of it silver-clear water bubbled from a reservoir with a gilded canopy supported on pillars—an indulgence well.

The crowning glory of the sun-baked site was the dim basilica with its five naves. Among a forest of marble pillars stood fifty-two altars, on which 700 candles burned day and night. Golden mosaics gleamed and sparkled on the walls and arches. A lofty baldacchino roofed over the tomb of the apostle. Among pilgrims it was the custom to lower handkerchiefs or other small objects into the tomb on a stick, in order that they might come in contact with the sarcophagus of St. Peter.

Agiulphus, Dean of Tours, visited the church about the year 600. His detailed description of what he saw has been preserved: "Saint Peter is buried in a church which since ancient times has been called the Vatican. His tomb, which lies under the altar, is very seldom entered. However, when anyone wishes to pray, the rails with which the place is surrounded are opened. He crosses over the tomb and then after he has opened a small window he puts his head inside and gives tongue to his anxiety and distress."

Probably St. Peter's grave was bit by bit completely walled in to protect it in troubled times from injury from the outer world. At all events, it disappeared from the horizon of the historians, and no further contemporary mention is made of it.

In the course of more than 1150 years the great wooden roof of the basilica became rotten, and the south wall above the old wall of the circus showed signs of dangerous subsidence, serious signs of old age, which made it imperative to rebuild the church. In 1506 it was decided to replace the old building, and a design was submitted by Bramante. Many famous names were included among the architects, such as that of Raphael and of Michelangelo, who was in charge of operations from 1547.

In 1594, when the architect Giacomo della Porta was busy with some work above the apostle's tomb, a large crack opened up unexpectedly at his feet, exposing to view a vault beneath. On hearing of this, Pope Clement VIII and three cardinals hastened to the scene and by the light of a flickering torch inspected the spot. The vault contained a gold cross about the height of a man. According to tradition the Emperor Constantine and his mother Helena laid this on St. Peter's tomb in 326. The crevice was closed up while Clement VIII was still present.

The pillars of the weighty baldacchino that was to be erected over the burial place demanded a solid foundation. Bernini, who in June, 1626, tested the floor of the crypt for that purpose, came upon remains of human skeletons—the floor of Constantine's basilica covered rows of graves.

Nothing of all this was made public. But the Vatican archives contain a painstaking record of this discovery by Urbaldi, then a prebendary of St. Peter's. This report was found there by Professor Armellini in 1891.

"They began digging the foundations for the second pillar in front of the confessio," says the account. "When they were little more than three feet down, they found on one side a large coffin made of sheets of marble. When they opened the end of it they were surprised to find in it ashes and a collection of bones. They all fitted together and were half burnt. These bones suggested the famous fire in the time of Nero, three years before the martyrdom of St. Peter, when the Christians who were accused of starting the fire met their deaths in Nero's circus. Two of the principal coffins were uncovered, and each of them contained two bodies. Their heads pointed toward the altar. They were clothed in long robes down to the ankle, dark in color, indeed, almost black with age, and they were wrapped in winding sheets like infants in swaddling clothes. The bodies had been laid side by side with great care. But they and all the others in the coffins dissolved into dust as soon as they were touched or moved. Nothing except some pieces of cloth withstood the least touch."

A sketch of the place showed quite clearly that the graves were arranged like the spokes of a wheel, pointing to a central spot which was under the old high altar. Apart from digging foundations for the four pillars of the baldacchino, everything else under the confessio was left intact. The new Basilica of St. Peter at Rome was completed, having taken rather more than a century to rebuild. The solemn dedication took place in 1626.

Three hundred years went past. Then at the beginning of 1949, Pope Pius XII mentioned casually in an address given to Roman students that the tomb of St. Peter lay under the center of the Basilica. His audience knew the old legends, but none of them had any idea that Pius XII in saying what he did was referring to the latest results of archaeological research, for up till then only a small circle of experts had been told of it.

To rule out the possibility of publishing premature results, all those involved had been sworn to strictest secrecy. Until there could be complete clarity and absolute certainty backed up by the opinions of international experts, and until the last trace of doubt had been removed as to the actual significance of the finds under St. Peter's, the world at large was not to be informed of it.

"Has the grave of St. Peter really been rediscovered?" came the voice of the Pope on December 23, 1950, in a broadcast which reached the ears of the whole world. He himself gave the answer: "Yes."

The Very Reverend Dr. Ludwig Kaas was a professor of ecclesiastical law in Germany and the instigator of the investigations under St. Peter's. Perhaps he would have become neither of these if he had not been born in Trier and received there his early and decisive impressions. In Trier, Helena, the mother of the Emperor Constantine, had built the first Christian church. Constantine himself had spent some time there. In Trier scholars were forever coming upon evidence of ancient Rome in the course of excavations.

Pius XI, the Pope with the strong Milanese sense of humor, put him in charge of the "underworld" of St. Peter's, all that "lay under the surface." When Kaas inspected his new kingdom for the first time, he was appalled at the vast confusion that reigned in the grottos of St. Peter's. He had some difficulty in finding his way about the vaults, among the multiplicity of stone and marble coffins, ancient tombstones, and remnants of monuments. Not only had anything and everything found its way into the crypt during the rebuilding of St. Peter's, but the confusion had become even greater in the centuries following, in that emperors and kings, 144 popes, and an endless stream of cardinals and courtiers had all been buried there, too. It was by no means easy to restore order, to distinguish the sarcophagus of the prefect of Rome dating from 359 from that of the Holy Roman Emperor Otto II or the red granite grave of the only English Pope Adrian IV from the grave of Queen Christina of Sweden, whose face was covered by a wonderfully preserved silver mask.

During the time-consuming and difficult business of restoring order among all this confusion, it was borne in upon Kaas what a worthwhile task it would be to investigate thoroughly once for all this quiet, forgotten realm under St. Peter's. Pius XI, however, did not welcome the idea. Nevertheless, it was his own last wish that he might rest from his earthly labors as near to Pius X as possible that set things in motion.

Two days before the funeral Kaas was looking round the crypt for a suitable place. While a heavy marble plaque was being removed from a wall, the wall caved in and exposed an ancient vault. When he saw it, Kaas exclaimed, "I know this! This is exactly the same as I have seen in Trier." The characteristic masonry of the early Christian method of building churches was unmistakable.

On the instructions of the new Pope Pius XII, he began the first scientific investigations under St. Peter's in the spring of 1939. Carried on under conditions of the strictest secrecy, the investigations were to last for years and resulted in a voyage of discovery into the past that went back to the beginning of the Christian Era.

As a consequence of considerable preliminary study the Director of the Papal Institute of Christian Archaeology, Professor Enrico Josi, had already come to the conclusion that any search for St. Peter's tomb must begin from the ground level of Constantine's basilica, a conclusion which proved to be correct as the digging proceeded.

The *sampietrini*[1] had not been plying their picks and spades for long before an ancient world, wrapped in mystery, came to light. St. Peter's was built on top of a cemetery which dates back to the early centuries of the Christian era. Step by step, the *sampietrini* dug up a vast city of the dead. The use of drills would have endangered not only the finds but also the foundations of the basilica. Large mausoleums and beautiful funerary urns concealed the mortal remains of pagan Romans. Later, however, the cemetery was used also by Christians as a burial place. A Christian mausoleum contains the oldest mosaics so far discovered with a Christian theme—Christ portrayed as the sun. These early Christian mosaics date from the third century and are therefore older than those hitherto known. Handsome sarcophagi date from later centuries of the Christian era.

Extremely revealing, too, was the discovery of how difficult it must have been to carry out building operations in Constantine's day, in that they had to keep the ground level of the old basilica, with its five naves, equal with the level of St. Peter's grave. That had forced the architects to build powerful supporting walls on the slopes of what had once been the Vatican hill. Part of the slope had to be dug away and the other part filled in. Since the law forbade the destruction of graves, many of the mausoleums had their roofs removed and were filled up to the top with soil. No trace was found of the walls of Nero's circus. But the monument of a Roman indicated the spot precisely. His last wish as expressed on the inscription was that he should be buried immediately next to the circus.

The further the work proceeded, the clearer it became that the great building was leveled unmistakably to a certain spot exactly under the high altar. The investigations now concentrated on this central point. Nearly twenty-five feet beneath the floor of St. Peter's the cautiously wielded spades came upon a tomb under the high altar. The tomb was like the small mausoleums, which are well known from other Roman burial grounds, except that it was decorated with Christian

---

[1] Vatican workmen.

mosaics. One of them depicted a fisherman with a rod (Peter), another the Good Shepherd, a third Jonah being swallowed by the whale.

Far below the high altar the excavators eventually uncovered a red rough-cast wall. The center of this "Red Wall" is still in good condition and embedded in it is a pillar. A memorial was said to have stood over the grave of the apostle on the slope of the Vatican hill. This pillar must have been part of it.

On the day on which the entrance to the apostle's tomb was rediscovered, the guards closed the doors of St. Peter's. Pius XII proceeded to the crypt to see with his own eyes the most important find in the history of Christian archaeology.

Repeated critical investigations have ruled out any doubts as to its identity. All the details of the excavation, all the essential facts which have a bearing on the date have been collected in the report on the discovery and reproduced in 1500 copies of a record, *Esplorazione sotto la Confessione di San Pietro in Vaticano*. Only after distinguished experts from all over the world had checked the report did the general public learn anything of it.

In the Vatican record dealing with the grave of St. Peter there is no mention of an urn of baked clay. It was found in the tomb and contained remains of human bones consisting of a thigh bone and a shin bone. Apart from these it contained many small scraps of purple cloth. Concealed in the masonry above there was a receptacle without a lid, into which the urn fitted exactly and which obviously served as a hiding place in which it would be safe in case of any danger of theft.

A pious tale, often classed in the category of a Christian legend, has found its historical confirmation in Rome.

Rebellion—The Jewish War—Fighting in Galilee—General Titus—80,000 Romans advance—The order to attack—Parade outside the gates—500 crucifixions daily—Jerusalem sealed off—The specter of famine—Castle of Antonia taken—The Temple in flames—The city is razed—Triumph in Rome

AND AS SOME SPAKE OF THE TEMPLE, HOW IT WAS ADORNED WITH GOODLY STONES AND GIFTS, HE SAID, AS FOR THESE THINGS WHICH YE BEHOLD, THE DAYS WILL COME, IN THE WHICH THERE SHALL NOT BE LEFT ONE STONE UPON ANOTHER, THAT SHALL NOT BE THROWN DOWN. . . . AND WHEN YE SHALL SEE JERUSALEM COMPASSED WITH ARMIES, THEN KNOW THAT THE DESOLATION THEREOF IS NIGH. . . . FOR THERE SHALL BE GREAT DISTRESS UPON THE LAND AND WRATH UPON THIS PEOPLE. AND THEY SHALL FALL BY THE EDGE OF THE SWORD, AND SHALL BE LED AWAY CAPTIVE INTO ALL NATIONS: AND JERUSALEM SHALL BE TRODDEN DOWN BY THE GENTILES. . . . (Luke 21:5, 6, 20, 23, 24)

Countless royal palaces and castles, cities, mansions, and temples, buildings whose foundations were laid in the first, second, or even third millennium before Christ, have been wrested from the past. At a cost of untold effort archaeology has used its spades and the sharp wits of its experts to free these buildings from the dust in which they have been buried. But the city and Temple of Jerusalem, whose importance for posterity cannot be rated too highly, have eluded the endeavors of the archaeologists. They have been blotted out forever from this earth; for barely within a generation after the crucifixion of Jesus, they suffered in "the days of vengeance" (Luke 21:22) the fate that Jesus prophesied for them.

Old Israel, whose history no longer included the

words and works of Jesus, the religious community of Jerusalem, which condemned and crucified Jesus, was extinguished in an inferno which is almost unparalleled in history—the so-called "Jewish War" in A.D. 66-70.

Louder and louder grew the protests against the hated Romans. In the party of the Zealots, fanatics and rebels banded themselves together, demanding incessantly the removal of the foreign power. Every one of them carried a dagger concealed under his cloak. Their deeds of violence disturbed the country. Autocratic encroachment by the Roman procurator heightened the tension. More and more supporters flocked to the side of the radicals.

This mounting anger broke into open revolt in May, 66, when the procurator Florus demanded seventeen talents from the Temple treasury. The Roman garrison was overrun. Jerusalem fell into the hands of the rebels. The prohibition of the daily sacrifices to the emperor meant an open declaration of war against the Roman world empire. Tiny Jerusalem threw down the gauntlet at Rome's feet and challenged the great Imperium Romanum.

This was the signal for the whole country. Rebellion flared up everywhere. Florus was no longer in command of the situation. The governor of the province of Syria, C. Cestius Gallus, marched to the rescue with one legion and a large number of auxiliary troops, but was forced to retire with heavy losses. The rebels controlled the country.

Being certain that Rome would strike back with all its might, they hastened to fortify the cities. They repaired the old defense walls and appointed military commandants. Joseph, later known as Josephus the historian, was appointed commander in chief of Galilee. On the Roman side, the Emperor Nero entrusted the command to General Titus Flavius Vespasianus, who had proved himself a brilliant soldier and had distinguished himself during the conquest of Britain.

Accompanied by his son Titus, three of the best legions in the army, and numerous auxiliaries, he attacked Galilee from the north.

The villages on the Lake of Galilee, where but a few

years earlier Jesus had been preaching to the fishermen, saw the first of the bloody butchery. The whole of Galilee was subdued by October, 67. Among the crowds of prisoners marched Josephus, the commander in chief. He was put in chains and conveyed to head-quarters at Vespasian's orders. From then on he saw the Jewish War from inside the enemy's camp. Six thousand Jews went as slaves to build the Corinth canal.

In the following spring the suppression of the rebels in Judaea was resumed. In the midst of the fighting news came which, for the time being, halted the campaign—Nero had committed suicide. Civil war broke out in Rome. Vespasian awaited developments. One after another three insignificant emperors lost their thrones and their lives. At last the legions in the East stepped in. A year after Nero's death the cry went up in Egypt, in Syria, in Palestine, throughout the whole of the Orient: "Vivat Caesar." Vespasian became master of the Roman Empire. From Caesarea on the coast of Palestine where the news reached him, he embarked without delay for Rome, leaving his son Titus to fin-ish the last act of the Jewish War.

Shortly before the full moon in the spring of 70, Titus appeared with an enormous army outside Jerusa-lem. Marching columns filled the highways and byways leading to the city such as Judaea had never seen be-fore. They were made up of the 5th, 10th, 12th, and 15th legions, accompanied by cavalry, engineers, and other auxiliary troops, almost 80,000 men.

The Holy City was swarming with people, for pil-grims had come from far and near to celebrate the Passover. Disputes between the extremists among the Zealots and the moderate party interrupted the devo-tions; the wounded and the dead remained untended.

Meantime the Romans moved into their camps in the environs of the city. A call to surrender was met with derisive laughter. Titus replied with the command to attack. The Roman artillery, *scorpiones* (quick-firing siege engines) and *ballistae* (stone throwers) closed in. Every one of these heavy weapons could throw stones weighing a hundredweight a distance of 600 feet. On the north side the engineers were cracking open the Achilles heel of the fortress. On the south, east, and west sharp precipices protected the ramparts. The north side was, however, unusually strongly fortified by three massive walls. Battering rams and siege engines began to crack and thunder as they attacked the foundations. Only when an incessant hail of great stones came hurtling into the city and when, night and day, the heavy thud of the battering rams could be heard did civil war end within the fortress. The rival factions came to terms. Simon bar Giora, leader of the moderates, took over the defense of the north side; John of Gischala, leader of the Zealots, took over the defense of the Temple area and the Tower of Antonia.

By the beginning of May the siege engines had in the space of two weeks made a gaping hole in the most northerly wall. In five more days the Romans were through the second wall. A determined counterattack put the defenders once more in possession of the wall, and it was several days before the Romans could recapture it. With that the northern suburb was firmly in Roman hands.

Convinced that in view of this situation Jerusalem would surrender, Titus called off the attack. The gran-

Fig. 75. Roman siege technique during the conquest of Jerusalem.

diose spectacle of a great parade of his forces immediately under the eyes of the beleaguered people would surely bring them to their senses.

The Romans doffed their battledress and polished their full-dress uniforms until they shone. The legionaries put on their armor, their coats of mail, and their helmets. The cavalry decked their horses with the richest caparisons, and amid loud blasts from the trumpets tens of thousands of warriors marched past Titus and received their pay and ample rations in full view of the garrison. For four days, from early morn till dusk, the tramping feet of these unbeaten Roman columns echoed in the air.

It achieved nothing. Packed tight along the old wall, on the north side of the Temple, on every roof, the people spat hatred down at the Romans. The demonstration had been useless. The beleaguered garrison had no thought of surrender.

Titus made one last attempt to win them round. He sent their captive countryman Flavius Josephus, the Jewish commander in chief in Galilee, to harangue them under the fortress walls.

Josephus' voice hailed them from below: "O hard hearted men, throw away your weapons, have pity on your country that stands on the edge of the abyss. Look round and behold the beauty of all that you are ready to betray. What a city! What a Temple! What gifts from so many nations! Who would dare to let all of this be given to the flames? Is there one of you who can wish for all this to be no more? What more precious treasure could have been given to man to preserve— You obdurate creatures, more unfeeling than these very stones!"

In heartrending words Josephus reminded them of the great deeds of the past, of their forefathers, of their history, of the mission of Israel—his exhortations and pleas fell on deaf ears.

The battle began anew from the second wall and surged against the Tower of Antonia. The front was pushed forward through the streets of the suburbs to the Temple area and the upper part of the city. The engineers built ramps and auxiliaries dragged trees for this purpose from far and near. The Romans proceeded with all their tried methods of siege warfare. Their preparations were constantly being sorely hampered by the determined efforts of the defenders to upset them. Apart from wild sorties, no sooner were their wooden ramparts in position than they went up in flames. When darkness set in, the Roman camp was surrounded by swarms of figures who had crept out of their hiding places or through subterranean passages or over the walls.

Titus ordered reprisals to be made against these half-starved ghostly figures and against deserters. Anyone caught outside—deserters, raiders, or foragers—was to be crucified. Mercenaries nailed 500 of them every day to crosses just outside the city. Gradually a whole forest of crosses sprang up on the hillsides till the lack of wood called a halt to the frightful practice.

Tree after tree was sacrificed for crosses, siege ramps, scaling ladders, and camp fires. The Romans had come into a flourishing countryside. Now the vineyards had disappeared as had the market gardens, the wealth of fig trees and olive trees; even the Mount of Olives no longer provided shade. An unbearable stench hung over the bare and desolate countryside. The corpses of those who had died of starvation and of those who had died in battle, thrown over the ramparts by the beleaguered garrison, were piled beneath the walls by the thousand. Who had the strength to bury them in the traditional way?

"No stranger who had seen Judaea of old, and the lovely suburbs of its capital, and now saw this devastation," mourned Josephus, "could have restrained his tears and lamentations at the hideous change. For the war had turned all that beauty into a wilderness. And no man who knew these places of old and suddenly saw them again could possibly have recognized them."

To seal off the city hermetically, Titus ordered the erection of a *circumvallatio*. Working night and day, the Romans constructed a massive high wall of earthwork in a wide circle round Jerusalem, strengthened by thirteen fortified strong points and guarded by a close chain of pickets. If so far it had been possible to smuggle supplies and provisions into the city by night by way of secret paths through tunnels or ditches, the *circumvallatio* stopped even this last meager reinforcement.

The specter of famine haunted the city, which was filled to overflowing with pilgrims, and death mowed them down in a dread harvest. The craving for food, no matter of what sort, drove men beyond all bounds and killed all normal feeling.

"The terrible famine that increased in frightfulness daily annihilated whole families of the people. The terraces were full of women and children who had collapsed from hunger, the alleys were piled high with the bodies of the aged. Children and young people, swollen with lack of food, wandered around like ghosts until they fell. They were so far spent that they could no longer bury anyone, and if they did they fell dead upon the very corpses they were burying. The misery was unspeakable. For as soon as even the shadow of anything eatable appeared anywhere, a fight began over it, and the best of friends fought each other and tore from each other the most miserable trifles. No one would believe that the dying had no provisions stored away. Robbers threw themselves upon those who were drawing their last breath and ransacked their clothing. These robbers ran about reeling and staggering like mad dogs and hammered on the doors of houses like drunk men. In their despair they often plunged into the same house two or three times in the one day. Their hunger was so unbearable that they were forced to chew anything and everything. They laid hands on things that even the meanest of animals would not touch, far less eat. They had long since eaten their belts and shoes and even their leather jerkins were torn to shreds and chewed. Many of them fed on old hay and there were some who collected stalks of corn and sold a small quantity of it for four Attic drachmas— But why should I describe the shame and indignity that famine brought upon men, making them eat such unnatural things?" asks Josephus in his *History of the Wars of the Jews*.

"Because I tell of things unknown to history, wheth-

Fig. 76. Jerusalem during the siege by Titus, 70 A.D.

er Greek or barbarian. It is frightful to speak of it and unbelievable to hear of it. I should gladly have passed over this disaster in silence, so that I might not get the reputation of recording something which must appear to posterity wholly degrading. But there were too many eyewitnesses in my time. Apart from that my country would have little cause to be grateful to me were I to be silent about the misery which it endured at this time."

Josephus, whose own family suffered with the defenders, was not afraid to describe an inhuman occurrence which proves that the raging famine had begun to cloud the brains of the blockaded citizens. Zealots were foraging through the lanes of the city in quest of food. From one house came the smell of roast meat. The men plunged into the house at once and were confronted by Maria, daughter of the noble line of Beth-Ezob in Transjordan, an extremely wealthy family. She had come to Jerusalem on pilgrimage for the Passover.

The Zealots threatened her with death unless she handed over the roast meat to them. With a wild look she gave them what they asked for. Aghast, they found themselves looking at a half-consumed infant—Maria's own child.

Soon not only had the whole city learned of this, but the news had also seeped out through the walls to the Roman camp. Titus swore that he would bury this dreadful deed under the ruins of the whole city.

Many fled from death by starvation under cover of darkness and ran into the arms of an equally cruel fate. The story had got around among the Romans' auxiliaries that fugitives from within the walls always carried gold and jewels, which they had swallowed in the hope of preserving them from being seized by strangers. If any of these unsuspecting people were caught, they were felled to the ground and their bodies slit open in the endless quest for plunder. In one night two thousand alone lost their lives in this way. Titus was furious. Without mercy he got his cavalry to decimate an auxiliary unit. An order of the day made the crime punishable by death. But it was of little avail; the slaughter continued secretly.

Meantime, day and night the battering rams were hammering on the suburbs of Jerusalem. New ramps were laid down. Titus was in a hurry. He wanted to end this frightful nightmare as quickly as possible. At the beginning of July his soldiers stormed the Tower of Antonia. The castle, on whose Pavement Jesus of Nazareth had been sentenced to death, was razed to its foundations. Its walls abutted on the north wall of the Temple.

It was now the turn of the Temple, that powerful and extremely well fortified complex of galleries, balustrades, and forecourts. The commander in chief discussed the situation with his officers. Many of them wanted to treat the Temple like a fortress. Titus opposed them. He wanted if possible to spare this famous sanctuary which was known throughout the empire. For the last time his heralds demanded that the rebels should surrender. Once more the answer was a refusal.

Titus then finally embarked upon the attack against the sacred precincts.

An incessant hail of heavy stones and a rain of arrows showered down upon its courts. The Jews fought like men possessed and did not yield an inch. They relied on Yahweh hastening to their aid at the last moment and protecting his shrine. More than once legionaries on scaling ladders reached the perimeter wall. Every time they were thrown back. Rams and siege engines were powerless against these walls. It was impossible to shatter the vast stone blocks of which Herod had built the Temple. In order to force an entry Titus set fire to the wooden Temple gates.

Hardly were they consumed when he gave instructions to put out the flames and make a passage for the legionaries to attack. Titus's order of the day read, "Spare the sanctuary." But during the night the fire had reached the inner court, and the Romans had their hands full to put it out. The beleaguered rebels profited by this favorable opportunity to make a violent attack. With remorseless slaughter the legionaries drove the Jews back and pursued them through the courts. In wild tumult the battle raged round the sanctuary. Carried away by excitement, "one of the soldiers, without waiting for orders and without any sense of the horror of his deed, or rather being driven by some evil spirit, seized a blazing torch and, hoisted on the shoulders of one of his comrades, flung it through the Golden Window that opened into the rooms which lay beside the Holy of Holies."

These rooms were paneled with old wood and contained, as well as highly inflammable materials for the sacrifices, jars of holy oil. The flaming torch found instantaneous and ample fodder. Titus saw the flames springing up and tried to check the spread of the fire.

"Caesar[1] then commanded that the fire should be put out, calling in a loud voice to the soldiers who were in the thick of the fighting and giving them a signal with his right hand. But they did not hear what he said for

---

[1] Titus became Emperor in 79.

all his shouting. . . . And since Caesar was unable to restrain the hot rage of the soldiery, and since the flames were spreading further and further, he entered the Holy Place in the Temple together with his commander and viewed it and all its contents. . . . But since the flames had not yet reached the inner rooms, and were still devouring the rooms that surrounded the Tabernacle, Titus, assuming, as was indeed the case, that the Tabernacle itself could still be saved, hurried away and made every effort to get the soldiers to put out the fire, giving orders to Liberalius the centurion and to one of his own body guard to beat the soldiers with staves if they refused and by every means to restrain them. But however great their enthusiasm for Caesar and their dread of what he had forbidden them to do, their hatred of the Jews and their eagerness to fight them was equally great.

"In addition the hope of booty spurred many of them on. They had the impression that all these rooms within were full of gold, and they saw that all around them was made of pure gold. . . . Thus the Holy Place was burnt down without Caesar's approbation."

In August of A.D. 70 Roman legionaries erected their banners in the sacred precincts and sacrificed before them. Although half of Jerusalem was in the hands of the enemy, although ominous black columns of smoke rose from the burning Temple, the Zealots would not surrender. John of Gischala escaped with quite a large band from the Temple area into the upper part of the city on the western hill. Others fled into the strong towers of Herod's palace. Once again Titus had to deploy his engineers, artillery, siege engines, and all his brilliant technical skill. In September these walls, too, were forced, and the last bastions conquered. Resistance was finally at an end.

Murdering and plundering, the victors took possession of the city that had so fiercely and bitterly resisted them and had cost them so much blood and time. "Caesar ordered the whole city and the Temple to be razed to the ground. He left standing only the towers of Phasael, Hippicus, and Mariamne and part of the city wall on the west side. This was to provide quarters for the garrison that was to remain behind."

The legion that occupied the garrison in this dreadful place for sixty long years bore the symbol "Leg XF," which meant "Tenth Fretensian Legion." Their home station was on the Fretum Siciliense, the Straits of Messina. They left behind them in and around Jerusalem thousands upon thousands of indications of their presence. Gardeners and peasants still find occasionally small tiles with the legion's number and its emblems of a galley and a boar.

The loss of life among the Jews was unimaginably high. During the siege, according to Tacitus, there were 600,000 people in the city. Josephus gives the number of prisoners as 97,000, not counting those crucified or ripped open, and adds that within a period of three months 115,800 corpses were taken out of one of the city gates alone by the Jews.

In the year 71 Titus paraded his great victory over Jerusalem in a gigantic triumphal procession through Rome. Among 700 Jewish prisoners, John of Gischala and Simon bar Giora were marched past in chains. Amid great rejoicing two costly trophies of pure gold were borne in procession, the seven-branched candlestick and the table of the shewbread from the Temple at Jerusalem. They found a new home in the Temple of Peace in Rome. Both these accessories of Jewish ritual can still be seen on the great Arch of Titus which was erected to commemorate his successful campaign.

On top of these desolate and cheerless ruins, on which neither Jews nor Christians were allowed to set foot on pain of death, the Emperor Hadrian[1] built a new Roman colony—Aelia Capitolina. The sight of a foreign settlement on this sacred Jewish soil provoked yet another open rebellion. Julius Severus was summoned to Judaea from his governorship in Britain and smashed the last desperate attempt of the Jews to regain their freedom. But it took him three years to do so. The Emperor Hadrian then erected a racecourse, two baths,

---

[1] A.D. 117-138.

and a large theater. A statue of Jupiter was enthroned above the ruins of the Jewish Temple as if in derision, and on the site that Christian tradition believed to be that of the Holy Sepulchre, strangers climbed the terraced steps to do homage at a shrine of the pagan goddess Venus.

The greatest part of the population of the Promised Land that was not massacred in the bloody Jewish War of 66-70 and in the Bar-Kokhba rebellion of 132-135 was sold into slavery. "And they shall fall by the edge of the sword and shall be led away captive into all nations."

Archaeologists have found no material evidence of Israel's existence in Palestine after the year 70, not even a tombstone with a Jewish inscription. The synagogues were destroyed, even the house of God in quiet Capernaum was reduced to ruins. The inexorable hand of destiny had drawn a line through Israel's part in the concert of nations.

But by then the teaching of Jesus was well started on its irresistible and victorious journey, uniting and giving new life to the nations.

III / Let There Be Light!

CHAPTER 1 / The Creation Story

Modern science calculates "The Beginning"—The expanding universe—The recession of the spiral nebulae—The age of the earth's crust: 5,000,000,000 to 10,000,000,000 years —A speech by Pope Pius XII

IN THE BEGINNING GOD CREATED THE HEAVEN AND THE EARTH. AND THE EARTH WAS WITHOUT FORM AND VOID: AND DARKNESS WAS UPON THE FACE OF THE DEEP. AND THE SPIRIT OF GOD MOVED UPON THE FACE OF THE WATERS. AND GOD SAID, LET THERE BE LIGHT: AND THERE WAS LIGHT. (Gen. 1:1-3)

The conception of the Age of Progress embraces an overwhelming wealth of inventions, developments, and discoveries. Man's restless, questing mind has succeeded in splitting matter. The mushroom-like clouds of horrifying atomic explosions have become familiar pictures. Electronic equipment replaces hundreds of mathematicians, construction engineers, and office workers. Robot installations direct fully automatic factories. Earth-satellites encircle the globe and the thought that very shortly manned space-ships may be making flights into remote parts of the universe hardly surprises the man in the street any more.

When people speak of progress, they generally mean technical progress. But really genuine, revolutionary advances are being made in the new insights and discoveries or physics and mathematics, of astronomy and many other branches of knowledge. In addition to altering radically our traditional conception of the world, they have opened up hitherto unimagined vistas into the cosmos, both the microcosm and the macrocosm.

In the age of progress the answer has also been found to a question that has always been of the deepest concern to mankind right from the beginning, namely, the ancient question as to the origin of our earth and of the universe. And the astonishing thing is that the answer

457

that science gives is essentially the same as the wonderful picture given by the Creation narrative in the Bible.

"All attempts to harmonise our Biblical story of the Creation of the world with the results of natural science have been useless and must always be so," wrote Professor Delitzsch, a German scholar, in his book *Babel and Bible,* published in 1902. He was by no means alone in this opinion; he merely voiced the scientific opinion of his day.

Today, only sixty years later, this view has been superseded, and the new insights and perceptions of science appear so irrefutable that even the Church no longer closes its doors to them. In Rome, which condemned Copernicus and Galileo, it would once have been thought impossible that the highest ecclesiastical dignitary of the Catholic Church should speak of the Creation story in the light of modern science. But in an address to the Papal Academy of Sciences at Rome, which aroused considerable attention, Pius XII gave his views on the bearing of recent scientific knowledge on the Biblical Creation story.

"When the scientist in the present-day world looks towards its future he is bound to recognize in microcosm and macrocosm that the world is aging. In the course of thousands of millions of years the apparently inexhaustible mass of atoms is losing its effective energy. Matter is approaching the condition, so to speak, of an extinct and scoriform volcano. If then the present world which is full of rhythm and pulsating life has no sufficient foundation for existence within itself, how much less will the world of the past possess it, that world over which the wings of death have passed.

"The further back into the past we go, the richer do we find matter to be in spontaneous energy as well as being the subject of great cosmic revolutions. Everything points to the fact that the material world, equipped with unimaginably great reserves of energy, had its beginning at a certain time. Two questions, therefore, present themselves to our minds: Can science say when the world had its great beginning? And what was the state of the world when it did begin?

"To follow up these questions, which can certainly be only in approximate order of importance, science adopts different methods, which are more or less independent of one another but converge in their results. These methods are briefly as follows:

"1. *The centrifugal movement of the spiral nebulae, or galactic systems.* The investigation of the numerous spiral nebulae, which has been carried out particularly by Edwin E. Hubble, at Mount Wilson Observatory, led to the conclusion that these remote galactic systems have a tendency to detach themselves from each other at such a rate that the distance between two such nebulae doubles itself in about 1300 million years. This process of an expanding universe suggests that at some time in the past, anything from 1000 to 10,000 million years ago the material of all the spiral nebulae was compressed together in a comparatively small space.

"2. *The age of the earth's crust.* To find the age of original radioactive substances, we may take with a reasonable degree of approximation the dates of the transformation of the isotope of uranium 238 into an isotope of lead (Ra G), of uranium 235 into actinium D (Ac D), and of the isotope of thorium 232 into thorium D (Th D). The mass of helium, which is thereby produced, can act as a check. The conclusion emerges that the average age of the oldest minerals is at the most 5000 million years.

"3. *The age of the meteorites.* The same method applied to meteorites to establish their age produces approximately the same figure of 5000 million years. This result has particular significance in that it is now generally held that meteorites are of interstellar origin.

"4. *The stability of binary systems and constellations.* The variations in gravitation to which these systems are subject (from outside themselves), such as the tides, fix their stability within limits of 5000 to 10,000 million years.

"These figures may be surprising, but they do not contain any different concept, even for the simplest believer, from that in the first words of Genesis—'In the beginning'—which means the beginning of things in time. The figures of the scientists give to these words of scripture a concrete, and at the same time a mathematical, expression.

"With the same sense of responsibility and a like freedom in the pursuit of knowledge scholars have considered the other and certainly more difficult question: the question about the nature and properties of the original material.

"Anyone examining these problems seriously from the point of view of modern scientific knowledge must give up the idea of wholly independent and autochthonous material, uncreated or self-created, and must reach the conception of a creative mind. With the same clear and critical eye with which he judges facts, he will recognize the work of a creative omnipotence, whose power, set in motion by a great fiat of the creative Spirit thousands of millions of years ago, distributes itself throughout the whole cosmos and by an act of love has brought into being the material universe with its bursting energy. Modern science seems to have been able to bridge the gulf of millions of centuries and to witness that first 'fiat lux' (Let there be light) when, with matter, a sea of light and radiance burst forth out of nothing while the particles of the chemical elements divided and reunited in millions of galactic systems.

"It is probably true that up to now the ascertainable facts do not provide so absolute a proof of creation in time as do the arguments from metaphysics and revelation regarding creation as such and of revelation regarding creation in time. The facts of science demand further research and confirmation, and the theories based on them demand further development and new proofs in order that they may provide a solid foundation for a discussion which by its very nature lies outside the province of natural science. Nevertheless, it is of the utmost significance that modern science considers the idea of a creation of the universe wholly reconcilable with the scientific attitude—and that on the grounds of its own researches.

"Only a few decades ago such a hypothesis was refuted as totally incompatible with the present position of science. As late as 1911 the famous physicist Svante Arrhenius declared: 'The view that something can be created out of nothing contradicts the present position of science which contends that matter is unalterable.'

"How different and how much more realistic is the view expressed by an outstanding scientist of our own day. Sir Edmund Whittaker said with reference to research into the age of the cosmos: 'Differing calculations converge in the conclusion that there was a time, 1000 to 10,000 million years ago, when, if the cosmos existed at all, it existed in a totally different way from things as we know them today. This time represents for us the furthest limit of knowledge. We can probably call it the time of creation. It provides the background for the view of the world, which has been borne in upon us by the facts of geology, namely, that every organism that exists on the earth had a beginning in time.'[1]

"What significance, then, has modern science for the proof of the existence of God, which depends on the fact that the cosmos is susceptible of change? Science by its accurate and detailed research into macrocosm and microcosm has greatly broadened and deepened the empirical foundations of this proof. From the fact that there is change we may conclude that there is an Absolute Being whose nature is unchangeable. Science has also traced the course and the direction of cosmic development and acknowledged that it must inevitably come to an end, just as it has recognized its beginning 5000 million years ago. Thereby it has, with the concreteness that belongs to physical proof, confirmed the principle of contingency and the conclusion based on it that at that time the cosmos came into being by the hand of the Creator.

"Creation in time! That presupposes a Creator, presupposes God! This declaration, even if it is no express and final declaration, is one which we demanded from science and which modern man expects from science. It is based on a mature and clear consideration of one single aspect of the universe—its mutability. But this aspect is sufficient to cause all mankind, the crown and

_____

[1] *Space and Spirit*, 1946, p. 118.

the rational expression of the macrocosm and the microcosm, to reflect upon his Creator, to recognize his activity in space and time, and to fall on his knees in worship before his sublime majesty."

What an incredible change! Right into the twentieth century no scientific hypotheses existed concerning the origin of the universe, since the basis for them was still lacking. That had not, however, prevented men from striving honestly to find the solution to the great problem. Indeed they even believed it was possible to supply exact dates.

In 1654 Archbishop Ussher, of Ireland, declared that the Creation took place at 9 A.M. on October 26 in the year 4004 B.C., basing his claim on a careful study of the scriptures. For more than a century this date, the result of conscientious calculations, was regarded as valid. Anyone who suggested an earlier date was considered a heretic.

Modern science has estimated the time that has elapsed since the creation of the universe. The speech of Pius XII means that the highest authority in the Catholic Church gives it his approval.

*Economic planning with the help of the Old Testament—
The wells of the patriarchs provide for the settlers—"Honey
out of the rock"—Stone walls to collect dew—Digging
again in Solomon's mines—Pioneering on the Biblical pattern*

No one would dispute that the Old Testament is filled
with that imponderable moral and spiritual power
which outlasts time and loses nothing with its passing.
But that its power should extend to the sober and
prosaic business of remolding the economy of a country
is a sensational development.

Since 1948, the Book of Books, now more than
3000 years old, has been playing the role of a trusted
adviser in the rebuilding of the modern state of Israel.
In the growth of both agriculture and industry the exact
historical information given in the Bible has proved to
be of the highest importance.

The territory of the new state covers about 8000
square miles. In 1948 it was only in the Plain of Jezreel
and the productive lowlands by the Lake of Galilee that
there seemed to be even a remote reflection of the
Biblical description of the Promised Land flowing with
milk and honey. Large areas in Galilee and almost the
whole of the Judaean highlands presented an entirely
different picture from that of Biblical times. Centuries
of mismanagement had even destroyed the grass roots.
Careless cultivation of olive and fig groves on the hillsides had dried them up. Increasing barrenness and
considerable erosion were the sequel.

The inexperienced settlers, to whom the country was
a completely unknown quantity, found the Old Testament of priceless assistance. It helped them to make
many a decision in questions of cultivation, afforestation or industrial development. It is nothing unusual
even for experts to consult it on doubtful problems.

"Fortunately," said Dr. Walter Clay Lowdermilk, an
expert on agricultural economics, "the Bible tells us

what plants can grow in particular places. We know
from the book of Judges that the Philistines grew corn,
for Samson tied foxes' tails together 'and put a fire-
brand in the midst between two tails' and 'let them go
into the standing corn of the Philistines.' In the same
manner he set fire to their olive groves, and as he was
on his way to visit his lady love he passed vineyards.
[Judges 15:5; 14:5] All these plants are now doing
well there."

Every attempt to settle in the Negeb must have
seemed hopeless. South of the mountains of Judah between Hebron and Egypt lay nothing but desert, inter-
spersed with wadis and barren of any vegetation.
Meteorological measurements showed an average annual rainfall of less than six inches. It was a discouraging prospect.

Nothing can grow with a rainfall as small as that.
But had the stories of the days of the patriarchs nothing of value to contribute? "And Abraham journeyed
from thence toward the south country, and dwelled between Kadesh, and Shur and sojourned in Gerar."
(Gen. 20:1) The father of the patriarchs was a shepherd, he kept close company with his large flock, and it
needed pasture and water.

A reconnaissance party spent weeks with geologists
scouring the desolate sand dunes and rocky hills of the
"south country."[1] They actually found what they were
looking for. And the Israeli did exactly what Isaac had
done. "And Isaac departed thence, and pitched his
tent in the valley of Gerar, and dwelt there. And Isaac
digged again the wells of water which they had digged
in the days of Abraham his father." (Gen. 26:17, 18)
Choked with sand, the ancient wells are still there and
still as before at the foot of them runs clear pure water,
"springing water," as Isaac's servants called it. They
meant by that drinking water, for otherwise the underground water in the Negeb—as was proved by testing
the soil—is brackish and unpalatable. Once again tents
stood on the same spots by the water holes. The well

[1]Negeb.

beside which Abraham's rejected bondwoman Hagar rested with her son Ishmael (Gen. 21:14-19) now supplies water for sixty families of settlers. Romanian Jews have settled on a nearby hillside only a mile or two from the Beersheba of the Bible.

In the same area there is another remarkable feature. The settlers have planted seedlings, slender young trees which are coming along famously. "The first tree which Abraham planted in the soil of Beersheba was a tamarisk," declared Dr. Joseph Weitz, the Israeli forestry expert. "Following his example we have planted 2,000,000 of them in this area. Abraham did absolutely the right thing. For the tamarisk is one of the few trees, as we have proved, that will flourish at all in the south where the annual rainfall is under 6 inches." Here, again, the Bible pointed the way: "And Abraham planted a tamarisk tree in Beersheba." (Gen. 21:33—R.V.)

Afforestation is an essential prerequisite in making a countryside that is short of water into a fertile land. Since the beginning of the return of the Jews to Palestine, the settlers have been planting forests. In choosing the types of trees they could rely on the observations of their forefathers just as much as in the choice of suitable areas. A few years ago, when the question arose as to whether the bare mountain slopes in the northern part of the country could be afforested, the book of Joshua gave them the answer. "And Joshua spake unto the house of Joseph, even to Ephraim and to Manasseh saying: Thou art a great people and hast great power: thou shalt not have one lot only: but the mountain shall be thine for it is a wood and thou shalt cut it down." (Josh. 17:17-18)

Both these tribes, it was known, settled north of Jerusalem from the mountain ridge of Bethel past Biblical Shechem at the foot of Mt. Gerizim right to the Plain of Jezreel. "Since trees are known to grow better in places where there have been trees before," argued Professor Zohary of the Hebrew University, "we are relying on the Book of Books."

Much discussion has centered round an extremely

obscure reference which until a few years ago was understood by nobody: "He made him (Jacob) . . . that he might eat the increase of the fields: and he made him to suck honey out of the rock, and oil out of the flinty rock." (Deut. 32:13) The riddle was solved when in the Negeb they came across thousands of little circular stone walls. There was no water in the neighborhood, neither springs nor any pools of underground water worth speaking of. When the sand was shoveled out of these stone walls, they found the remains of the roots of ancient olive trees and vines. The stone walls had served their ancestors as valuable collectors of dew.

Their construction indicated an astonishing practical knowledge of the process of condensation. The stones in the circles were loosely stacked to ensure that the wind could blow through them. In this way the moisture from the air was deposited inside. This moisture was enough to feed an olive tree or a vine. Inside each wall there was always one tree only. The sweet juice of the grapes was often extolled in ancient times as "honey." The olive tree produces oil. Honey and oil were sucked "out of the rock . . . out of the flinty rock." Present-day Israeli set great store by these serviceable little dew collectors in the redevelopment of their agriculture.

In the second half of 1953, for the first time in Israel 3000 tons of copper were mined. Where the houses of Solomon's workmen and slaves stood 3000 years ago, new miners' houses stand today. Copper mining still pays. The geologist Dr. Ben Tor had the ancient copper mines tested in 1949 as to their mineral resources and their possibilities as an economic proposition. Experts estimated that there was enough ore to provide 100,000 tons of copper. According to their calculations the ramifications of the mines could produce at least another 200,000 tons. Since then, "Eziongeber, which is beside Eloth on the shores of the Red Sea" (I Kings 9:26) has been a hive of activity. Jeeps and trucks scurry around, churning up clouds of yellow dust, and gangs of sunburned men ply pick and shovel. "Wherever the ore is particularly rich," maintains a mining engineer, "we come upon the slag and furnaces of Solomon's miners. It often seems as if they had just left the place."

In the company's main office there is a text hanging on the wall. It reads: "For the Lord thy God bringeth thee into a good land . . . a land whose stones are iron, and out of whose hills thou mayest dig brass." (Deut. 8:7, 9)

Iron is, however, not yet being mined. But the outcrops have already been recorded. Not far from Beersheba, exactly where the iron-smelting Philistines lived, Dr. Ben Tor noticed steep hillsides with reddish-black veins, the sign of iron-ore deposits. Investigation showed that they amounted to 15,000,000 tons on a rough estimate. Most of this is ore of inferior quality, but in the course of the survey excellent ores were discovered with between 60 and 65 per cent of pure iron.

Another very well known Biblical passage kept running in the mind of Xiel Federmann, a shrewd businessman. It was the sentence in which the destruction of Sodom and Gomorrah is described ". . . and lo, the smoke of the country went up as the smoke of a furnace." (Gen. 19:28) He could get no peace. Did these conflagrations not indicate subterranean gas? And where there is underground gas there are also deposits of oil, as has long been recognized. A company was formed and the experts who were sent to the Dead Sea confirmed completely Federmann's guess. On November 3, 1953, the first Israeli oil well was drilled.

More than fifty farming communities have sprung up again between the sites of the Biblical settlements of Dan and Beersheba. Almost every one of them possesses a small modern pumping station above a spring or a well dating from ancient times. Gradually many parts of the country are coming to resemble once more the cheerful picture of Old Testament times.

It is a hard task that the young state of Israel has set itself. But its people are fully convinced that they and their descendants will overcome all difficulties—not least thanks to the Bible—and that the prophecy of Ezekiel to the children of Israel will be fulfilled—"And the desolate land shall be tilled, whereas it lay desolate in the sight of all that passed by. And they shall say, this land that was desolate is become like the garden of Eden." (Ezek. 36:34-35)

A lost lamb—The Dead Sea scrolls—Harding and de Vaux in Wadi Qumran—Archbishop Samuel goes to Chicago—Nuclear physicists assist with the dating—Testing linen in the "atomic clock"—In the valley of the pirate diggers—A text that corresponds after 2000 years

THE GRASS WITHERETH, THE FLOWER FADETH: BUT THE WORD OF OUR GOD SHALL STAND FOR EVER. (Isa. 40:8)

The discovery of the Dead Sea scrolls is only one of the many vital findings in Biblical archaeology, but it has become the most popular of the recent discoveries. A great deal has already been written about the scrolls. The final evaluation, however, is yet to come.

In the spring of 1947, Mohammed Dib, a Bedouin shepherd of the tribe of Ta'Amireh, shared the experience of young Saul, who set out to find his father's asses, which were lost, and acquired a kingdom. (I Sam. 9:10) Mohammed was combing the rocky ravines on the western shore of the Dead Sea in quest of a lost lamb when he unwittingly came upon a veritable royal treasure in the form of Biblical material. He had been clambering to no purpose for several hours up and down the clefts and gullies of the ridge, which had many a time served as a hideout for hermits and sectaries, to say nothing of bandits, when he spied a dark crevice above his head in the rock face of Wadi Qumran. Could his lost lamb have taken refuge there? A well-aimed stone whistled through the air. But instead of the sharp crack which he expected in reply, a dull rumbling noise came from the cave instead. Mohammed Dib fled in terror and fetched two of his fellow tribesmen to the scene. They approached the cave with great caution and eventually squeezed their way through its narrow entrance. To their amazement they saw in the dim light of the little vault some clay jars. Treasure was their first thought and the three

469

shepherds pounced on the jars and smashed them. But to their disappointment they contained neither jewels, nor gold, nor coins: nothing appeared but battered looking written scrolls of ancient leather and papyrus, wrapped in linen. In their annoyance they threw their finds carelessly aside, trampling on many of them, until it suddenly dawned on them that there might, after all, be money in them. At all events they took a few of the best looking scrolls to see if perhaps they had some cash value. With that, the ancient documents set out on a remarkable journey.

They were smuggled into Bethlehem and came by means of the black market into the hands of antique dealers. Jewish and Arab collectors bought some of the scrolls, and a bundle of four came into the possession of the Orthodox Archbishop of Jerusalem, Yeshue Samuel, for a handful of coins. The archbishop had no idea how precious was the treasure he had acquired until experts from the American Schools of Oriental Research paid a visit to St. Mark's Monastery, where the documents were stored. A cursory examination convinced the archaeologists that they were dealing with Biblical documents of an uncommonly early date. A twenty-three-foot-long scroll with the complete text of the book of Isaiah in Hebrew was among them. A short published report by the Americans on their find aroused incredulous astonishment among experts all over the world. The immediate question, however, as to the exact age of the leather and the papyrus could best be solved by examining the place where they were discovered.

With endless trouble and patience the origin of the documents was therefore traced back through the dealers and the black market in Bethlehem to the Arabs of the Ta'Amireh tribe and so eventually to the cave in Wadi Qumran. But access to the cave was prohibited, for, following on the establishment of the new state of Israel, Arab-Jewish warfare had broken out in 1948, and the whole of Palestine was a hotbed of unrest.

The persistence of a Belgian United Nations observer in Jerusalem finally helped to overcome all difficulties. Captain Philippe Lippens had studied papyrology at the ancient University of Louvain. At the end of 1948 he established contact with Gerald Lankester Harding, the British director of antiquities in Amman, the capital of Jordan. Their united efforts succeeded in interesting officers of the Arab Legion in the cave where the discovery was made. Thirty miles in a jeep from Amman to Wadi Qumran presented no problems. After several fruitless quests among the numerous caves, they eventually found the right one. The entrance to the cave was guarded by sentries until in February, 1949, G. L. Harding and Father Roland de Vaux, Dominican director of the French École Biblique et Archéologique at Jerusalem, arrived at the spot in person.

Their hopes were, however, dashed. They found neither complete scrolls nor undamaged jars. Everything pointed to the fact that in the meantime others had rummaged through the mysterious cave on their own. With infinite patience and labor the two scholars examined the floor of the cave, literally with their finger nails, in search of even the tiniest remains of manuscripts or of clay jars. What they collected in the way of fragments permitted them nevertheless to draw some important conclusions. The potsherds were uniformly Greco-Roman, dating from 30 B.C. to A.D. 70. Six hundred tiny scraps of leather and papyrus made it possible to recognize Hebrew transcriptions from Genesis, Deuteronomy, and the book of Judges. Pieces of linen fabric that had served to wrap up the scrolls completed the meager spoils.

In response to an American invitation Archbishop Yeshue Samuel took his precious scrolls to the United States in the summer of 1949 and submitted them for examination to the Oriental Institute in Chicago. A violent dispute broke out among the experts on the question of the age and authenticity of the documents. To settle the matter, one of them proposed a course which was still unfamiliar to archaeologists, namely, to invite the assistance of a nuclear physicist. This was all the easier since the Oriental Institute is next door to the

University of Chicago, where nuclear physicists had begun to determine the age of organic substances with the aid of Geiger counters.

Professor Willard F. Libby, of the Chicago Institute of Nuclear Physics, had already carried out his first astonishingly accurate calculations of age by the use of the so-called "atomic calendar" which he had evolved. The idea behind this method is as follows: As a result of the bombardment of cosmic rays, which are constantly penetrating our atmosphere from outer space, nitrogen is transformed into the radioactive isotope of carbon C14. Every living organism—men, animals, plants—absorbs this C14 with its food and the air it breathes every day until it dies. In the course of 5600 years this carbon loses half of its original radioactivity. In the case of any dead organic substance a highly sensitive Geiger counter can establish how much radiation has been lost from its content of C14. This makes it possible to calculate how many years it has been since it absorbed carbon for the last time.

Professor Libby was asked to conduct an investigation. He took pieces of the linen in which the Isaiah scroll had been wrapped, burned them to ashes, put them into a battery of Geiger tubes, and came to an astonishing conclusion. The linen had been made from flax which had been harvested in the time of Christ. The documents that had been wrapped in it must therefore have been older still. After exhaustive and minute examination the papyrologists came to the same conclusion. The text of Isaiah from the cave at Qumran had actually been copied about 100 B.C., as Professor Albright had been first to recognize.

This discovery means more than simply a scientific sensation. To estimate the importance of the Dead Sea scrolls, it is necessary to remember that the oldest text of the Bible that we possess in the Hebrew language— the so-called Masoretic Text (Masora = tradition), which is the work of rabbinical scribes—dates from no earlier than the fifth to tenth century of the Christian Era. The chief sources for our version of the scriptures are the Septuagint, the Greek translation, and the Vulgate, the Latin translation of St. Jerome (fourth century). Our knowledge of the text of the Bible rested for a long time on nothing but these two translations and the very late Hebrew manuscript. But with the discovery of the Dead Sea scroll of Isaiah we have a Hebrew text of the Bible which is a thousand years older. And the remarkable and wonderful fact is that that ancient scroll of Isaiah, just like the book of the prophet in any printed Bible, whether in Hebrew, Greek, Latin, German, or any other language, has sixty-six chapters and agrees with our present-day text.

Seventeen sheets of leather sewn together into a length of almost twenty-three feet—this must have been what the roll of the prophet looked like as it was handed to Jesus in the synagogue at Nazareth so that he might read from it to the congregation. "And there was delivered unto him the book of the prophet Esaias." (Luke 4:16, 17) "Every movement of Jesus' hands is brought closer to us," writes Professor André Parrot, "for we can still see on the reverse side of the leather the marks of the readers' fingers."

That first chance find made by a Bedouin in 1947 at Qumran was to lead to a whole series of most astonishing and highly significant discoveries. Soon after, for the first time a systematic investigation of the Judaean hills was undertaken with a view to finding more documents and further historical evidence. Expeditions were mounted both in Israel and Jordan. Hundreds upon hundreds of lonely gullies and hitherto unexplored caves in the Dead Sea area were searched. Many a time it was a race between the experts and unofficial explorers, because it had very quickly become clear to the natives that there was big money in these unlikely scraps of parchment and papyrus with any hint of writing on them. The result was that within ten years a whole host of documents and written records, including many Old Testament writings, came to light, providing a vast amount of new knowledge about Biblical and post-Biblical times.

In Khirbet Qumran, near the cave where the first discoveries were made, scholars came upon the ruins of a settlement and a cemetery of the Jewish sect of Essenes, of whose existence we had only previously

known from the accounts given by ancient writers—
Philo, Josephus, and Pliny. The Essenes—first mentioned in the time of Jonathan, brother of Judas Maccabaeus (160-143 B.C.)—were members of an ascetic
order who lived strictly in accordance with the law.
They formed communities which were completely self-
supporting and refused to do military service. The particular group at Qumran survived up to the Roman
invasion in A.D. 68. Presumably it was members of this
group who were responsible for many of the copies of
the books of the Old Testament which have been rescued from caves in the adjacent hills, since a proper
scriptorium was discovered among the ruins of the settlement. This Jewish monastic order, as their records
now disclose, recognized as their head a "Teacher of
Righteousness" who had revealed to them a secret rule
of life. Some scholars were at first inclined to say that
Qumran had strongly influenced John the Baptist, Jesus,
and the early Church. This view, which caused a stir
at the time, has on closer investigation proved to
be unfounded.

Almost at the same time as the Dead Sea scrolls
were discovered, a collection of manuscripts was found
not far from Luxor in Egypt which was to prove highly
significant for our understanding of early Christianity.
Fellaheen had discovered at Nag Hammadi, near the
ancient Chenoboskion, a clay jar containing thirteen
leather-bound volumes with about 1000 leaves. These
papyrus manuscripts written in Coptic, dating from the
third and fourth centuries A.D., and including a collection of the Sayings of Jesus ascribed to the Apostle
Thomas, "the Gospel according to Thomas," shed light
on an early Christian Gnostic sect of which, apart from
the writings of the early Christian Fathers, we hitherto
knew little or nothing. The Fathers attacked the Gnos-
tics as heretics since they tried to combine Egyptian,
Babylonian, Greek, Persian, and Jewish mysticism with
Christian doctrine. The Nag Hammadi manuscripts,
apart altogether from what further research discloses as
to the authenticity of the teaching of Jesus which they
contain, give us some idea of the formidable opposition

and competition which the early Christian teachers had to face.

Following on the finds at the Dead Sea which aroused world-wide interest came the discovery in 1952 of two inscribed copper scrolls in a cave to the north of the ruined monastery of Qumran. When eventually in the winter of 1955-56, after careful chemical experiments, experts in the Manchester College of Technology succeeded in opening them, the contents, about which everyone had been agog, turned out to be a curious inventory of hidden treasure. While the experts are still far from clear as to the real significance of this list, a geographical reference in the text confirmed the reliability of a piece of topographical information contained in the Fourth Gospel. According to John 5:2 "there is at Jerusalem by the sheep market a pool, which is called in the Hebrew tongue Bethesda, having five porches. . . ." The accuracy of this description was questioned until quite recently, when Bethesda was cleared of the rubble of centuries and brought once more to the light of day a vast double pool covering over 5000 square yards to the north of the Temple area. It had in fact five colonnades. Four of these surrounded the whole place, but the fifth porch, in which the sick folk lay waiting to be healed, stood on a ridge of rock which divided the two pools. The text of the copper scroll makes it quite clear that the layout at Bethesda consisted of two pools, since one of the hiding places is given as the smaller of the two reservoirs.

In the ancient Jewish fortress of Massada on the Dead Sea, Israeli scholars, in 1956, came upon armories and storehouses of Herod the Great. A fragment of papyrus was discovered inscribed with Hebrew characters and written in black ink. According to Dr. Aharoni, the fort and Herod's palace which crowned it were destroyed by the Romans in A.D. 73 after the end of the Jewish War.

Other expeditions have made interesting discoveries which shed an odd ray of light here and there on the Jewish rebellion under Simon Bar-Kokhba, which took place after the Biblical period. Hitherto, all that was known of this great revolt of the Jews against the emperor Hadrian and their struggle against the legions of Julius Severus consisted of comments in later Jewish writings, in the works of the Greek historian Dio Cassius, and the Christian Fathers Eusebius and Jerome.

In 1951 Professor Lankester Harding and Father de Vaux had retrieved original letters of the leader of the revolt dating from A.D. 130—including several copies of a document proclaiming the liberation and issued by Bar-Kokhba—from caves to the south of Qumran in Wadi Murabba'at, one of the most desolate spots in Palestine. Then in 1960 a group of archaeologists under the direction of Professor Yigael Yadin of Jerusalem University found army orders from the leader to his subordinates in caves in the Hever Ravine. The original letters deal with arrests, confiscation of crops and removal of population from Tekoa, the birthplace of the prophet Amos. A second expedition led by Professor Yadin in 1961 found in the same place a bundle of documents—papyri in Hebrew, Greek and Aramaic. It is thought that these are minutes dating from the year A.D. 134 from the archives of the commandant of the stronghold at En-Gedi by the Dead Sea who had been installed there by Bar-Kokhba. Together with coins of the "Son of a Star"—which was Bar-Kokhba's title—and pieces of crockery, a gruesome discovery awaited the archaeologists: skeletons of rebels indicated the desperate last act of this historical tragedy. Women and men who had taken refuge there had obviously died of starvation in their hide-out.

With all these discoveries since the first finds in 1947, quite apart from the recovery of numerous Biblical manuscripts, the period immediately after Biblical times has for the first time been illuminated in a way which no one a few years ago would have dared to hope.

So far the total number of manuscripts discovered at the Dead Sea amounts to over 400, including 100 Biblical manuscripts. Apart from the Book of Esther every book of the Old Testament is represented. The best known is the complete scroll of the book of Isaiah. The scrolls and fragments which come from Qumran date from about 200 B.C. to A.D. 68; those from Wadi Murabba'at go up to A.D. 132-135.

These unexpected discoveries in the words of Professor Lankester Harding are "perhaps the most sensational archaeological event of our time. It will take a whole generation of Biblical scholars to assess the value of these manuscripts."

APPENDIX

The Oldest Manuscripts
of the Bible

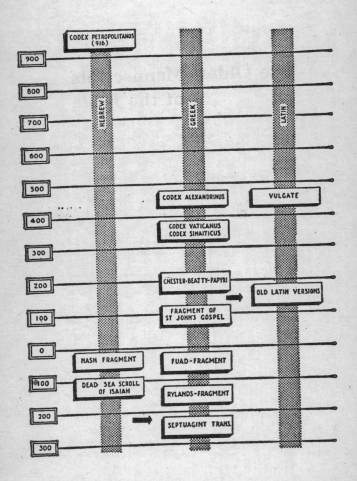

The oldest and most complete texts of the Old and New Testaments were, until recently, the famous Codex Vaticanus and Codex Sinaiticus dating from the fourth century A.D., supplemented in 1931 by the Chester Beatty papyri dating from the second and third century A.D. Besides these, there were some fragments of the Old Testament from pre-Christian times (Fuad and Rylands Fragments). But all of these documents are in Greek, that is to say translations as far as the Old Testament is concerned. The oldest and fullest MS in Hebrew was the Codex Petropolitanus dating from 916 A.D. By the discovery of the leather scroll of Isaiah at the Dead Sea the Hebrew text has been carried back to almost exactly a thousand years before. In 1935 a part of St. John's Gospel in Greek—the famous Bodmer papyrus—dating from the time of Trajan (98-117) was discovered. These old MSS are the most convincing answer to all doubts as to the genuineness and reliability of the text that we have in our Bibles today.

Index of
Biblical References

Index of Biblical References

OLD TESTAMENT

Bibliography and
Illustration Credits

Bibliography

Abel, F.-êM.: Géographie de la Palestine I (1933), II (1938), Histoire de la Palestine depuis la conquete d'Alexandre jusqu'à l'invasion Arabe I/II (1952).

Adams, J. M. K.: Ancient Records and the Bible (1946).

Albright, W. F.: Archaeology and the Religion of Israel (1953), Recent Discoveries in Bible Lands (1936), Exploring Sinai with the University of California (1948), Archaeology of Palestine (1954), Von de Steinzeit zum Christentum (1949).

Alt, A.: Die Herkunft der Hyksos in neuer Sicht (1954), Kleine Schriften zur Geschichte des Volkes Israel I/II (1953).

Andrae, W.: Das wiedererstandene Assur (1938).

Bailey, A. E.: Daily Life in Bible Times (1943).

Barrois, A. G.: Manuel d'archéologie biblique I/II (1939/53).

Bauer, H.: Die alphabetischen Keilschrifttexte von Ras-Shamra (1936).

Begrich, J.: Die Chronologie der Könige von Israel und Juda (1929).

Benzinger, I.: Hebräische Archäologie (1927).

Biblisches Nachschlagewerk, Stuttgarter (1955).

Bittel, K.: Die Ruinen von Bogazköy (1937).

Bittel, K., und R. Naumann: Bogazköy (1938).

Bodenheimer, Fr. S. u. O. Theodor: Ergebnisse der Sinai-Expedition 1927 (1929).

Bossert, H. Th.: Altanatolien (1942).

Breasted, J. H.: The Dawn of Conscience (1933), Ancient Records of Egypt I-V (1906/07), Geschichte Ägyptens (1936).

Budge, W. E. A.: The Babylonian Story of the Deluge and the Epos of Gilgamesh (1920).

Burrows, M.: What Mean These Stones? (1941).

Caiger, S. L.: Bible and Spade (1936).

Canyon, Fr.: Bible and Archaeology (1955).

Carleton, P.: Buried Empires (1939).

Chase, M. E.: Die Bibel und der Mensch von heute (1951).

Clay, A. T.: Business Documents of Murashu Sons (1898).

Clemen, C.: Die phönikische Religion nach Philo von Byblos (1939).

Clermont-Ganneau, C. S.: La Stèle de Mésa (1887).

Collart, Philippes ville de Macedoine.

Contenau, G.: La civilisation phénicienne (1949), La vie quotidienne á Babylone et en Assyrie (1953), Les civilisations

495

ancienne du Proche Orient (1945), Manuel d'Archéologie orientale I-IV (1927/47).

Crowfoot, J. W.: a. o. The Buildings at Samaria (1942).

Cuneiform Texts: Hrsg. British Museum.

Dalman, G.: Heilige Stätten und Wege (1935), Licht vom Osten (1923), Arbeit und Sitte in Palästina I-VII (1928/42).

Dalmas, G.: Die talmud. Texte über Jesu (1900).

Davis, J. D.: Dictionary of the Bible (1953).

Davis, J. D. and H. S. Gehman: The Westminster Dictionary of the Bible (1944).

Delitzsch Fr.: Babel und Bibel (1903).

Dobschütz, E. v.: Die Bibel im Leben der Völker (1954).

Dougherty, R. P.: Nabonitus and Belshazzar (1929).

Duncan, G.: Digging up Biblical History I/II (1931).

Dussaud, R.: Les Découvertes de Ras Shamra et l'Ancien Testament (1941).

Ebeling, E. u. B. Meissner: Reallexikon der Assyriologie I/II (1932/38).

Eberhard, E. G.: Bible-Thesaurus (1953).

Eisfeldt, O.: Handbuch zum Alten Testament (1935), Philister und Phönizier, Der Alte Orient (1930).

Ephesus, Forschungen in Veröffentl. v. Österr. Archäol. Inst. (1937).

Eusebius, Historica ecclesiastica, hrsg. v. E. Schwartz (1914), Das Leben von Constantin.

Finegan, J.: Light from the Ancient Past (1954).

Frayzel, S.: A History of the Jews (1952).

Gadd, E.: The Fall of Nineveh (1923).

Galling, K.: Biblisches Reallexikon (1937), Textbuch zur Geschichte Israels (1950).

Gardiner, A. H. and E. Peet: The Inscriptions of Sinai (1952).

Garis-Davies, N. de: The Tomb of Rekh-mi-re at Thebes (1943).

Garstang, J. B. E.: The Story of Jericho (1940).

Gerke, S.: Die christl. Sarkophage d. vorkonstantin. Zeit (1940).

Glueck, N.: The Other Side of the Jordan (1940), The River Jordan (1946).

Goldschmidt, L.: Der Babylonische Talmud (1935).

Gordon, C. H.: The Living Past (1941), Ugaritic Literature (1949).

Götze, A.: Hethiter, Churitter u. Assyrer (1936).

Gressmann, H.: Die älteste Geschichtsschreibung und Prophetie

Israels (1921), Altorientalische Texte und Bilder zum Alten Testament (1927).

Gunkel, H., W. Stark u. a.: Die Schriften des Alten Testaments in Auswahl I-VII (1921/25).

Guthe, H.: Bibelatlas (1926), Palästina, Monographien zur Erdkunde 21 (1927).

Harper: Bible Dictionary (1952).

Heitel, A.: The Gilgamesh-Epos and the Old Testament (1953).

Herodots von Halikarna β' Geschichte (1829).

Hogarth, D. G.: Excavations in Ephesus (1908).

Honor, L. L.: Sennacherib's Invasion of Palestine (1926).

International Standard Bible Encyclopaedia (1952).

Jansen, H. L.: Die Politik Antiochus' IV (1943).

Jirku, A.: Die ägypt. Listen palästinens, u. syr. Ortsnamen (1937).

Josephus, Flavius: Altertümer, Jüdischer Krieg.

Junge, P. J.: Dareios I., König der Perser (1944).

Kaufmann, C. M.: Handbuch der christl. Archäologie I-III (1922).

Klausner, J.: Jesus von Nazareth (1950), Von Jesus zu Paulus (1950).

Knopf, Lietzmann, Weinel: Einführung in das Neue Testament (1949).

Knudtzon, J. A.: Die El-Amarna-Tafeln I/II (1908/15).

Koeppel, P. R.: Palästina (1930).

Kohl und Watzinger: Antike Synagogen in Galiläa (1916).

Koldewey, R.: Das wiedererstehende Babylon (1925).

Kraeling, E. G.: Gerasa, City of the Decapolis (1938).

Kugler-Schaumberger: Sternkunde und Sterndienst in Babel (1935).

Laible, H.: Jesus Christus im Talmud (1900).

Layard, A.: Discoveries in the Ruins of Nineveh and Babylon (1853).

Lefebre, G.: Romans et Contes Egyptiens de l'époque Pharaonique (1949).

Lentzen, H. J.: Die Entwicklung der Ziggurat (1942).

Lepsius, C. R.: Königsbuch der alten Ägypter (1858), Denkmäler aus Ägypten und Äthiopien (1849/56).

Lietzmann, H.: Petrus und Paulus in Rom (1927).

Loud, G.: Megiddo Ivories (1939), Megiddo II (1948).

Macalister, R. A. S.: Gezer I-III (1912), The Excavations of Gezer (1912), A Century of Excavations in Palestine (1925).

Mari, Archives royales de, hrsg. Musée du Louvre I-V.

McCown, C. C.: The Ladder of Progress in Palestine (1943), a. o. Tell-en-Nasbeh I/II (1947).

Meyer, Ed.: Der Papyrusfund von Elephantine (1912), Geschichte des Altertums I-III (1925/37).

Miller, M. S. and J. L.: Encyclopedia of Bible Life (1944).

Moldenke, H. N. and A. L.: Plants of the Bible (1952).

Moret, A.: The Nile and Egyptian Civilisation (1927).

Montet, P.: Les nouvelles fouilles de Tanis (1929/32, 1933), Avaris, Pi-Ramsès, Tanis (Syria XVII 1936), Tanis (1942).

Morton, H. V.: Through Lands of the Bible (1954), In the Steps of the Master (1953).

Moscati, S.: Geschichte und Kultur der semitischen Völker (1953).

Newberry, P. E.: Beni Hasan I (1893).

Noth, M.: Die Welt des Alten Testaments (1953), Geschichte Israels (1954).

Origines: Contra Celsum I, 32.

Orlinski, H. M.: Ancient Israel (1954).

Otto, E.: Agypten (1953).

Otto, W.: Handbuch der Altertumswissenschaft (1928).

Parrot, A.: Mari une ville perdue (1936), Archéologie méso-potamienne, Les Etapes I (1946), Entdekung begrabener Welten (1954), Studia Mariana (1950).

Petrie, Fl.: Researches in Sinai (1906).

Pfeiffer, R. H.: History of New Testament Times (1949), Introduction to the Old Testament (1948).

Pingré, M.: Cométographie I (1783).

Pius XII., Papst: Die Gottesbeweise im Lichte der modernen Naturwissenschaft (Universitas, Okt. 1952).

Plutarch: Das Leben Alexanders.

Post, G. E.: Flora of Syria, Palestine and Sinai (1933).

Pottier, E.: Musée du Louvre, Catalogue des Antiquités As-syriennes No. 165.

Pritchard, J. B.: Ancient Near Eastern Texts Relating to the Old Testament (1950), The Ancient Near East in Pictures (1954).

Ramsay, W. M.: The Cities of St. Paul (1900).

Reisner, Th., H. and W. O. E. Oesterley: Excavations at Samaria I-II (1924).

Ricciotti, G.: Storia d'Israele I-II (1949).

Reimschneider, M.: Die Welt der Hethiter (1954).

Rowe, A.: The Topography and the History of Beth-Shan (1930), The Four Canaanite Temples of Beth-Shan I (1940).

Rowley, H. H.: The Re-discovery of the Old Testament (1945), The Old Testament and Modern Study (1952), From Joseph to Joshua (1948).

Sanchuniathon: Urgeschichte der Phönizier.
Schaeffer, C. F. A.: The Cuneiform Texts of Ras Shamra-Ugarit (1939), Ugaritica I-II (1939/49).
Scharff, A.: Handbuch der Archäologie I (1939).
Scharff, A.: Moortgat, A.: Ägypten und Vorderasien im Altertum (1950).
Schmidt, E. F.: The Treasury of Persepolis and Other Discoveries in the Homeland of the Achaemenians (1939).
Schnabel, P.: Berossos u. d. babylon.-hellenist. Literatur (1923).
Schott, A.: Das Gilgamesch-Epos (1934).
Sellin, E.: Wie wurde Sichem israelitische Stadt? (1923), Geschichte des israel.-jüd. Volkes I-II (1924/32).
Sethe, K.: Die Ächtungstexte feindl. Fürsten, Völker u. Dinge auf altägypt. Tongefäßscherben d. Mittl. Reiches (APAW 1926, Nr. 5), Zur Geschichte der Einbalsamierung b. d. alten Agyptern (1934).
Simons, J.: Opgravingen in Palestina (1935).
Soden, W. v.: Leistung und Grenze sumerischer u. babylon. Wissenschaft, Welt als Geschichte II (1936), Das altbabylon. Briefarchiv v. Mari, Die Welt des Orients (1948).
Speiser, E. A.: Introduction to Hurrian (1941).
Starkey, J. L.: Excavations at Tell ed-Duweir 1933/34 (1934).
Starr, R. F. S.: Nuzi, Report on the Excavations at Yorgan Tepa near Kirkuk I-II (1937/39), Nuzi I (1939).
Steindorf, G., K. C. Seele: When Egypt Ruled the East (1942).
Strabo: Geographie.
Sukenik, E. L.: Ancient Synagogues in Palestine and Greece (1934), a. o. The Third Wall of Jerusalem (1930).
Svenskt Bibliskt Uppslagsverk (hrsg. I. Engnell u. A. Fridrichsen, 1948).

Torczyner, H.: Lakish I, The Lakish Letters (1938).

Unger, E.: Babylon, die heilige Stadt (1931).
Ungnad, A.: Reallexikon der Assyriologie (1938), Die neue Grundlage f. d. altoriental. Chronologie (1940).

Vincent, L. H.: Canaan d'après l'exploration récente (1914), Jericho et sa chronologie (1935), L'Archéologie et la Bible (1945).

Watzinger, C.: Denkmäler Palästinas I-II (1933/35).
Weißbach, F. H.: Die Keilschriften der Archämeniden (1911).

Wolff, H. W.: Eine Handbreit Erde (1955).

Wood, J. T.: Modern Discoveries on the Side of Ancient Ephesus (1890).

Woolley, C. L.: Abraham, Recent Discoveries and Hebrew Origins (1936), Ur Excavations; V The Ziggurat and Its Surroundings (1939), Ur of the Chaldees (1954).

Wreszinski, Atlas zur ägyptischen Kulturgeschichte I-III (1923/40).

Wright, S. E. and Fl. V. Filson: The Westminster Historical Atlas to the Bible (1953).

Zeitschriften: Annual of American Schools of Oriental Research (AASOR), Der Alte Orient (AO), American Journal of Archaeology (AJA), Biblical Archaeologist (BA), Bulletin of the American Schools of Oriental Research (BASOR), Beiträge zur Wissenschaft vom Alten u. Neuen Testament (BWANT), Illustrated London News, Israel Exploration Journal, Journal of the Society of Oriental Research (JSOR), Picture Post, London, Zeitschrift des Deutschen Palästinavereins (ZDPV), Revue Biblique (RB), Syria.

Illustration Credits

General Index

General Index

505

ABOUT THE AUTHOR

DR. WERNER KELLER, born in 1909 on a farm near Zerbst, Anhalt, Germany, is without a doubt one of the contemporary scientific journalists of stature. He studied in Zurich, Geneva, and Jena, and lived in Berlin until 1945, where he published his first articles in the *Berliner Tageblatt*. For many years, the results of current research and science have been the subject of his numerous articles, which he published in leading newspapers and magazines, often under a pen name, and of his many lectures on radio and TV. His main interest lies in the areas of archaeology and anthropology. He studied practical aspects of these subjects on his travels to Italy, the Balkans, and the Near East. The plan for a book on the almost inexhaustible array of finds and excavations at Biblical sites was the result of his studies in 1950 of the sensational reports on the discovery of the ancient Phoenician maritime city of Ugarit and the home of the Patriarchs of the Kingdom of Mari at the Euphrates. He compiled the excavation reports—unknown but to a small number of experts—of American, British, French, Scandinavian, and German explorers and made them available to the general public in his international bestseller THE BIBLE AS HISTORY. This work has been translated into all major languages and his sold over 3½ million copies.

ABOUT THE AUTHOR

DR. WERNER KELLER, born in 1909 on a farm near Zerbst, Anhalt, Germany, is without a doubt one of the contemporary scientific journalists of stature. He studied in Zurich, Geneva, and Jena, and lived in Berlin until 1945, where he published his first articles in the *Berliner Tageblatt*. For many years, the results of current research and science have been the subject of his numerous articles, which he published in leading newspapers and magazines, often under a pen name, and of his many lectures on radio and TV. His main interest lies in the areas of archaeology and anthropology. He studied practical aspects of these subjects on his travels to Italy, the Balkans, and the Near East. The plan for a book on the almost inexhaustible array of finds and excavations at Biblical sites was the result of his studies in 1950 of the sensational reports on the discovery of the ancient Phoenician maritime city of Ugarit and the home of the Patriarchs of the Kingdom of Mari at the Euphrates. He compiled the excavation reports—unknown but to a small number of experts—of American, British, French, Scandinavian, and German explorers and made them available to the general public in his international bestseller THE BIBLE AS HISTORY. This work has been translated into all major languages and his sold over 3½ million copies.

LOOKING IN

Books that explore Eastern and Western spirituality and examine man's concepts of God and the universe.

INTIMATE REFLECTIONS

Thoughts, ideas, and perceptions of life as it is.

Heartwarming Books
of
Faith and Inspiration

Bantam Book Catalog

Here's your up-to-the-minute listing of over 1,400 titles by your favorite authors.

This illustrated, large format catalog gives a description of each title. For your convenience, it is divided into categories in fiction and non-fiction—gothics, science fiction, westerns, mysteries, cookbooks, mysticism and occult, biographies, history, family living, health, psychology, art.

So don't delay—take advantage of this special opportunity to increase your reading pleasure.

Just send us your name and address and 50¢ (to help defray postage and handling costs).